Innovation Management for a Resilient Digital Economy

Miltiadis D. Lytras
The American College of Greece, Greece & Computer Science Department, College of Engineering, Effat University, Saudi Arabia

Patricia Ordonez
University of Oviedo, Spain

Afnan Alkhaldi
Arab Open University Kuwait, Kuwait

Andreea Claudia Serban
Bucharest University of Economic Studies, Romania

IGI Global
Scientific Publishing
Publishing Tomorrow's Research Today

Published in the United States of America by
IGI Global Scientific Publishing
701 East Chocolate Avenue
Hershey, PA, 17033, USA
Tel: 717-533-8845
Fax: 717-533-8661
Website: https://www.igi-global.com E-mail: cust@igi-global.com

Library of Congress Cataloging-in-Publication Data

Names: Lytras, Miltiadis D., 1973- editor.
Title: Innovation management for a resilient digital economy / [edited by] Miltiadis Lytras, Patricia Ordóñez de Pablos, Afnan Alkhaldi, Andreea Claudia Șerban.
Description: Hershey, PA : IGI Global Scientific Publishing, [2025] | Includes bibliographical references and index. | Summary: "The primary objective of the book is to bridge the gap between emerging technological advancements and their practical applications in business and society. This book aims to provide a comprehensive analysis of how innovation management can leverage technologies such as artificial intelligence, blockchain, and big data analytics to create resilient and sustainable business models"-- Provided by publisher.
Identifiers: LCCN 2024055657 (print) | LCCN 2024055658 (ebook) | ISBN 9798369383575 (hardcover) | ISBN 9798369383582 (paperback) | ISBN 9798369383599 (ebook)
Subjects: LCSH: Technological innovations--Economic aspects. | Technological innovations--Management.
Classification: LCC HC79.T4 .I54668 2025 (print) | LCC HC79.T4 (ebook) | DDC 338/.064--dc23/eng/20250124
LC record available at https://lccn.loc.gov/2024055657
LC ebook record available at https://lccn.loc.gov/2024055658

British Cataloguing in Publication Data
A Cataloguing in Publication record for this book is available from the British Library.

Table of Contents

Preface x

Chapter 1
Developing Sustainable Business Models: Integrating Circular Economy, Social Entrepreneurship, and Green Technologies 1
S. Sudhakar, LEAD College of Management, Palakkad, India
Sadaf Anwar, M.S. Ramaiah Institute of Management, Bengaluru, India
Parul Wadhwa, DPG Degree College, Gurugram, India
Narender Singh, Rungta College of Science and Technology, Bhilai, India

Chapter 2
From Industrial to Digital Economy: The Role of Digital Transformation in Building a Resilient Qatari Economic Future 23
Ahmed Badran, Qatar University, Qatar

Chapter 3
Analyzing E-Participation Index as an Indicator of Digital Transformation: A Bibliometric Analysis 55
Laura Anesti Ayu Kirana, Universitas Muhammadiyah Makassar, Indonesia
Haeria A. Mardhatillah, Universitas Muhammadiyah Makassar, Indonesia
Muhammad Younus, Universitas Muhammadiyah Yogyakarta, Pakistan
Aqmal Reza Amri, Universitas Muhammadiyah Makassar, Indonesia
Andi Luhur Prianto, Universitas Muhammadiyah Makassar, Indonesia
Ahmad Harakan, Universitas Muhammadiyah Makassar, Indonesia
Achmad Nurmandi, Universitas Muhammadiyah Yogyakarta, Indonesia
Umar Congge, Universitas Muhammadiyah Sinjai, Indonesia
Timothy Apriyanto, Universitas Muhammadiyah Yogyakarta, Indonesia
Sekson Yongvanit, Khon Kaen University, Thailand

Chapter 4
AI in Tourism: Business and Economic Perspectives 81
Farhana Yeasmin Lina, Daffodil International University, Bangladesh
Mohammad Badruddoza Talukder, International University of Business Agriculture and Technology, Bangladesh

Chapter 5
Enhancing Consumer Trust Through Transparent Data Practices and Ethical Data Management in Business 105
Saher Hassan El-Annan, International American University, Los Angeles, USA
Rawan Hassoun, International American University, Los Angeles, USA

Chapter 6
Factors Affecting the Implementation of Cloud-Based ERP Systems in the South African Gold Mining Industries 149
Tlou Maggie Masenya, Durban University of Technology, South Africa
Oluwasegun Julius Aroba, Durban University of Technology, South Africa

Chapter 7
Innovation Management Landscape for Digital Economy Transformation Through Innovation Resilience in Ethiopia 177
Metasebia Adula, Bule Hora University, Ethiopia
Shashi Kant, Bule Hora University, Ethiopia
Haro Duloma Geda, Bule Hora University, Ethiopia

Chapter 8
Securing the Digital Supply Chain: Challenges, Innovations, and Best Practices in Cybersecurity 205
Pratik Nahta, University of Cumberlands, USA

Chapter 9
Innovative Pedagogies for a Digital World 231
Fareeha Javed, Lahore College for Women University, Pakistan

Compilation of References 261

About the Contributors 307

Index 313

Detailed Table of Contents

Preface x

Chapter 1
Developing Sustainable Business Models: Integrating Circular Economy, Social Entrepreneurship, and Green Technologies 1
S. Sudhakar, LEAD College of Management, Palakkad, India
Sadaf Anwar, M.S. Ramaiah Institute of Management, Bengaluru, India
Parul Wadhwa, DPG Degree College, Gurugram, India
Narender Singh, Rungta College of Science and Technology, Bhilai, India

This chapter is focused on the process of integrating Circular Economy, Social Entrepreneurship, and Green Technologies into sustainable business models. As the environmental and social issues combating the world progress, organizations are changing the ways they do business and implementing changes that support waste minimization, social perspective, and green technology. The chapter begins by defining these key concepts and examining their individual roles in promoting sustainability. Thus, using case examples, it shows successful instances of application and reveals the advantages and limitations of each method. Because of these elements, a proposed framework to integrate these elements emphasize on how these elements complement each other to bring about a comprehensive framework for business. Moreover, the chapter stresses that is crucial to continuously develop and invites businesses, entrepreneurs, and policymakers to fighting for sustainability as a competitive challenge for futures success.

Chapter 2
From Industrial to Digital Economy: The Role of Digital Transformation in Building a Resilient Qatari Economic Future 23
Ahmed Badran, Qatar University, Qatar

this chapter addresses the issue of the digital economy from a public policy perspective by focusing on the strategies applied in the State of Qatar to emphasize the importance of the knowledge and innovation. In this context, information technology is a key in achieving comprehensive, sustainable and resilient economic development. The chapter starts from a main research question: To what extent do the current strategies of the State of Qatar contribute to the successful transition towards the digital economy? To answer this question, the chapter relies on the idea of methodological integration by combining the use of the descriptive analytical approach and the case study approach. The aim is to provide a critical analytical reading of previous literature in addition to determining the effectiveness of the strategies applied by the Qatari government to transform from traditional to digital economy.

Chapter 3
Analyzing E-Participation Index as an Indicator of Digital Transformation: A Bibliometric Analysis 55
Laura Anesti Ayu Kirana, Universitas Muhammadiyah Makassar, Indonesia
Haeria A. Mardhatillah, Universitas Muhammadiyah Makassar, Indonesia
Muhammad Younus, Universitas Muhammadiyah Yogyakarta, Pakistan
Aqmal Reza Amri, Universitas Muhammadiyah Makassar, Indonesia
Andi Luhur Prianto, Universitas Muhammadiyah Makassar, Indonesia
Ahmad Harakan, Universitas Muhammadiyah Makassar, Indonesia
Achmad Nurmandi, Universitas Muhammadiyah Yogyakarta, Indonesia
Umar Congge, Universitas Muhammadiyah Sinjai, Indonesia
Timothy Apriyanto, Universitas Muhammadiyah Yogyakarta, Indonesia
Sekson Yongvanit, Khon Kaen University, Thailand

This paper's goal is to provide information about Indonesia's E-Participation Index analysis as a digital transformation indicator for the year 2022. After that, we were able to ascertain the effects of digital revolution on Indonesian individuals as well as the modifications that were made to the way they thought about politics. "Qualitative research" is the methodology employed by the researchers working in this field. The research's data was collected from the United Nations website, Dimension AI, and Google Scholar, and it was then presented in a descriptive manner. The research presented in this paper raises awareness of the ways that electronic engagement in society influences Indonesia's digital transformation. This paper will only cover the extent to which each change's component is explained in detail; it will also examine potential fixes for problems that the public has identified and how best to go about putting them into practice.

Chapter 4
AI in Tourism: Business and Economic Perspectives.. 81
Farhana Yeasmin Lina, Daffodil International University, Bangladesh
Mohammad Badruddoza Talukder, International University of Business Agriculture and Technology, Bangladesh

Artificial Intelligence is redefining the tourism industry by ensuring the accumulation of technologies in business operations and tourism-related activities and fostering economic growth and financial outcomes. From the automated reservation system, AI is increasing its branches toward personalized marketing, setting dynamic pricing models, and offering tailored experiences per guests' requirements. Tourism and hospitality-related services can strengthen smarter decision-making, certify efficient operations, and enhance service delivery to tourists. This chapter scrutinizes the sequential development of AI in tourism, examining assorted AI applications that have been applied to the tourism industry. AI creates new job opportunities, increasing efficiency at work, enhancing competitiveness, and encouraging economic expansion and growth, especially in developing markets. This chapter offers a thorough overview of the transformative role of AI in tourism-related business, economic development, and advancement challenges and opportunities AI presents to the industry.

Chapter 5
Enhancing Consumer Trust Through Transparent Data Practices and Ethical Data Management in Business 105
Saher Hassan El-Annan, International American University, Los Angeles, USA
Rawan Hassoun, International American University, Los Angeles, USA

This chapter evaluates the relationship between TDP and PT on consumer trust in digital business models mediated by ethical data management (EDM). The study applies an exploratory research design with two structured surveys addressing consumers and professionals to gather quantitative insights regarding these connections. The research shows that transparent data practices increase consumer trust, and perceiving transparency strengthens this influence. The management of data with integrity significantly strengthens trust. The research outcomes match Trust Transference and Social Contract Theory theories and show that upholding transparency and ethics significantly enhances consumer trust. The relevance of straightforward communication to improve perceived transparency among businesses is emphasized in the analysis. This research presents important suggestions for companies and regulators to improve data management and consumer trust in the digital market.

Chapter 6
Factors Affecting the Implementation of Cloud-Based ERP Systems in the South African Gold Mining Industries 149
Tlou Maggie Masenya, Durban University of Technology, South Africa
Oluwasegun Julius Aroba, Durban University of Technology, South Africa

South Africa is one of the nations in Africa that has contributed to the mining industry due to the mineral substances found within the nation. However, the current enterprise resource planning (ERP) system that is used in the mining sector dramatically impacts the way gold mines function and their effectiveness. Most of South African Gold Mines are still using old cloud-based ERP system. The aim of this chapter is to investigate the implementation of cloud-based enterprise resource planning (ERP) within the South African gold mining industries by looking at the variables that influence the move from a conventional or traditional ERP framework to a cloud-based framework. The study identified the factors affecting the effective implementation of cloud-based ERP system including cyber threat, cost of deployment, flexibility, more space storage, time and shortage of highly skilled local worker force. This chapter recommends that a hybrid strategy incorporating a cloud-based ERP system with the support services system would be beneficial.

Chapter 7
Innovation Management Landscape for Digital Economy Transformation Through Innovation Resilience in Ethiopia 177
Metasebia Adula, Bule Hora University, Ethiopia
Shashi Kant, Bule Hora University, Ethiopia
Haro Duloma Geda, Bule Hora University, Ethiopia

This chapter explores the role that innovation resilience techniques play as a mediator in the link that exists between Ethiopia's digital economy's transformational potential and the innovation management environment. A survey was conducted with 400 participants, comprising digital economy specialists, innovation ecosystem players, and technology entrepreneurs. To find the underlying dimensions, exploratory factor analysis (EFA) and confirmatory factor analysis (CFA) were used. The data's appropriateness for factor analysis was evaluated using Bartlett's test of sphericity and the Kaiser-Meyer-Olkin (KMO) measure of sampling adequacy. The mediating function of innovation resilience methods was then investigated using structural equation modeling (SEM). The study's conclusions provide direction for Ethiopian players in the digital economy about how to best take advantage of the connections between innovation resilience, innovation management, and the transformative potential of the sector to promote sustainable development.

Chapter 8
Securing the Digital Supply Chain: Challenges, Innovations, and Best Practices in Cybersecurity 205
Pratik Nahta, University of Cumberlands, USA

This paper explores the significant cybersecurity challenges facing modern supply chains within an increasingly digitized and interconnected business environment. It outlines the current threat landscape, highlighting issues like ransomware, phishing, and nation-state cyber threats, and examines their potential impacts on supply chain operations. The research identifies critical vulnerabilities, including third-party risks and IoT device weaknesses, while also discussing the dual nature of emerging technologies such as blockchain and artificial intelligence, which offer both opportunities and new security challenges. Additionally, the paper reviews mitigation strategies, evaluating frameworks like the NIST Cybersecurity Framework and Zero Trust Architecture, and draws lessons from recent high-profile cyber-attacks, such as the Colonial Pipeline incident. Finally, it identifies future research areas, including quantum-resistant cryptography and securing AI/ML models, aiming to provide organizations with actionable insights to strengthen their supply chain cybersecurity posture.

Chapter 9
Innovative Pedagogies for a Digital World 231
Fareeha Javed, Lahore College for Women University, Pakistan

This chapter aims to provide a thorough analysis of the ways in which innovative pedagogies can adapt to the ever-changing demands of future competencies and skills in a digital world. In an attempt to offer perceptive guidance on how to alter education to better prepare students for the problems that lie ahead, the chapter offers helpful recommendations, case studies, and in-depth research. With its enormous potential to revolutionize education, the field of creative pedagogies for the digital era is vibrant and constantly evolving. By implementing these innovative strategies, educators may design more successful, inclusive, and captivating learning opportunities that equip students for the demands of the twenty-first century. Although there are many obstacles to overcome, implementing cutting-edge digital pedagogies has the potential to greatly enhance learning experiences. Successful deployment necessitates a thorough strategy that addresses infrastructure, teaching strategies, digital literacy, inclusivity, and ethical considerations.

Compilation of References 261

About the Contributors 307

Index 313

Preface

In the dynamic and ever-evolving digital economy, the role of innovation management has never been more critical. As economies worldwide grapple with rapid technological advancements and unprecedented challenges, innovation serves as the linchpin for resilience, adaptability, and growth. This book, *Innovation Management for a Resilient Digital Economy*, delves into the transformative potential of emerging technologies, data-driven models, and innovative strategies in building economies that are not only robust but also inclusive and sustainable.

The chapters presented in this volume explore a wide array of themes, ranging from the integration of circular economy principles and AI-driven tourism to the challenges of cybersecurity in supply chains and the implementation of cutting-edge pedagogies for the digital world. By combining theoretical frameworks with real-world applications, this book provides actionable insights for policymakers, technologists, researchers, and industry professionals.

PURPOSE AND VISION

The aim of this book is to bridge the gap between technological advancements and practical applications, empowering stakeholders to harness the power of innovation for economic and societal resilience. It aspires to:

- Advance the discourse on innovation management in the digital economy.
- Promote sustainable business practices that align with global development goals.
- Foster multidisciplinary collaboration among academia, industry, and policymakers.
- Provide actionable strategies for navigating disruption and driving growth.

By addressing key topics such as AI, blockchain, big data analytics, and ethical technology adoption, this book seeks to inspire a deeper understanding of the critical intersection between innovation and economic resilience.

COVERAGE OF TOPICS

The chapters in this book span several thematic areas:

- **Innovation Strategies**: Exploring frameworks and metrics for fostering innovation in digital economies.
- **Emerging Technologies**: Examining the impact of AI, blockchain, IoT, and big data analytics on business models and societal outcomes.
- **Sustainable Business Models**: Investigating the integration of circular economy, green technologies, and social entrepreneurship into resilient business strategies.
- **Data-Driven Applications**: Highlighting the role of data in predictive analytics, operational efficiency, and customer-centric models.
- **Policy and Regulatory Frameworks**: Addressing ethical considerations, innovation policies, and global standards for the digital economy.
- **Future Trends**: Anticipating the implications of technological innovation on education, work, and economic inclusivity.

OVERVIEW OF THE CHAPTERS

This section provides an overview of the chapters in *Innovation Management for a Resilient Digital Economy*, summarizing their core themes, approaches, contributions, and implications for advancing innovation management in the digital economy.

Chapter 1: Introduction to the Theme

This chapter sets the stage for the book, introducing the importance of innovation management in fostering resilience within the digital economy. It highlights the transformative role of emerging technologies and sustainable practices in driving economic growth and social impact.

Approach: Lays the conceptual groundwork for exploring the intersection of innovation, technology, and economic resilience.

Contribution: Provides an overarching framework for the discussions and analyses presented in subsequent chapters.

Implications: Offers readers a foundational understanding of the critical role of innovation in shaping resilient digital economies.

Chapter 2: Developing Sustainable Business Models: Integrating Circular Economy, Social Entrepreneurship, and Green Technologies

This chapter examines how organizations can incorporate circular economy principles, social entrepreneurship, and green technologies into sustainable business models. Using case studies, it highlights successes, challenges, and opportunities in implementing these practices.

Approach: Combines conceptual analysis with case-based exploration to propose an integrative framework for sustainability-driven business models.

Contribution: Demonstrates how integrating environmental and social perspectives fosters competitive advantage and long-term success.

Implications: Encourages businesses, policymakers, and entrepreneurs to adopt innovative approaches for achieving sustainability goals.

Chapter 3: From Industrial to Digital Economy: The Role of Digital Transformation in Building a Resilient Qatari Economic Future

This chapter addresses Qatar's transition from a traditional to a digital economy through knowledge and innovation-driven strategies. It evaluates the effectiveness of governmental policies in promoting digital transformation.

Approach: Employs a methodological integration of descriptive and case study analyses to assess Qatar's digital economy strategies.

Contribution: Provides insights into how policy frameworks and IT infrastructure enable resilience and sustainable growth in digital economies.

Implications: Serves as a model for other nations seeking to navigate the complexities of digital transformation.

Chapter 4: Analyzing E-Participation Index as an Indicator of Digital Transformation: A Bibliometric Analysis

This chapter explores Indonesia's E-Participation Index as a metric for digital transformation, analyzing its influence on citizens' engagement and political perspectives.

Approach: Uses bibliometric and qualitative analysis to link e-participation with digital transformation outcomes.

Contribution: Highlights the role of digital engagement in fostering inclusive and participatory governance.

Implications: Provides policymakers with actionable insights for leveraging e-participation to drive societal digitalization.

Chapter 5: AI in Tourism: Business and Economic Perspectives

This chapter investigates how AI is transforming the tourism sector, enabling personalized services, dynamic pricing, and operational efficiencies. It examines AI's potential to drive growth in developing markets.

Approach: Presents a detailed analysis of AI applications in tourism, supported by case studies and industry trends.

Contribution: Highlights the economic benefits and transformative role of AI in enhancing competitiveness in tourism.

Implications: Encourages stakeholders to adopt AI to boost innovation and economic performance in the tourism sector.

Chapter 6: Enhancing Consumer Trust Through Transparent Data Practices and Ethical Data Management in Business

This chapter evaluates how transparent data practices (TDP) and ethical data management (EDM) influence consumer trust in digital business models.

Approach: Combines survey-based quantitative research with theoretical frameworks like Trust Transference and Social Contract Theory.

Contribution: Demonstrates that ethical transparency in data management strengthens consumer trust in the digital economy.

Implications: Offers actionable recommendations for businesses to improve data practices and build stronger consumer relationships.

Chapter 7: Factors Affecting the Implementation of Cloud-Based ERP Systems in the South African Gold Mining Industries

This chapter investigates the challenges and opportunities of adopting cloud-based ERP systems in South Africa's gold mining sector.

Approach: Combines exploratory research with case studies to identify key variables influencing cloud ERP adoption.

Contribution: Proposes a hybrid strategy for implementing cloud ERP systems to enhance flexibility and operational efficiency.

Implications: Guides mining companies and technologists in transitioning to cloud-based ERP systems for improved performance.

Chapter 8: Innovation Management Landscape for Digital Economy Transformation Through Innovation Resilience in Ethiopia

This chapter examines the mediating role of innovation resilience in linking Ethiopia's digital economy potential with its innovation management environment.

Approach: Employs survey-based research with exploratory and confirmatory factor analysis, supported by structural equation modeling (SEM).

Contribution: Identifies strategies to strengthen innovation resilience as a driver of digital transformation in developing economies.

Implications: Provides policymakers and industry leaders with a roadmap for leveraging innovation resilience to achieve sustainable growth.

Chapter 9: Securing the Digital Supply Chain: Challenges, Innovations, and Best Practices in Cybersecurity

This chapter addresses cybersecurity challenges in modern supply chains, focusing on vulnerabilities and mitigation strategies.

Approach: Combines threat landscape analysis with evaluations of cybersecurity frameworks like NIST and Zero Trust Architecture.

Contribution: Highlights best practices for enhancing supply chain security in a digitized business environment.

Implications: Offers organizations actionable insights for safeguarding supply chains against evolving cyber threats.

Chapter 10: Innovative Pedagogies for a Digital World

This chapter explores how innovative pedagogies can prepare students for future competencies in a rapidly digitizing world. It emphasizes inclusivity, infrastructure, and ethical considerations in designing effective learning experiences.

Approach: Combines case studies with theoretical analysis to propose strategies for integrating digital pedagogies into education.

Contribution: Highlights the transformative potential of creative teaching methods in equipping learners for the 21st century.

Implications: Encourages educators and policymakers to adopt innovative approaches to enhance learning experiences and outcomes.

FRAMEWORK FOR INNOVATION MANAGEMENT FOR A RESILIENT DIGITAL ECONOMY

This framework summarizes the book's structure, highlighting its key themes, areas of focus, and contributions. It provides a comprehensive view of how innovation management drives resilience in the digital economy, emphasizing sustainable practices, technological integration, and forward-thinking strategies.

1. Coverage

The book spans diverse thematic areas, capturing the essence of innovation management in various contexts. It begins with foundational frameworks for resilience, exploring how innovation strategies contribute to adaptability and economic stability. The integration of emerging technologies like AI, blockchain, and cloud ERP systems is extensively discussed, showcasing their transformative potential in critical sectors such as tourism, education, and supply chain management.

Sustainability and inclusivity are pivotal themes, emphasizing circular economy principles, social entrepreneurship, and digital engagement. The chapters also address the regulatory and ethical dimensions of innovation, preparing stakeholders for the future challenges of the digital economy. Together, these themes present a holistic view of the interplay between innovation, technology, and policy.

Table 1.

Thematic Area	Chapters Covered	Key Focus Areas
Innovation Strategies for Resilience	Chapters 1, 2, 8	Frameworks for innovation, sustainable business models, and strategies for resilience in economic transformation.
Technological Integration and Transformation	Chapters 3, 7, 9	Adoption of emerging technologies such as cloud ERP systems, digital transformation strategies, and cybersecurity.
Sector-Specific Applications	Chapters 5, 6	Innovation in tourism, consumer trust in digital business models, and innovative pedagogies for the digital era.
Sustainable and Inclusive Practices	Chapters 2, 4, 8	Emphasizing circular economy principles, digital engagement, and inclusive digital transformation efforts.
Policy and Future Trends	Chapters 3, 9	Exploring regulatory, ethical, and educational dimensions to prepare for disruptions in the digital economy.

2. Impact

The impact of this book extends across multiple stakeholder groups, addressing both theoretical and practical needs. Academics and researchers gain a deeper understanding of innovation management frameworks, while business leaders and industry professionals receive actionable insights to navigate disruptions and implement innovative strategies effectively.

For policymakers and regulators, the book emphasizes ethical technology adoption and policy frameworks for inclusive growth. Educators and students benefit from discussions on digital pedagogies and preparing future generations for the challenges of the digital economy. Finally, society at large is positioned to benefit from inclusive and sustainable innovation practices that drive equity and economic growth.

Table 2.

Stakeholder Group	Impact
Academics and Researchers	Advances theoretical understanding of innovation management and its role in resilient digital economies.
Business Leaders and Industry Professionals	Provides practical tools, case studies, and strategies to navigate disruptions and implement innovative approaches.
Policymakers and Regulators	Highlights policy frameworks and ethical considerations for promoting equitable and sustainable digital economies.
Educators and Students	Offers innovative pedagogies and strategies to equip future generations with digital literacy and resilience.
Society at Large	Demonstrates how inclusive innovation practices drive sustainable development, social equity, and economic growth.

3. Contribution

The contributions of this book are multidimensional, combining theory, practice, and policy insights to provide a comprehensive resource for navigating the digital economy. Theoretical advancements focus on resilience strategies and the integration of technology with economic goals. Practical applications include frameworks, case studies, and real-world examples that demonstrate how innovation management can be implemented across industries.

Policy insights highlight the importance of ethical and inclusive innovation practices, offering guidelines for regulators and industry leaders. Sustainable innovation is a recurring theme, promoting long-term economic success through the adoption of green technologies and social entrepreneurship. Finally, the book anticipates future disruptions, equipping stakeholders with strategies to address emerging challenges in cybersecurity, education, and digital transformation.

Table 3.

Dimension	Details
Theoretical Advancements	Expands understanding of resilience strategies, innovation metrics, and the interplay of technology and economics.
Practical Applications	Provides actionable frameworks, real-world examples, and case studies for implementing innovative strategies.
Policy Insights	Proposes guidelines for ethical technology adoption, innovation policies, and regulatory standards.
Sustainable Innovation	Highlights the role of circular economy principles, green technologies, and social entrepreneurship in economic resilience.
Future-Ready Solutions	Anticipates trends in education, cybersecurity, and technology integration to prepare for future disruptions.

KEY THEMES OF THE FRAMEWORK

The themes of the book highlight the critical dimensions of innovation management and its role in fostering resilience in the digital economy. Resilience through innovation underscores the adaptability required to navigate disruptions, while technology as an enabler showcases the transformative potential of tools like AI, blockchain, and IoT. Inclusivity and equity are emphasized as essential to ensuring broad societal benefits, and sustainability remains a core focus for achieving long-term success. Finally, preparing for the future equips stakeholders with the strategies needed to thrive in an ever-changing digital landscape.

Table 4.

Theme	Description
Resilience Through Innovation	Leveraging innovation management to build adaptable and sustainable economies.
Technology as an Enabler	Integrating AI, blockchain, IoT, and cloud systems for transformative impacts.
Inclusivity and Equity	Ensuring innovation benefits all stakeholders and promotes inclusivity and social equity.

continued on following page

Table 4. Continued

Theme	Description
Sustainability as a Priority	Embedding green technologies and circular economy principles in business practices.
Preparing for the Future	Equipping businesses, governments, and educators to navigate the challenges of digitization.

ACKNOWLEDGMENTS

This volume would not have been possible without the dedication and expertise of the contributing authors, whose work represents diverse perspectives and insights from across the globe. We extend our gratitude to our editorial team, reviewers, and supporters, whose efforts have enriched this endeavor.

Invitation to Readers

We invite you to engage with the chapters in this book, which offer a blend of theoretical insights and practical applications for navigating the challenges of the digital economy. It is our hope that this volume serves as both a guide and an inspiration for fostering innovation, resilience, and inclusivity in an increasingly complex and interconnected world.

Miltiadis D. Lytras

The American College of Greece, Greece & Computer Science Department, College of Engineering, Effat University, Saudi Arabia

Patricia Ordonez

University of Oviedo, Spain

Afnan Alkhaldi

Arab Open University Kuwait, Kuwait

Andreea Claudia Serban

Bucharest University of Economic Studies, Romania

Chapter 1
Developing Sustainable Business Models: Integrating Circular Economy, Social Entrepreneurship, and Green Technologies

S. Sudhakar
https://orcid.org/0009-0006-4435-8452
LEAD College of Management, Palakkad, India

Sadaf Anwar
https://orcid.org/0000-0002-6964-3739
M.S. Ramaiah Institute of Management, Bengaluru, India

Parul Wadhwa
https://orcid.org/0009-0008-8751-6128
DPG Degree College, Gurugram, India

Narender Singh
https://orcid.org/0009-0001-4690-3710
Rungta College of Science and Technology, Bhilai, India

ABSTRACT

This chapter is focused on the process of integrating Circular Economy, Social Entrepreneurship, and Green Technologies into sustainable business models. As the environmental and social issues combating the world progress, organizations are changing the ways they do business and implementing changes that support waste minimization, social perspective, and green technology. The chapter begins by defining these key concepts and examining their individual roles in promoting

DOI: 10.4018/979-8-3693-8357-5.ch001

sustainability. Thus, using case examples, it shows successful instances of application and reveals the advantages and limitations of each method. Because of these elements, a proposed framework to integrate these elements emphasize on how these elements complement each other to bring about a comprehensive framework for business. Moreover, the chapter stresses that is crucial to continuously develop and invites businesses, entrepreneurs, and policymakers to fighting for sustainability as a competitive challenge for futures success.

1.INTRODUCTION

Recently, several issues on sustainability management have emerged as prominent top-priority concepts for companies to implement them in their activity due to the existing global environmental and social concerns. The increasing impacts of climate change, as highlighted in the latest IPCC report, emphasize the urgent need for businesses to adopt sustainable models. Without such changes, environmental degradation will continue at an alarming pace (Masson-Delmotte et al., 2021). The IPCC report outlines several critical issues: rising global temperatures, increasing frequency of natural disasters, and shrinking natural resources. These findings reinforce the immediate need for businesses to adapt to sustainable models to mitigate environmental damage. There is general consensus that the linear model of economy which could be described by the "take-make-dispose" principle is highly unsustainable, as it implies resource depletion and pollution (Kirchherr, Reike, & Hekkert, 2017). This model is particularly ironical given that the ecosystems and economies of the world are now interconnected such that actions of one part have implications on another part.

In response, companies are now waking up to the reality that sustainability has to be a core part of strategies. This change is motivated by ethic and rationale reasons as sustainable approach has become a key driver of competitive advantage (Portery & Kramer, 2018). The Circular Economy has been proposed as a solution towards these challenges due to promoting resource loop –ability or utilizing resources and reducing waste (Esposito et al., 2017). Similarly, the realization of Social Entrepreneurship shows how business enterprise can also work towards solving existing social challenges and at the same time generate profits (Doherty, Haugh, & Lyon, 2014). Secondly, the application of Green Technologies has provided real strategies for minimizing the impact of the business activities on the environment (Koutoudjian et al., 2021).

Other global practices like the UN's Sustainable Development Goals also emphasize the centrality of business in solving global challenges especially the call for the promotion of sustainable consumption and production patterns. Thus, the strategies based on the sustainability approaches are not only the effective reactions to the environment issues and social problems, but the relevant and effective solutions for the further successful business development.

To identify how sustainability can be incorporated into business strategies, it is relevant to clarify the meaning of Circular Economy, Social Entrepreneurship, and Green Technologies.

Circular Economy is an economic model that aims to reduce waste to the lowest possible levels or even eliminate it completely throughout the economic cycle for goods and services. In contrast to the linear economy, the circular economy draws on the concept of closing the Loop so that products and processes are designed for reuse and recycling thus reducing ecosystem impact (Geissdoerfer et al., 2020). The limitations of the linear economy, such as resource depletion and waste, have prompted a shift toward the Circular Economy. This model, unlike the linear one, emphasizes closing resource loops through reuse, recycling, and reducing ecosystem impacts. It is one with added sustainability in terms of its environmental impact and saves costs of forming new products, markets, and focuses on freeing itself from the clutches of scarce resources (Ogunmakinde et al., 2021). Shift towards the circular economy is viewed as a major element to foster the achievement of sustainable development objectives (Ghisellini et al., 2016).

Social Entrepreneurship therefore ranges from creating new and unique models of business ventures that seek to solve social issues. In contrast to conventional business owners for whom the main goal is the generation of financial returns, social entrepreneurs aim at creating social impact and increasing the welfare of society (Zahra et al., 2014). Social enterprises are organizations that seek to pursue social objectives while at the same time being profitability conscious and as such possess characteristics of both for-profit and nonprofit entities (Doherty et al., 2014). This approach enables social impact to be grown sustainably and thereby meet the goals of addressing the chronic social problems.

Green Technologies can therefore be defined as any technology advancement that seeks to solve environmental issues. These technologies include renewable energy technologies like wind and solar energy technologies other innovations in energy efficiency, eco-waste management and improved utilization of resources (Koutoudjian et al., 2021). In this case, the advanced green technologies play a crucial role to those organizations that seek to build sustainable green business and minimize their impact to the environment. Current developments in this area have enabled organizations to include green innovations in their operations hence enhancing environmental and economic sustainability (Demirel et al., 2019).

Thus, the main focus of this chapter is to discuss how Circular Economy, Social Entrepreneurship and Green Technologies can be utilized in viable and sustainable business strategies. Through the analysis of these three factors, the goal of this chapter is to propose an integrated framework that may be used by businesses in order to create sustainable value in the long run. Incorporation of these concept is not just a process of reacting to environment or social pressures but more so a process of seizing opportunities for creation of new value in a business environment that is rapidly changing and becoming ever more competitive.

2. LITERATURE REVIEW

Sustainable business models originate from several theories and frameworks that help business consider environmental, social, and economic aspects. Some of them include the Triple Bottom Line Framework which was proposed by Elkington (1999) where he posited that companies should work on people, planet and profit as opposed to measuring organization performance in terms of profit alone. This idea has played a crucial role in changing corporate values towards the organization's health and the environment. More than 20 years later, Elkington reflected on this concept and the need for businesses to reimagine and transform TBL to suit the present day sustainability issues (Elkington, 2018).

Extending the TBL, the RBV of the firm as proposed by Hart and Dowell (2011) postulates that the competitive advantage of a firm is resilient where the resources, which are valuable, rare and imitable by competitors, are well managed. This theory is particularly important in sustainability as both environmental and social assets become considered as valuable resources.

Recently Abdelkafi et al. (2023) contribute to this discussion by reviewing the existing literature concerning sustainable business model patterns and call for integrated approaches. Their work establishes the importance of integrating multiple sustainability components into components that are executable strategies for organizations.

Therefore, before exploring the various strategies for sustainable business, there is a need to identify and discuss the concept of sustainability, its major issues, and trends in the subject. The following Table1. provides a concise overview of these critical elements, highlighting how sustainability in business has evolved, the role of the circular economy and social entrepreneurship, the importance of green technologies, and the ongoing debates and innovations driving the future of sustainable business models.

Table 1. Overview of key concepts, challenges, and emerging trends in sustainable business practices

Topic	Key Concepts	Challenges/Gaps	Emerging Trends
Sustainability in Business	• Developed from CSR to integrated sustainability into business strategies (Carroll, 1999). • Promotes innovation and sustainable business value (Amini and Bienstock, 2014; Ashrafi et al., 2018). • Green product innovation as a strategic decision: Evidence from consumer electronics firms (Dangelico, 2016).	• Need for deeper integration of social and environmental goals. • Limited long-term impact case studies.	Growing focus on green product innovation as a strategic advantage (Dangelico, 2016).
Circular Economy (CE)	• Encourages resource re-use in a bid to reduce resource wastage (MacArthur, 2013; Geissdoerfer et al., 2017). • They challenge the traditional 'extract-consume-dispose' mode of consumerism. • Important for innovation and resource utilization (Korhonen et al., 2018).	• Complexity in closing resource loops. • Rebound effects and scaling issues.	Digital tech (IoT, blockchain) supports CE practices (Pappas et al., 2019).
Social Entrepreneurship	• Contains both business and social purposes (Battilana & Lee, 2014). • Combats societal issues with issues of sustainable profitability (Doherty et al., 2014). • Possibilities of mission drift (Ebrahim, Battilana, & Mair, 2014).	• Balancing social missions with financial sustainability. • Scalability remains challenging.	Hybrid organizations are bridging for-profit and non-profit models (Battilana & Lee, 2014).
Green Technologies	• Lowers impacts and/or emissions related to the finish environment and raises productivity (Dangelico, 2016). • They may be in the areas of renewable power, energy conservation, use of environment friendly materials. • It becomes a requirement in order to conform to certain standards and to meet the needs of the market (Hojnik & Ruzzier, 2016).	• High initial costs and technological complexity. • Needs better integration into business strategies.	Investment in green tech driven by carbon neutrality goals and digital optimization tools (Pappas et al., 2019).

3. UNDERSTANDING CIRCULAR ECONOMY IN BUSINESS MODELS

A circular economy (CE) is the idea of developing economic models that reduce the amount of waste produced and thereby keep materials within closed loops. According to Bocken et al. (2016), it is important that the principles of circular economy exclude the connection between resource consumption and economic growth by using longevity, renewability, reuse, repair, upgrade, refurbishment and recirculation. Business models that are circular, as described by Geissdoerfer et al. (2020), eliminate environmental harm and generate value at the same time by prolonging the lifecycle of products and using waste as inputs. This approach is a shift from the linear economy, in which products are manufactured, used, and then discarded, which results in wastage of resources.

The paper by Kirchherr, Reike, and Hekkert (2017) presents a systematic review of 114 definitions of the circular economy and advocated for system change in product design, production, and use. They claim that for a business to practice CE, it means rethinking operations, supply chains, and value proposition, with a focus on keeping material in use for as long as possible.

3.1 Examples and Case Studies

- A great example of applying the concepts of circular economy is the case of **Patagonia**, which is described by Chouinard and Stanley (2013). Currently Patagonia has incorporated circular economy concepts into its business strategy through campaigns such as Worn Wear campaign that seeks to reform, renew and recycle used clothes. This program fits well into CE in aspects of product life extension as well as the minimization of wastes produced thus showing how a firm can grow its profits without compromising the environment.
- Another example is the paper by Erasmus et al. (2024) on the role of end-of-life fishing nets, lines, and ropes in the **Namibian** circular economy. In this regard, the researchers examine how such waste materials can be reused to become sources of value. Besides, the initiative of turning these end-of-life materials to new products also helps to fight against pollution and generate job opportunities especially in coastal areas where fishing industries dominate.
- Rizos et al. (2016) focus their study on analysing the existing and potential application of circular economy business models among **SMEs**. These specify the external and internal factors influencing the decision to engage in CE practices pointing to the fact that while SMEs have restrictions in terms of capital and know-how, they also have a vast potential to stand out in the market through the implementation of circular processes. For instance, some of the SMEs have ensured they have

circular business models by ensuring that product design enables easy disassembly and recycling of the product in a sustainable economy.

3.2 Circular Economy: Challenges vs. Opportunities

Adopting Circular Economy practices in business models presents both significant challenges and promising opportunities. Table 2 below presents a summary of these key points, with the view to providing a balanced perspective of the state of the transition towards sustainable business practices.

Table 2. Challenges vs. opportunities

Challenges	Opportunities
Initial High Costs Upfront investments in redesigning products, supply chains, and business processes can be significant. (Lewandowski, 2016)	**Cost Savings** Long-term savings through resource efficiency, waste reduction, and product longevity. (Zhu et al., 2022)
Complexity in Implementation Integrating circular practices into existing linear models requires complex changes and coordination. (Rizos et al., 2016)	**Innovation & Differentiation** Opportunity to innovate in product design, processes, and models, leading to market differentiation. (Bocken et al., 2019)
Consumer Behavior & Market Acceptance Slow market acceptance and the need for consumer education on circular products. (Chouinard & Stanley, 2013)	**Enhanced Brand Reputation** Strengthening brand reputation among environmentally conscious consumers. (Tudor & Dutra, 2021)
Regulatory & Policy Barriers Navigating diverse regulations and the lack of supportive policies. (Zhu et al., 2022)	**New Market Opportunities** Expanding into emerging markets focused on sustainability. (Erasmus et al., 2024)
Supply Chain Dependencies Challenges in collaborating closely with suppliers and partners for circular practices. (Rizos et al., 2016)	**Collaboration & Partnerships** Shared resources, knowledge, and innovation through strategic partnerships. (Bocken et al., 2016)
Technological Limitations Limited access to or development of necessary technologies. (Lewandowski, 2016)	**Resource Security & Resilience** Strengthening resource security and business resilience by reducing dependency on finite resources. (Zhu et al., 2022)

4. SOCIAL ENTREPRENEURSHIP: ALIGNING BUSINESS WITH SOCIAL IMPACT

Social entrepreneurship is a model of operating that aims at addressing social challenges with a strong reference to the business ventures' strategies, integrating the values of social benefits with the organizational effectiveness of business enterprises. Saebi, Foss, and Linder (2019) pointed out that while social entrepreneurship also entails an orientation to the greater good, it is different from pure philanthropy as well as business with primary focus on profit. Such dual characteristics enable social enterprises to solve multifaceted issues that include poverty, unemployment, and pollution.

Yunus (2017) defines social entrepreneurship using a powerful image of the world with no poverty, no unemployment, and no net carbon emissions making it necessary to embrace change and recognize that social entrepreneurship can be the way to make the change. Social business runs on the belief that commerce indeed has the potential to bring out positive changes in society and every business should be financially sustainable.

Hybrid organizing as provided by Battilana and Lee (2014) is a critical in explaining social entrepreneurship. The organizations of this type use features of both for-profit and nonprofit organizations, giving equal importance to the social mission and financial sustainability. This balance is important so that social entrepreneurship can be able to be financially stable for it to support its operations and expand its social impact. This ensures that the social entrepreneurs have the capacity to balance and harness this dual feature.

4.1 Case Studies

This is done through sharing of several examples that show how social entrepreneurship can be developed into the existing business models in order to give out social relevance. These examples demonstrate that there is no 'best practice' model for social entrepreneurship and the creative ways used by people to solve society's problems.

The methods of Muhammad Yunus and the Grameen Bank provides a good example of where microfinance originated from. According to Yunus (2017), Grameen Bank channels small loans to the needy, especially women, without any security deposit. Thus, this model has help millions of people to become their own bosses and surface themselves from poverty level a true sign of social entrepreneur and power of entrepreneurship in supporting economic growth and social equity.

Yet another example is the work of Westley et al. (2014), which focuses on the scaling up of social innovations by nonprofit organizations in Canada. The authors outline five generic approaches to scaling social impact, which include the diffusion approach, the bridging approach, and the integration approach. These cases show that the extension of the experience and the implementation of the diversification of the approach allows social enterprise to improve their results and affect a wider population.

Santos, Pache, and Birkholz (2015) offer additional information on how to connect the business model with organizational design for social enterprises to create social impacts. Based on their studies of hybrid organizations, they conclude that organizational oversight is critical in enhancing correspondence between business strategies and social objectives in order to foster long-term sustainability of social impact. It also enhances the strategies of social enterprises in order to meet their efficiency and objectives without compromising the aims of social entrepreneurship.

4.2 Challenges in Scaling Social Impact

While scaling up social enterprises, there are lots of issues that need to be solved, especially when it comes to achieving both the goals of social impact and financial performance. Eiselein and Dentchev (2021) noted that as social enterprises expand and develop, there is usually a danger in which organizations become too embedded in more financial objectives, which may influence mission drift in hybrid organisations that have both, social and economic objectives. Bloom and Chatterji (2009) also focus on resource limitations as one of the main problems, stating that compared to traditional businesses, social enterprises have a small amount of capital and contacts to access more and reach more people, especially in developing countries.

Another challenge is the difficulty of scaling up the implementation of successful models across different contexts. In their paper, Smith, Kistruck, and Cannatelli (2016) present the ethical challenges that are associated with scaling decisions, whereby the social entrepreneurs have to make sure that their efforts to expand their activities do not harm the core purpose of achieving a social mission. In response to these challenges, impact investing as defined by Bugg-Levine and Emerson (2011) can be considered as a strategic approach of aligning investors' motives with the social purposes of ventures to provide required capital for growth as well as integrating financial incentives with social returns. Nevertheless, social entrepreneurship presents great potential to reconnect business with the social good as long as the alignment strategies and more importantly socially innovative financing instruments are carefully used.

5. ROLE OF GREEN TECHNOLOGIES IN SUSTAINABLE BUSINESS MODELS

Green technologies are important as they support sustainable business strategies because they reduce negative effects on the environment and adapt innovations. These technologies include, but are not limited to, renewable power generation technologies such as wind, water and solar energy, improved methods of water desalination and water recycling. In the current discourse, Komazawa (2023) defines that the promotion of renewable energy remains the key focal area of discourse on sustainable development covering the transition to clean energy systems and green infrastructure. There is also an increase in the utilization of technologies like Carbon Capture and Storage (CCS), which Bui, Ishkanov, and Rivero (2018) mentioned can greatly ensure the reduction of carbon emissions from various activities in industries. Also, the integration of technology in green innovation is changing the landscape of industries and enterprises. This is according to Li et al. (2023) who suggest that the innovation of business models especially in manufacturing has continued to support the use of green technologies hence making production more sustainable.

5.1 Integration into Business Practices

The management of green technologies as practices in business organizations calls for a strategic approach that defines these practices in relation to the larger organizational sustainability frameworks. For instance, there has been a general acceptance of circular economy as a method used by organizations in the modern organization in the quest for minimizing waste and optimizing resource throughput. In their paper published in 2019, De Sousa Jabbour et al. also talk about the way circular economy business models can be adopted in operations management for efficiency and sustainable operations. It also includes water aspects Gude (2017) on desalination, which is one of the technologies that holds the potential in addressing shortage of fresh water in the world. In addition, several firms are now utilizing technology to increase the efficiency of implementing green technologies. Li et al. (2023) explain how open business models in Haier COSMOPlat affect knowledge management and green technology in the manufacturing industry.

5.2 Innovations and Future Trends

The future belongs to the further development of green technologies and their use in other spheres of activity. Liu, Thurasamy, and Hati (2024) have highlighted the factor and consequences of green technology innovation adoption by third-party logistics firms in China, how innovation can help these firms improve their environmental performance and have competitive advantage. Such contemporary technologies like blockchain are also being considered for application in development and sustenance of the sustainable supply chains. According to Kouhizadeh, Saberi, and Sarkis (2021), there are potential barriers to blockchain adoption in sustainable supply chain and if these hurdles are crossed there will be improvement in supply chains. Furthermore, Jacobson et al.'s (2017) study on 100% clean, renewable energy for 139 countries showed that complete transition to green energy sources is possible and could transform energy systems worldwide while helping achieve sustainable development goals.

6. INTEGRATING CIRCULAR ECONOMY, SOCIAL ENTREPRENEURSHIP, AND GREEN TECHNOLOGIES

The integration of the circular economy (CE), social entrepreneurship, and green technologies (GT) offers a modern path to sustainability by combining environmental care with social responsibility and innovation. CE aims at minimizing waste and recycling as much as possible, whereas GT builds on this through tools, such as efficient energy use, energy from renewable sources, and sustainable material use. Social entrepreneurship does this while targeting the social and environmental objectives in addition to revenues. As Mazzucato (2021) noted, companies need to establish purpose for transforming global challenges on a systemic level. Elkington's (1999) three Ps of people, planet, and profit most aptly fit this model, thus creating value for business as well as for the society and the planet. This creates a synergy, which leads to more sustainable and effective business models.

This Figure 1. depicts the interrelation between Circular Economy (CE), Green Technologies (GT), and Social Entrepreneurship (SE) as the pillars for sustainable business model. The figure 1. shows the effectiveness of CE in reducing waste and enhancing resource utilization, the applicability the GT in offering solutions such as efficient energy, and the incorporation of SE, where social aspects are combined with sustainability. The connections between these elements – Enhanced Sustainability, Innovative Solutions, and Triple Bottom Line Impact, show how their coherence results in sustainable business models, therefore encouraging a systemic change and ensuring that operations involve people, the planet, and profits in equal measure. CE, GT, and SE are interconnected concepts that support each other in creating a holistic approach to solving global challenges by adopting sustainable processes and ideas.

Figure 1. Integrated framework for sustainable innovation by author

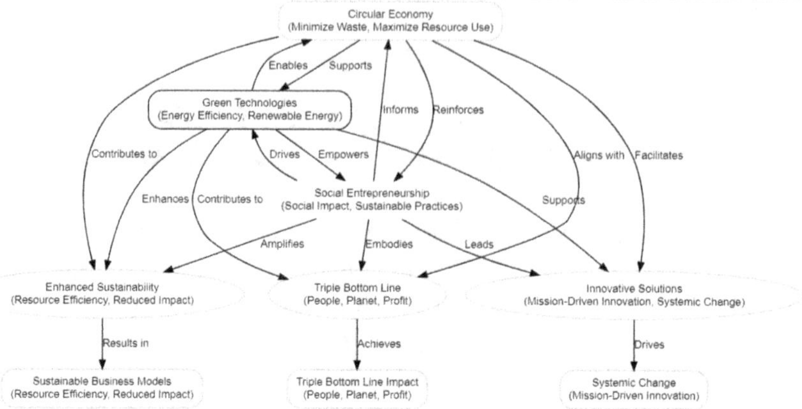

6.1 Proposed Framework for Integration

CE, social entrepreneurship, and GT have to be integrated, and this requires a good and strong framework. According to Boons and Lüdeke-Freund (2013) the focus should be made on sustainable business model, including the linkage of innovation to sustainable development. They suggest that instead of pursuing shareholder value, it should be about value creation where all stakeholders, the environment, and the society, are considered and valued. This may be done by implementing CE principles, which enable reuse, refurbishment and recycling of materials to minimize waste and resource consumption.

On this basis, there are suggestions by Bocken et al. (2016) on the design and business models in relation to the CE. The CE components include designing products for longevity, modularity, and recyclability, as pointed out by the authors. These strategies can be implemented within the Business Model which also emphasizes the Social Entrepreneurship aspects of the business, addressing, therefore, the social perspective of business activity alongside the environmental one. For example, Tariqullah (2024) presents the concept of Circular-ESG, a model of Business regeneration combining ESG parameters. Thus, this model can serve as a reference model for companies that are trying to shift from being traditional to adopting CE principles, using GT, and having social objectives.

The following Figure 2. provides a Proposed Framework for Integration of how Circular Economy, Social Entrepreneurship, and Green Technologies can be aligned to deliver sustainable solutions. Thereby proving that the Circular Economy, Social Entrepreneurship, and Green Technologies all play a part in the Sustainable Business

Models, Product Design Strategies, and the Circular-ESG Model. These integration strategies then lead to key outcomes: The Three Pillars," which are Positive Societal Impact, Environmental Sustainability and Economic Viability." It shows influence flow where overall strategy is informed and supported by each of these components to improve the societal worth, environmental return on investment and economic profitability." This structural approach centers on how these components contribute to the generation of sustainability and value.

Figure 2. Proposed framework for integration by author

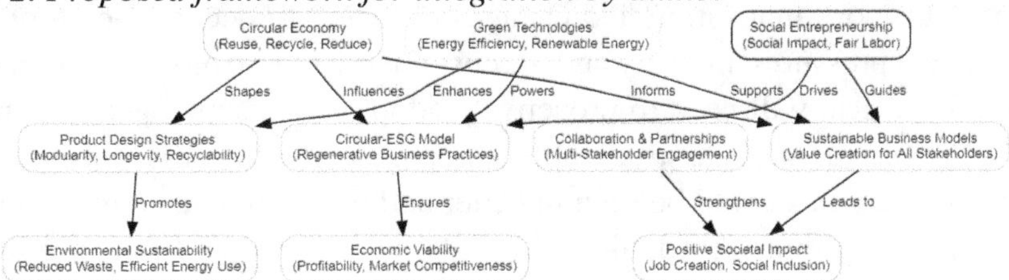

6.2 Case Studies and Best Practices

A few examples of companies that illustrate how CE, social entrepreneurship, and GT can be implemented in practice are provided below.

- **Social Enterprises in Ukraine:**Redko (2023) also focuses on Ukrainian social enterprises that are most advanced in implementing CE strategies. They also provide solutions to multiple environmental practices like the reduction of waste, the recycling procedures besides solving social issues like that of unemployment and social exclusion by creating job opportunities and interacting with the society.
- **Smart Grids and CE Integration:**Reindl et al. (2024) elaborate the implementation of CE principles in smart grids, one of the pillars of GT. the use of smart grids improve the usage of energy and thus encourages the shift from traditional sources of energy to renewable sources. This integration doesn't only eliminate the environmental issue but also brings chances of social innovation to offer energy to remote areas of the world.

These case studies illustrate the potential for businesses to successfully integrate CE, social entrepreneurship, and GT, creating value for both society and the environment while maintaining economic viability.

7. CONCLUSION

This chapter has focused on the implementation of circular economy, social entrepreneurship, and green technology as the sustainability framework of businesses. It was highlighted how these elements can prompt innovation, the increase in competitiveness, and overall sustainability. Interconnection between these ideas was demonstrated, as it is important to recognize their further possibilities for developing new business model and making companies more sustainable and ethical.

Moving forward, the future of sustainable business models will likely not be stagnant with more innovation and changes expected to occur. Therefore, as the environmental pressures intensify and the customers become more environmentally conscious, the firm will need to proactively adopt new technologies, reformulate its value-chain, and integrate sustainable, comprehensive business objectives. Even further improvements could be seen in better and more complex circular business models and stronger implementation of social impacts into key strategic directions.

Lastly, it is pertinent to emphasize that there should be an appeals to action where all the business, the entrepreneurial, and policymaking entities should promote environmental sustainability. In this way, managing them they are not only able to cope with the outstanding global issues but also open new opportunities for future development in the constantly changing world.

REFERENCES

Abdelkafi, N., Xu, J., Pero, M., Ciccullo, F., & Masi, A. (2023). Does the combination of sustainable business model patterns lead to truly sustainable business models? Critical analysis of existing frameworks and extensions. *Journal of Business Economics*, 93(4), 597–634. DOI: 10.1007/s11573-023-01140-0

Amini, M., & Bienstock, C. C. (2014). Corporate sustainability: An integrative definition and framework to evaluate corporate practice and guide academic research. *Journal of Cleaner Production*, 76, 12–19. DOI: 10.1016/j.jclepro.2014.02.016

Ashrafi, M., Adams, M., Walker, T. R., & Magnan, G. (2018). How corporate social responsibility can be integrated into corporate sustainability: A theoretical review of their relationships. *International Journal of Sustainable Development and World Ecology*, 25(8), 672–682. DOI: 10.1080/13504509.2018.1471628

Battilana, J., & Lee, M. (2014). Advancing research on hybrid organizing–Insights from the study of social enterprises. *The Academy of Management Annals*, 8(1), 397–441. DOI: 10.5465/19416520.2014.893615

Bloom, P. N., & Chatterji, A. K. (2009). Scaling social entrepreneurial impact. *California Management Review*, 51(3), 114–133. DOI: 10.2307/41166496

Bocken, N., Strupeit, L., Whalen, K., & Nußholz, J. (2019). A review and evaluation of circular business model innovation tools. *Sustainability (Basel)*, 11(8), 2210. DOI: 10.3390/su11082210

. Bocken, N. M., De Pauw, I., Bakker, C., & Van Der Grinten, B. (2016). Product design and business model strategies for a circular economy. Journal of industrial and production engineering, 33(5), 308-320.

Bocken, N. M., Short, S. W., Rana, P., & Evans, S. (2014). A literature and practice review to develop sustainable business model archetypes. *Journal of Cleaner Production*, 65, 42–56. DOI: 10.1016/j.jclepro.2013.11.039

Boons, F., & Lüdeke-Freund, F. (2013). Business models for sustainable innovation: State-of-the-art and steps towards a research agenda. *Journal of Cleaner Production*, 45, 9–19. DOI: 10.1016/j.jclepro.2012.07.007

Bugg-Levine, A., & Emerson, J. (2011). *Impact investing: Transforming how we make money while making a difference*. John Wiley & Sons.

Bui, M., Adjiman, C. S., Bardow, A., Anthony, E. J., Boston, A., Brown, S., Fennell, P. S., Fuss, S., Galindo, A., Hackett, L. A., Hallett, J. P., Herzog, H. J., Jackson, G., Kemper, J., Krevor, S., Maitland, G. C., Matuszewski, M., Metcalfe, I. S., Petit, C., & Mac Dowell, N. (2018). Carbon capture and storage (CCS): The way forward. *Energy & Environmental Science*, 11(5), 1062–1176. DOI: 10.1039/C7EE02342A

Carroll, A. B. (1999). Corporate social responsibility: Evolution of a definitional construct. *Business & Society*, 38(3), 268–295. DOI: 10.1177/000765039903800303

Chouinard, Y., & Stanley, V. (2013). *The responsible company: What we've learned from Patagonia's first 40 years*. Patagonia.

Dacin, P. A., Dacin, M. T., & Matear, M. (2010). Social entrepreneurship: Why we don't need a new theory and how we move forward from here. *The Academy of Management Perspectives*, 24(3), 37–57.

Dangelico, R. M. (2016). Green product innovation: Where we are and where we are going. *Business Strategy and the Environment*, 25(8), 560–576. DOI: 10.1002/bse.1886

de Sousa Jabbour, A. B. L., Luiz, J. V. R., Luiz, O. R., Jabbour, C. J. C., Ndubisi, N. O., de Oliveira, J. H. C., & Junior, F. H. (2019). Circular economy business models and operations management. *Journal of Cleaner Production*, 235, 1525–1539. DOI: 10.1016/j.jclepro.2019.06.349

Demirel, P., Li, Q. C., Rentocchini, F., & Tamvada, J. P. (2019). Born to be green: New insights into the economics and management of green entrepreneurship. *Small Business Economics*, 52(4), 759–771. DOI: 10.1007/s11187-017-9933-z

Doherty, B., Haugh, H., & Lyon, F. (2014). Social enterprises as hybrid organizations: A review and research agenda. *International Journal of Management Reviews*, 16(4), 417–436. DOI: 10.1111/ijmr.12028

Ebrahim, A., Battilana, J., & Mair, J. (2014). The governance of social enterprises: Mission drift and accountability challenges in hybrid organizations. *Research in Organizational Behavior*, 34, 81–100. DOI: 10.1016/j.riob.2014.09.001

. Eiselein, P., & Dentchev, N. A. (2021). Scaling social impact: What challenges and opportunities Await social entrepreneurs. Social Entrepreneurship, 145-172.

Elkington, J. (2018). 25 years ago I coined the phrase "triple bottom line." Here's why it's time to rethink it. *Harvard Business Review*, 25(2-5).

Elkington, J., & Rowlands, I. H. (1999). Cannibals with forks: The triple bottom line of 21st century business. *Alternatives Journal*, 25(4), 42.

Erasmus, V. N., Johannes, F. N., Amutenya, N., & James, N. A. (2024). The potential contribution of end-of-life fishing nets, lines and ropes to a circular economy: The Namibian perspective. *Frontiers in Sustainability*, 5, 1356265. DOI: 10.3389/frsus.2024.1356265

Esposito, M., Tse, T., & Soufani, K. (2017). Is the circular economy a new fast-expanding market? *Thunderbird International Business Review*, 59(1), 9–14. DOI: 10.1002/tie.21764

Geissdoerfer, M., Pieroni, M. P., Pigosso, D. C., & Soufani, K. (2020). Circular business models: A review. *Journal of Cleaner Production*, 277, 123741. DOI: 10.1016/j.jclepro.2020.123741

Geissdoerfer, M., Savaget, P., Bocken, N. M., & Hultink, E. J. (2017). The Circular Economy–A new sustainability paradigm? *Journal of Cleaner Production*, 143, 757–768. DOI: 10.1016/j.jclepro.2016.12.048

Ghisellini, P., Cialani, C., & Ulgiati, S. (2016). A review on circular economy: The expected transition to a balanced interplay of environmental and economic systems. *Journal of Cleaner Production*, 114, 11–32. DOI: 10.1016/j.jclepro.2015.09.007

Giglio, F., Grillo, E., & Sansotta, S. (2023, September). Integration of Circular and Green Technologies for the Adaptive Reuse of Public Space. In Mediterranean Architecture and the Green-Digital Transition: Selected Papers from the World Renewable Energy Congress Med Green Forum 2022 (pp. 339-353). Cham: Springer International Publishing. DOI: 10.1007/978-3-031-33148-0_27

Gude, V. G. (2017). Desalination and water reuse to address global water scarcity. *Reviews in Environmental Science and Biotechnology*, 16(4), 591–609. DOI: 10.1007/s11157-017-9449-7

Hart, S. L., & Dowell, G. (2011). Invited editorial: A natural-resource-based view of the firm: Fifteen years after. *Journal of Management*, 37(5), 1464–1479. DOI: 10.1177/0149206310390219

Hazen, B. T., Boone, C. A., Ezell, J. D., & Jones-Farmer, L. A. (2014). Data quality for data science, predictive analytics, and big data in supply chain management: An introduction to the problem and suggestions for research and applications. *International Journal of Production Economics*, 154, 72–80. DOI: 10.1016/j.ijpe.2014.04.018

Hojnik, J., & Ruzzier, M. (2016). What drives eco-innovation? A review of an emerging literature. *Environmental Innovation and Societal Transitions*, 19, 31–41. DOI: 10.1016/j.eist.2015.09.006

Jabbour, C. J. C., de Sousa Jabbour, A. B. L., Sarkis, J., & Godinho Filho, M. (2019). Unlocking the circular economy through new business models based on large-scale data: An integrative framework and research agenda. *Technological Forecasting and Social Change*, 144, 546–552. DOI: 10.1016/j.techfore.2017.09.010

Jacobson, M. Z., Delucchi, M. A., Bauer, Z. A., Goodman, S. C., Chapman, W. E., Cameron, M. A., Bozonnat, C., Chobadi, L., Clonts, H. A., Enevoldsen, P., Erwin, J. R., Fobi, S. N., Goldstrom, O. K., Hennessy, E. M., Liu, J., Lo, J., Meyer, C. B., Morris, S. B., Moy, K. R., & Yachanin, A. S. (2017). 100% clean and renewable wind, water, and sunlight all-sector energy roadmaps for 139 countries of the world. *Joule*, 1(1), 108–121. DOI: 10.1016/j.joule.2017.07.005

Kirchherr, J., Reike, D., & Hekkert, M. (2017). Conceptualizing the circular economy: An analysis of 114 definitions. *Resources, Conservation and Recycling*, 127, 221–232. DOI: 10.1016/j.resconrec.2017.09.005

KOMAZAWA. (2022). Y. (2023). Renewables 2023 Global Status Report Collection Energy Systems & Infrastructure-Key. *Headlines (Lagos)*.

Korhonen, J., Honkasalo, A., & Seppälä, J. (2018). Circular economy: The concept and its limitations. *Ecological Economics*, 143, 37–46. DOI: 10.1016/j.ecolecon.2017.06.041

Kouhizadeh, M., Saberi, S., & Sarkis, J. (2021). Blockchain technology and the sustainable supply chain: Theoretically exploring adoption barriers. *International Journal of Production Economics*, 231, 107831. DOI: 10.1016/j.ijpe.2020.107831

. Koutoudjian, G., Diniz, L., Cespedes, R., & UNDP, V. G. (2021). About IRENA The International Renewable Energy Agency (IRENA) is an intergovernmental organisation that supports countries in their transition to a sustainable energy future, and serves as the principal platform for international co-operation, a centre of excellence, and a repository of policy, technology, resource and financial knowledge on renewable energy. IRENA promotes the. IRENA promotes the, 24.

Lewandowski, M. (2016). Designing the business models for circular economy—Towards the conceptual framework. *Sustainability (Basel)*, 8(1), 43. DOI: 10.3390/su8010043

Li, H., Yang, Z., Wang, H., & Li, Y. (2023). Digitalization of business models, knowledge management and green technology innovation of Chinese manufacturing enterprises: A mixed analysis based on the Haier COSMOPlat ecosystem. *Asia Pacific Business Review*, •••, 1–29. DOI: 10.1080/13602381.2023.2282116

Liu, S., Thurasamy, R., & Hati, S. R. H. (2024). Determinants and Outcomes of Green Technology Innovation Adoption among Third-Party Logistics Firms in China: A SEM-ANN Analysis. *Systems*, 12(9), 331. DOI: 10.3390/systems12090331

MacArthur, E. (2013). Towards the circular economy. *Journal of Industrial Ecology*, 2(1), 23–44.

Masson-Delmotte, V. P., Zhai, P., Pirani, S. L., Connors, C., Péan, S., Berger, N., . . . Scheel Monteiro, P. M. (2021). Ipcc, 2021: Summary for policymakers. in: Climate change 2021: The physical science basis. contribution of working group i to the sixth assessment report of the intergovernmental panel on climate change.

Mazzucato, M. (2021). *Mission economy: A moonshot guide to changing capitalism.*

Nicholls, A. (2010). The legitimacy of social entrepreneurship: Reflexive isomorphism in a pre–paradigmatic field. *Entrepreneurship Theory and Practice*, 34(4), 611–633. DOI: 10.1111/j.1540-6520.2010.00397.x

Ogunmakinde, O. E., Sher, W., & Egbelakin, T. (2021). Circular economy pillars: A semi-systematic review. *Clean Technologies and Environmental Policy*, 23(3), 899–914. DOI: 10.1007/s10098-020-02012-9

Pappas, I. O., Mikalef, P., Dwivedi, Y., Jaccheri, L., Krogstie, J., & Mäntymäki, M. (2019). *Digital transformation for a sustainable society in the 21st century*. Springer International Publishing. DOI: 10.1007/978-3-030-29374-1

Porter, M. E., & Kramer, M. R. (2018). Creating shared value: How to reinvent capitalism—And unleash a wave of innovation and growth. In *Managing sustainable business: An executive education case and textbook* (pp. 323–346). Springer Netherlands.

Rajpoot, S. (2024). Eco-Friendly Solutions for Sustainable Waste Management: An Approach Towards a Cleaner and Greener Future. In Waste Management and Life Cycle Assessment for Sustainable Business Practice (pp. 43-64). IGI Global.

Raworth, K. (2017). *Doughnut economics: Seven ways to think like a 21st-century economist*. Chelsea Green Publishing.

. Redko, K. (2023). Social enterprises leading as the way in the circular economy in Ukraine.

Reindl, K., Dalhammar, C., & Brodén, E. (2024). Circular Economy Integration in Smart Grids: A Nexus for Sustainability. *Circular Economy and Sustainability*, 4(3), 1–27. DOI: 10.1007/s43615-024-00375-5

Rizos, V., Behrens, A., Van der Gaast, W., Hofman, E., Ioannou, A., Kafyeke, T., Flamos, A., Rinaldi, R., Papadelis, S., Hirschnitz-Garbers, M., & Topi, C. (2016). Implementation of circular economy business models by small and medium-sized enterprises (SMEs): Barriers and enablers. *Sustainability (Basel)*, 8(11), 1212. DOI: 10.3390/su8111212

Saebi, T., Foss, N. J., & Linder, S. (2019). Social entrepreneurship research: Past achievements and future promises. *Journal of Management*, 45(1), 70–95. DOI: 10.1177/0149206318793196

Santos, F., Pache, A. C., & Birkholz, C. (2015). Making hybrids work: Aligning business models and organizational design for social enterprises. *California Management Review*, 57(3), 36–58. DOI: 10.1525/cmr.2015.57.3.36

Santos, F. M. (2012). A positive theory of social entrepreneurship. *Journal of Business Ethics*, 111(3), 335–351. DOI: 10.1007/s10551-012-1413-4

Smith, B. R., Kistruck, G. M., & Cannatelli, B. (2016). The impact of moral intensity and desire for control on scaling decisions in social entrepreneurship. *Journal of Business Ethics*, 133(4), 677–689. DOI: 10.1007/s10551-014-2447-6

. Tariqullah, K. (2024). Circular-ESG Model for Regenerative Transition.

Tudor, T., & Dutra, C. J. (Eds.). (2021). *The Routledge handbook of waste, resources and the circular economy*. Routledge.

Westley, F., Antadze, N., Riddell, D. J., Robinson, K., & Geobey, S. (2014). Five configurations for scaling up social innovation: Case examples of nonprofit organizations from Canada. *The Journal of Applied Behavioral Science*, 50(3), 234–260. DOI: 10.1177/0021886314532945

Yunus, M. (2017). *A world of three zeros: the new economics of zero poverty, zero unemployment, and zero net carbon emissions.*

Zahra, S. A., Newey, L. R., & Li, Y. (2014). On the frontiers: The implications of social entrepreneurship for international entrepreneurship. *Entrepreneurship Theory and Practice*, 38(1), 137–158. DOI: 10.1111/etap.12061

Zeng, S., Li, G., Wu, S., & Dong, Z. (2022). The impact of green technology innovation on carbon emissions in the context of carbon neutrality in China: Evidence from spatial spillover and nonlinear effect analysis. *International Journal of Environmental Research and Public Health*, 19(2), 730. DOI: 10.3390/ijerph19020730 PMID: 35055553

Zhu, B., Nguyen, M., Siri, N. S., & Malik, A. (2022). Towards a transformative model of circular economy for SMEs. *Journal of Business Research*, 144, 545–555. DOI: 10.1016/j.jbusres.2022.01.093

Chapter 2
From Industrial to Digital Economy:
The Role of Digital Transformation in Building a Resilient Qatari Economic Future

Ahmed Badran
https://orcid.org/0000-0002-9346-1927
Qatar University, Qatar

ABSTRACT

this chapter addresses the issue of the digital economy from a public policy perspective by focusing on the strategies applied in the State of Qatar to emphasize the importance of the knowledge and innovation. In this context, information technology is a key in achieving comprehensive, sustainable and resilient economic development. The chapter starts from a main research question: To what extent do the current strategies of the State of Qatar contribute to the successful transition towards the digital economy? To answer this question, the chapter relies on the idea of methodological integration by combining the use of the descriptive analytical approach and the case study approach. The aim is to provide a critical analytical reading of previous literature in addition to determining the effectiveness of the strategies applied by the Qatari government to transform from traditional to digital economy.

DOI: 10.4018/979-8-3693-8357-5.ch002

1. INTRODUCTION: STATEMENT OF PROBLEM AND RESEARCH QUESTION

The global economy is witnessing a radical shift from industrial to digital models driven by rapid developments in information and communications technology, the spread of big data and the integration of artificial intelligence. This transformation, known as the Fourth Industrial Revolution, emphasizes the critical importance of digital transformation as a tool to enhance economic resilience, stimulate innovation and ensure sustainable growth globally. Countries are exploiting digital technologies to diversify their economies, increase productivity and reduce the challenges resulting from external shocks. For resource-rich countries such as Qatar, which have historically relied on hydrocarbons, the shift towards a digital economy represents an opportunity and a challenge to redefine their economic path and build a resilient and sustainable economy.

Despite the growing recognition of the importance of digital transformation, current literature often focuses on its effects in advanced economies with limited attention to its role in emerging markets, especially in countries that rely on natural resources. In this context, many current studies address the technical and infrastructural aspects of digital transformation, but they lack a comprehensive definition of its strategic role in achieving economic resilience. In addition, despite the significant progress achieved by Qatar in its digital agenda as part of its National Vision 2023, the relationship between digital transformation and economic resilience in the Qatari context has not received sufficient research. This chapter seeks to bridge these gaps by examining how digital transformation contributes to driving Qatar's transformation from an industrial economy to a digital economy while simultaneously building a resilient economy. Focusing on the unique social, economic and political context of the State of Qatar, this research aims to provide an in-depth understanding of the opportunities and challenges associated with this transformation in this context. The research is guided by the following question: How can digital transformation contribute to building a resilient and sustainable economic future in the State of Qatar as it transitions from an industrial economy to a digital economy? The research problem revolves around the tension between Qatar's dependence on hydrocarbon revenues and its ambition to diversify and modernize its economy. While digital transformation provides a path to economic diversification and resilience, its successful implementation requires addressing structural challenges such as developing a skilled workforce, enhancing digital infrastructure, and fostering innovation environments. These challenges are exacerbated by global economic uncertainty, rapid technological change, and the need to align with sustainable development goals.

As such, this chapter contributes to the growing literature on digital transformation by providing an in-depth analysis of its role in economic downturns, particularly in the context of emerging markets. It also addresses Qatar's strategic initiatives, identifies key enablers and barriers to digital transformation, and provides practical, applicable insights to guide policymakers, businesses, and researchers in harnessing digital technologies for sustainable economic development. By bridging the current gaps in the literature, this chapter aims to advance the theoretical and practical understanding of digital transformation as a foundation for building resilient economies in the digital age.

This chapter is organized into several main sections to provide a comprehensive exploration of the role of digital transformation in building a resilient economy in the State of Qatar. After the introduction, in which we explained the global importance of the topic, identified gaps in the current literature, and presented the research question and the research problems of the study, the second section of the chapter identifies the data, methods, and quantitative techniques used in this chapter. This section also clarifies the data sources and analytical frameworks adopted. The literature review section addresses relevant theories and concepts, with a focus on the transition from industrial to digital economies and their impact on the concept of economic resilience. The case study section presents practical applications of digital transformation and highlights initiatives and strategies that illustrate Qatar's efforts to build a resilient economy. Finally, the concluding section provides a comprehensive analysis of the results, with a focus on managerial, practical, and theoretical implications, in addition to policy recommendations to support the digital transformation journey in Qatar. The chapter concludes by identifying future research directions to enhance the understanding of digital transformation in similar emerging markets.

2. DATA AND METHODS

This study adopts a qualitative research design to explore the role of digital transformation in building a resilient economy in the State of Qatar. The methodology combines a case study approach and a descriptive analytical framework to provide a deep understanding of the processes, challenges, and outcomes associated with Qatar's transition from an industrial economy to a digital economy. At the theoretical perspective, the study is based on the Resource-Based View (RBV) theory, which emphasizes the importance of intangible assets such as knowledge, innovation, and digital capabilities as key factors for achieving a sustainable competitive advantage (Cuervo-Cazurra et al., 2021; Robinson, 2004). This perspective is particularly relevant to analysing how Qatar uses its digital infrastructure, human capital, and innovation ecosystems to enhance economic resilience and adapt to global economic changes.

At the analytical level, a qualitative approach was used to interpret data collected from multiple sources. The analysis focuses on identifying patterns, themes, and relationships that provide insights into the strategic role of digital transformation in the State of Qatar. The analysis aims to reveal how digital initiatives contribute to enhancing economic resilience and achieving national development goals. In terms of Case Study, this approach allows for an in-depth examination of the unique socio-economic context of Qatar and its efforts to transform into a digital economy. Qatar was chosen as a case study due to its ambitious digital transformation initiatives such as those outlined in the Qatar National Vision 2030 and related policies. This approach enables the exploration of specific examples and strategies that highlight the successes and challenges in achieving the idea of digital economic resilience. Regarding the descriptive analytical approach, the descriptive analytical approach is used to provide a comprehensive understanding of the digital transformation journey in Qatar through a systematic linkage of policies, initiatives and outcomes. This approach helps to highlight the broader implications of digital transformation for the idea of economic resilience in Qatar and similar contexts.

The study also relied on the documentary analysis method, as policy documents constitute a primary source of data in this study. Document analysis was conducted to assess the content, objectives and impacts of key policy frameworks, including the Qatar National Vision 2030, which provides a strategic roadmap focused on Economic diversification and sustainability with a focus on exploiting digital technologies. The study also analysed Qatar's National Development Strategy, which highlights digital transformation as a fundamental pillar for achieving the idea of economic resilience and sustainable development. Among the policy documents that were also analysed is Qatar's Digital Government Strategy, which aims to modernize public services through digital platforms and enhance government efficiency, in addition to ICT policies and strategies that focus on building a strong digital infrastructure, fostering innovation and supporting digital economy growth. These documents provide valuable insights into the strategic priorities and policy measures adopted to facilitate digital transformation in Qatar. To complement the analysis of the documents, informal discussions were held with key stakeholders including policymakers, industry experts and academia. These discussions provided insights into the challenges and opportunities associated with digital transformation in Qatar. The insights gained from these conversations helped contextualize the findings and refine the analysis. This multi-methodological approach ensures a comprehensive understanding of Qatar's digital transformation journey and its implications for building a resilient micro-economy. The combination of theoretical foundation, case study analysis, and document review and stakeholder inputs allows for a comprehensive examination of the research question.

3. LITERATURE REVIEW

The transition from an industrial economy to a digital economy has received significant attention in recent years due to its profound impacts on economic resilience, innovation, and sustainable growth. The literature on this topic spans several disciplines, including economics, public policy, and organizational studies, highlighting the transformative role of digital technologies in reshaping economic structures and processes. While global discourse largely focuses on advanced economies, limited attention has been paid to the unique challenges and opportunities faced by resource-rich emerging economies such as Qatar. This literature review aims to analyse current knowledge on digital transformation and its impact on economic resilience, with a focus on how these concepts intersect and evolve in the context of Qatar's transition from a digital economy. By drawing together insights from theoretical frameworks, empirical studies, and regional analyses, this section provides a basis for addressing the research question and situating the study within the broader academic and policy context.

3.1. Digital Transformation: Concept, Opportunities and Challenges

3.1.1. Conceptualising Digital Transformation

Over the past decade, technological advancements and innovation have been crucial in shaping contemporary society. Information, serving as a crucial element for development, has become integral to social, economic, and technical processes. In this chapter, digital transformation is conceptualized as the integration of digital technology across all facets of business operations. This integration induces profound changes in organizational functioning and the manner in which value is delivered to customers (Rackwitz & Van Doninck, 2024). In that sense, digital transformation encompasses the disposition of various digital technologies, including cloud computing, artificial intelligence, and the Internet of Things, aimed at optimizing operations and enhancing customer experience. This transformation facilitates the automation of numerous routine processes, enabling employees to concentrate on more strategic tasks. Consequently, digital transformation can lead to increased productivity, cost reduction, and improved employee satisfaction. In this context, digital transformation provides a holistic process necessitating strategic planning, innovation, and collaboration at different organizational levels to achieve significant change and generate sustainable value (H. Rykkja et al., 2024). Recent technological advancements such as artificial intelligence and integrated smart services have significantly influenced social and economic activities on a global scale. Additional innovations such as augmented reality and 3D printing further exemplify the transformative impact of these technologies. The integration of digital advancements into traditional structures highlights the substantial progress made in global technological development. Consequently, considerable attention is given to the processes via which products and services are introduced into economic markets and social domains. This in turn reflects the deep changes driven by technologies and innovations (Lips, 2024).

The interest of decision-makers and researchers in digital policies and issues related to digital transformation in the Arab world has significantly increased recently, particularly in the wake of the Covid-19 crisis. This global pandemic has compelled rapid acceleration of digital transformation across various sectors and highlighted several critical considerations for digital policy formulation. The first consideration emphasizes the inseparability of digital and real-world policies. While these policies share common goals, they differ in their spatial domains: digital policies operate within cyberspace, whereas traditional policies function within the tangible world of citizens. The second consideration advocates for an integrative perspective on digital policies, recognizing that they intersect with cultural, technical, social, economic, and political spheres (Margetts & Dunleavy, 2013). The third consideration acknowledges the global context of digital policies. Despite being rooted in the framework of the nation-state, the international dimension within which these policies operate cannot be overlooked (Abdel-Ghani, 2022).

Amidst the rapid changes occurring in the Arab region, digital transformation has become an urgent economic necessity. These shifts underscore the need to diversify Arab economies, particularly those reliant on oil and natural gas exports, to mitigate the effects of global energy market fluctuations. Digital transformation, therefore, can be seen as a catalyst aimed at enhancing productivity and competitiveness across Arab markets by leveraging advancements in information technology across various economic sectors. Implementing digital transformation policies can significantly increase the flexibility of these economies, enabling them to adapt more swiftly to economic changes. Furthermore, digital transformation can accelerate economic performance and create more job opportunities for the growing youth population (Yassin & El Nahlawy, 2023).

3.1.2. Digital Transformation: the Opportunities

While acknowledging the difficulty of generalizing to all Arab countries due to varying contextual factors, it is evident that numerous opportunities can be realized through digitization processes. In the realm of government services, digital transformation can significantly enhance the quality of services provided to citizens by leveraging the speed and efficiency that technology offers in service delivery. Smart government initiatives, which have been adopted by many Arab countries, are particularly notable in this regard. These initiatives aim to achieve integration and inclusivity in government services, ensuring that they are accessible to citizens around the clock—24 hours a day, 7 days a week, 365 days a year (Badran, 2019). As such, digital transformation enhances the governance of service design and delivery. By capitalising on digital technologies, it can improve transparency and accountability in government and businesses activities, thereby reducing the potential for financial and administrative corruption. This transformation promotes more efficient, reliable, and equitable services, fostering trust between citizens and the state.

At the economic level, digital transformation is closely tied to the concept of the digital economy. This concept enables small and medium-sized enterprises (SMEs) to access global markets through e-commerce platforms. Furthermore, the integration of technology across various sectors can foster a culture of entrepreneurship and innovation, driving economic growth and diversification (Windrum, 2008). In this context, digital transformation can encourage the establishment of companies that adopt creative ideas through business incubators specifically designed for this purpose. From a financial standpoint, digital transformation facilitates financial inclusion. Digital services such as electronic payments, loan applications, and insurance services provided by smart banking applications can significantly benefit individuals and businesses in society. These advancements make financial services more accessible, efficient, and inclusive, thereby supporting broader economic participation and growth (Grozea, 2023).

At the social level, digital transformation plays a crucial role in advancing key sectors such as education and healthcare. In education, digital transformation enhances distance-learning processes, access to educational materials, and fostering quality educational opportunities through electronic platforms. Similarly, in healthcare, digital transformation improves the quality and accessibility of healthcare services, offering alternative methods such as remote medical consultations that enhance user comfort. Technological advancements facilitate the efficient collection, organization, and storage of healthcare information, enhancing patient care. Electronic medical records enable seamless access for healthcare providers, streamlining review and follow-up processes. Additionally, smart applications for booking medical appointments, viewing test results, and managing prescriptions offer effective avenues for accessing patient information and benefiting from healthcare services (Gong & Ribiere, 2023)

At the technological level, recent advancements in artificial intelligence and big data analytics have significantly enhanced the potential for successful digital transformation in Arab countries. Decision-makers and stakeholders across various sectors can utilise these technologies to identify general trends and key patterns of societal behaviour by analysing vast databases and training diverse algorithms to monitor and track these behavioural patterns. This analytical approach enables informed decision-making, facilitates targeted interventions, and enhances overall efficiency in implementing digital transformation initiatives (Pencheva et al., 2018). These analyses are instrumental in designing government services, enabling policy-makers to determine optimal methods of service delivery. Despite the relatively recent introduction of artificial intelligence into our contemporary world, its applications have proliferated rapidly (Badran, 2021b). Nearly every sector today incorporates some form of artificial intelligence applications. It is noteworthy that the current revolution in artificial intelligence represents only the beginning. In the coming years and decades, we can anticipate further propagation of artificial intelligence applications, particularly with the emergence of generative artificial intelligence. These technological advancements offer significant opportunities to enhance and enrich individuals' lives and improve the operational efficiency (Nadkarni & Haider, 2022; Pencheva et al., 2018). Nevertheless, they also present several challenges, which will be discussed later on.

Embracing the concept of digital transformation contributes to the development of a country's technological infrastructure, including high-speed communication and internet networks. The effective implementation of digital transformation necessitates the establishment of data storage and cloud computing centres, which serve as essential repositories for the operation of smart applications. These applications facilitate the formulation and execution of public policies within the country. Collectively, these digital advancements would promote the diversification of Arab countries' economies, reducing their reliance on the extraction and export of natural resources. In essence, digital transformation should aid Arab economies in addressing instability in global markets stemming from fluctuations in raw material prices (Al-Roubaier et al., 2020).

3.1.3. Digital Transformation: the Challenges

The aforementioned benefits and opportunities presented by digital transformation for Arab countries should not overshadow the fact that this transformative process is not without its difficulties and challenges. Chief among these challenges is the absence of comprehensive digital transformation and digitization strategies in many countries. While countries such as Qatar, the United Arab Emirates, and the Kingdom of Saudi Arabia have made significant progress towards digital transformation and smart governance, others still encounter obstacles in fulfilling the fundamental requirements for digitization (Alabbasi, 2018). Furthermore, in examining the digital infrastructure sector, it becomes evident that many countries in the region continue to grapple with challenges in providing high-speed internet services and expanding coverage to encompass the entire territory of the country. These technological prerequisites serve as the foundation for the successful implementation of digital transformation initiatives. Additionally, an assessment of human capital in some countries within the region reveals a significant absence of basic digital skills among a large segment of the workforce, particularly within government agencies. This deficiency in fundamental digital skills poses obstacles to advancing digital transformation initiatives and hinders the maximization of associated benefits (Al-Roubaie, 2019).

Information security and safeguarding users' privacy represent significant challenges in addition to those previously mentioned. In an era where information has become one of the most valuable commodities and with the multiplying of open cyberspace, there are growing risks concerning Arab countries' ability to protect users' data and privacy. For instance, if government databases are compromised by cyber-attacks, it could lead to severe consequences for individuals' privacy, as unauthorized third parties may access their information. Given the critical role of data in the information age, databases have become prime targets for continuous hacking attempts by malicious actors. Consequently, cybersecurity and information security have emerged as crucial priorities for Arab governments. In response, some countries have implemented appropriate legislative and regulatory frameworks aimed at safeguarding information security and user privacy. These measures reflect the recognition of the importance of protecting sensitive data and ensuring the trust and confidence of citizens in digital services and platforms (Badran, 2024). Nonetheless, concerning the legislative and legal frameworks essential for advancing digital transformation, disparities among countries in the region are apparent. While some nations have endeavoured to establish clear regulatory frameworks for digitization processes, achieving this entails harmonizing existing legislation with the requirements of digital transformation and enacting new legislation where necessary. Conversely, in other countries, there is a deficiency in essential legislation for digitization, coupled with conflicts between existing and new regulations, impeding the digital transformation process. (Mahmoud, 2023).

From a social perspective, digital transformation processes may exacerbate levels of social inequality within Arab societies, potentially widening the gap between the affluent and the economically disadvantaged. Moreover, digital transformation could intensify disparities between urban and rural areas within the same country

(Yusuf, 2021). Another significant challenge is the promotion of a digital culture and the transition away from traditional methods of conducting activities or accessing services, which poses considerable hurdles for certain Arab countries. In many government organizations, for instance, the prevailing organizational culture does not incentivize the adoption of digital practices. Embracing digital culture requires acquiring new skills and adopting a different, more innovative approach to service delivery—an adjustment that may not align with established norms and practices (Badran, 2019, 2021a). Government employees perceive this as an additional burden, requiring them to alter their accustomed methods of conducting daily organizational activities. Similarly, certain segments of Arab societies, particularly the elderly and those less proficient in modern technology, encounter significant challenges in accessing services provided through digital platforms (Al Thani et al., 2021). These cultural shifts—both within the organizational culture of government agencies and among community members in adopting digital practices—are integral to the success of the digital transformation process in any country.

From a financial perspective, certain countries in the region may encounter challenges in allocating sufficient funds to complete the digital transformation process as needed (Alharbi, 2020). As previously mentioned, digital transformation necessitates significant investments in digital infrastructure, communication networks, high-speed internet access, and the establishment of information storage and cloud computing centres. While wealthy Arab countries have been able to make such investments, economically disadvantaged nations are still striving to secure the necessary funding for such projects, often resorting to borrowing from international financing institutions. However, the intricacies of international borrowing procedures and associated conditionalities exacerbate the reliance of many countries in the region on foreign technology to fulfil digital transformation initiatives. This dependence underscores the importance of strategic financial planning and resource allocation to ensure the successful implementation of digital transformation agendas.

Social sciences advance continuously and add new branches through research and innovation. Because economics is one of the branches of social sciences, it has a continuous tendency to evolve. The traditional economy in its well-known sectors- agriculture, industry and trade- has contributed to achieving development in many countries. However, with the revolution in the field of information and communications, it has become necessary for the traditional economy to develop to focus on the production and employment of knowledge in achieving development in its various dimensions. This revolution paved the way for the emergence of the knowledge economy.

3.2. Knowledge Economy: Conceptual and Theoretical Debates

3.2.1. The Evolution of Knowledge Economy

The concept of knowledge-based economy emerged in the second half of the twentieth century, driven by rapid developments in information technology, which revolutionized economic practices and changed the role of knowledge in achieving economic growth. Historically, the development of the economy reflects different stages of economic models. The agricultural economy based on agricultural activity and crops emerged, and the industrial economy was linked to the industrial revolution and the use of machinery in the production process. The commercial economy also emerged as a complementary activity to the agricultural and industrial economy. In contrast, the knowledge-based economy represents a modern stage characterized by a focus on investment in human capital and the strategic application of knowledge to drive economic growth.

What distinguishes this modern era is how to deal with knowledge and use it through the tools of the knowledge-based economy to develop the economies of different countries. With the emergence of the third industrial revolution and the widespread reliance on digital technologies, knowledge, innovation and intellectual capital became more important than natural resources and traditional labour as basic drivers of economic development. Since then, knowledge has become considered one of the valuable economic assets that can be used to generate wealth and enhance the competitiveness of countries on the global stage. The knowledge-based economy has witnessed remarkable development since the nineties of the last century with increasing interest in research, development and innovation as drivers of growth. In the last two decades, the spread of the Internet, the development of information and communications technology, the adoption of big data, advanced analytics and artificial intelligence have led to an increase in the importance of the knowledge-based economy. International organizations such as the Organization for Economic Cooperation and Development and the World Bank have played a pivotal role in spreading this concept and promoting it as pillars of sustainable economic development at the global level.

The concept of knowledge-based economy is closely related to information science, as both occur to invest data to achieve development goals such as improving education and community growth. However, the knowledge-based economy focuses more on explicit knowledge, which depends largely on the ability of individuals to generate, store and share information effectively. In this sense, the knowledge-based economy can be considered an advanced version of the information economy, as it shifts from investing in traditional capital such as machinery and equipment to investing in human capital. Individual knowledge is the foundation on which the knowledge-based economy and the digital economy are based, which enables the transformation of traditional production methods through modern technology and innovation. By strategically employing community knowledge and taking advantage of the global technological transformation, the knowledge-based economy contributes to bringing about comprehensive change in economic systems and their modernization (Al -Hashemi and Al -Azzawi, 2010).

3.2.2. The Knowledge Economy in the Arab Region

The knowledge-based economy is a relatively new concept in the Arab world in general and in Qatari society in particular. This concept has recently spread in some Arab countries that have relied on successful experiences from Western countries in this field. In recent years, some Arab countries have begun to transform from traditional economies to a digital economy by developing national visions aimed at facilitating this transformation and putting in place the necessary measures to overcome challenges. Researchers in various Arab countries have analysed experiences of transformation in the field of the knowledge-based economy and revealed many obstacles facing this transformation and provided policy recommendations to help decision-makers address these challenges. The diversity of definitions and measurement methods reflects the multiplicity of aspects of the knowledge-based economy. For example, Kanana (2017) defined the knowledge-based economy as a modern branch of the humanities that relies primarily on the level of knowledge in society and its impact on the growth of its wealth. On the other hand, some other sources have differentiated between the knowledge economy and the knowledge-based economy, as the former focused on developing the economic system to become more responsive to the changes resulting from Globalization, while the second concept focused on employing community knowledge to enhance national wealth.

Despite this diversity in definitions, there is a common understanding that revolves around the basic characteristics of the knowledge-based economy. These characteristics include the focus on investment in human capital rather than natural resources, reliance on innovation in services and production methods, as well as the need for a strong scientific societal structure based on technological expansion and development. The knowledge-based economy also highlights the need to combine traditional economic models with a knowledge-based approach to create a strong and comprehensive economic system in the Arab context. The knowledge-based economy focuses on building a strong scientific societal foundation based on technological development and knowledge dissemination. Studies agree on the importance of good governance as a key tool for regulating and adopting information and communication technology, encouraging open markets for innovation, and creating value-added opportunities for economic development. The knowledge-based economy highlights its ability to achieve innovation and creativity through research and development, with a focus on investment in human capital as a key factor for growth. This literature review confirms the transformative potential of the knowledge-based economy, especially in the Arab region, and through the integration of societal knowledge with Modern technological tools enable Arab countries to develop comprehensive strategies to overcome obstacles and achieve sustainable economic growth.

4. BUILDING A RESILIENT ECONOMIC FUTURE FOR THE STATE OF QATAR: CASE STUDY ANALYSIS AND DISCUSSION

4.1. Contextualisation

Following on from the aforementioned theatrical discussion of Digital transformation, this section of the paper focuses on the analysis of the Digital government and its applications in Qatar. The aim is to examine and reflect on the overall policy and regulatory framework that has been developed in order to facilitate the digital transformation process. The discussion in this section will be guided with the theoretical insights and the results of the previous research discussed in section two. Motivated by the expected gains of digital transformation, Qatar has put several plans into place to improve its government services and to become a digital nation. These plans require government departments to join forces in order to speed-up digital government efforts. The aim is for the Qatari government to become more effective, efficient, accessible, and citizens-centric.

Qatar's transition from an industrial economy to a digital economy is a vital aspect of its long-term strategy to diversify its economy and reduce its dependence on hydrocarbon revenues. As part of the Qatar National Vision 2030, Qatar has prioritized the development of a knowledge-based economy, with digital transformation a key driver of economic resilience and sustainability (General Secretariat for Development Planning, 2008). This transformation is particularly important given Qatar's unique economic and social context, characterized by its wealth of natural resources, ambitious development goals, and rapid urbanization. This section of the chapter examines Qatar's efforts to implement digital transformation initiatives, focusing on how these initiatives align with its national development strategy and global trends. This section highlights key projects and policies that illustrate Qatar's approach to integrating digital technologies across multiple sectors, including government, education, and industry. By focusing on these initiatives, the case studies presented provide insights into the opportunities and challenges associated with the transition to a digital economy in a material-rich emerging market. Through this analysis, the study sheds light on the broader implications Qatar's journey in digital transformation offers valuable lessons for similar economies seeking to enhance resilience and competitiveness in an increasingly digital world. This context ensures that outcomes are rooted in Qatar's specific economic and political environment while also contributing to the global discourse on digital transformation and economic resilience.

4.2. Digital Transformation and Knowledge Economy in Qatar: Policies, Strategies, and Regulatory Framework

Qatar has made significant progress in harnessing digital transformation as a fundamental pillar of its strategies for economic diversification and building a resilient economy. These efforts have been directed through comprehensive policies, an ambitious strategy, and a strong regulatory framework aimed at strengthening the knowledge-based economy, increasing technology adoption, and ensuring sustainability. At the policy level, key national policies form the basis for the digital transformation process in Qatar, emphasizing the integration of digital technologies into all sectors. The most prominent of these policy frameworks is Qatar National Vision 2023, which represents the strategic framework that sets this transition to a diversified knowledge-based economy and prioritizes the development of human capital, innovation, and the adoption of technology as essential elements for achieving economic resilience. Qatar National Vision 2030 provides the blueprint for all government agencies. The vision develop the guidelines for policy-makers by focusing on four main pillars: human, economic, social and environmental development. With regard to human development, the vision emphasises the importance of developing and implanting policies, which result in an educated and healthy population both physically and mentally in addition to a capable and motivated workforce. Economically speaking, the vision has focused on developing sound economic management and responsible exploitation of oil and gas in order to reach suitable economic diversification. At the social level, the vision underlined the need to provide social care and protection through a sound social structure and international cooperation. A balance between developmental needs and protecting the environment has been pointed out in the vision as a cornerstone (General Secretariat for Development Planning, 2008).

In addition, multiple national development strategies emerged from Qatar National Vision 2030. These strategies define the process of integrating digital technologies into specific areas such as education, healthcare, and governance, with a focus on enhancing efficiency and sustainability. With regard to strategies supporting digital initiatives, it can be noted that Qatar has launched several targeted strategies to accelerate digital transformation. The most prominent of these strategies is the Qatar Digital Government Strategy, which aims to digitize government services, improve the efficiency of government performance, and enhance citizen interaction through easy-to-use digital platforms. The strategy seeks to enhance transparency and simplify administrative processes. We will present some examples of these initiatives in the next section of the paper. There is also the Qatar Information and Communications Technology Strategy, which focuses on building a strong digital infrastructure, encouraging innovation, and supporting digital entrepreneurship to ensure economic and social development. There is also the Smart Qatar Initiative, which represents a pioneering program that aims to exploit emerging technologies such as the Internet of Things, artificial intelligence, and big data to address national challenges in sectors such as transportation, healthcare, and the environment (Ministry of Communications & Information Technology, 2020).

Regarding the regulatory framework governing the transformation process, it can be noted that to successfully implement its digital transformation, Qatar has developed a strong regulatory framework that includes a set of laws and regulations. For example, Qatar issued comprehensive cybersecurity legislation to protect digital assets, secure data, and ensure the security of vital national infrastructure (ictQATAR, 2014). The Qatari government also issued a set of data protection regulations aimed at enhancing trust in digital platforms by ensuring the privacy and security of personal data in line with international best practices (Emiri Diwan, 2016). In addition, Qatar issued the Telecommunications Law, which defines the regulatory framework and operation of the telecommunications sector in the State of Qatar, which facilitates competition and encourages investment in digital infrastructure. This regulatory framework has been supported by a set of institutional initiatives that highlighted the role played by some institutions in implementing policies and strategies. At the forefront of the institutions concerned with the digital transformation process and building a knowledge economy in the State of Qatar is the Ministry of Communications and Information Technology, as it is responsible for implementing digital transformation initiatives and promoting an environment conducive to technological innovation. Added to this, Qatar Science and Technology Park was also established, which represents a centre for research, development and innovation that supports emerging partnerships and enhances cooperation between academia, industry and government. There is also the National Cybersecurity Agency, which is tasked with overseeing the cybersecurity landscape and ensuring resilience against any cyber threats that may be exposed to government websites. Qatar's digital transformation efforts have resulted in notable achievements, including the digitization of government services, the deployment of 5G networks, and the successful integration of technology into sectors such as education and healthcare. Ongoing initiatives such as TASMU and the Digital Government Strategy continue to drive innovation and efficiency (Ministry of Communications & Information Technology, 2020). Through these policies, strategies and regulatory frameworks, Qatar is positioning itself as a regional leader in digital transformation, which contributes not only to achieving economic resilience but also to achieving long-term sustainability and enhancing global competitiveness.

4.3. Towards a Resilient Knowledge Economy via Digital Transformation in Qatar: Current Initiatives and Projects

Following on from these broad policy guidelines, different government agencies have embarked on several projects and initiatives in numerous policy domains including digital transformation. With respect to the human development pillar of the vision, the Ministry of Communications and Information Technology (MCIT) has focused on improving the population's digital awareness and skills through education and training. To this end, MCIT has launched the National Skilling Program in 2022. The aim of this initiative is to accelerate the human sustainable development and digital transformation in Qatar. The National Skill Development Program was introduced at the same time as the first-ever Digital Centre of Excellence in Qatar. The centre is working with several renowned global universities to provide top-notch training programmes. It also collaborates with LinkedIn, the largest professional network, to enhance participants' educational journeys through targeted seminars. As such, the Digital Centre of Excellence is anticipated to be essential in creating the skill pool necessary to hasten the digital transformation of Qatari government agencies and private sector businesses. As reported by the Assistant Undersecretary of Information Technology, at MCIT:

The human development pillar of Qatar National Vision 2030 motivates us on a daily basis to empower and equip the people of Qatar with the skills needed to develop the country into an advanced society capable of sustaining its development and providing a high standard of living for its people. The launch of the National Skilling Program and the opening of the Digital Centre of Excellence will be key to this effort, providing advanced knowledge of modern technology and cloud computing that will empower all demographics (Arabian Business 2022).

In education, *the Centralized Connectivity in the Schools Network* initiated by the Ministry of Education and Higher Education (MOEHE) of Qatar provides a good example of improving efficiency and cost cutting. In this regard, MOEHE has invested heavily in modernising existing educational infrastructure and technologies in order to meet the educational need of the nation's fast-growing population. For all Government Schools and Kindergartens around the country, MOEHE is now able to provide a high-speed, centralised, monitored, secure, dependable, scalable internet infrastructure. This is accomplished by consolidating the present dispersed independent connections to the internet and MPLS line into a strong, integrated, secure, cost-effective, performance-based architecture with 200 Mpbs per School and 60 Mbps per Kindergarten with the Centralized Internet solution. Every school and kindergarten in the country has been included in this effort, including those in rural and metropolitan locations. For security, monitoring, and wireless management, cutting-edge technology has been used. Over 151,000 users (students, teachers, and staff) are served by the 200 schools and 70 kindergartens that make up this strategic project's stakeholder base. Only Government Schools and Kindergartens are served by the network, which was designed as a separate zone. Anyone in Qatar can easily connect to the network without much reliance on other services. Modern multi-vendor technology that is scalable for the upcoming few years is used to deliver a single policy, blacklist, and patch for all the entities indicated above.

The *Single Window platform* provides a good example of improving service quality and customer satisfaction. The platform is offering a unified interface of the State of Qatar to all investors seeking to launch or manage their businesses. The platform's technological aspect is essential to its success. The digital platform is made up of the following components: knowledge portal, smart application, digital signature, approval portal, company information centre, and performance monitoring and management dashboard. As such, the Single Window platform introduces a fully integrated digital transformation of government services, improved user experience, and decreased expenses of company licencing for both investors and the government. The platform makes use of technology to deliver quick, effective, and user-friendly government services, making service delivery overall easier. By combining, packaging, and re-engineering more than 180 services into 31 comprehensive services, there has been a significant reduction in the complexity and ambiguity of the government services' processes. Additionally, the platform reduced the unnecessary use of paper by combining more than 100 applications into one digital smart form, thereby reducing the waste of time and resources. These improvements are to save an estimated 165,000 USD, which represents the cost of printing and preserving paper documents. In addition to cost cutting, the platform helps achieving the notion of government integration and improve the overall performance of the integrated unites. More than 22 government agencies and systems are combined into a single platform. Furthermore, using computerised tools to handle and review the application will reduce human mistake. By establishing a clear and transparent performance-monitoring dashboard the platform is expected to gauge government agencies' commitment to providing their services effectively, allowing for accountability, transparency, and the ability to take wise and fact-based corrective actions to improve the quality of the government services. Taken together, all of the aforementioned measures will raise public satisfaction levels, foster greater public confidence in government policies, and decrease the number of complaints and violations.

The open data portal is an example par excellence for the implementation of government openness notion. In 2014, the Qatari government declared the implementation of open government principles. A project was therefore started to create an open data platform that would enable the agencies to publish and manage their datasets as well as the recipients to find and utilise the datasets in one location. To this end, the open data portal that was created in April 2019 in order to enable the government agencies in Qatar to publish their datasets in an open format ready for utilisation. As such, individuals, organisations, and companies will be able to openly access datasets that were not previously accessible.

The notion of social inclusion has been asserted by several government initiatives in Qatar. MADA - *Assistive Technology Center Qatar* that was established by the Ministry of Transport and Communications in 2010 is case in point. Through its Innovation Program and Accreditation Service, Mada promotes the expansion of digital inclusion to help the elderly and people with disabilities satisfy their ICT accessibility needs. The vision and mission of Mada include "Enhancing ICT accessibility in Qatar and beyond" and "Unlocking the potential of persons with functional limitations, persons with disabilities, and the elderly - through enabling ICT accessible capabilities and platforms". To this end, Mada collaborates closely with important Qatari stakeholders to advance greater digital accessibility while adhering to the legal guidelines established by the United Nations Convention on the Rights of Persons with Disabilities. This is accomplished by locating areas where policies are lacking and formulating suggestions based on global best practises and fruitful case studies in the area of digital accessibility. These initiatives have increased the participation of students with disabilities in the educational system and encouraged equal and inclusive access to digital platforms and services for people with disabilities and the elderly (https://mada.org.qa/).

Another research-based programme was launched in 2015 under the name *Better Connections* in order to address the digital divide that workers in Qatar. Contextual research revealed that 67% of temporary employees lacked access to ICT resources, which limited their knowledge of technology and the advantages that came with possessing ICT abilities. The programme is based on establishing ICT facilities inside the workers' residences to reduce travel time. These facilities are furnished and connected to the internet with donated, refurbished computers that are loaded with content catered to their needs in the five most popular languages among the workers' communities. The program is a public-private partnership including government and private counterparts working together in order to improve the quality of life of migrant workers and to help them integrate into the digital community and larger society, it gives them access to technology and helps them develop their ICT skills (https://www.motc.gov.qa/en/ditoolkit/migrant-workers/better-connections-program).

The *Nationwide Digitalization Project* (NDP) provides an example of digitisation in the Qatari government. The MOTC initiated the NDP in accordance with Qatar Vision 2030. Through the digitization of current and historical physical records, the initiative aims to assist Qatar's government sector in undergoing a digital transformation. A variety of digitization and record management services are offered by the project. The following are the program's main components: digitization of physical documents; using Enterprise Content Management (ECM); keeping physical papers in specially designed, highly secure facilities, and securely destroying records and data tape management and media storage disposal that is secure and safe. Consequently, the following occurred:

- Easy access to these documents. With just a few keywords, a user can quickly and simply find the document they need.
- Several people accessing the same documents at once
- Time is saved by eliminating the need for filing, retrieval, and refiling.
- Documents may be distributed among different government departments.

In order to save resources, lower the price of keeping physical documents and use less paper.

- Prevent government documents from being accidentally lost or destroyed.
- Manage and keep an eye on who has access to private information.

Metrash2 is one of the smart electronic services provided by the Ministry of Interior as an example of services integration in government. This service is a free application available on mobile phones and other smart devices, which saves a lot of effort and time for users. The Ministry of Interior in Qatar is introducing many developments on this application in order to serve citizens, residents, companies and institutions around the clock and without interruption from anywhere and at any time. Through Metrash2 services, the government in the State of Qatar can notify users of the services performed and alerts related to official documents and traffic violations, by sending text messages to phones. In addition, customers with the various government agencies of the Ministry of Interior can carry out their transactions through the smart application without the need to visit these places, after completing the paperwork and procedures required to provide the service.as such, the Metrash2 application allows its users to access more than 150 services provided by the Ministry of Interior. Through the application, the user can pay service fees directly, which saves time and effort for service subscribers. The application also helps to accelerate the pace of completion of the ministry's services and achieve Qatar's vision for the year 2030.

As noted by Information systems consultant at the General Administration of Information Systems, Ministry of the Interior, the service was launched in September 2012 and the number of subscribers is currently 330,000 subscribers. The average monthly transactions are 200,000 transactions per month. The total number of transactions to date is 4,800,000 transactions. The total number of query transactions to date is 17,216,701 million.

Traffic services: These services include traffic violations, renewal of a driver's license, issuance of a damaged driver's license, vehicle exit permit, transfer of vehicle ownership, transfer of ownership of a distinctive number, traffic certificates, no objection to a driver's license, inquiring about a vehicle with the base number, auction of distinctive plates, View featured license plates, release vehicle mortgage.

Residency services: These services include renewal of residency, cancellation of residency, transfer of residency to the new passport, separation of a companion from a passport, issuance of a new residency with the entry visa number, reactivation of a previous residency, a report on the names of workers in an establishment.

These experiences combined demonstrate that the State of Qatar has been able to achieve significant progress in the transition towards a knowledge economy by activating digital transformation strategies.

4.4. Challenges Facing Digital Transformation in Qatar

Even though Qatar has made great strides in its shift from an industrial to a digital economy, a number of obstacles still stand in the way of its attempts to create a robust and sustainable economy. These challenges are distributed across technical, social, economic and regulatory fields, reflecting the complexities inherent in transforming a resource-based economy into a knowledge-based and digital-based economy. Understanding and addressing these challenges is critical to ensuring the success of Qatar's digital transformation agenda. At the forefront of these challenges is workforce development and the digital skills gap, which is one of the most prominent challenges facing Qatar. Despite significant investments in education and training, there is still a gap between the skills required in the digital economy and those currently available in the labour market. This problem is particularly prominent in specialized fields such as data analysis, cybersecurity and artificial intelligence. In addition, the heavy reliance on the expatriate workforce adds challenges to ensuring the continuity of skills development and aligning the workforce's capabilities with national digital strategies (Al Thani et al., 2021).

Another challenge facing Qatar is its reliance on hydrocarbons. The Qatari economy remains heavily dependent on hydrocarbon revenues, making it vulnerable to fluctuations in global energy markets (PwC, 2024). This reliance represents a dual challenge. Although energy revenues have helped finance investments in digital infrastructure, the continued dominance of the hydrocarbon sector slows the pace of economic diversification. There is also the challenge of the limited local innovation system. Despite Qatar's significant efforts over the years to promote innovation, the local system for digital entrepreneurship and technological development is still in its early stages. Start-ups, small and medium-sized enterprises (SMEs) face challenges such as limited access to finance, market constraints, and a lack of mentoring opportunities. Building a strong ecosystem that supports local entrepreneurs and integrates them into the national digital economy is a critical challenge. Gaps in infrastructure and technology represent another challenge in addition to the previous challenges. Although Qatar has an advanced digital infrastructure, there are disparities in accessibility and quality of services across sectors and regions. For example, some industries and public services have not fully adopted digital technologies in its operations. In addition, there is a continuous need to update the current infrastructure to keep pace with global technological advances, especially in areas such as 5G networks, smart systems and cloud computing. Among the challenges facing Qatar are cybersecurity and data protection. With the increasing reliance on digital systems, the risks associated with cyber threats and data leakage have increased. Ensuring strong protection of sensitive information and national infrastructure is an ongoing challenge (Dagnino & Armaroli, 2019; Emiri Diwan, 2016). In addition, although Qatar has implemented data protection regulations, their alignment with international standards and addressing public concerns about privacy still require further development (Alhaimer, 2024).

Social and cultural resistance is one of the challenges facing Qatar in its journey towards a knowledge-based economy. Digital transformation often requires changes in social norms and cultural practices, which leads to resistance from some segments of society to these changes (Al Thani et al., 2021). For example, the adoption of digital public services and smart technologies may face rejection due to lack of trust in digital platforms or limited digital literacy among some groups. Bridging this gap requires intensive awareness campaigns and easy-to-use digital solutions that meet the needs of all members of society. In addition, the fragmentation of policies and regulations is one of the most important challenges facing Qatar in its journey towards digital transformation. Although Qatar has implemented several policies and strategies to support digital transformation, as shown in the previous section of the chapter, challenges remain to ensure coordination and consistency between different government agencies and sectors. Policy fragmentation can lead to duplication of efforts, inefficiency, and implementation gaps (Badran, 2024). Having a unified regulatory framework that integrates digital transformation initiatives across all sectors is essential to achieving national goals from a sustainability perspective. Balancing sustainability and digital growth is one of the challenges facing the State of Qatar now, as the overlap between sustainability and digital transformation poses a unique challenge to the Qatari government. While digital technology can enhance efficiency and reduce the environmental footprint, its deployment can significantly increase energy consumption (Mohammed et al., 2022). Perhaps the most prominent example of this is large data centres and smart grids, and what this transformation requires in terms of increasing demand for energy, which may harm the environment. Therefore, aligning digital transformation with sustainability goals requires careful planning and investment in green technologies and renewable energy sources (Elidrisy, 2024).

On the technical front, reliance on imported technologies from abroad represents one of the most important challenges facing Qatar in its journey towards a knowledge-based economy and digital transformation. Digital transformation in Qatar relies heavily on imported technologies and expertise, which may create weaknesses related to technological dependence. This dependence may limit the country's ability to develop local solutions and adapt technologies to meet local needs. Building local capabilities in technology development and reducing reliance on foreign expertise is also a critical challenge. From the same technological perspective, adapting to the rapid technological change witnessed by the world represents one of the unique challenges facing Qatar. The bills of rapid technological progress represent an ongoing challenge to Qatar's efforts in digital transformation. Rapid innovation in areas such as artificial intelligence, blockchain technologies, and quantum computing require continuous adaptation and proactive policies to remain competitive. Delays in adopting or integrating these technologies could hinder Qatar's ability to achieve its goals in the digital economy and the transformation towards a knowledge-based economy (Mohtar, 2015).

Overcoming these challenges requires a multi-dimensional approach that includes strengthening education and training systems, encouraging public-private partnerships, improving regulatory frameworks, and fostering a culture of innovation. In addition, aligning digital transformation efforts with national sustainability goals and ensuring inclusive adoption of digital technology is essential to building a sustainable and resilient economy. By strategically addressing these obstacles, Qatar can continue its progress towards becoming a leading digital economy in the region and beyond, enhancing its economic resilience and improving its competitiveness in an increasingly digital world.

5. CONCLUSION

In the pursuit of digital transformation within governmental and private sectors, numerous Arab countries have aimed to leverage digitization processes. The aim is to enhance benefits and address the challenges inherent in digital policies implementation. This chapter examines the opportunities and challenges associated with implementing digital transformation in the Arab region. Recognizing the diverse political, economic, and social contexts of Arab nations, the chapter focuses on the most significant opportunities and challenges that digital transformation presents to Arab economies. The paper underscores that digital transformation has the potential to significantly boost economic growth and strengthen the economies of Arab countries. Yet, various obstacles and challenges should be addressed to ensure the security and stability of electronic service delivery. The chapter highlights the importance of increased investment in technological infrastructure and the strengthening of cybersecurity measures to protect data and electronic transactions from escalating cyber threats.

Following on from the above discussion it can be concluded that digital transformation signifies a fundamental paradigm shift in the operations of both government entities and businesses. Essentially, digital transformation necessitates a comprehensive re-evaluation of existing service design and delivery mechanisms, aimed at fostering a more integrated model. Moreover, digital transformation revolves around citizens and other stakeholders in society, utilizing smart technologies and applications to facilitate their closer engagement with centres of policy and decision-making. Within digital transformation models, societal stakeholders transition from being passive recipients of public services to active participants in their design and delivery through ongoing interactions with governmental administrative structures. The digital government of the future is envisioned as customer-centric, operating around-the-clock to provide services in the most effective manner possible. From this perspective, it is evident that digital transformation and its applications have the potential to contribute significantly to the realization of sustainable development goals. By instigating fundamental changes in governmental and business operations, digital transformation paves the way for enhanced efficiency, transparency, and responsiveness, thereby fostering progress towards sustainable development objectives.

5.1. Managerial Implications

The transition from an industrial economy to a digital economy represents great opportunities for managers and decision-makers in Qatar to build a sustainable economic future. This digital-led transformation depends on strategic planning, investment in digital infrastructure, and developing workforce skills to maximize its benefits. The main managerial implications for strengthening the Qatari economy through digital transformation are evident in a set of factors, most notably investment in digital infrastructure. In this context, managers must prioritize investing in advanced digital infrastructure such as high-speed internet, data centres, and secure cloud systems to facilitate digital operations with three pillars. A strong infrastructure enhances business continuity and increases the sustainability of the national economy in the face of potential economic challenges. It is also necessary to focus on developing the workforce and updating skills. As Qatar moves towards a digital economy, managers must implement continuous education programs and skills development initiatives that focus on digital competencies. Training employees in areas such as data analytics, cybersecurity, and artificial intelligence can help prepare the workforce for the requirements of new technologies and enhance their contribution to the digital economy. Strengthening Digital innovation and entrepreneurship is another important factor as managers across sectors are encouraged to foster a culture of digital innovation and support employees to explore digital solutions to business challenges (Mohtar, 2015). By supporting entrepreneurship initiatives, companies can foster a digital mind-set and the ability to quickly adapt to changing market dynamics in their decision-making process. Improving the mechanism through which decisions are made based on data is an important factor that managers and decision-makers in Qatar should focus on in this regard. Digital transformation provides large amounts of data, which allows for data-driven decisions. In this context, managers should focus on developing strong data governance frameworks to effectively exploit data analytics, which provides insights that enhance operational efficiency, customer satisfaction, and strategic planning. Cybersecurity and risk management also play an important role in the role of technology in developing services and building a sustainable economy. As digital reliance increases, cybersecurity risks increase, and managers must therefore implement comprehensive risk management protocols (ictQATAR, 2014). From a management perspective, public-private partnerships are essential to building a resilient economy in Qatar. Managers should pursue partnerships that support digital infrastructure, provide training, and facilitate knowledge exchange. Such government-private partnerships can accelerate digital transformation initiatives and ensure that different sectors are aligned with national economic goals. Finally, managers must direct digital transformation strategies in line with Qatar National Vision 2030 by integrating government initiatives that focus on economic diversification, sustainability and technological advancement in a way that enables institutions to effectively contribute to achieving the national agenda and enhancing economic stability.

5.2. Practical Implications

The transition from an industrial economy to a digital economy has important practical implications for companies, policymakers and educational institutions in the State of Qatar. By focusing on the following areas, stakeholders can support a strong digital economy and enhance resilience in the face of future economic challenges: First, the need to adapt business strategies. Companies need to adapt their business models to include digital technologies and data-driven decision-making. Practical steps include investing in digital tools that enhance customer engagement, streamline operations and improve supply chain management. Companies should consider adopting e-commerce platforms and AI analytics to remain competitive in the digital economy. Second, developing digital skills and training programs. Educational institutions and employers should collaborate to develop specialized training programs that equip the workforce with digital skills. Practical initiatives include establishing partnerships with universities, offering training opportunities in digital sectors and providing on-the-job training for employees to enhance their proficiency in areas such as programming, data analysis and cybersecurity. Third, implementing data governance. With the increase in digital data, organizations must develop effective data governance policies to manage, protect, and use data responsibly. Practical steps include establishing clear protocols for data collection, storage, and use, as well as investing in data security measures to protect against breaches. This is essential to building consumer trust and ensuring regulatory compliance. Fourth, encouraging innovation hubs and emerging partnerships. Policymakers can support a vibrant innovation environment by creating incentives for start-ups and establishing digital innovation hubs. Practical policies may include tax exemptions for technology start-ups, grants for digital technology research and development, and support for incubators and accelerators to help digital companies grow. Fifth, promoting sustainable digital infrastructure. As Qatar shifts towards a digital economy, investing in a sustainable and resilient digital infrastructure is essential. Practical steps include expanding high-speed internet coverage, enhancing cloud-computing facilities, and developing smart city initiatives that align with environmental and economic goals. Sixth: Integrating digital initiatives between the public and private sectors. Digital initiatives in public-private cooperation can be added to the previously discussed practical implications of the idea of digital transformation. In practice, this can include establishing joint projects that benefit from public funding and private expertise to develop smart systems in areas such as healthcare, education and telecommunications, which benefits society and improves the process of providing services. Seventh: Focus on cybersecurity preparedness. As digital transformation increases, the importance of cybersecurity increases. Practical applications include the need for regular training for employees in the field of cybersecurity, developing plans to respond to incidents and investing in cybersecurity infrastructure to protect digital assets and sensitive information. Finally, there is a need to comply with national and international digital standards. In order for Qatar to fully benefit from the advantages of the digital economy, compliance with global digital standards and policies is essential. This practically requires staying up to date with international best practices and adopting frameworks that facilitate operational compatibility, digital trade and regulatory compliance, which ensures Qatar remains competitive in the global digital arena

5.3. Theoretical Implications

The transition from an industrial economy to a digital economy in Qatar has several theoretical implications for the study of economic resilience, digital transformation, and innovation policies, especially in emerging markets. By identifying this digital transition, this research contributes to expanding the theoretical understanding of these areas with regard to enhancing the theory of economic resilience. This study provides a new perspective on the concept of resilience from an economic perspective in the context of digital transformation, proposing that resilience is not limited to economic recovery and traditional adaptation, but also includes digital readiness and infrastructure. The results support an expanded theoretical framework for the concept of economic resilience, as digital capability is a key factor in the economy's ability to adapt to economic shocks. The findings of this study also contribute to the existing debate in the literature on innovation by demonstrating how digital transformation can be a catalyst for broader economic transition and sustainability in emerging markets. From this perspective, this research reinforces theoretical discussions on the stages and factors of digital transformation, demonstrating that political will, consistency of national strategies, and investment in infrastructure are critical components in this context. This research also provides an addition to public policy theories by exploring how government strategies can accelerate digital transformation and enhance economic resilience. Qatar's approach highlights the role of policy frameworks, government incentives, and regulation in shaping digital systems, indicating that a proactive public policy framework can be essential to achieving a resilient and diversified economy. In addition, by analysing digital infrastructure, skilled labour, and data resources as key assets for building a competitive advantage in the digital economy, this study can contribute to the debate on resource theory. The results demonstrate that the application of the traditional resource perspective must be adapted to include digital and data resources as assets. Sustainable economic centrality, especially in knowledge-based economies. The theoretical implications of this research also include expanding theories of sustainable development in emerging markets, as the research expands the theory of sustainable development by positioning digital transformation as a tool for achieving long-term economic sustainability in resource-dependent economies. This indicates the need to integrate digitalization into the development of sustainable development in emerging markets as a means to reduce dependence on non-renewable resources and enhance economic diversification. Another theoretical contribution of the research is the combination of institutional theory and digital transformation, as this research contributes to institutional theory by exploring how to adapt institutional structures in Qatar to support digital transformation. The results indicate that institutional theory can be expanded by studying how to develop regulatory bodies, educational institutions, and public-private partnerships to meet the requirements of the digital economy.

5.4. Policy Recommendations

Based on the discussion presented in this paper, a set of policy recommendations can be made to facilitate Qatar's transition to a resilient digital economy. *First*, developing a national digital resilience strategy. Qatar should create a comprehensive digital resilience strategy that is aligned with the Qatar National Vision 2023. This strategy should focus on strengthening digital infrastructure, encouraging innovation, and supporting economic diversification to ensure that the economy remains resilient to external shocks. *Second*, investing in digital education and develop workforce skills to meet the demands of the digital economy. It is essential to equip the workforce with the necessary digital skills. Policymakers should foster partnerships between government, educational institutions, and the private sector to develop digital skills programs that target current and future workers. *Third*, encouraging public-private partnerships in digital innovation. The government can foster a strong innovation ecosystem by stimulating public-private partnerships that focus on digital transformation. Policies should encourage collaboration in research and development, data sharing, and adoption of digital solutions across industries. *Fourth*, providing incentives for small and medium-sized enterprises (SMEs). Policies should support SMEs in adopting digital tools and technologies by providing financial incentives, grants and subsidies. This will help small businesses embrace the digital transformation and contribute to a diversified and resilient economy. *Fifth*, strengthening cybersecurity policies and infrastructure. As digital activity increases, it becomes imperative to take strong cybersecurity measures. Policymakers should improve cybersecurity standards and frameworks across sectors to protect digital access and ensure data integrity. *Sixth*, promote sustainable digital infrastructure. Qatar should prioritize sustainable practices in developing digital infrastructure, including energy-efficient data centres and smart city initiatives. These measures will support the transition to a low-carbon digital economy in line with Qatar's sustainability goals. Seventh, aligning with international digital standards and practices to enhance competitiveness. Qatar should align its digital policies with international standards in data protection, digital trade and frameworks. This regulatory alignment will facilitate cross-border digital cooperation and help integrate Qatar into the global digital economy.

5.5. Future Directions of Research

This chapter sheds light on the transition from an industrial economy to a digital economy in Qatar. The framework of the earlier conversations might be used to provide a number of potential areas for future research. These areas can enhance our understanding of economic resilience, digital transformation, and sustainable growth in emerging markets. The main directions for future research on this topic are conducting comparative studies with Gulf countries and other emerging economies. Comparative studies between Qatar and other GCC countries or emerging economies can provide a broader understanding of the unique and common challenges of digital transformation. These studies can explore how diverse economic policies, cultural factors, and resources affect the success of digital initiatives and the readiness and efforts to enhance economic resilience. Another area of future research is analysing digital transformation at the sector level within Qatar. While this study addresses the macroeconomic perspective, future research can focus on specific sectors such as healthcare, education, and finance to understand the details of digital transformation within different industries. Exploring how each sector adapts to digitalization and its impact on economic resilience can provide insights. Value for targeted policy interventions Future studies could also focus on assessing and developing policies related to cybersecurity and data governance. Given the increase in digital activity, future studies could assess the effectiveness of cybersecurity and data governance policies in ensuring economic resilience and protecting digital assets. Studies could analyse the adequacy of current regulations and explore best practices for risk management. In addition, the social and environmental impacts of digital transformation are one dimension that could be focused on in future studies. In addition to economic outcomes, future research should consider the social and environmental impacts of digital transformation. This could include studying how digitalization affects quality of life, access to public services, and environmental sustainability in Qatar, and identifying potential trade-offs and unintended effects.

REFERENCES

Abdel Ghani, S. M. (2022). The impact of digital transformation on enhancing economic growth in Egypt. *Journal of Political Economy*, 15(14), 44–79.

Al-Roubaie, A. (2019) Building capacity for digital development in the Arab world. Role Educ. Int. J. Eng. Adv. Technol. (IJEAT) 8(2249–8958, 5C), 1530–1537

Al-Roubaier, A., Hamdan, A., & Sarea, A. M. (2020). Economic Diversification in a Digital Economy. In: Hassanien, AE., Azar, A., Gaber, T., Oliva, D., Tolba, F. (eds) Proceedings of the International Conference on Artificial Intelligence and Computer Vision (AICV2020). AICV 2020. Advances in Intelligent Systems and Computing, vol 1153. Springer, Cham. DOI: 10.1007/978-3-030-44289-7_62

Al Thani, D., Hassan, A., Chalghoumi, H., Othman, A., & Hammad, S. (2021). Addressing the Digital Gap for the Older Persons and their caregivers in the State of Qatar: A Stakeholders' Perspective. *2021 8th International Conference on ICT & Accessibility (ICTA)*, 01–06. DOI: 10.1109/ICTA54582.2021.9809430

Alabbasi, M. (2018), Digital Transformation and Change Management Practices in Qatari Organizations: Challenges and Recommendations [pdf], http://tinyurl.com/3hd3veff

Alhaimer, R. (2024). Exploring the Attitudes of Kuwait's Residents Toward the Role of Corruption and Anti-Corruption Entities (Nazaha) in Kuwait. *Public Integrity*, 26(3), 305–321. DOI: 10.1080/10999922.2023.2176054

Alharbi, A. S. (2020), Challenges in Digital Transformation in Saudi Arabia Obstacles in Paradigm Shift in Saudi Arabia, *6th International Conference on Computing for Sustainable Global Development (INDIACom)*, New Delhi, India, pp. 1287-1291.

Badran, A. (2019). Smart-Governments for Smart Cities: The Case of Dubai Smart-Government. In Samad, W. A., & Azar, E. (Eds.), *Smart Cities in the Gulf* (pp. 59–82). Springer Nature Singapore., DOI: 10.1007/978-981-13-2011-8_5

Badran, A. (2021a). Developing Smart Cities: Regulatory and Policy Implications for the State of Qatar. *International Journal of Public Administration*, •••, 1–14. DOI: 10.1080/01900692.2021.2003811

Badran, A. (2021b). Thoughts and Reflections on the Case of Qatar: Should Artificial Intelligence Be Regulated? In Azar, E., & Haddad, A. N. (Eds.), *Artificial Intelligence in the Gulf* (pp. 69–92). Springer Singapore., DOI: 10.1007/978-981-16-0771-4_5

Badran, A. (2024). Regulating Cyberspace for Children: Reflections on the Qatari Case. *British Journal of Cyber Criminology*, 3(1). https://www.pubtexto.com/pdf/?regulating-cyberspace-for-children-reflections-on-the-qatari-case

Cuervo-Cazurra, A., Dieleman, M., Hirsch, P., Rodrigues, S. B., & Zyglidopoulos, S. (2021). Multinationals' misbehavior. *Journal of World Business*, 56(5), 101244. DOI: 10.1016/j.jwb.2021.101244

Dagnino, E., & Armaroli, I. (2019). A Seat at the Table: Negotiating Data Processing in the Workplace: A National Case Study and Comparative Insights Automation, Artificial Intelligence, & Labor Law. *Comparative Labor Law & Policy Journal*, 41(1), 173–196.

Elidrisy, A. (2024). Leveraging Cloud Services & Digital Transformation for Sustainability: Insights from Cases of Qatar. *Journal of Innovative Research*, 2(1), 20–28. DOI: 10.54536/jir.v2i1.2398

Emiri Diwan. (2016). *Law No. (13) of 2016 on Protecting Personal Data Privacy.* https://assurance.ncsa.gov.qa/sites/default/files/library/2020-11/Law%20No.%20%2813%29%20of%202016%20%20on%20Protecting%20Personal%20Data%20Privacy%20-%20English.pdf

General Secretariat for Development Planning. (2008). *Qatar National Vision 2030.* https://www.mdps.gov.qa/en/knowledge/HomePagePublications/QNV2030_Arabic_v2.pdf

Gong, C., & Ribiere, V. (2023). A historical outline of digital transformation. In *Digital Transformation in Healthcare in Post-Covid-19 Times* (pp. 3–25). Elsevier., DOI: 10.1016/B978-0-323-98353-2.00016-2

Grozea, I.-L., & Troancă, D. (2023). Digital Transformation and the Financial Sector: A Comprehensive Perspective. *Sciendo*, 56(2), 56–63. DOI: 10.2478/saec-2023-0018

ictQATAR. (2014). *Qatar National Cyber Security Strategy.*

Lips, M. (2024). Digital transformation in the public sector. In Verhoest, K., Hammerschmid, G., Rykkja, L. H., & Klijn, E. H. (Eds.), *Collaborating for Digital Transformation* (pp. 13–30). Edward Elgar Publishing., DOI: 10.4337/9781803923895.00010

Mahmoud, N. (2023). Prospects of Digital Transformation in the Arab World. *Arab and Regional Horizons*, 8(14), 0–0. DOI: 10.21608/afar.2023.238807.1021

Margetts, H., & Dunleavy, P. (2013). The second wave of digital-era governance: A quasi-paradigm for government on the Web. *Philosophical Transactions of the Royal Society A: Mathematical, Physical and Engineering Sciences, 371*(1987), 20120382. DOI: 10.1098/rsta.2012.0382

Ministry of Communications & Information Technology. (2020). *TASMU Experience Policy*. https://www.mcit.gov.qa/sites/default/files/tasmu_experience_policy_en_v1.0.pdf

Mohammed, S., Desha, C., & Goonetilleke, A. (2022). Investigating low-carbon pathways for hydrocarbon-dependent rentier states: Economic transition in Qatar. *Technological Forecasting and Social Change*, 185, 122084. DOI: 10.1016/j.techfore.2022.122084

Mohtar, R. H. (2015). Opportunities and Challenges for Innovations in Q atar. *Muslim World (Hartford, Conn.)*, 105(1), 46–57. DOI: 10.1111/muwo.12079

Nadkarni, S., & Haider, I. (2022). Digital transformation, operational efficiency and sustainability: Innovation drivers for hospitality's rebound in the United Arab Emirates. *Worldwide Hospitality and Tourism Themes*, 14(6), 572–578. DOI: 10.1108/WHATT-05-2022-0054

Pencheva, I., Esteve, M., & Mikhaylov, S. J. (2018). Big data and AI – A transformational shift for government: So, what next for research? *Public Policy and Administration*, •••, 1–21.

PwC. (2024). *Qatar Economy Watch 2024*.

Robinson, R. (2004). Liner Shipping Strategy, Network Structuring and Competitive Advantage: A Chain Systems Perspective. *Research in Transportation Economics*, 12, 247–289. DOI: 10.1016/S0739-8859(04)12008-8

Windrum, P. (2008). Innovation and entrepreneurship in public services. In Windrum, P., & Koch, P. (Eds.), *Innovation in Public Sector Services*. Edward Elgar. DOI: 10.4337/9781848441545.00009

Yassin, F. E., & El Nahlawy, H. (2023). *Driving digital transformation in the Arab region*. UNDP. https://www.undp.org/arab-states/stories/driving-digital-transformation-arab-region

Yusuf, S. (2021). *Digital Technology and Inequality: The Impact on Arab Countries* (ERF Working Papers Series). https://erf.org.eg/app/uploads/2021/09/1632920263_470_2894109_1486.pdf

Chapter 3
Analyzing E-Participation Index as an Indicator of Digital Transformation:
A Bibliometric Analysis

Laura Anesti Ayu Kirana
Universitas Muhammadiyah Makassar, Indonesia

Haeria A. Mardhatillah
Universitas Muhammadiyah Makassar, Indonesia

Muhammad Younus
https://orcid.org/0000-0001-9654-1546
Universitas Muhammadiyah Yogyakarta, Pakistan

Aqmal Reza Amri
Universitas Muhammadiyah Makassar, Indonesia

Andi Luhur Prianto
Universitas Muhammadiyah Makassar, Indonesia

Ahmad Harakan
Universitas Muhammadiyah Makassar, Indonesia

Achmad Nurmandi
Universitas Muhammadiyah Yogyakarta, Indonesia

Umar Congge
Universitas Muhammadiyah Sinjai, Indonesia

Timothy Apriyanto
Universitas Muhammadiyah Yogyakarta, Indonesia

Sekson Yongvanit
Khon Kaen University, Thailand

ABSTRACT

This paper's goal is to provide information about Indonesia's E-Participation Index analysis as a digital transformation indicator for the year 2022. After that, we were able to ascertain the effects of digital revolution on Indonesian individuals as well as

DOI: 10.4018/979-8-3693-8357-5.ch003

the modifications that were made to the way they thought about politics. "Qualitative research" is the methodology employed by the researchers working in this field. The research's data was collected from the United Nations website, Dimension AI, and Google Scholar, and it was then presented in a descriptive manner. The research presented in this paper raises awareness of the ways that electronic engagement in society influences Indonesia's digital transformation. This paper will only cover the extent to which each change's component is explained in detail; it will also examine potential fixes for problems that the public has identified and how best to go about putting them into practice.

1. INTRODUCTION

In the contemporary landscape of governance and public administration, digital transformation has emerged as a critical factor influencing the efficiency, transparency, and inclusivity of governmental operations. The pervasive integration of digital technologies into various sectors has ushered in a new era of governance characterized by enhanced citizen engagement and streamlined public services. At the heart of this transformation lies e-participation, a concept that reflects the ways in which digital tools and platforms enable and facilitate citizen involvement in the decision-making processes of government and other institutions (Yao & Xu, 2022). The E-Participation Index (EPI), a metric designed to gauge the extent and effectiveness of e-participation initiatives, has become a pivotal indicator of how digital transformation is reshaping governance.

1.1 Background

Digital transformation represents a profound shift in the way organizations and governments operate, driven by the adoption and utilization of digital technologies. This transformation encompasses various facets, including improved service delivery, increased operational efficiency, and enhanced citizen engagement (Hinsberg, 2010). E-participation, a critical component of this transformation, involves leveraging digital platforms to involve citizens in policy-making, service delivery, and governance processes. The E-Participation Index serves as a quantitative measure to evaluate the extent of citizen engagement through digital means and the effectiveness of e-participation initiatives.

The concept of e-participation has evolved significantly over the past two decades, driven by advancements in information and communication technologies (ICTs) and the increasing emphasis on participatory governance. E-participation platforms range from online surveys and forums to social media and mobile applications, each offering distinct opportunities for citizen involvement (Sacchi et al., 2022). The EPI, developed to assess the effectiveness of these platforms, provides valuable insights into how well governments and organizations are leveraging digital tools to foster citizen engagement and participation.

1.2 Problem Formulation

Despite the growing importance of e-participation and the E-Participation Index as a measure of digital transformation, there remains a gap in the comprehensive understanding of the EPI's role and impact. While numerous studies have explored individual aspects of e-participation, such as citizen engagement through specific platforms or the effectiveness of particular digital tools, there is a lack of a holistic analysis that synthesizes these findings into a broader understanding of how the EPI reflects digital transformation (Quintana et al., 2022). This gap in the literature necessitates a thorough bibliometric analysis to examine the evolution of research on the EPI, identify key trends and patterns, and assess the overall impact of e-participation on digital transformation.

Additionally, existing research often focuses on specific regions or contexts, leading to fragmented insights that may not capture the global dynamics of e-participation. There is a need for a comprehensive review that consolidates research across various geographical and institutional contexts to provide a more nuanced understanding of how the EPI serves as an indicator of digital transformation (Aman & Jan, 2022). This research is crucial for policymakers, practitioners, and scholars who seek to understand the broader implications of e-participation and its role in shaping the future of governance.

1.3 Research Objective

The primary objective of this research is to conduct a bibliometric analysis of the E-Participation Index as an indicator of digital transformation. This analysis aims to achieve several specific goals. First, it seeks to map the evolution of research on the EPI, identifying key publications, authors, and research trends over time. By examining the growth of literature and the development of theoretical and empirical perspectives, this research will provide a comprehensive overview of how EPI has been studied and understood in the context of digital transformation.

Second, the study aims to uncover the thematic focus of existing research, highlighting the key areas of interest and investigation within the field of e-participation. This includes analyzing the various dimensions of e-participation that have been explored, such as citizen engagement, policy outcomes, and technological innovations. Understanding these thematic trends will offer insights into the current state of research and identify potential areas for future exploration.

Third, the research will assess the impact of e-participation on digital transformation by evaluating how the EPI reflects broader changes in governance and public administration. This includes examining the relationship between e-participation initiatives and the overall effectiveness of digital transformation efforts. By integrating findings from diverse studies, this analysis will provide a nuanced understanding of how the EPI serves as a measure of progress in digital governance.

Overall, this research aims to fill the existing gap in the literature by providing a comprehensive bibliometric analysis of the E-Participation Index. The findings will contribute to a deeper understanding of e-participation as a key indicator of digital transformation, offering valuable insights for policymakers, practitioners, and researchers interested in the intersection of technology and governance.

This article is organized as follows: After the introduction, the literature review section discusses the key concepts related to e-participation, digital transformation, and governance, offering a comprehensive overview of existing research. The research methodology section outlines the qualitative bibliometric analysis used to study the E-Participation Index as an indicator of digital transformation, describing the data collection and analysis techniques. The results section presents the findings from the bibliometric analysis, including trends, key themes, and patterns in the literature. The discussion elaborates on the significance of these findings, highlighting the impact of e-participation on digital transformation. Finally, the conclusion summarizes the key insights and suggests areas for future research.

2. LITERATURE REVIEW

2.1 What is Government

Government is a structured system through which authority and power are exercised to regulate the social, economic, and political life of a society. It encompasses various functions, including legislative, executive, and judicial roles, while also acting as a policy-maker and service provider (Cha et al., 2005; Zato et al., 2012). The concept of government is deeply rooted in historical and philosophical contexts, reflecting the evolution of governance practices over time.

A government is defined as a group of individuals responsible for exercising power and authority within a state, ensuring the rule of law and sovereignty (Vieira, 2013). It operates through distinct branches: legislative (making laws), executive (enforcing laws), and judicial (interpreting laws). The term "government" originates from the Greek word "kyvernites," meaning steersman, indicating its role in guiding society. Philosophers like Aristotle have historically debated the virtues of government, emphasizing its moral implications (Gill et al., 2016; Kostopoulos, 2004).

Governance involves decision-making processes that reflect societal expectations, highlighting the relationship between the government and its citizens. The role of government can vary significantly, from serving citizens' rights in liberal democracies to enforcing state authority in more authoritarian regimes (Svirina et al., 2021). In contrast, some perspectives argue that the effectiveness of government can be hindered by bureaucratic inefficiencies or miscommunication, as seen in public health advisories that may need to be followed correctly. This highlights the complexities and challenges inherent in governance.

2.2 What is E-Government

E-Government represents a transformative approach to public administration, leveraging information and communication technologies (ICT) to enhance government operations and citizen engagement. It aims to streamline service delivery, improve transparency, and foster greater participation in governance (Gregor et al., 2014). E-Government utilizes digital platforms to provide government services and information, making it accessible to citizens without bureaucratic barriers. It encompasses a range of services, from taxation to law enforcement, facilitated through the Internet (Yuhertiana et al., 2020).

The implementation of e-government can lead to increased efficiency, improved public services, and enhanced political participation (Hobololo & Mawela, 2017; Shen et al., 2022). It also promotes accountability and trust between governments and citizens, contributing to a more inclusive society. While e-government holds significant promise, its success often hinges on existing institutional frameworks and political will, particularly in developing regions where such reforms may face resistance (Hobololo & Mawela, 2017).

2.3 What is E-Participation

E-Participation refers to the engagement of citizens in governance processes through Information and Communication Technologies (ICTs), enhancing democratic participation and decision-making. It aims to overcome barriers to traditional participation, such as time and distance and is increasingly recognized for its potential to foster transparency and inclusivity in governance (Yao & Xu, 2022). E-participation enables citizens to influence public policy and decision-making, promoting a more open and collaborative government environment[3]. It is essential for enhancing democratic engagement, particularly for marginalized groups, by providing accessible platforms for participation (Hobololo & Mawela, 2017).

Trust is a critical factor influencing citizen participation in e-participation initiatives. Factors such as technology reliability and participatory processes significantly affect this trust[2]. Successful e-participation initiatives, like “Decide Madrid,” highlight the importance of political leadership and collaboration in fostering citizen engagement (Bhatia & Mabillard, 2022). Despite its potential, e-participation has faced challenges related to inclusivity, often needing to engage diverse demographics. The proposed Digital Citizen Participation framework aims to address these shortcomings by integrating user-centered design and technological innovations (Linhartova, 2022). In summary, while e-participation holds promise for enhancing democratic processes, it must address issues of trust, inclusivity, and effective implementation to realize its full potential.

2.4 What is E-Participation in Indonesia

E-participation in Indonesia refers to the use of digital platforms to enhance public engagement in governance, facilitating access to information, consultations, and decision-making processes. “E-Participation” Digital Dialogue Initiatives: Indonesian provincial governments have successfully utilized social media to foster public participation, ensuring citizens' voices are heard in governmental decisions (Hinsberg, 2010).

Indicators of E-Participation: The framework includes E-Information, E-Consultation, and E-Decision Making, with studies indicating that E-Information is the most utilized aspect, while E-Decision Making remains the least engaged (Yao & Xu, 2022). Decentralization and E-Participation: Effective management of funds, such as the Tobacco Excise Production Sharing Fund, requires enhanced e-participation to align with decentralization principles, promoting stakeholder involvement (Androniceanu et al., 2020). Public Engagement During Crises: Initiatives like 'Warga Bantu Warga' during the pandemic illustrate how digital media can mobilize community support and solidarity, reflecting a form of civic patriotism (Lim, 2021).

Challenges and Readiness: Despite the potential, e-participation faces challenges such as inadequate infrastructure and socio-economic barriers, impacting its effectiveness (Mohamed & Han, 2022). While e-participation presents opportunities for enhanced governance, it also faces significant hurdles that must be addressed to realize its full potential in Indonesia.

Table 1. Taxonomy of research data

Papers	Summarized Abstract	Results
Mengukur E-Participation Masyarakat di Era Transformasi Digital dengan Metode Multi Factor Evaluation Process (MFEP)	- Study on E-Participation in the digital transformation era. - The MFEP method is used to identify indicators and determine the level of E-Participation.	- The study identifies indicators and criteria used in E-Participation. - The level of E-Participation in Central Java is average.
Toward e-participation: Measuring and explaining performance	- Examines e-participation implementation and attributes that explain variation across countries. - Measures the efficiency of technology infrastructure conversion and e-participation development.	- The development of e-participation depends on governance stability and quality of regulation. - Efficient conversion of technology infrastructure depends on human capital availability.
Toward e-participation: Measuring and explaining performance	- Examines variation in e-participation implementation across countries - Identifies factors influencing efficiency in technology infrastructure and e-participation conversion	- The efficiency of e-participation depends on governance stability and quality of regulation. - The efficiency of technology infrastructure conversion depends on the availability of human capital.
Transforming e-participation: VR-dialogue – building and evaluating an AI-supported framework for next-gen VR-enabled e-participation research	- The study explores whether VR can enhance e-participation and overcome communication obstacles. - Authors propose AI-supported VR analytics infrastructure for e-participation research.	- The authors developed a novel framework for analyzing VR engagements in e-participation. - The AI-powered VR analytics infrastructure demonstrated good performance in classifying behavioral scenarios.
Social Media and E-Participation Research	- Social media tools promote citizens' engagement and participation in public affairs. - Research on social media and e-participation is still immature, and further research is needed.	- Research on social media and e-participation has increased in recent years. - Further research is needed to understand the true impacts of social media tools in e-participation.
Dimensions of e-Participation: Levels of Participation and Citizen Configurations	The study examines digital methods and tools for participatory processes in national government. - Findings reveal the concentration of tokenism and the absence of deepened citizen participation.	- Concentration of participatory activities associated with tokenism - Deepened forms of citizen participation were largely absent in the data
E-participation in lawmaking: background, promises & challenges	- E-participation initiatives aim to transform traditional lawmaking processes. - E-participation promises inclusiveness, transparency, and legitimacy in lawmaking.	- The paper identifies the context and attributes of e-participation in lawmaking. - The paper discusses the promises and challenges of e-participation in lawmaking.
E-participation in contemporary China: A comparison with conventional offline participation	- The study compares e-participation and offline participation in China. - E-government and online platforms offer equal participation opportunities to disadvantaged citizens.	- Traditional resources such as money and civic skills positively influence e-participation and offline political participation. - Communist party members and elites are more likely to participate in conventional offline political activities.

continued on following page

Table 1. Continued

Papers	Summarized Abstract	Results
What explains the degree of e-participation? A comparison of the adoption of digital participation platforms in Oslo, Melbourne, and Madrid	- Comparative case study of e-participation platforms in Oslo, Melbourne, and Madrid. - Develop an explanatory framework using institutional entrepreneurship and change theories.	- Conventional adoption theory cannot explain differences in e-participation platforms. The degree of e-participation is influenced by change agents, institutional discretion, and resources.
Framework for analysis of the management and organization of e-participation initiatives	- Research design and analytical model for exploring e-participation initiatives - Analytical framework with five aspects for evaluating e-participation platforms	- The paper presents an analytical model for exploring e-participation initiatives. - The framework can be useful for further research and government practitioners.

3. RESEARCH METHOD

3.1 Types of Research

The objective of this article is to comprehend the Analyzing E-Participation Index as an Indicator of Digital Transformation: A Bibliometric Analysis. Accordingly, we believe that the "Qualitative Research" method is suitable for this kind of research topic since it enables a thorough examination of the theme that incorporates unbiased viewpoints and experiences.

3.2 Research Locations

The United Nations website and scholarly journals served as our article's primary sources of information. However, our analysis shows that academic journals—which offer in-depth analyses of expert research—have emerged as a reliable source of data and knowledge. We obtained Academic Journal-related data from several online database sources, including Dimension AI, Google Scholar, Scopus, and so on. The data were subjected to peer assessment, guaranteeing their dependability and accuracy.

3.3 Data Collection Techniques

As researchers, we collected our data by doing a literature review, which enabled us to compile the body of current knowledge. Our comprehension of the data was successful because of the information that was gathered. We identified the research gaps and the crucial insights for our brainstorming. The first stage in conducting a literature review for us was to specify the parameters of our investigation; in this case, that meant identifying the keywords we would use to look for information pertaining to the article's issue, such as "e-government," "e-participation," etc. Additionally, we restricted our search to articles published in the previous five years. Following a preliminary review, we quickly perused the collected papers' abstracts to make sure they were pertinent to our piece.

Figure 1. Filters and keywords used for research

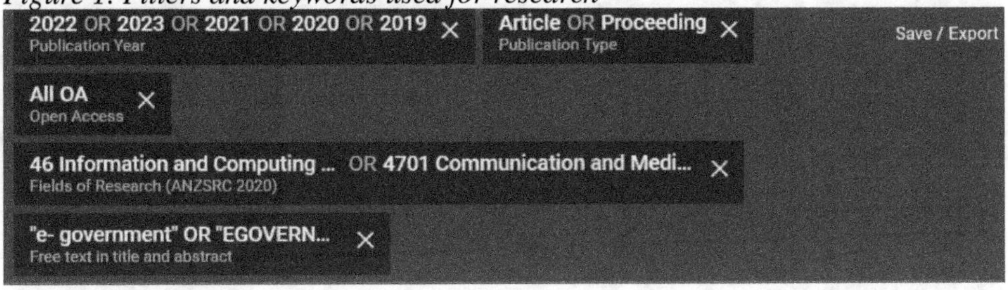

Source. Dimension AI

3.4 Data Analysis Techniques

A great desktop program for bibliometric analysis and research data visualization is called VOSViewer. It is now a useful resource for our literature review as well. In order to begin the analysis, we first loaded the research data into the VOSViewer program in the RIS format. After the data was successfully imported, we performed bibliometric analysis, which allowed us to determine which themes were the most influential. The ability to build maps with VOSViewer that illustrate the connections between various themes found in the study data is one of its key advantages. These maps are also useful for finding gaps in the research, which will greatly add to the significance of our article's findings.

Figure 2. Density visualization of research

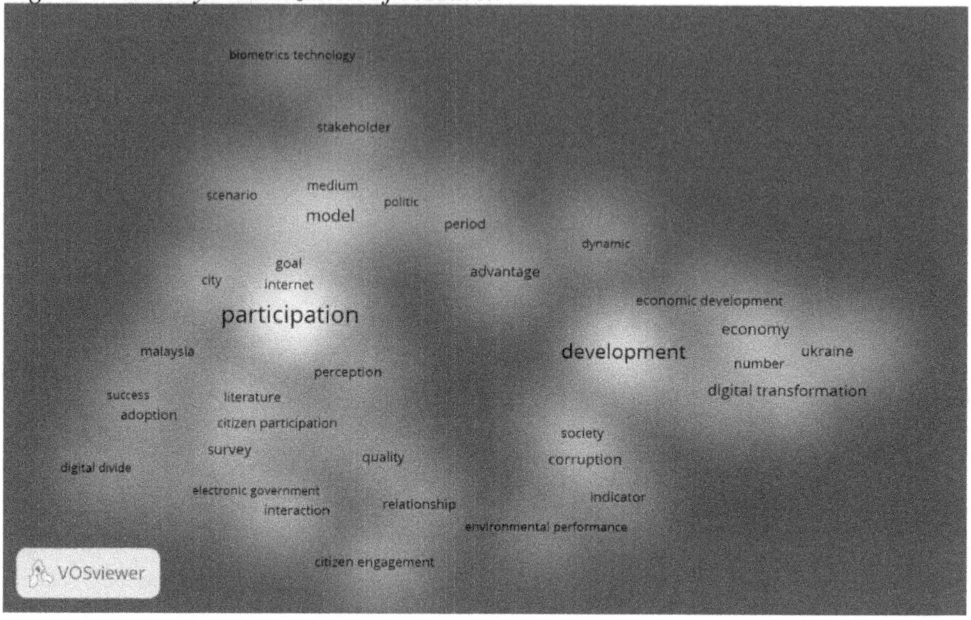

Source. Created by Author

3.5 Validity

The validity of this study is grounded in the careful selection of data sources and the application of established bibliometric analysis tools. The use of data from reputable databases such as the United Nations website, Dimension AI, Google Scholar, and Scopus ensures that the research draws from a comprehensive and credible pool of academic publications. To enhance content validity, the study focuses on widely accepted concepts and indicators, such as the E-Participation Index (EPI) and digital transformation, which are well-documented in the literature. The chosen keywords and search filters were carefully crafted to capture the breadth of the field without over-exclusion or inclusion, ensuring that the research is representative of the relevant body of knowledge.

Furthermore, the use of VOSviewer, a recognized and widely used bibliometric analysis tool, adds to the construct validity of the research, as it allows for systematic mapping of themes and trends in a rigorous and transparent manner. The methodology aligns with previous bibliometric studies, further reinforcing the validity of the research framework.

3.6 Reliability

The reliability of this study is reinforced by the reproducibility of its data collection and analysis procedures. The detailed description of how data were sourced—using specific databases, search terms, and inclusion/exclusion criteria—ensures that future researchers can replicate the study. The use of peer-reviewed journals and high-quality academic sources ensures consistency and reliability in the information gathered.

Moreover, the application of VOSviewer for bibliometric analysis adds to the internal reliability of the study. The software's robust algorithms for mapping bibliographic data ensure that the findings are not subject to subjective bias, and the visualizations (network, overlay, and density maps) produced can be replicated using the same dataset and parameters. To enhance external reliability, this study draws on literature from multiple regions and sectors, which broadens the applicability of its findings beyond a single context.

3.7 Research Approach

To ensure the robustness of this study, careful attention was given to both the validity and reliability of the research methods used. **Validity** was enhanced through the careful selection of data sources from reputable platforms such as the United Nations website, Dimension AI, Google Scholar, and Scopus. These platforms provided access to a wide range of academic publications, ensuring that the research drew from a broad and credible body of knowledge. The keywords and search terms were deliberately chosen to reflect key concepts like e-participation and digital transformation, thereby ensuring that the study captured the most relevant literature. This careful design maximizes the **content validity** of the research.

Furthermore, the study employed **VOSviewer**, a well-established bibliometric analysis tool, to map relationships between publications and key themes. This approach strengthens the **construct validity**, ensuring that the chosen metrics and visualizations accurately reflect the underlying structures of the data. By aligning with previous bibliometric studies, the study further supports its theoretical validity and connection to established research frameworks.

In terms of **reliability**, the methods were designed for replicability. The detailed description of the search strategies, inclusion/exclusion criteria, and data sources ensures that the research can be repeated with consistent results, contributing to the study's **internal reliability**. The use of peer-reviewed journals and high-quality academic sources further strengthens the reliability of the data. VOSviewer's systematic algorithm for bibliometric analysis minimizes subjective biases, while the visualizations (network, overlay, and density maps) can be reproduced by future researchers using the same dataset and methods, ensuring the **external reliability** of the findings.

4. RESULTS AND DISCUSSION

4.1 Results

4.1.1 Document Publication by Year

Figure 3. Publication of documents by years, source, dimension AI

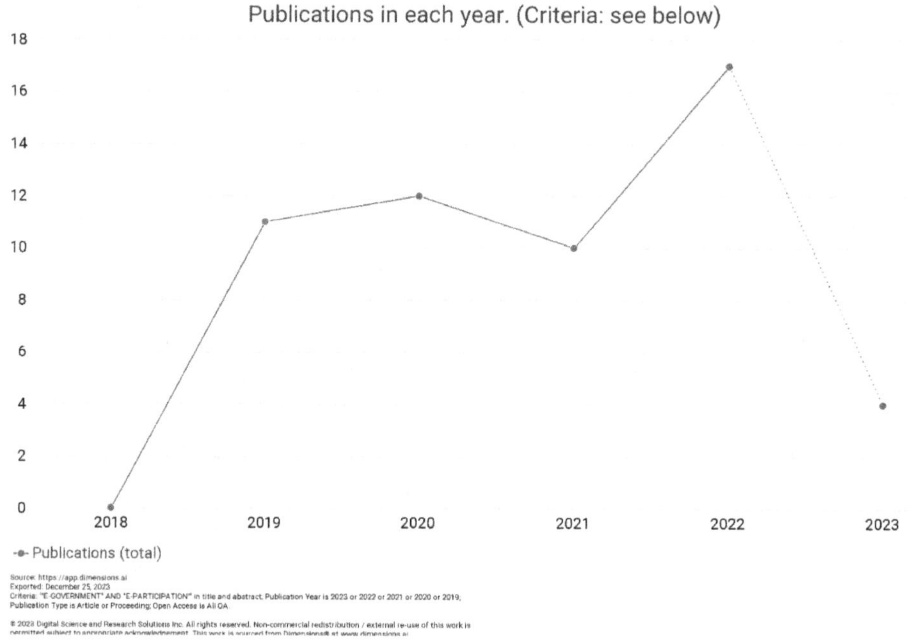

Figure 3. presents a visual representation of the number of publications related to "E-GOVERNMENT" and "E-PARTICIPATION" from 2018 to 2023. The data, sourced from Dimensions, highlights a significant increase in publications in this field over the years. While the number of publications in 2018 was relatively low, it experienced a substantial surge in 2019 and 2020, reaching a peak in 2022. However, a decline was observed in 2023, suggesting a potential temporary decrease in research activity or a change in publication trends. Overall, the data indicates a growing interest and research focus on "E-GOVERNMENT" and "E-PARTICIPATION" within the academic community.

4.1.2 Document Publication by Subject Area

Figure 4. Publication of documents by subject area, source, dimension AI

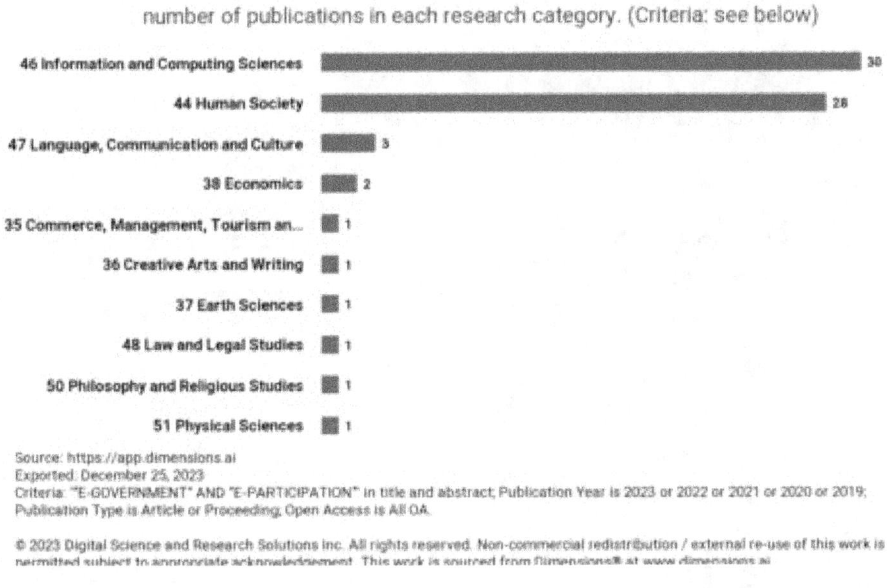

Figure 4. presents a bar chart illustrating the distribution of publications in various research categories related to "E-GOVERNMENT" and "E-PARTICIPATION" from 2019 to 2023. The data, sourced from Dimensions, reveals that the majority of publications fall within the "Information and Computing Sciences" category, followed by "Human Society." This suggests a strong focus on technological aspects and societal implications of "E-GOVERNMENT" and "E-PARTICIPATION." While the remaining categories have fewer publications, they contribute to a diverse understanding of the field. Overall, the chart highlights the interdisciplinary nature of research in this area, encompassing a range of perspectives from different academic disciplines.

4.1.3 Document Publication by Author

Figure 5. Publication of documents by author, source, dimension AI

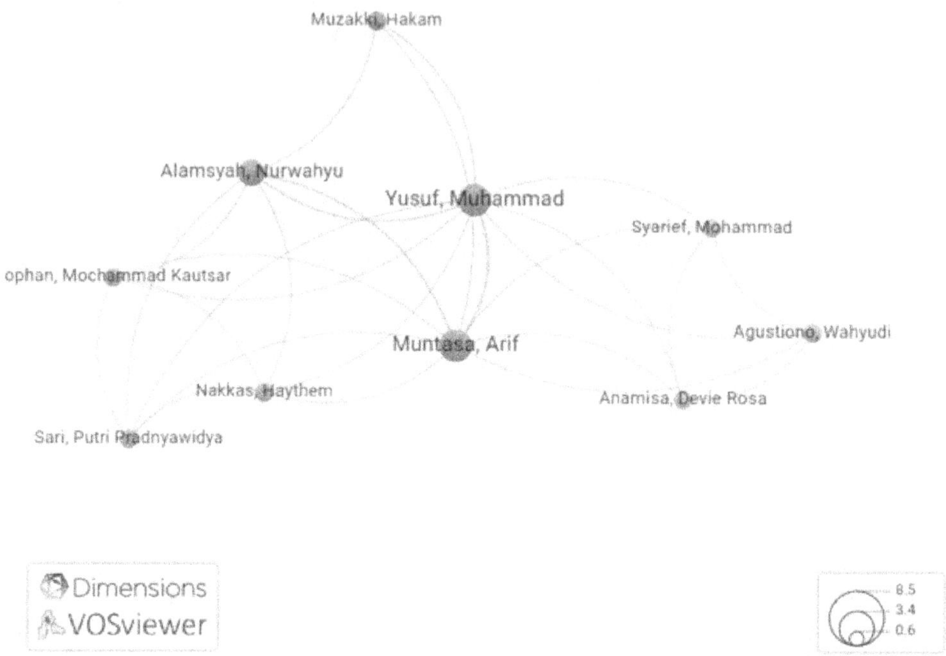

Figure 5. presents a network visualization of co-authorship relationships among researchers involved in “E-GOVERNMENT” and “E-PARTICIPATION” research. The nodes represent individual researchers, while the edges indicate collaborative connections. The size of each node corresponds to the number of publications, and the thickness of the edges reflects the frequency of collaboration. The visualization reveals a central cluster of researchers with strong interconnections, suggesting a core group of collaborators in the field. The network also highlights peripheral researchers with fewer connections, potentially indicating emerging or less established research communities. Overall, the figure provides insights into the collaborative landscape of “E-GOVERNMENT” and “E-PARTICIPATION” research, identifying key collaborators and potential areas for future research partnerships.

4.2 Discussion

4.2.1 Network Visualisation

Figure 6. Network visualization or research

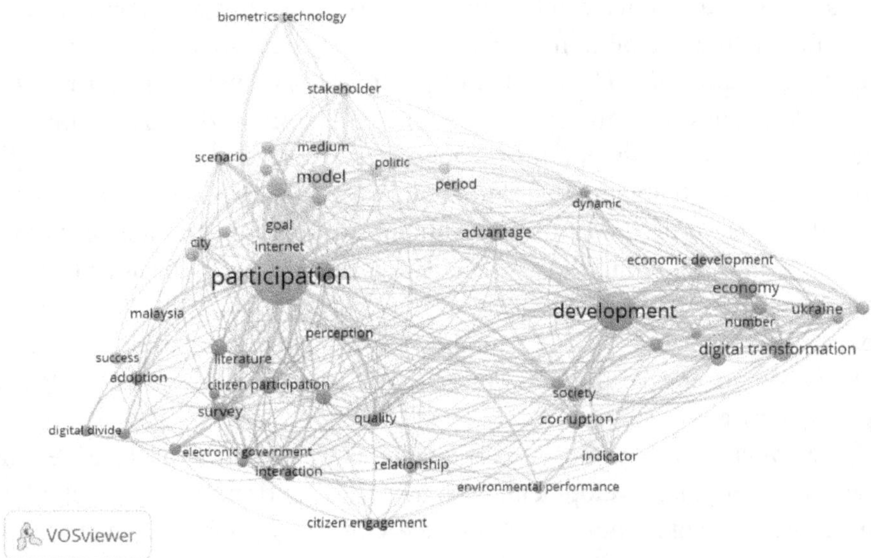

Source, Created by Author

Via the creation of network, overlay, and density visualizations using VosViewer, the bibliometric study of the network connecting subjects in 122 documents acquired from dimension AI was completed. The elements of a bibliometric network are edges and nodes. Publications, journals, or keywords are examples of nodes, which are represented as circles, while relationships between nodes are shown by edges. It displays the connection between two nodes. Distance serves as a symbol of edge, which is also the strength of the bond. The correlation between nodes is more substantial the closer they are to one another.

It is impossible to separate the topics of development, digital transformation, and analysis of the e-participation Index as an indicator of digital transformation. The examination of the e-participation index as a gauge of digital transformation is intimately linked to the growth of e-participation and the broader phenomenon of digital transformation. A measure of participation in the growth and advancement of a nation's or region's digital transformation is the e-participation index, which shows how much individuals participate in decision-making online. Governments and stakeholders can find possibilities and obstacles in promoting public participation, assisting with development, and quickening the digital transformation process by comprehending and evaluating this index. The following results of the VOS viewer study provide a network visualization with the issue of analyzing the e-participation Index as an indicator of digital transformation.

The color of the cluster is indicated by the cluster label on the image, which displays keywords or terms that appear frequently. While grouping is used to get an understanding or a summary of bibliometric groupings, image mapping is used to obtain a full picture of a bibliometric network. Every circle denotes a commonly occurring term or keyword. The number of publications related to the term in the document title is shown by the size of the circle. The more documents that are pertinent to that term or keyword, the bigger the circle's size.

As seen in Figure 6 above, e-participation is a significant node size or term. Moreover, the terms "e-participation," "development," and "digital transformation" are pertinent when examining the e-participation Index as an indicator of digital transformation. The picture above illustrates the cluster relationship between the topics of e-government and e-participation by the variation in the color of the connecting lines. Moreover, five clusters comprising all other terms are visualized, with a relationship between each keyword.

First place went to the keyword "e-participation," which had 84 occurrences and 76 overall link strength. Development, with 67 total occurrences and 60 total link strengths, came in second. Third place went to digital transformation, which had 45 overall link strength and 58 total appearances. An analysis of the e-participation index as an indicator of digital transformation reveals a substantial correlation between keywords based on the number of occurrences and total link strength.

With five occurrences and two total link strengths, "electronic government facility" is the keyword with the lowest order. Information technology came in second with five appearances and three link strengths overall. Third place goes to an e-government service with up to six appearances and five overall link strengths.

4.2.2 Overlay Visualisation

Figure 7. Overlay visualization of research

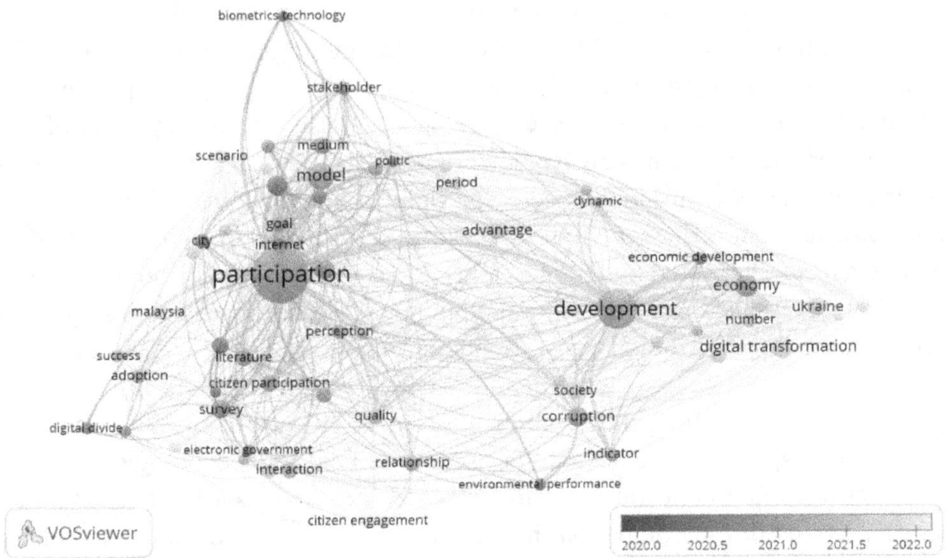

Source. Created by Author

Figure 7. presents a network visualization of bibliographic coupling among documents related to “E-GOVERNMENT” and “E-PARTICIPATION” from 2020 to 2022. The nodes represent individual documents, while the edges indicate the degree of similarity between them based on shared references. The size of each node corresponds to the number of citations received, and the thickness of the edges reflects the strength of the bibliographic coupling. The visualization reveals a dense cluster of documents centered around the concepts of “participation,” “development,” and “electronic government.” This suggests a strong interconnectivity and knowledge base within this research area. The other clusters, including those related to “biometrics technology,” “stakeholder,” and “economy,” also exhibit significant connections, indicating their relevance and integration within the broader field of “E-GOVERNMENT” and “E-PARTICIPATION.” The temporal distribution of the documents, represented by the color gradient, provides insights into the evolution of research trends over the study period.

4.3 Implication

4.3.1 Theoretical Implications

The findings of this study provide a deeper understanding of the evolving role of the E-Participation Index (EPI) as a key indicator of digital transformation. This research confirms the theoretical framework suggesting that e-participation is not merely a tool for enhancing citizen engagement but also a critical measure of how digital governance structures evolve. The study extends existing theories by demonstrating that the relationship between e-participation and digital transformation is multi-dimensional, influencing policy-making, service delivery, and transparency in governance. These findings suggest a need to revisit existing theoretical models of digital governance to incorporate the nuanced role of e-participation, particularly in contexts where digital transformation is unevenly distributed. Additionally, this research identifies gaps in the literature concerning regional disparities in EPI performance, highlighting the need for future theoretical frameworks to consider more context-specific variables, such as socio-political and technological factors.

The theoretical implications of this study stem from its contribution to the academic discourse on e-participation and digital transformation. The research provides insights into the evolving theoretical understanding of the E-Participation Index (EPI) as a metric for gauging the success of digital governance. Specifically, the findings validate and extend existing theories by demonstrating how e-participation can influence multiple dimensions of governance, including transparency, efficiency, and citizen engagement. Furthermore, the study uncovers a gap in current theoretical models, particularly regarding regional differences in the application and impact of e-participation. This suggests the need for further refinement of theoretical frameworks to account for socio-economic, technological, and political factors that affect e-participation on a local scale. In conclusion, this study offers new avenues for theoretical exploration, especially in terms of how digital inclusion and e-participation metrics are interpreted in various contexts of digital transformation.

4.3.2 Practical Implications

From a practical standpoint, this study highlights actionable insights for policymakers and government agencies aiming to enhance digital governance through e-participation. The bibliometric analysis reveals that e-participation initiatives, when effectively implemented, can significantly improve citizen engagement and decision-making processes. This finding underscores the importance of investing in digital infrastructure and citizen-centered platforms to facilitate greater involvement in governance. Moreover, the study provides evidence that improving the EPI can serve as a strategic tool for tracking progress in digital governance and addressing gaps in e-participation, particularly in underrepresented areas. Governments can utilize these insights to design more inclusive and accessible e-participation tools, thus fostering more equitable digital transformation across regions. The results also suggest that successful e-participation efforts require political leadership, reliable digital platforms, and trust-building mechanisms, offering practical guidance for stakeholders looking to implement effective e-government strategies.

From a practical perspective, the findings offer actionable insights for policymakers and practitioners involved in digital governance and public administration. The study highlights that improving e-participation infrastructure can lead to more effective citizen engagement and better decision-making processes. Practically, this suggests that governments should invest in more robust digital platforms that facilitate e-participation, ensuring they are inclusive, accessible, and secure. Furthermore, the results emphasize the importance of establishing trust and reliability in these platforms to encourage higher levels of citizen involvement. Governments can use the EPI as a diagnostic tool to identify weaknesses in their e-governance systems and address specific challenges, such as the digital divide or lack of transparency in certain regions. These practical recommendations provide a clear path for enhancing public participation through digital tools, ultimately promoting a more inclusive and responsive form of governance.

4.4 Limitations and Future Research

4.4.1 Limitations

While this study provides valuable insights into the role of the E-Participation Index (EPI) in digital transformation, several limitations should be acknowledged. First, the study relies primarily on bibliometric analysis, which limits its ability to explore the qualitative nuances of how e-participation is implemented in different political and social contexts. Additionally, the scope of the research is confined to the analysis of published literature, potentially omitting relevant gray literature, policy reports, or case studies that might offer more practical insights. Furthermore, the study focuses on global trends, which may obscure region-specific challenges and opportunities in e-participation. Lastly, the temporal scope of the analysis may limit the ability to capture emerging trends in the rapidly evolving field of digital governance.

4.4.2 Future Research

Future research should address these limitations by incorporating qualitative methods, such as case studies or interviews, to provide a deeper understanding of the mechanisms through which e-participation affects governance in specific contexts. Expanding the scope to include unpublished or gray literature would also enhance the comprehensiveness of future analyses. Additionally, future studies should focus on region-specific examinations of e-participation to uncover the unique socio-political factors that influence digital transformation in different parts of the world. Researchers may also explore the impact of new and emerging technologies, such as artificial intelligence and blockchain, on e-participation and its effectiveness. Finally, longitudinal studies that track the evolution of e-participation over time would be beneficial to identify long-term trends and assess the sustainability of digital governance initiatives.

5. CONCLUSION

To sum up, this study has shed light on e-government in a useful way. By conducting a thorough analysis of E-participation, we have added to the corpus of knowledge already available on E-government. Our findings have ramifications for pertinent domains or uses of e-participation, exposing the advantages and disadvantages of e-government. However, our research has illuminated certain aspects that are crucial to acknowledge the possible constraints, such as insufficient expertise of the facilitator, insufficient productivity, and Language barrier. Subsequent investigations ought to delve into the implementation of participatory budgeting and revamp the public planning procedure, consolidating our current understanding to augment our comprehension of e-government. In summary, the present study highlights the significance of ongoing research and deliberate discussion on e-participation in order to promote progress that benefits pertinent stakeholders and communities.

REFERENCES

Adnan, M., Ghazali, M., & Othman, N. Z. S. (2022). E-participation within the context of e-government initiatives: A comprehensive systematic review. *Telematics and Informatics Reports*, 8, 100015. DOI: 10.1016/j.teler.2022.100015

nAl-Dwairi, R., & Jditawi, W. (2022). The Role of Cloud Computing on the Governmental Units Performance and EParticipation (Empirical Study). *International Journal of Advances in Soft Computing and Its Applications*, 14(3), 79–93. DOI: 10.15849/IJASCA.221128.06

Aljazzaf, Z. M., Ayad, S., & Sarfraz, M. (2020). E-Participation Model for Kuwait e-Government. *International Journal of Advanced Computer Science and Applications*, 11(2). Advance online publication. DOI: 10.14569/IJACSA.2020.0110226

Aman, S., & Jan, M. A. (2022). Are we moving towards a managerial model of e-governance? building a case for citizen centric e-participation in Khyber Pakhtunkhwa, Pakistan. *Journal of Humanities* [JHSMS]. *Social and Management Sciences*, 3(1), 500–523. DOI: 10.47264/idea.jhsms/3.1.35

Androniceanu, A., Kinnunen, J., & Georgescu, I. (2020). E-government clusters in the eu based on the gaussian mixture models. *Administratie Si Management Public*, 2020(35), 6–20. DOI: 10.24818/amp/2020.35-01

Basri, N. H., Adnan, W. A. W., & Baharin, H. (2019). An exploratory study of users' experiences with e-participation: A case study of Malaysia. *Indonesian Journal of Electrical Engineering and Computer Science*, 15(3), 1138–1143. DOI: 10.11591/ijeecs.v15.i3.pp1138-1143

Bhatia, I., & Mabillard, V. (2022). How do cities use their communication channels? A study of social media adoption in two European federal states. *Electronic Government*, 18(2), 119–136. DOI: 10.1504/EG.2022.121970

Cha, S.-C., Tung, H.-W., Lee, H.-C., Tsai, T.-M., Lin, R., & Hsu, C.-H. (2005). Robalo: A risk-oriented job dispatching mechanism for workforce management system. In *IFIP Advances in Information and Communication Technology* (Vol. 189, pp. 559–570). Springer New York LLC. DOI: 10.1007/0-387-29773-1_37

Dias, G. P. (2020). Determinants of e-government implementation at the local level: An empirical model. *Online Information Review*, 44(7), 1307–1326. DOI: 10.1108/OIR-04-2020-0148

Gill, A. Q., Phennel, N., Lane, D., & Phung, V. L. (2016). IoT-enabled emergency information supply chain architecture for elderly people: The Australian context. *Information Systems*, 58, 75–86. DOI: 10.1016/j.is.2016.02.004

Gounopoulos, E., Kontogiannis, S., Kazanidis, I., & Valsamidis, S. (2020). The Impact of the Digital Divide on the Adoption of e-Government in Greece. *KnE Social Sciences*, 401–411–401–411. DOI: 10.18502/kss.v4i1.6002

Gregor, S., Imran, A., & Turner, T. (2014). A "sweet spot" change strategy for a least developed country: Leveraging e-Government in Bangladesh. *European Journal of Information Systems*, 23(6), 655–671. DOI: 10.1057/ejis.2013.14

Hinsberg, H. (2010). A community of fans, friends and power-users sustainable e-participation in Estonia. *EJournal of EDemocracy and Open Government*, 2(2), 111–118. DOI: 10.29379/jedem.v2i2.45

Hobololo, T. S., & Mawela, T. (2017). Exploring the use of mobile phones for public participation in the Buffalo City metropolitan municipality. *AGRIS On-Line Papers in Economics and Informatics*, 9(1), 57–68. DOI: 10.7160/aol.2017.090105

Kostopoulos, G. K. (2004). E-government in the Arabian Gulf: A vision toward reality. *Electronic Government*, 1(3), 293–299. DOI: 10.1504/EG.2004.005553

Lim, I. (2021). Exploring experience at the intersection of migration and digital democracy in South Korea. *Asiascape: Digital Asia*, 8(3), 139–163. DOI: 10.1163/22142312-bja10019

Linhartova, V. (2022). The Role of E-Government in the Evaluation of the Quality of Governance in the Countries of the European Union. *Croatian and Comparative Public Administration*, 22(2), 267–287. DOI: 10.31297/hkju.22.2.4

Mohamed, S., & Han, S. (2022). Translating Human Values to Design Requirements: The Case of Developing Digital Government Collaborative Platform (DGCP) for Environmental Sustainability in Sri Lanka. In H. L., S. M., & H. S. (Eds.), *23rd Annual International Conference on Digital Government Research: Intelligent Technologies, Governments and Citizens, DGO 2022* (pp. 54–61). Association for Computing Machinery. DOI: 10.1145/3543434.3543455

Musiał-Karg, M., & Kapsa, I. (2019). Citizen e-Participation as an Important Factor for Sustainable Development. *European Journal of Sustainable Development*, 8(3), 210. DOI: 10.14207/ejsd.2019.v8n3p210

Palacin, V., Zundel, A., Aquaro, V., & Kwok, W. M. (2023). *Reframing E-participation for Sustainable Development*. 172–180. DOI: 10.1145/3494193.3494218

Proposing an Index for Cross-District Comparison for Citizen e-Services Provision. (2019). *International Journal of Recent Technology and Engineering, 8*(2S11), 3601–3605. DOI: 10.35940/ijrte.B1450.0982S1119

Quintana, A. G., Urquía-Grande, E., & Delgado Jalón, M. L. (2022). Strategic Conceptual Theories and Sustainable Cooperation Among Stakeholders in E-government, E-participation, and Social Media. *Central European Journal of Public Policy*, 16(2), 46–63. DOI: 10.2478/cejpp-2022-0007

Quintana, A. G., Urquía-Grande, E., & Jalón, M. L. D. (2022). Strategic Conceptual Theories and Sustainable Cooperation Among Stakeholders in E-government, E-participation, and Social Media. *Central European Journal of Public Policy*, 16(2), 46–63. DOI: 10.2478/cejpp-2022-0007

Revyakin, S., & da Rocha, A. (2021). AN EMPIRICAL INVESTIGATION OF E-GOVERNMENT ADOPTION IN RUSSIA: ACCESS, RIGHTS, TRUST AND CITIZENS' EXPERIENCE. *Public Administration Issues*, 0(5), 137–160. DOI: 10.17323/1999-5431-2021-0-5-137-160

Rodríguez-Martínez, C. C., García-Sánchez, I. M., Vicente-Galindo, P., & Galindo-Villardón, P. (2019). Exploring Relationships between Environmental Performance, E-Government and Corruption: A Multivariate Perspective. *Sustainability (Basel)*, 11(22), 6497. DOI: 10.3390/su11226497

Sacchi, A., Santolini, R., & Schneider, F. (2022). On the effects of e-participation on shadow economy: A worldwide empirical analysis. *German Economic Review*, 23(3), 463–491. DOI: 10.1515/ger-2021-0076

Shen, Y., Cheng, Y., & Yu, J. (2022). From recovery resilience to transformative resilience: How digital platforms reshape public service provision during and post COVID-19. *Public Management Review*. Advance online publication. DOI: 10.1080/14719037.2022.2033052

Shofia, S., Trisetyarso, A., Abbas, B. S., & Suparta, W. (2023).. . *E-Participation Platform Model for E-Government Case Study in Karawang City*, 354–357. Advance online publication. DOI: 10.2991/assehr.k.200303.085

Shofia*, S., Meyliana*, Hidayanto, A. N., & Prabowo, H. (2020). Critical Success Factors E-Participation for E-Government. *International Journal of Recent Technology and Engineering (IJRTE), 8*(5), 4010–4016. DOI: 10.35940/ijrte.E6246.018520

Stratu-Strelet, D., Gil-Gómez, H., Oltra-Badenes, R., & Oltra-Gutierrez, J. V. (2021). Critical factors in the institutionalization of e-participation in e-government in Europe: Technology or leadership? *Technological Forecasting and Social Change*, 164, 120489. DOI: 10.1016/j.techfore.2020.120489

Suardi, I. (2021). E-Government, Governance and Corruption in Asian countries. *Emerging Markets : Business and Management Studies Journal*, 8(2), 137–150. DOI: 10.33555/embm.v8i2.180

Sudirman, F. A., & Saidin, S. (2022). Pemerintahan Berbasis Elektronik (E-Government) dan Pembangunan Berkelanjutan: Reviu Literatur Sistematis. *Nakhoda: Jurnal Ilmu Pemerintahan*, 21(1), 44–58. DOI: 10.35967/njip.v21i1.269

Susanti, E., Harta, R., Diana, B. A., & Utami, S. B. (2021). E-Readiness and The Effectiveness of E-Participation in Indonesia. *MIMBAR : Jurnal Sosial Dan Pembangunan*, 37(1). Advance online publication. DOI: 10.29313/mimbar.v37i1.6931

Svirina, A., Appalonova, N., Garanin, D., Lukashevich, N., & Koshkin, I. (2021). Fintech developmental trends: The role and influence of sustainable digital logistics. In K. V. (Ed.), *2021 Ural Environmental Science Forum on Sustainable Development of Industrial Region, UESF 2021* (Vol. 258). EDP Sciences. DOI: 10.1051/e3sconf/202125802019

Tawakkal, G. T. I. (2022). A POTENTIAL FOR CAUSALITY IN DEVELOPMENT COUNTRIES (TRACKING E-PARTICIPATION AND E-GOVERNMENT IN SOUTHEAST ASIAN COUNTRIES). *Politico (Pavia, Italy)*, 22(2), 58–70. DOI: 10.32528/politico.v22i2.8176

UN, & Le Blanc, D. (2020). *E-participation: A Quick Overview of Recent Qualitative Trends*. DOI: 10.18356/a39cdf00-en

Usmanova, A. A. (2023). *Does a Higher E-Government Development Index Mean a Higher GDP Growth Rate?* 467–472. DOI: 10.1145/3508072.3508168

Vieira, J. B. (2013). The impact of public transparency in fighting corruption a study on brazilian municipalities e-government. *EJournal of EDemocracy and Open Government*, 5(1), 80–106. DOI: 10.29379/jedem.v5i1.140

Xu, P., Johnson, K., & Rundlett, A. (2022). E-participation in contemporary China: A comparison with conventional offline participation. *Chinese Public Administration Review*, 13(3), 150–161. DOI: 10.1177/15396754221107115

Yao, Y., & Xu, P. (2022). E-participation decision across different channels. *Information Technology & People*, 35(3), 956–976. DOI: 10.1108/ITP-05-2020-0314

Yildirim, K.YILDIRIM. (2022). A REVIEW OF LOCAL AND NATIONAL E-GOVERNMENT DEVELOPMENT MODELS AND THEIR DETERMINANTS. *Akademik Yaklaşımlar Dergisi*, 13(1), 270–297. DOI: 10.54688/ayd.1103488

Yuhertiana, I., Izaak, W. C., & Arifin, J. (2020). E-government and e-finance on African countries. *Journal of Advanced Research in Dynamical and Control Systems, 12*(6 Special Issue), 184–204. https://doi.org/DOI: 10.5373/JARDCS/V12SP6/SP20201023

Yusuf, M., Muntasa, A., Agustiono, W., Anamisa, D. R., & Syarief, M. (2020). A Novel Conceptual Model of e-Participation using Biometrics Technologies. *Journal of Physics: Conference Series*, 1569(2), 22069. DOI: 10.1088/1742-6596/1569/2/022069

Yusuf, M., Sophan, M. K., Muntasa, A., Alamsyah, N., Nakkas, H., & Sari, P. P. (2020). E-government learning media through augmented reality technology. *Bulletin of Social Informatics Theory and Application*, 4(1), 12–20. DOI: 10.31763/businta.v4i1.258

Zato, C., De Luis, A., Bajo, J., De Paz, J. F., & Corchado, J. M. (2012). Dynamic model of distribution and organization of activities in multi-agent systems. *Logic Journal of the IGPL*, 20(3), 570–578. DOI: 10.1093/jigpal/jzr005

Chapter 4
AI in Tourism:
Business and Economic Perspectives

Farhana Yeasmin Lina
https://orcid.org/0009-0006-8308-5549
Daffodil International University, Bangladesh

Mohammad Badruddoza Talukder
https://orcid.org/0009-0008-1662-9221
International University of Business Agriculture and Technology, Bangladesh

ABSTRACT

Artificial Intelligence is redefining the tourism industry by ensuring the accumulation of technologies in business operations and tourism-related activities and fostering economic growth and financial outcomes. From the automated reservation system, AI is increasing its branches toward personalized marketing, setting dynamic pricing models, and offering tailored experiences per guests' requirements. Tourism and hospitality-related services can strengthen smarter decision-making, certify efficient operations, and enhance service delivery to tourists. This chapter scrutinizes the sequential development of AI in tourism, examining assorted AI applications that have been applied to the tourism industry. AI creates new job opportunities, increasing efficiency at work, enhancing competitiveness, and encouraging economic expansion and growth, especially in developing markets. This chapter offers a thorough overview of the transformative role of AI in tourism-related business, economic development, and advancement challenges and opportunities AI presents to the industry.

DOI: 10.4018/979-8-3693-8357-5.ch004

INTRODUCTION

AI technologies are transforming the nature and characteristics of different industries, including tourism and hospitality (Talukder, 2020). Various forms of these AI technologies, such as machine learning, natural language processing, and computer vision, are transforming business operations and creating new ways of effective interaction with guests and travellers. As the tourism industry is working as the catalyst for creating a super-smart society, it needs to ensure the amalgamation of AI technologies and AI integration in every sphere (Cheng & Zhang, 2020). The revolutionary power of AI can analyze and process vast amounts of data, identify working patterns, and make effective and efficient decisions. It triggers the transformation of the business environment and the industry, too. For the economic development of any country and to contribute to the global economy, the tourism industry plays a vital role as it generates substantial revenue, creates millions of jobs, and drives cultural exchange (M.-H. Huang et al., 2019). Including AI in the tourism industry influences improving business operations and efficiency, increasing customer experience, and steering innovation(Mohammad et al., 2024). By analyzing vast databases, AI technologies can find the inherent insights to understand the needs and demands of consumers and their behavioural patterns, optimizing the quality of service based on the market with greater accuracy and efficiency (Robinson et al., 2020).

Artificial Intelligence (AI) in tourism includes utilizing advanced technologies and applications to intensify the service quality provided by the travel and hospitality industry (A. Huang et al., 2022). With the advancement of AI technologies and applications, the tourism industry is expanding its branches and enabling its related sectors to adapt to the upgraded consumer preferences and serve them more efficiently (Doborjeh et al., 2022). It contemplates using machine learning, natural language processing (NLP), robotics, and other intelligent systems and applications to ensure personalized service per guest requirements, increase work efficiency, and optimize tourism-related operations. The adoption of advanced AI-driven technologies is assisting various sectors, including airlines, hotels, travel agencies, and online travel platforms to expedite their services by doing predictive analytics to make proper decisions, providing visual and automated customer service, and also enhancing efficiency and customer satisfaction (Ivanov & Webster, 2019). AI-driven technologies benefit tourism businesses by increasing efficiency at work, minimizing operating costs, increasing personalized marketing, increasing revenue from business operations, and driving economic growth (Qin et al., 2024). This chapter highlights the interconnectedness of AI and tourism, the significance of AI applications in the tourism business, the economic contribution, and the future possibilities. Tourism-related service providers used computerized reservation systems and fundamental data analysis in the early days. Still, in the modern era of advanced technologies, AI is transforming the whole pattern of the tourism industry as it includes machine learning, natural language processing, and robotics for service provision (Shmarkov et al., 2019). Tourism businesses and destinations are enabling themselves to offer personalized experiences, enhance operational efficiency, and maximize revenue by utilizing these advancements. The tourism industry is ever-evolving as it connects people worldwide, and now, this industry is transforming itself to cope with the technological revolution (Kumar et al., 2024). AI encompasses a variety of technologies that utilize machines to perform tasks with minimal time and in a structured way utilizing human intelligence, such as learning, reasoning, and self-correction. AI can play a revolutionary role in the tourism industry by changing business patterns, enhancing guest satisfaction, and boosting economic growth (Makridakis, 2017; Sawon et al., 2024). This chapter examines the in-depth analysis of the usages of AI in tourism and the business and financial implications of the connection. The chapter also indicates the adoption of AI in various aspects of the tourism industry and the economic impact on tourism-related business growth, efficiency, and competitiveness.

LITERATURE REVIEW

The incorporation of AI in tourism has attained significant consideration from academic and industry interests for the positive contribution extracted by the business and economic sectors. This literature review integrates the key findings of the existing research to understand AI's role in the tourism industry.

The use of AI in the service-providing or tourism and hospitality industry is bringing considerable changes in the customer experience level (Youssef et al., 2025). AI-driven technologies and applications such as chatbots and virtual assistants assist customers with instant, if needed, virtual assistance, ultimately ensuring instant customer support and personalized recommendations (Masum et al., 2025). AI-driven technologies are facilitating travellers by providing real-time information regarding their hotel stay information, schedule of flights, and details about the destinations and surroundings and increasing the satisfaction level of the travel by ensuring instant and real-time responses and services (Gupta et al., 2023; Kabir et al., 2024)).

Including AI in extensive data analysis can assist in understanding individual traveller preferences and selecting the appropriate marketing strategies to serve travellers effectively (Stone et al., 2020). By analyzing customer data, AI algorithms can include detailed traveller profiles, mentioning their likes, dislikes, preferences, demands, and other requirements (Talukder et al., 2023). By examining the algorithms, businesses can select proper promotional activities and methods and design customized travel itineraries for travellers. Providing tailored experiences and personalization of the services can increase customer loyalty and satisfaction (Buhalis et al., 2019).

The application of AI technologies is streamlining tourism operations by improving operational processes, focusing on revenue management, considering demand forecasting, and analyzing strategies for dynamic pricing (Guizzardi et al., 2021). AI-driven revenue management systems utilized by hotels, airlines, and other organizations use historical data and predictive analytics to identify suitable pricing for providing services and inventory allocation to ensure real-time experiences that work for the maximization of revenues (Buhalis & Sinarta, 2019).

The literature also highlights that the engagement of AI accelerates business process automation and optimizes operational efficiency (Buhalis & Sinarta, 2019). Businesses utilize new modes of innovation, such as AI-powered robots and virtual assistants, to provide customer services, maintain routine tasks such as check-ins and check-outs, manage room service requests, and instantly fulfil information queries (Pillai & Sivathanu, 2020). This automation expedites the quality of regular operations. It enables employees to focus on essential work that needs direct human interaction and improves service quality and operational efficiency (Ng et al., 2021).

Implementing AI technologies in the tourism industry has substantial economic repercussions as it streamlines productivity and economic growth by focusing on personalized service delivery and appropriately enhancing the utilization of available resources (M. Li et al., 2021; Singh et al., 2025). AI-driven automation assists in minimizing operational costs and increasing efficiency, and it facilitates the organization or business in increasing profitability and economic conditions. The deployment of AI can facilitate business organizations in creating new employment opportunities and transform the overall structure of the tourism industry. Including AI threatens humans but creates new job positions such as AI development, data analysis, and digital marketing, among other areas (Nam et al., 2021).

The literature acknowledges a variety of positive impacts of the application of AI and some challenges and ethical considerations as it analyzes big data sets related directly to travellers and their preferences (Wirtz et al., 2019). Large volumes of personal data are examined with AI applications to find solutions and identify proper business models that can sometimes hamper data privacy and security concerns. Business organizations must ensure conformity towards data privacy and protection regulations such as the General Data Protection Regulation (Di Vaio et al., 2020).

AI algorithms-based activities require proper training as they deal with real-time data. Ethical considerations must be considered as they can create biased decisions and discrimination among different parties, as well as customer experiences and brand reputation (Fusté-Forné & Jamal, 2021). Proper utilization of AI algorithms with transparency and accountability can boost the efficiency work of business organizations.

The ever-evolving nature of AI technologies has been working to transform businesses with AI-powered predictive analytics, natural language processing (NLP), and robotics, contributing to the provision of sophisticated and personalized tourism services (Doborjeh et al., 2022). AI is responsible for managing destinations by promoting sustainable tourism practices and optimizing the proper use of businesses' resources (Balsalobre-Lorente et al., 2023).

By collaborating on the positive impacts of AI applications, the tourism industry can ensure sustainability and accessibility for tourists. Public-private partnerships and cross-industry collaborations are necessary to identify the possible challenges and manage them by minimizing negative impacts (Vosman et al., 2023). By creating innovative ecosystems, tourism businesses can facilitate the overall development and use AI technologies based on the industry's unique demands. So, using AI can ensure numerous benefits in terms of customer experience, operational efficiency, economic growth, and innovation.

CONCEPTUAL FRAMEWORK FOR AI IN THE TOURISM INDUSTRY FROM BUSINESS AND ECONOMIC PERSPECTIVES

Figure 1. Conceptual framework for AI in the tourism industry from business and economic perspectives

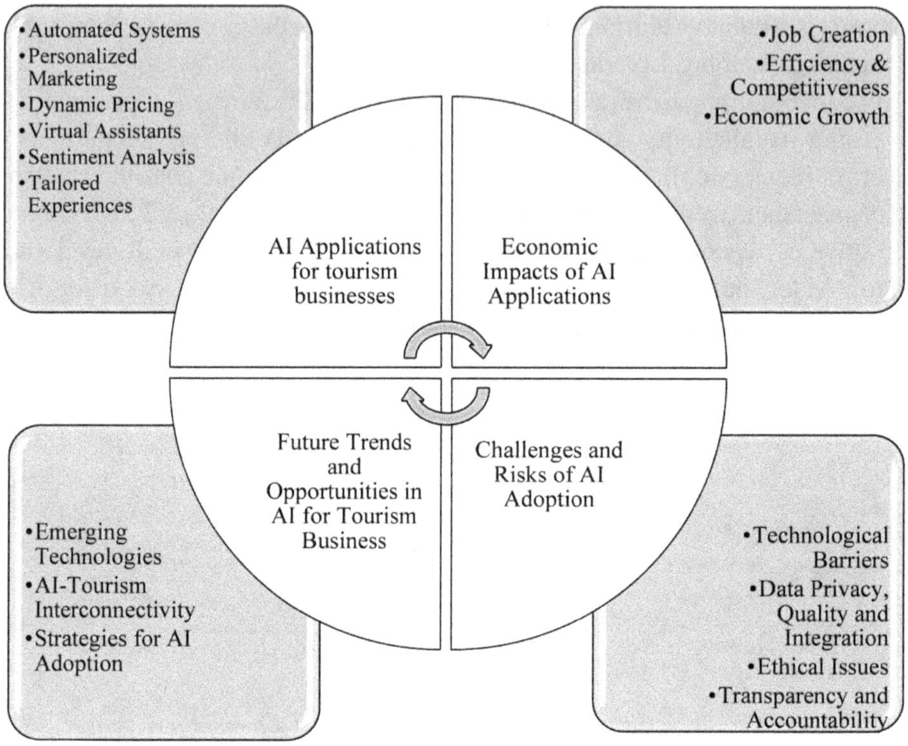

(Author's Compilation)

Evolution of AI in Tourism

Historical Development of AI in Tourism

The amalgamation of tourism and technology began with computerized reservation systems that assisted business organizations in optimizing the reservation and booking system and inventory management. The incorporation of technology in tourism began with the innovation of computerized reservation systems (CRS) in the 1960s, allowing travel agencies and airlines to introduce a new concept to serve clients more efficiently and design the booking system and inventory management more effectively.

The emergence of digitalized online travel agencies (OTAs) and travel search engines was seen between the 1970s and 1980s, which initiated the automation of booking systems and somehow allowed the provision of a minimal level of personalized recommendations based on available resources. With time and technological progression, the inclusion of AI in tourism and its capabilities has been increased for the betterment of tourism businesses and economic development. With time, how the inclusion of AI emerged in tourism is mentioned below:

Table 1. Significant sequential evolution of AI in tourism

Time Frame	Significant Sequential Evolution of AI in Tourism	Sources
End of the 20th century, 1980s-1990s	The introduction of new technology, global distribution systems (GDS), enabled travel agencies to reach their customers within a shorter period and provide them with real-time flight information, which changed the booking system's previous capability. The evolution of this system assisted in creating an integrated and interconnected travel ecosystem that stimulates the travel experiences of tourists and connects different airlines, hotels, car rentals, and other companies.	(Vosman et al., 2023), (Buhalis & Leung, 2018)
Turn of the millennium, 2000s	Implementing the Internet and e-commerce has changed travel agencies' whole work arrangement and operational pattern as they started to work as online travel agencies. Online travel agencies (OTAs) enable customers to get customer-centric recommendations. Customer-facing AI tools such as automated response and recommendation providers, mobile-friendly travel services, and chatbots stimulated the company's personalized user experiences.	(Polytechnic Institute of Porto et al., 2019) (Sawon et al., 2024),
2010s, The 2010–2019 period	Machine learning and big data analytics appeared within this time frame, introducing more personalized customer experiences. These processes assisted businesses in understanding the customers more closely by analyzing various forms of data through predictive analytics. By scrutinizing big data and utilizing data processing technologies, businesses started to understand their needs and preferences more effectively and designed effective marketing strategies and personalized offers.	(Miah et al., 2017), (Piccoli et al., 2017)
The decade of the 2020s and onwards	Up-to-date AI applications and technologies are converting business operations by including computer vision, robotics, natural language processing, and automated decision-making. Incorporating AI in tourism has drastically changed the operational pattern and service provision quality by digitalizing them.	(Jabeen et al., 2022)

(Author's Compilation)

Technological Advancements Enabling AI in Tourism

Several technological advancements and AI applications are transforming tourism and related service-providing businesses to enhance the efficiency of work and increase personalized customer experiences with the help of data analytics and extensive data analysis, cloud computing, natural language processing, machine learning, IoT devices, robotics and automation, computer vision and facial recognition, and utilization of VR and AR technologies.

Table 2. Technological advancements and usages of AI applications in tourism

AI applications	Technological advancements and usages of AI applications in tourism	Sources
Data Analytics and Big Data	Data analytics and big data refer to analyzing large amounts of data to determine suitable insights based on the data and assist in making decisions regarding any issues. Examining the vast amount of data collected from different sources, business organizations can determine suitable strategies based on travel patterns, market trends, and customer preferences.	(J. Li et al., 2018)
Cloud Computing	With the help of cloud computing, business organizations have become more efficient in storing and processing large amounts of data more securely. This procedure facilitates the applications to operate effectively and utilize those data resources when required. Cloud computing minimizes the additional cost of purchasing hardware or storing devices and boosts the use of sophisticated AI algorithms per the tourism business requirements.	(Wei et al., 2020)
Natural Language Processing (NLP)	Natural language processing, or NLP, has enabled the tourism industry to communicate and respond to tourists in real-time and instantaneously through chatbots and virtual assistants. The interconnection of these AI applications focuses on improving customer engagement and satisfaction by analyzing customer feedback from reviews and social media and ensuring the required services meet guests' demands.	(Álvarez-Carmona et al., 2022)
Machine Learning (ML)	Machine learning is generally used to scrutinize large amounts of data to make decisions in different areas, such as revenue management, understanding customer preferences, influencing market demands, and providing personalized travel recommendations. Business organizations also use it to predict market trends, understand the demand and supply conditions, and, if necessary, assist in setting effective pricing for the business products or services and tactics to maximize profitability.	(Egger, 2022)
Internet of Things (IoT)	Integrating IoT devices in tourism businesses enhances the communication and connectivity between the guests and the business organizations. It assists in providing and collecting data in real-time and more efficiently. Today, intelligent hotels use IoT devices to automatically control the room ambience, lighting, and temperature, depending on guests' preferences. It can help track the guests' movement and behavioural patterns and utilize them to design personalized marketing and service delivery.	(Car et al., 2019)

continued on following page

Table 2. Continued

AI applications	Technological advancements and usages of AI applications in tourism	Sources
Robotics and Automation	In airports, hotels, and other service-providing organizations, automated robots do routine tasks such as luggage checking, floor cleaning, concierge services, check-ins, and check-outs. Using robotics increases the effectiveness and efficiency of service-providing businesses and provides unique experiences to satisfy guests.	(Ivanov & Webster, 2020)
Computer Vision and Facial Recognition	Different organizations use computer vision and facial recognition to maintain security and personalization. Hotels and airports are using these technologies to provide automated services directly to guests in a more personalized way. Such as check-in, ticket booking, and getting boarding passes directly by automated facial analysis. Different businesses are using computer vision to ensure the safety of tourists by monitoring the flow of tourists, controlling carrying capacity, and maintaining balanced, sustainable services.	(González-Rodríguez et al., 2020)
Virtual Reality (VR) and Augmented Reality (AR)	The utilization of VR and AR technologies assists destinations in showing their actual beauty virtually to tourists and assisting them in selecting their preferred destinations. It provides information and virtual tours with immersive experiences that include interactive information.	(Yung & Khoo-Lattimore, 2019)

(Author's Compilation)

Economic Impact of AI on Tourism

AI's Contribution to Economic Growth

With the help of different mechanisms, AI contributes to the economic growth in the tourism sector. Businesses ensure productivity and operational efficiency by utilizing automation and AI in routine tasks. The amalgamation of AI in the tourism sector is optimizing resource use, reducing costs drastically, and increasing productivity, all of which ultimately contribute to GDP, financial benefits, and overall economic growth (Gökovali & Bahar, 2006). However, there is a threat of jobs being replaced by AI. The transformation creates new job opportunities, such as AI development, data analysis, and digital marketing.

AI-Driven Innovation and Market Expansion

AI technologies boost innovation and assist businesses in expanding the tourism market by designing new business models and creating new markets. Developing new AI applications can help organizations understand and predict demand and develop innovative business models to offer personalized and efficient services (Soni et al., 2019). Travel agencies, airlines, and hotels use AI to arrange virtual tours, show their available resources or services, and assist guests with virtual travel assistance. AI tools also facilitate businesses to help guests with bookings, recommendations, and travel arrangements. New market segments, customer segments, current trends, guest preferences, and demands can be identified with the help of AI tools and technologies.

Impact on Small and Medium-Sized Enterprises (SMEs)

Small and Medium-Sized enterprises are getting numerous opportunities with the help of AI applications. AI technologies are creating cost-effective solutions to make services more accessible and affordable for tourists. Using AI tools allows SMEs to compete with big competitors by providing services more efficiently and personally and enhancing the service's quality (Baabdullah et al., 2021). With the help of AI-driven marketing tools, SMEs can design personalized marketing strategies within a Budget and reach their desired audience without requiring large marketing budgets. AI assists SMEs in providing personalized experiences to guests and setting dynamic pricing to enhance competitiveness in a crowded market.

AI in Sustainable Tourism Development

AI technologies are assisting in creating sustainable tourism development by utilizing available resources more effectively and minimizing the negative environmental impacts (Sharpley, 2020). Utilizing AI algorithms can find new energy sources and optimize energy use in different businesses such as hotels, resorts, and other organizations, ensuring energy efficiency and proper resource management. AI-driven technologies are creating new energy management systems to analyze resource and energy usage patterns to control and optimize guest consumption and support sustainability goals. With the help of AI tools, extensive data analysis is possible to promote sustainable tourism practices and encourage businesses to focus on and arrange eco-friendly accommodations and activities.

Figure 2. Economic impact of AI on tourism

AI's Contribution to Economic Growth	• Increased Productivity and Efficiency • Job Creation and Transformation • Enhanced Competitiveness
AI-Driven Innovation and Market Expansion	• New Business Models • Expansion into New Markets
Impact on Small and Medium-Sized Enterprises (SMEs)	• Cost-Effective Solutions • Personalized Marketing on a Budget
AI in Sustainable Tourism Development	• Energy Efficiency and Resource Management • Promoting Sustainable Practices

(Author's Compilation)

CHALLENGES AND RISKS OF AI ADOPTION

Technological Challenges and Data Privacy Issues

Several technological challenges and data privacy concerns have been created with the emergence of AI adoption in tourism. The effectiveness and efficiency of AI solutions, the quality of data, and data integration highly depend on high-quality resources and proper AI adoption techniques (Bulchand-Gidumal et al., 2024). Adopting and implementing AI technologies require significant investment in data infrastructure to arrange everything properly. AI systems are related to large amounts of personal data, so the privacy and security of the data must be ensured to protect those personal data. AI systems are vulnerable to cyberattacks, so proper security measures must be designed by businesses before dealing with AI solutions and providing a continuous monitoring system to manage threats and cyberattacks.

Ethical Considerations in AI Implementation

AI implementation must ensure the use of massive data sets that include detailed information about guests, their preferences, needs, and wants. As AI algorithms deal with personalized data collected from guests, some threats, such as bias and discrimination, might occur. Prejudice and discrimination can impact the whole result and hamper decision-making, customer experiences, and brand reputation (Jabeen et al., 2022). To maximize customer trust and reliability and minimize the negative impacts, AI systems must be designed and operated by trained staff to ensure fair and unbiased distribution of information and transparency and accountability among different parties. Customer trust and regulatory compliance must be ensured to maintain trust and confidence in decision-making processes.

Financial Investment and ROI Challenges

Businesses need to invest a lot of money initially to acquire and implement AI applications and technologies. Financial considerations are significant in implementing, updating, and maintaining AI technologies. As the initial investment is very high, sometimes it creates barriers for small and medium enterprises to utilize AI applications. Using AI can benefit companies differently, but the return on investment for AI is still unpredictable and uncertain. The return on investment for AI applications dramatically depends on the successful implementation and integration with effective processes (Camisón et al., 2016). To manage, operate, and maintain the AI systems, skilled personnel need to be hired and trained as per the requirements of the businesses. Still, it may seem overly costly for small organizations.

Resistance to Change within the Industry

Employees and management may not be aware of the benefits of AI for both the business and its employees, and that is why this perception can create resistance to change in AI adoption. Fear of replacement from the job and lack of proper knowledge about AI's benefits may hinder the acceptance of AI adoption (Talukder, 2021). To ensure smooth AI integration and minimize resistance, businesses must design and implement effective change management strategies. Providing necessary training about the AI adoption process, involving them in the AI adoption process, developing essential skills, and demonstrating the value of AI in improving their work can encourage employees to encourage AI adoption.

RECOMMENDATIONS FOR ADOPTING AI TECHNOLOGIES IN TRANSFORMING TOURISM BUSINESSES AND ENSURING ECONOMIC GROWTH

Figure 3. Recommendations for adopting AI Technologies in Transforming Tourism Businesses and ensuring Economic growth

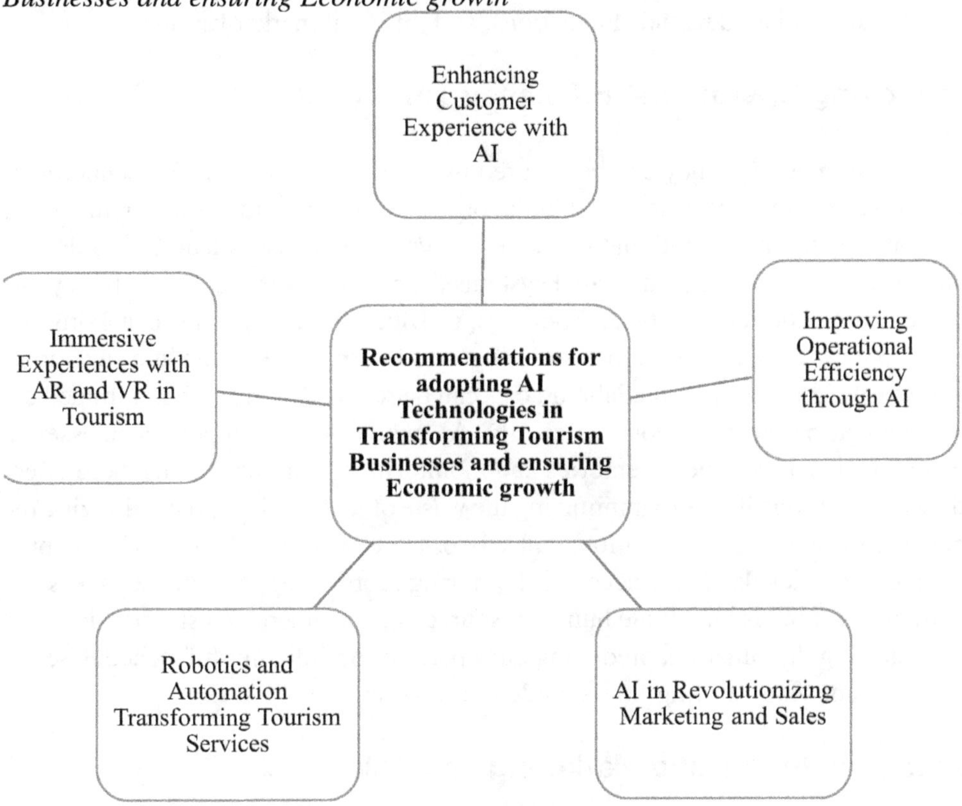

(Author's Compilation)

Enhancing Customer Experience with AI

Incorporating AI applications in different forms, such as Chatbots, Virtual assistants, Personalized recommendation engines, and Dynamic pricing models, assists business organizations in enhancing customer experiences. With the help of chatbots and virtual assistants, businesses provide instant travel advice and customer support, respond to booking queries, and provide accurate information quickly (Pillai & Sivathanu, 2020). These technologies facilitate the customers by providing prompt services and, if necessary, assisting the guests in getting compensation for delays or cancellations of flights or other bookings. By examining vast amounts of data, AI can provide personalized travel suggestions as per the demands of the guests and create customized itineraries as per their requirements. This process encourages the guests to engage more effectively (Casillo et al., 2019). Analyzing the AI algorithms can find out the current trends of the markets and the behavioural patterns of the guests and assist the management in making decisions regarding dynamic pricing, competitor pricing, demand fluctuations, and different market variables.

Improving Operational Efficiency Through AI

Operational efficiency can be ensured by the incorporation of AI technologies in tourism-related businesses as it assist organizations in automating routine tasks and optimizing the operational processes to work fast (Tussyadiah, 2020). Hotels and airlines are creating automated systems for customers through which they can ensure automatic room or ticket bookings, provide boarding passes, check-ins and outs, room service requests, food ordering, and housekeeping schedule selections. With the help of automation, labour costs can be reduced, and swift and immediate service can be ensured more efficiently. AI analytics can support businesses in managing resources and inventories and monitoring the supply chains more effectively, which contributes to minimizing the waste of inventories and maximizing the benefits from resource utilization. It also boosts the operational process by keeping track of stock levels and, if necessary, ensuring reorder supplies and seamless operations. AI can also facilitate human resources management and staff deployment by analyzing the situation, predicting busy periods, optimizing shift schedules, and ensuring adequate staffing levels while minimizing costs.

AI in Revolutionizing Marketing and Sales

With the help of AI, the trends and preferences of targeted potential travellers, advertising campaigns, and marketing and sales strategies can be easily identified. Marketing and sales strategies in tourism are transforming drastically with the help of AI technologies, which collaborate with different applications such as targeted advertising, sentiment analysis for brand management, and customer relationship management (CRM) to reshape marketing and sales activities. AI technologies can analyze customer reviews and social media to predict the preferences and sentiment toward a brand and focus proactively on serving the customers as per the requirements. Some applications can allow real-time sentiment analysis, which helps businesses respond to guest queries quickly and effectively. Customer relationship management (CRM) utilizes AI applications to provide insights into customer behaviour and preferences, which can guide organizations in enabling personalized communication and strengthening customer relationships.

Robotics and Automation Transforming Tourism Services

The utilization of robotics in tourism is growing because of the benefits it can bring to ensure novelty and efficiency in different activities. Hotels and airports use robots for regular tasks such as luggage handling, room service delivery, and customer information. The employment of robotics supports businesses in improving efficiency and reducing labour costs while offering a unique customer experience. Autonomous vehicles and drones are also used by service-providing businesses to test guided tours and deliveries, offer aerial sightseeing tours, provide an innovative way to experience the city and manage transportation within tourism destinations. These robotic-based applications offer new possibilities for service delivery to different destinations quickly and more efficiently.

Immersive Experiences with AR and VR in Tourism

The utilization of VR and AR technologies is growing within tourism business activities to improve customer engagement. With the help of virtual tours and AR experiences, travellers can explore destinations and hotel rooms without even going there and virtually within a very short time. This process encourages travellers to accelerate the decision-making process and increases business bookings. Some applications provide immersive virtual tours to show their available resources or services, creating appeal among their targeted groups, helping them visualize their stays, and making informed choices. Proper work knowledge must improve service quality and secure service provision. VR is used to train employees from different institutions in real time, which helps create a realistic and immersive learning environment that enhances the preparedness of the employees and assists them in improving customer interactions, emergency procedures, and service efficiency.

CONCLUSION AND FUTURE STUDY

Artificial Intelligence (AI) has been the transformative force within the tourism industry, enabling business operations to enjoy the benefits of significant advancements, exponential economic growth, and substantial economic development. This chapter has analyzed the evolution and application of AI in tourism, focusing on its essential role in enhancing customer service, personalized marketing, dynamic pricing, and operational efficiency. By utilizing different applications of AI technologies such as virtual assistants, data-driven insights, and sentiment analysis, businesses in the tourism sector can create a more efficient work environment and make smarter decisions, optimizing service delivery based on the needs and demands of the customers. AI applications and technology adoption can foster job creation, improve competitiveness, and drive economic expansion by extending effectiveness and efficiency at work, improving operational efficiency, enhancing customer satisfaction, and promoting more innovative business strategies. With the bringing of economic growth and benefits, AI adoption and implementation can bring some challenges, too, such as technological barriers, data privacy concerns, data management, and maintaining ethical considerations (Wang et al., 2020). The economic impact of AI is also evident as it creates new job opportunities and increases the efficiency of employees and organizations. Integrating AI technologies into the tourism industry can bring sustainable business growth and economic development by embracing AI's capabilities and utilizing them in business activities for long-term success and continued economic growth. Future research can delve into the long-term effects of AI on employment within the tourism industry and identify a sustainable way for AI adoption to ensure economic benefits by managing ethical considerations or data security. AI assists in revolutionizing the tourism industry and tourism-related businesses by taking adaptive strategies and frameworks to work effectively and maximize their potential, ultimately encouraging innovation and economic growth for businesses.

REFERENCES

Álvarez-Carmona, M. Á., Aranda, R., Rodríguez-Gonzalez, A. Y., Fajardo-Delgado, D., Sánchez, M. G., Pérez-Espinosa, H., Martínez-Miranda, J., Guerrero-Rodríguez, R., Bustio-Martínez, L., & Díaz-Pacheco, Á. (2022). Natural language processing applied to tourism research: A systematic review and future research directions. *Journal of King Saud University. Computer and Information Sciences*, 34(10), 10125–10144. DOI: 10.1016/j.jksuci.2022.10.010

Baabdullah, A. M., Alalwan, A. A., Slade, E. L., Raman, R., & Khatatneh, K. F. (2021). SMEs and artificial intelligence (AI): Antecedents and consequences of AI-based B2B practices. *Industrial Marketing Management*, 98, 255–270. DOI: 10.1016/j.indmarman.2021.09.003

Balsalobre-Lorente, D., Abbas, J., He, C., Pilař, L., & Shah, S. A. R. (2023). Tourism, urbanization and natural resources rents matter for environmental sustainability: The leading role of AI and ICT on sustainable development goals in the digital era. *Resources Policy*, 82, 103445. DOI: 10.1016/j.resourpol.2023.103445

Buhalis, D., Harwood, T., Bogicevic, V., Viglia, G., Beldona, S., & Hofacker, C. (2019). Technological disruptions in services: Lessons from tourism and hospitality. *Journal of Service Management*, 30(4), 484–506. DOI: 10.1108/JOSM-12-2018-0398

Buhalis, D., & Leung, R. (2018). Smart hospitality—Interconnectivity and interoperability towards an ecosystem. *International Journal of Hospitality Management*, 71, 41–50. DOI: 10.1016/j.ijhm.2017.11.011

Buhalis, D., & Sinarta, Y. (2019). Real-time co-creation and nowness service: Lessons from tourism and hospitality. *Journal of Travel & Tourism Marketing*, 36(5), 563–582. DOI: 10.1080/10548408.2019.1592059

Bulchand-Gidumal, J., William Secin, E., O'Connor, P., & Buhalis, D. (2024). Artificial intelligence's impact on hospitality and tourism marketing: Exploring key themes and addressing challenges. *Current Issues in Tourism*, 27(14), 2345–2362. DOI: 10.1080/13683500.2023.2229480

Camisón, C., Forés, B., & Puig-Denia, A. (2016). Return on capital in Spanish tourism businesses: A comparative analysis of family vs non-family businesses. *European Journal of Management and Business Economics*, 25(3), 91–110. DOI: 10.1016/j.redeen.2016.04.002

Car, T., Pilepić Stifanich, L., & Šimunić, M. (2019). *Internet of things (iot) in tourism and hospitality: opportunities and challenges*. DOI: 10.20867/tosee.05.42

Casillo, M., Clarizia, F., Colace, F., Lombardi, M., Pascale, F., & Santaniello, D. (2019). An Approach for Recommending Contextualized Services in e-Tourism. *Information (Basel)*, 10(5), 180. DOI: 10.3390/info10050180

Cheng, L., & Zhang, J. (2020). Is tourism development a catalyst of economic recovery following a natural disaster? An analysis of economic resilience and spatial variability. *Current Issues in Tourism*, 23(20), 2602–2623. DOI: 10.1080/13683500.2019.1711029

Di Vaio, A., Palladino, R., Hassan, R., & Escobar, O. (2020). Artificial intelligence and business models in the sustainable development goals perspective: A systematic literature review. *Journal of Business Research*, 121, 283–314. DOI: 10.1016/j.jbusres.2020.08.019

Doborjeh, Z., Hemmington, N., Doborjeh, M., & Kasabov, N. (2022). Artificial intelligence: A systematic review of methods and applications in hospitality and tourism. *International Journal of Contemporary Hospitality Management*, 34(3), 1154–1176. DOI: 10.1108/IJCHM-06-2021-0767

Egger, R. (2022). Machine Learning in Tourism: A Brief Overview: Generation of Knowledge from Experience. In Egger, R. (Ed.), *Applied Data Science in Tourism* (pp. 85–107). Springer International Publishing., DOI: 10.1007/978-3-030-88389-8_6

Fusté-Forné, F., & Jamal, T. (2021). Co-Creating New Directions for Service Robots in Hospitality and Tourism. *Tourism and Hospitality*, 2(1), 43–61. DOI: 10.3390/tourhosp2010003

Gökovali, U., & Bahar, O. (2006). Contribution of Tourism to Economic Growth: A Panel Data Approach. *Anatolia*, 17(2), 155–167. DOI: 10.1080/13032917.2006.9687184

González-Rodríguez, M. R., Díaz-Fernández, M. C., & Pacheco Gómez, C. (2020). Facial-expression recognition: An emergent approach to the measurement of tourist satisfaction through emotions. *Telematics and Informatics*, 51, 101404. DOI: 10.1016/j.tele.2020.101404

Guizzardi, A., Pons, F. M. E., Angelini, G., & Ranieri, E. (2021). Big data from dynamic pricing: A smart approach to tourism demand forecasting. *International Journal of Forecasting*, 37(3), 1049–1060. DOI: 10.1016/j.ijforecast.2020.11.006

Gupta, S., Modgil, S., Lee, C.-K., & Sivarajah, U. (2023). The future is yesterday: Use of AI-driven facial recognition to enhance value in the travel and tourism industry. *Information Systems Frontiers*, 25(3), 1179–1195. DOI: 10.1007/s10796-022-10271-8 PMID: 35529102

Huang, A., Chao, Y., De La Mora Velasco, E., Bilgihan, A., & Wei, W. (2022). When artificial intelligence meets the hospitality and tourism industry: An assessment framework to inform theory and management. *Journal of Hospitality and Tourism Insights*, 5(5), 1080–1100. DOI: 10.1108/JHTI-01-2021-0021

Huang, M.-H., Rust, R., & Maksimovic, V. (2019). The Feeling Economy: Managing in the Next Generation of Artificial Intelligence (AI). *California Management Review*, 61(4), 43–65. DOI: 10.1177/0008125619863436

Ivanov, S., & Webster, C. (2019). Conceptual Framework of the Use of Robots, Artificial Intelligence and Service Automation in Travel, Tourism, and Hospitality Companies. In S. Ivanov & C. Webster (Eds.), *Robots, Artificial Intelligence, and Service Automation in Travel, Tourism and Hospitality* (pp. 7–37). Emerald Publishing Limited. DOI: 10.1108/978-1-78756-687-320191001

Ivanov, S., & Webster, C. (2020). Robots in tourism: A research agenda for tourism economics. *Tourism Economics*, 26(7), 1065–1085. DOI: 10.1177/1354816619879583

Jabeen, F., Al Zaidi, S., & Al Dhaheri, M. H. (2022). Automation and artificial intelligence in hospitality and tourism. *Tourism Review*, 77(4), 1043–1061. DOI: 10.1108/TR-09-2019-0360

Kabir, F., Talukder, M. B., & Kumar, S. (2024). Exchange of Cultures in the Field of Gastronomy Tourism: Evidence of Bangladesh. In Castanho, R., & Franco, M. (Eds.), *Cultural, Gastronomy, and Adventure Tourism Development* (pp. 142–159). IGI Global., DOI: 10.4018/979-8-3693-3158-3.ch006

Kumar, S., Talukder, M. B., & Kaiser, F. (2024). Artificial Intelligence in Business: Negative Social Impacts. In *Demystifying the Dark Side of AI in Business* (pp. 81-97). IGI Global. DOI: 10.4018/979-8-3693-0724-3.ch005

Li, J., Xu, L., Tang, L., Wang, S., & Li, L. (2018). Big data in tourism research: A literature review. *Tourism Management*, 68, 301–323. DOI: 10.1016/j.tourman.2018.03.009

Li, M., Yin, D., Qiu, H., & Bai, B. (2021). A systematic review of AI technology-based service encounters: Implications for hospitality and tourism operations. *International Journal of Hospitality Management*, 95, 102930. DOI: 10.1016/j.ijhm.2021.102930

Makridakis, S. (2017). The forthcoming Artificial Intelligence (AI) revolution: Its impact on society and firms. *Futures*, 90, 46–60. DOI: 10.1016/j.futures.2017.03.006

Masum, M. Y., Faruq, M. O., Mia, M. N., & Talukder, M. B. (2025). Implementing Waste Management Solutions in Tourist Destinations. In Talukder, M., Kumar, S., & Haghi, A. (Eds.), *Application of Waste-to-Energy Innovations in Tourism* (pp. 1–28). IGI Global., DOI: 10.4018/979-8-3693-7605-8.ch001

Miah, S. J., Vu, H. Q., Gammack, J., & McGrath, M. (2017). A Big Data Analytics Method for Tourist Behaviour Analysis. *Information & Management*, 54(6), 771–785. DOI: 10.1016/j.im.2016.11.011

Mohammad Badruddoza Talukder. Sanjeev Kumar, I. R. Das. (2024). Implications of Blockchain Technology- Based Cryptocurrency in the cloud for the Hospitality Industry. In *Emerging Trends in Cloud Computing Analytics, Scalability, and Service Models* (p. 19). DOI: 10.4018/979-8-3693-0900-1.ch018

Mohammad Badruddoza Talukder. Sanjeev Kumar, I. R. Das. (2024). Perspectives of Digital Marketing for the Restaurant Industry. In *Advancements in Socialized and Digital Media Communications* (p. 17). DOI: 10.4018/979-8-3693-0855-4.ch009

Nam, K., Dutt, C. S., Chathoth, P., Daghfous, A., & Khan, M. S. (2021). The adoption of artificial intelligence and robotics in the hotel industry: Prospects and challenges. *Electronic Markets*, 31(3), 553–574. DOI: 10.1007/s12525-020-00442-3

Ng, K. K. H., Chen, C.-H., Lee, C. K. M., Jiao, J., & Yang, Z.-X. (2021). A systematic literature review on intelligent automation: Aligning concepts from theory, practice, and future perspectives. *Advanced Engineering Informatics*, 47, 101246. DOI: 10.1016/j.aei.2021.101246

Piccoli, G., Lui, T.-W., & Grün, B. (2017). The impact of IT-enabled customer service systems on service personalization, customer service perceptions, and hotel performance. *Tourism Management*, 59, 349–362. DOI: 10.1016/j.tourman.2016.08.015

Pillai, R., & Sivathanu, B. (2020). Adoption of AI-based chatbots for hospitality and tourism. *International Journal of Contemporary Hospitality Management*, 32(10), 3199–3226. DOI: 10.1108/IJCHM-04-2020-0259

Pinto, I., & Castro, C.Polytechnic Institute of Porto. (2019). Online travel agencies: Factors influencing tourist purchase decision. *Tourism & Management Studies*, 15(2), 7–20. DOI: 10.18089/tms.2019.150201

Qin, Y., Xu, Z., Wang, X., & Skare, M. (2024). Artificial Intelligence and Economic Development: An Evolutionary Investigation and Systematic Review. *Journal of the Knowledge Economy*, 15(1), 1736–1770. DOI: 10.1007/s13132-023-01183-2

Robinson, S., Orsingher, C., Alkire, L., De Keyser, A., Giebelhausen, M., Papamichail, K. N., Shams, P., & Temerak, M. S. (2020). Frontline encounters of the AI kind: An evolved service encounter framework. *Journal of Business Research*, 116, 366–376. DOI: 10.1016/j.jbusres.2019.08.038

Sawon, Md. M. H., Lina, F. Y., & Hossain, Md. A. (2024). AI in the Tourism and Hospitality Industry in Bangladesh: Challenges and Ways Forward. In M. B. Talukder, S. Kumar, & P. K. Tyagi (Eds.), *Advances in Hospitality, Tourism, and the Services Industry* (pp. 84–102). IGI Global. DOI: 10.4018/979-8-3693-6755-1.ch005

Sawon, M. M., Lina, F. Y., Talukder, M. B., & Hossain, M. A. (2025). Waste-to-Energy Integration Strategies in the Tourism Industry: Evidence of Bangladesh. In Talukder, M., Kumar, S., & Haghi, A. (Eds.), *Application of Waste-to-Energy Innovations in Tourism* (pp. 55–74). IGI Global., DOI: 10.4018/979-8-3693-7605-8.ch003

Sharpley, R. (2020). Tourism, sustainable development and the theoretical divide: 20 years on. *Journal of Sustainable Tourism*, 28(11), 1932–1946. DOI: 10.1080/09669582.2020.1779732

Shmarkov, M. S., Shmarkova, L. I., & Shmarkova, E. A. (2019). Digital technologies in the organization and management of tourist organizations. *Proceedings of the 1st International Scientific Conference "Modern Management Trends and the Digital Economy: From Regional Development to Global Economic Growth" (MTDE 2019)*. Proceedings of the 1st International Scientific Conference "Modern Management Trends and the Digital Economy: from Regional Development to Global Economic Growth" (MTDE 2019), Yekaterinburg, Russia. DOI: 10.2991/mtde-19.2019.18

Singh, K., Kumar, S., & Talukder, M. B. (2025). Digital Transformation and Its Impact on Tourism Business in India. In Albattat, A., Azman, N., Valeri, M., & Singh, A. (Eds.), *Tracking Tourism Patterns and Improving Travel Experiences With Innovative Technologies* (pp. 215–230). IGI Global., DOI: 10.4018/979-8-3693-9636-0.ch010

Soni, N., Sharma, E. K., Singh, N., & Kapoor, A. (2019). *Impact of Artificial Intelligence on Businesses: From Research, Innovation, Market Deployment to Future Shifts in Business Models* (Version 1). arXiv. DOI: 10.48550/ARXIV.1905.02092

Stone, M., Aravopoulou, E., Ekinci, Y., Evans, G., Hobbs, M., Labib, A., Laughlin, P., Machtynger, J., & Machtynger, L. (2020). Artificial intelligence (AI) in strategic marketing decision-making: A research agenda. *The Bottom Line (New York, N.Y.)*, 33(2), 183–200. DOI: 10.1108/BL-03-2020-0022

Talukder, M. B. (2020). An Appraisal of the Economic Outlook for the Tourism Industry, Specially Cox's Bazar in Bangladesh. *i-manager's Journal on Economics & Commerce,* 2(1), 23-35. DOI: 10.26634/jecom.2.1.17285

Talukder, M. B. (2020). The Future of Culinary Tourism: An Emerging Dimension for the Tourism Industry of Bangladesh. I-Manager's. *Journal of Management*, 15(1), 27. DOI: 10.26634/jmgt.15.1.17181

Talukder, M. B. (2021). An assessment of the roles of the social network in the development of the Tourism Industry in Bangladesh. *International Journal of Business, Law, and Education*, 2(3), 85–93. DOI: 10.56442/ijble.v2i3.21

Talukder, M. B., Das, I. R., & Afchar, M. N. (2025). Impact of Social Media on the Development of Religious Tourism Industry. In Jermsittiparsert, K., Wekke, I., & Suanpang, P. (Eds.), *Business Sustainability Practices in Society 5.0* (pp. 359–378). IGI Global., DOI: 10.4018/979-8-3693-9230-0.ch018

Talukder, M. B., & Hossain, M. M. (2021). Prospects of Future Tourism in Bangladesh: An Evaluative Study. I-Manager's. *Journal of Management*, 15(4), 1–8. DOI: 10.26634/jmgt.15.4.17495

Talukder, M. B., Kabir, F., & Jibon, F. A. (2025). AI-Driven Personalized Room Management in the Modern Hotel Industry. In Chiwaridzo, O., & Masengu, R. (Eds.), *AI Technologies for Personalized and Sustainable Tourism* (pp. 59–82). IGI Global., DOI: 10.4018/979-8-3693-5678-4.ch003

Talukder, M. B., Kabir, F., Kaiser, F., & Lina, F. Y. (2024). Digital Detox Movement in the Tourism Industry: Traveler Perspective. In *Business Drivers in Promoting Digital Detoxification* (pp. 91-110). IGI Global. DOI: 10.4018/979-8-3693-1107-3.ch007

Talukder, M.B., & Kumar, S. (2024). Revisiting intention in food service outlet of five-star hotels:A quantitative approach based on food service quality. Sport i Turystyka. Środkowoeuropejskie Czasopismo Naukowe, 7(1), 137–156. DOI: 10.16926/sit.2024.01.08

Talukder, M. B., Kumar, S., Sood, K., & Grima, S. (2023). Information Technology, Food Service Quality and Restaurant Revisit Intention. *International Journal of Sustainable Development and Planning*, 18(1), 295–303. DOI: 10.18280/ijsdp.180131

Talukder, M. B., & Swarna, D. A. (2025). Economic Perspectives on Hotel Occupancy and Tourist Movement Patterns. In Albattat, A., Azman, N., Valeri, M., & Singh, A. (Eds.), *Tracking Tourism Patterns and Improving Travel Experiences With Innovative Technologies* (pp. 231–258). IGI Global., DOI: 10.4018/979-8-3693-9636-0.ch011

Talukder, M. B., Swarna, D. A., & Khan, M. R. (2025). Kuakata Reimagined: Forecasting Economic Growth and Future Potential of Coastal Hub in Bangladesh. In Jermsittiparsert, K., Wekke, I., & Suanpang, P. (Eds.), *Business Sustainability Practices in Society 5.0* (pp. 419–434). IGI Global., DOI: 10.4018/979-8-3693-9230-0.ch021

Talukder, M. B., Swarna, D. A., & Khan, M. R. (2025). The Allure of Tranquillity: How Less-Crowded Destinations in Bangladesh are Captivating International Tourists. In Jermsittiparsert, K., Wekke, I., & Suanpang, P. (Eds.), *Business Sustainability Practices in Society 5.0* (pp. 399–418). IGI Global., DOI: 10.4018/979-8-3693-9230-0.ch020

Tussyadiah, I. (2020). A review of research into automation in tourism: Launching the Annals of Tourism Research Curated Collection on Artificial Intelligence and Robotics in Tourism. *Annals of Tourism Research*, 81, 102883. DOI: 10.1016/j.annals.2020.102883

Vosman, L., Coenen, T. B. J., Volker, L., & Visscher, K. (2023). Collaboration and innovation beyond project boundaries: Exploring the potential of an ecosystem perspective in the infrastructure sector. *Construction Management and Economics*, 41(6), 457–474. DOI: 10.1080/01446193.2023.2165695

Wang, J., Huang, X., Gong, Z., & Cao, K. (2020). Dynamic assessment of tourism carrying capacity and its impacts on tourism economic growth in urban tourism destinations in China. *Journal of Destination Marketing & Management*, 15, 100383. DOI: 10.1016/j.jdmm.2019.100383

Wei, C., Wang, Q., & Liu, C. (2020). Research on Construction of a Cloud Platform for Tourism Information Intelligent Service Based on Blockchain Technology. *Wireless Communications and Mobile Computing*, 2020, 1–9. DOI: 10.1155/2020/8856271

Wirtz, B. W., Weyerer, J. C., & Geyer, C. (2019). Artificial Intelligence and the Public Sector—Applications and Challenges. *International Journal of Public Administration*, 42(7), 596–615. DOI: 10.1080/01900692.2018.1498103

Youssef, A. B., Dutta, P., Doshi, R., & Sajnani, M. (Eds.). (2025). *AI, blockchain, and metaverse in hospitality and tourism Industry 4.0: Case studies and analysis* (1st ed.). C&H/CRC Press.

Yung, R., & Khoo-Lattimore, C. (2019). New realities: A systematic literature review on virtual reality and augmented reality in tourism research. *Current Issues in Tourism*, 22(17), 2056–2081. DOI: 10.1080/13683500.2017.1417359

Chapter 5
Enhancing Consumer Trust Through Transparent Data Practices and Ethical Data Management in Business

Saher Hassan El-Annan
https://orcid.org/0000-0001-8456-2024
International American University, Los Angeles, USA

Rawan Hassoun
https://orcid.org/0009-0002-4858-4984
International American University, Los Angeles, USA

ABSTRACT

This chapter evaluates the relationship between TDP and PT on consumer trust in digital business models mediated by ethical data management (EDM). The study applies an exploratory research design with two structured surveys addressing consumers and professionals to gather quantitative insights regarding these connections. The research shows that transparent data practices increase consumer trust, and perceiving transparency strengthens this influence. The management of data with integrity significantly strengthens trust. The research outcomes match Trust Transference and Social Contract Theory theories and show that upholding transparency and ethics significantly enhances consumer trust. The relevance of straightforward communication to improve perceived transparency among businesses is emphasized in the analysis. This research presents important suggestions for companies and regulators to improve data management and consumer trust in

DOI: 10.4018/979-8-3693-8357-5.ch005

the digital market.

1. INTRODUCTION

1.1 Research Background

Due to the advancement of technology and the emergence of new markets, the digital economy is experiencing significant growth, and this has resulted in the collection of large amounts of data and its analysis to improve the customer experience. (Sturgeon, 2019). However, this kind of data gathering has also brought many controversies regarding the issue of data privacy and security. Due to numerous data breaches and misuse cases, consumers are more sensitive to how their information is used. In this connection, the 'proper use of data' concept has become one of the most important levers to help create and sustain trust between consumers and businesses. Transparency concerning company data management can go a long way in shaping people's attitudes and actions. (Martin & Murphy, 2016)

Data disclosure and privacy rules differ greatly depending on the industry, influencing how an organisation addresses consumer data. For instance, in healthcare, HIPAA regulations regulate what can be done with patient data, emphasising that providers must inform users about what they do with data and ensure that unauthorised individuals do not access it. This transparency requirement ensures the patient knows how their health information will be used. In this way, there is increased confidence in the healthcare system due to providing a channel through which privacy can be protected through downstream regulation. (Office for Civil Rights, 2015).

Likewise, in the financial industry, the Financial Industry Regulatory Authority (FINRA) has made it mandatory for firms to maintain data accuracy and be transparent while dealing with critical economic data. FINRA's rules require firms to explain to consumers how their information is collected, used and protected, providing extra protection. It reduces the risk of financial fraud and creates a trust between the financial institutions and their customers. (Financial Industry Regulatory Authority, 2019)

The GDPR in the EU takes these requirements across different industries by focusing on data subject rights and control. Consumers are provided with extensive information on how their personal information is processed under GDPR, the right to erasure or to obtain data, which establishes the principle of transparency as a core of data management. Such different regulatory requirements prove the need for flexibility in transparency practices for various industries to fulfil legal obligations and customers' expectations. (European Union, 2016)

However, examples of how businesses manage data transparency and the lessons that can be learned from them show that ethical data management is necessary. For example, Apple uses privacy as one of its values and markets itself by ensuring customers that the company does not exploit their data. Apple's "Privacy. The simple slogan "That is iPhone." effectively, and Strategy communicates its data protection practices and reasserts the role of the iPhones in protecting customer data. (Apple Inc., 2019). On the other hand, the Cambridge Analytica case with Facebook is a case in which the company lost consumer trust through data misuse. Facebook has been used for political manipulation of the samples of user data, showing that the lack of transparency can be very costly to the company. These examples illustrate that transparency, even in data management, can significantly influence consumer attitudes and stress the importance of transparent actions for constructing long-term confidence in digital business models.(Isaak & Hanna, 2018).

1.2 Research Problem

While data transparency and ethical data management are critical for the digital economy, the role and interactions of each factor still need to be better understood. The variation in the regulatory requirements across industries creates various problems for digital firms in achieving transparency and compliance. Each of the companies presented above, from Apple to Facebook, demonstrates the importance of appropriate treatment of consumer data as one of the foundation stones of consumer confidence. This chapter investigates the role of data transparency in fostering consumer trust, addressing the central research question:

Main Research Question: How does data transparency affect consumer trust in digital business models?

Sub-questions:

1. How does perceived transparency moderate the relationship between transparent data practices and consumer trust?
2. In what way does ethical data management mediate the impact of transparent data practices on consumers' trust?
3. Which factors impact the consumer's perception of transparency and ethics regarding data?

1.3 Research Objectives

The objectives of this chapter are threefold: First, to investigate the effect of transparent data practices on consumers' trust in digital businesses. Second, to examine how perceived transparency acts as a moderator in this relationship. Third, to assess the mediating effect of ethical data management practices in either amplifying or reducing the impact of transparency on consumer trust.

1.4 Research Aim and Significance

The purpose of this chapter is to present the findings of the literature review and discuss the key factors that influence the creation of consumer trust through the use of transparent data practices. Thus, by exploring the two dimensions of perceived transparency and ethical data management, the chapter provides valuable recommendations for businesses to adapt their data practices to consumers' expectations and legal requirements. The chapter will also benefit the existing literature since it will help explain the interactions between these variables. Moreover, it will offer specific suggestions to the practitioners and legislators who want to establish a reliable digital ecosystem. The results of the study are expected to contribute to the formulation of policies and standards on ethical conduct in the management of data.

1.5 Chapter Organization

Introduction: This chapter starts by outlining the significance of consumer trust in the digital economy, the emerging issues with data privacy, and the part played by explicit data conduct. They include the formulation of the leading research problem, questions, objectives, and the significance of the study that creates a background to the other sections.

Literature Review: The literature review section focuses on previous research on data transparency and consumer trust and evaluates the findings. This paper discusses different theoretical perspectives that have been advanced to explain perceived transparency and ethical data management. The review also highlights areas that require further research and fills this gap by highlighting these areas.

Theoretical Framework and Hypotheses Development: This section builds on the research propositions established to show how the constructs of transparent data practices, perceived transparency, ethical data management, and consumer trust are related. It also defines the nature of the hypotheses used in the empirical analysis and thus offers a clear research agenda.

Methodology: The present chapter explains the quantitative research method used in the study. It describes the survey, the process of data collection, and the population under study. The chosen approach is meant to provide strict and systematic research of the hypotheses, thus, the reliability and validity of the results.

Data Analysis and Results: This chapter provides the statistical analysis findings on the survey data. It covers the study of the interconnection between the variables, the verification of the stated hypotheses, and the analysis of the results. The findings offer empirical support for the influence of transparent data practices on consumers' trust through perceived transparency and the moderation of ethical data management.

Discussion and Implications: The discussion section aligns the results with the existing literature to establish the study's relevance and contributions. The paper also discusses the findings' application for businesses and policymakers and provides guidelines for applying transparent and ethical data practices.

Conclusion and Future Research Directions: The final chapter briefly reviews the study's main findings and discusses their implications for further developing social entrepreneurship theory and practical application. It examines the study's impact and indicates areas for future research, thus inviting more research on the topic as data management and consumer trust develop.

2. LITERATURE REVIEW

2.1 Literature Landscape

In the new economy based on the usage of digital technologies, issues related to the transparency of data practices have emerged as a central concern for both theoretical and empirical investigations. This has been caused by the fact that as modern organisations gather and process vast volumes of data, transparency and ethical use of data have become more critical. This paper aims to review the literature on the correlation between data transparency and consumers' trust concerning the available theoretical and empirical literature.

2.1.1 Transparency of Data and Consumer Confidence

Data collection is crucial in strengthening consumers' trust and countering power relations in the sale of consumer products. This depends on the ability to explain to individuals exactly how data is obtained, managed and processed to avoid privacy infringement and, hence, gain trust in electronic commerce. People have focused on the fact that improved data transparency practices can help mitigate perceived power imbalance, which is relevant in areas like IoT where data misuse, for example, in health, can lead to critical privacy violations (Kim & Lee, 2018).

It has also been noted as a mechanism that can also be useful in promoting transparency and consumer confidence. In developing economies, prótégé traceability systems with the indicated sectors, such as the food supply chain, demonstrated improved transparency and enhanced consumer trust through real-time information tracking through blockchain technology (Yap et al., 2023).

Also, fields like finance and banking need clarity regarding the rules governing them and their protection measures to encourage the use of online facilities in financial activities. Gupta and Shukla (2023) further show that transparent data protection policies in digital financial services are essential to trust relationships.

Healthcare, too, is a case where transparent data practices are a pressing concern. Privacy and transparency are critical in that they have a massive impact on consumer trust, with a focus on information sharing concerning health information in particular. Funnel communication suggests that broad communication and efficient data utilisation unveil solutions to these concerns and foster trust in data-oriented healthcare institutions (Hutchings et al., 2020).

Scholars in the modern makeup industry show that perceived transparency—the extent consumers believe they are aware of sponsored content—regulates their trust in endorsements. Reality and clarity of information in advertisements lead to better brand-consumer relations (Satur et al., 2024).

Hence, it reveals the data handling concerns of users' confidence in IoT, health care, and finance sectors, but equally relevant in food delivery and other online business platforms.

The transparency of data practices is critical in restoring the balance of power between consumers and businesses. When companies openly communicate how they handle data, consumers are more likely to feel secure, fostering a positive relationship. Several studies highlight the importance of transparency in this aspect. For example, Kim and Lee (2018) explored how transparency in privacy policies within the Internet of Things (IoT) increases consumer confidence. Their findings indicate that consumers who understand how their data is collected and used are more willing to trust businesses. Moreover, transparency mitigates perceived power asymmetry, a critical issue in the digital economy.

Expand on how other sectors, such as e-commerce, finance, or healthcare, are applying transparent data practices to gain consumer trust. You could explore industries or sectors where data transparency has significantly impacted consumer loyalty or businesses that have faced challenges due to a lack of transparency (e.g., the Facebook-Cambridge Analytica scandal).

Data transparency is essential to any field since regulation and consumer expectations differ significantly across industries. Explants of the healthcare, financial, and technology industries describe each industry's outstanding transparency issues and approaches.

In healthcare, privacy and use of data are regulated by laws such as HIPAA; the rule ensures that the recipient of healthcare services is informed on how data collected from them will be used or shared with third parties, and there is a limitation placed on the accesses made by users of such data. Evidence shows that the clarity of data usage improves patient trust because patients will be comfortable knowing how their health information is handled (Wager et al., 2017). Gold and McLaughlin (2016) point out that organisations that strictly follow HIPAA rules have higher consumer confidence. Patients are ready to participate in digital health services if they trust the organisation with their data.

In the financial sector, FINRA regulations demand clarity in processing financial data, especially in protecting this information from fraudulent acts. The rules set by FINRA require firms to inform their customers about how their financial information is used and protected, which has been proven to enhance its usage as well as customer loyalty (Wang & Lee, 2017). Also, transparency decreases perceptions of power relations between financial institutions and consumers, leading to increased and more effective digital interactions in the financial sector (Chen & Lee, 2021).

Transparency plays another role across industries through the General Data Protection Regulation (GDPR) regulation. Studies show that EU consumers are more comfortable dealing with firms that observe the GDPR because these regulations provide users with rights to access, delete, and manage their data (Voigt and Von dem Bussche, 2017). Through the emphasis on transparency, GDPR has made firms improve their data practices, improving the consumer's right to data protection and trust in digital business models (Voigt & Von dem Bussche, 2017).

New technology tools that help increase transparency in data management include explainable artificial intelligence and blockchain. These tools are widely used to solve transparency and privacy issues in many fields.

To address the problem of lack of transparency in decision-making, Explainable AI (XAI) provides a solution. In contrast to prior AI methods that tend to be opaque and difficult to interpret, explainable AI models enable firms to explain why a specific decision was made (Doshi-Velez & Kim, 2017). It has found its application in various sectors, such as finance and healthcare because decision-making based on AI algorithms must be transparent. According to the current literature, consumers' trust in AI recommendations increases when firms explain how decisions were made, thereby supporting AI use (Binns et al., 2018).

Similarly, the article demonstrates that blockchain provides a solution for making records of interactions seamless and transparent. The use of blockchain in sectors such as finance, supply chain and healthcare systems provides a decentralised ledger that provides a clear and unalterable data record, increasing trust for data management (Zheng et al., 2018). For example, blockchain applications in food supply chain traceability enable consumers to trace products' origin and guarantee their authenticity, thus enhancing trust since data is encrypted at each touchpoint in the system (Saberi et al., 2019). Further, the study also shows that by transparency, blockchain's advantages could be precious in heavily regulated industries since they offer companies ways to prove compliance and ethical use of data (Casino, Dasaklis, & Patsakis, 2019).

2.1.2 Perceived Transparency as a Determinant of the Role

These categories are perceived transparency, which involves how consumers rate a particular firm based on the truthfulness of their data processing. Consumers are more likely to trust businesses that feel transparent in their interactions concerning data use and practices, even though actual transparency might be low. Thus, according to Lee and Li (2021), consumer trust depends on the exact level of data business transparency and the consumer's perceived levels of such transparency. This perceived transparency moderates trust where consumers may not fully understand a company's data processes.

Such perceived transparency needs to be understood in terms of sound real-life examples. For instance, a study focusing on the DTC genetic testing firms noted that the more the consumer understood that the company was being honest about the tests, the more they tended to have a positive attitude towards the genetic tests (Abitbol et al., 2022). In the same way, perceived transparency predictably influences consumer trust and purchase intention for an online retailing company more than perceived company reputation (Feng, 2020).

In a health context, Esmaeilzadeh (2020) observed that perceived privacy policy transparency improves cognitive and affective trust in Health Information Exchanges. The findings showed consumers would opt-in and reveal personal health information if only privacy policies were clear.

This is an essential factor in digital marketing, as its lack entails significant issues with consumer trust in the content produced by influencers. Sincere and clique-inspired sponsored-content marketing increases consumers' confidence in makeup products (Satur et al., 2024). In the same vein, Teodorescu et al. (2023) show that perceived transparency strongly affects consumer trust in artificial intelligence algorithms used in e-commerce and proposed that clarity regarding the use of AI may enhance trust.

Perceived transparency also fits into the agenda of financial policies. Cabello et al. (2020) established that consumers are more likely to trust tax decisions when they are made clear through proper communication and comprehension, implying broader applicability to consumers' trust in institutional decision-making.

Total, perceived transparency is the critical factor businesses can utilise to establish and develop consumer trust, especially in industries where data security is essential. Organisational communication management in everyday crises, such as data breaches, can assist organisations in regaining perceived transparency.

Examples of what actual world data practices (or the lack thereof) can do to affect consumer trust are provided. For instance, Apple has a core value company as a value that has something to do with privacy, and they also keep telling people that we have things to do with privacy, like privacy. That is iPhone." It has played a role in Apple's brand image as a privacy company and helps generate consumer trust by clearly telling them how Apple protects its data. According to Feng (2020), companies with good privacy practices and communication with consumers tend to have higher brand loyalty and trust.

For instance, the Cambridge Analytica scandal with Facebook is another example which shows the communicative burden of insufficient data transparency. In Facebook's case, the data of millions of users was improperly accessed and then used for political profiling. Everyone openly castigated Facebook with public hue and cry, and the regulator also sniffed around. After the incident, the scandal showed the dire consequences of the obtrusiveness of data practices and the erosion of trust that Facebook users experienced after the occurrence (Isaak & Hanna, 2018). This is a case in point of why corporate and consumer trust relies on transparent data practices.

2.1.3 Ethical Data Management

Practical, ethical data management is even more important for businesses interested in creating a positive consumer perception of their organisation by adhering to consumers' right to privacy and data protection. Practical implementation of ethical standards reduces risk factors associated with confidentiality and increases public confidence in business entities. Asgarinia et al. (2023) note that emerging technologies that decentralise data management have resulted in fresh ethical issues requiring the interdisciplinary creation of clear and admissible data protection policies. Holding machine-readable policies makes organisations more transparent in handling data, improving consumers' trust.

Examples include GDPR and CCPA, which set ethical data management ideals from which others can learn or emulate. These regulations bestow enhanced control in the hands of consumers and add much responsibility to different organisations. For instance, Sharma and Sharma (2024) stated that GDPR and CCPA help build trust mainly because they compel businesses to be more transparent regarding their use of data. Companies that fail to operate within these frameworks may suffer a loss of corporate reputation and customer trust.

This book review also points out that ethical data management goes beyond compliance. Ethical transparency is essential in digital marketing to correctly uphold appropriate standards. Daoud et al. (2023) noted that consumers' sensitivity to moral considerations in targeted advertising makes it crucial to pursue high transparency. Ethical standards include issues concerning consumers, especially data handling, and Porter's report shows that consumer trust is boosted by a brand's commitment to such standards during crises. For instance, organisations that shine on social responsibility towards data management are more likely to bounce back from disasters and have long-term sustainability (Kang et al., 2023).

Although properly implementing ethics in managing business data is a noble cause, the outcome could be better when these standards are followed minutely. An example of what can happen when an organisation is hacked can be described with the help of the Equifax data breach that occurred in 2017. It focused on what happens when data management is wrong and where confidence goes when such ethical mistakes occur. Similarly, Shaikh et al. (2024) also focused on the moral issue in AI-aided Customer Relationship Management (CRM). They postulated that the prudent use of AI in consumer-related processes is a critical reason for consumer trust.

Proper data management has been described as an ethical, never-ending process, as businesses must be keen and go the extra mile in handling data. It may also cause the organisation and its clients to suffer, damaging the image and consumer trust. On the other hand, organisations that have made ethical transparency their core values are most likely to build customer loyalty and confidence in the business in the long run.

2.1.4 Impact on Consumer Trust

Research studies conducted for various industries reveal that consumer confidence is highly influenced when there are no blurs in data policies and administrative action. To sum up, we argue that disclosure transparency about applied encryption measures and data processing policies is essential for building consumer perceptions of the protected data in the context of the fintech industry. Singh (2024) observed that improved data security by pointing out the fundamental conceptual advancements of fintech services increases consumer confidence because of the overall decrease in privacy concerns. Transparent data management increases consumers' attention and dedication, whereas reckless or non-transparent actions, such as data leakage, reduce consumers' trust.

The kind of transparency that can win customers' trust in the e-commerce sector is another thing that can support this argument. Thus, according to Tr ng (2024), the strict rules of data protection contribute to consumer trust in Internet stores by protecting data and trust, promoting purchases through the World Wide Web. Transparency, primarily through regulations like GDPR and the CCPA, has dramatically impacted digital marketing since it makes companies conform to ethical data usage. Not only does this increase customer confidence, but it also results in the creation of brand ambassadors due to compliance (Obudho, 2024).

AI marketing requires the transparent disclosure of the types of data being gathered and the method followed to arrive at generic conclusions about customers. According to Sharma et al. (2023), it could increase customer trust in details concerning the use of AI algorithms and the method of processing personal data on marketing applications because AI is getting popular in marketing. In the same vein, privacy concerns and personalisation in the recommendation ads diminish drastically when the ad is transparent, and thus increases the purchase intention and intentions to start a relationship: it underscores the need to be ethical when collecting and using data from customers (Böhler, 2024).

Conversely, they are much more likely to incur severe trust losses due to a failure to manage their data transparently. Some companies, such as Facebook, were affected by the scandal with CAMBRIDGE ANALYTICA and lost part of their consumer trust since the company did not show consumers how it was storing and using their information. Some companies, such as Apple, clearly follow privacy as their key policies and utilise clear data policies as their selling point to boost consumer confidence.

These instances show how useful it is to be transparent when seeking the public's trust when conducting business in fintech, digital marketing, and e-commerce. Privacy is an essential and sufficient method of gaining consumers' trust and positively affects further consumer interaction, devotion, and satisfaction; therefore, it should be considered an integral component of long-term customer-oriented strategies.

2.1.5 Challenges and Future Directions

Although it is taken for granted that transparency is a critical factor that will enhance consumer trust, a complete application of this aspect is still a big challenge. Thuermer et al. (2024) have rightfully noted that data collected through the participation of the public are frequently not well understood because documentation of their process is technical and written by experts for experts. This schism between technical documentation and public comprehension is a significant obstacle to creating transparency in data stewardship. In addition, technological advances such as blockchain provide new opportunities to increase transparency, which, however, come with new forms of ethical and practical difficulties.

Blockchain, despite increasing the transparency of records by cutting their accessibility and modifying possibilities, has some issues. As Loukil et al. (2020) observed, platforms for sharing IoT data, including PATRIoT based on blockchain technology, experience challenges in developing user-centred solutions for privacy and compliance. Other blockchain-based systems in healthcare, such as HealthLock, employ smart contracts and homomorphic encryption for good visibility. However, these systems have challenges in managing who has access to the data and the audit trails (Ali et al., 2023). Moreover, transparency underlying the blockchain's nature sometimes violates privacy requirements, raising questions about what information should be available in shared ledgers.

For instance, real estate and vendor sectors are evident where blockchain promises transparency in addressing cases of data alteration and safe handling of property financing, as posted by Junaid, Ke et al. in 2024. On the other hand, employing appropriately transparent systems frequently involves surmounting massive logistical issues that include compliance across different legal systems and the high costs of implementing blockchain technology (Avancha et al., 2024).

Transparency is again an issue, especially with Artificial intelligence (AI). While AI is a technology that can enhance decision-making to make marketing decisions more transparent, the former needs to be simplified so that consumers can comprehend how their data is being processed. Self-explanatory methods used within and for AI systems are essential to increasing the transparency of decisions made by an AI system. However, the ethical issues regarding such systems should be managed to ensure the continued reliance of consumers.

For this reason, future research must establish a framework for the best integration of blockchain with AI to improve transparency while considering the privacy rights and ethical issues involved. More integration of insights derived from the underlying blockchain technology and AI features regarding the use of consumer data is needed. Therefore, one of the future developments should be the generation of a synergy that would provide consumers with more transparency and understanding of their data usage. There is also a requirement for more precise documentation for consumers to understand and usability tools to assist the unsophisticated user in applying data structures. These will be imperative in the future to shed light on the gap between the technical framework of transparency and the ability of consumers to understand transparent data practices.

2.1.6 Literature Conclusion

Several studies in data transparency and consumer trust support how transparency leads to improved trust in business to consumers and business to the business environment. It ranges from implementing transparency in the IoT and healthcare sectors to e-commerce and fintech – that is, any industry requires an understanding of power distortion and privacy. Research by Kim and Lee (2018) reveals that consumers trust businesses more when they know how their data is collected and processed, especially in those fields that could potentially harm their privacy.

According to Lee and Li, perceived transparency engulfs an essential social component, particularly trustworthiness. Sometimes, the actual transparency we can achieve may be slight; however, it can serve as a significant foundation for trust relative to consumers' perceptions. This is especially the case where shoppers remain highly sensitive to an organisation's practices in handling consumer data, especially in digital marketing and healthcare sectors. Consumer behaviour research shows that perceived transparency is essential for consumers to make purchase decisions and to agree to share their data (Esmaeilzadeh, 2020).

Another consideration in ethical consumer data management is another indispensably significant benefit of the approach. Stringent legal requirements of rights to consumer privacy, like GDPR and CCPA, compel business organisations to be more open, thus improving consumer trust (Sharma & Sharma, 2024). Ethical transparency, specifically in organisational crises, allows organisations to regain the public's trust and prove that the organisation possesses sound data management principles (Kang et al., 2023). On the other hand, when data is being used unethically, as the Equifax data breach demonstrates, the level of trust consumers have for a company drastically reduces.

The reality is that the influence of transparent data practices on consumer trust is observed in contexts of fintech, e-commerce and digital marketing. Singh (2024) proved that defined data management protects privacy in fintech services, which leads to higher trust. The research in the e-commerce context indicates that adherence to data protection regulations creates more consumer engagement and trust (Tr ng, 2024). Another aspect is also essential in AI-based marketing, where the degree of information transparency positively impacts consumers' trust and purchasing disposition (Sharma et al., 2023).

As evidenced above, there are many benefits to the full implementation of transparency. Nevertheless, achieving the goal is not easy. Thuermer et al. (2024) point out that there might be a challenging gap between data transparency and understanding what is going on by crowds, as technical documentation literature predetermines non-expert audience detection and exclusion. They argued that emerging technologies, including blockchain and AI, have opened new avenues of transparency, though creating ethical and pragmatic issues for development, particularly regarding privacy and technical complexity (Ali et al., 2023; Loukil et al., 2020).

Future research should target the area between technical disclosure and consumer understanding. Future studies must investigate how the blockchain capability can be applied together with AI to increase transparency while protecting the consumer's right to privacy and regulating the proper application of data. Also, clear documentation and user-friendly instruments are required to initiate non-professionals in meaningful and diversified data management systems to create transparency, transforming not only into a governmental requirement but also a comprehensible concept for consumers. Such steps will help build long-term trust for the business models to gain acceptance in the digital economy.

2.2 Study Variables

2.2.1 Independent Variable

Since TDPI is the independent variable, it is the event that stimulates responses from other variables; therefore, we want to investigate in more detail. The various data practices are:

This entails a firm's steps to inform consumers regarding how it collects, stores, processes, and shares data. It encompasses whether companies make privacy policies readily available, share information about data usage in terms that regular people can comprehend and how openly the latter company notifies its customers about changes in the rules that pertain to consumer data.

2.2.2 Moderator Variable

The moderating independent variable is perceived transparency, defined here as the level of clarity that insiders and outsiders have regarding the organisation's internal workings.

This was fabricated in construct since perceived transparency approximates the consumers' views toward how much transparency they think a company takes when providing data. This perception stems from past experiences with the consumer and business, how well the company communicates with those consumers, and the consumer's knowledge of how businesses use data. It measures not only the actual level of transparency of a particular company but also how this level is reconstructed through the prism of customer experience and communication management.

2.2.3 Mediator Variable

Ethical data management is the mediating variable through which the effects of the inverted U-shape relationship between the amount of task autonomy and job performance were explained.

Ethical data management is an action taken to ensure compliance with ethical measures and legal concerns regarding consumer data. This includes principles associated with data security, data privacy and protection policies to be followed, and, generally, recognising consumer rights and privacy on data. It concerns itself with those who protect consumer data from misuse and those who assure that data handling processes are fair and accurate.

2.2.4 Dependent Variable

Consumer trust is the reliance placed by the consumer on the organisation to manage the consumer's private information. It covers consumers' confidence in a firm to observe the necessary ethical standards in collecting and managing consumers' data comprehensively. This essence of trust is a fundamental precondition for achieving a long-term communication relationship. It determines the readiness of consumers to disclose their data and participate in other digital services of the company.

2.3 Theoretical Framework

2.3.1 Trust Transference Theory

Trust Transference Theory, an extension of the psychology of influence and perception, describes how trust can be transferred from one entity to another through cues or behaviours. Although it is based on and associated with interpersonal relationships, it is relevant in organisational behaviour, especially in how firms address consumer information. Trust transference is particularly important in industries in which privacy is a significant issue since transparency plays an important and unique function, being a powerful cue which results in increased trust.

Trust Transference Theory holds that we can transfer trust to one entity from another and anything indicating that we trust the other (McKnight et al., 2002). In digital business models, trust transference is relevant, as consumers tend to trust one part of an organisation's practice, such as data transparency, to other, less transparent parts. For example, companies that proactively share how they collect and use customer data may see increased trust even from those who do not have the luxury of open transparency (e.g., company's proprietary algorithms) (Stewart, 2003). Across industries like finance and health, where data is susceptible, businesses are learning that transparency about how you treat data can help you build a reputation as a trustworthy data custodian (Feng, 2020). Trust transference is based on the organisation's capacity to communicate and maintain transparency as a core part of its business model, which results in goodwill that will be transferred to other company practices (Chen & Lee, 2021).

For instance, organisations that disclose how they manage data are more credible in a digital economy. The consumer views this openness as a voluntary adoption of certain consumer rights and protection of their privacy, which the company transfers to the perceptions of reliability and appropriate ethical business practices.

The following hypothesis emerges from the Trust Transference Theory, emphasising how transparent data practices influence consumer trust:

H1: The current data transparency practice enhances consumer trust, as the consumer will extend his perception of the company to transparency in its operations and intents.

By providing information about data management, companies engage the consumer's psychological identification process and peg them closer to the business, hence establishing goodwill. This process is crucial where data misuse issues are becoming new factors affecting customer choice. (Cobb, 2023)

2.3.2 Information Asymmetry Theory

The information asymmetry theory stipulates that individuals have varying information regarding an economic transaction.

Information Asymmetry Theory focuses on the information imbalance between related organisations and indicates that minimising this imbalance will likely benefit relationalism. When applied to digital business models, the present theory is crucial in promoting trustful data actions since there is usually mistrust if data practices are hidden or obscure.

When applied in e-commerce, openness fosters a situation where consumers' perception matches the corporate reality. This eliminates mistrust and promotes the use of online markets.

Information Asymmetry Theory is concerned with information asymmetry between the parties involved in a transaction and how reducing the gap between the two parties can improve relational trust (Akerlof, 1970). This theory is critical in the case of digital business models, where data practices are often opaque to the consumers. Companies can strengthen consumer trust by proactively informing data collection, processing and storage practices through information asymmetry reduction (Wang & Lee, 2017). For instance, GDPR's data handling disclosures requirements for explicit disclosures help to close the knowledge gap between businesses and consumers by creating trust in consumers' knowledge of their data rights (Voigt & Von dem Bussche, 2017). In e-commerce and finance, trust depends on the consumers feeling fully informed about data usage, and information asymmetry reduction is critical.

The following hypothesis is derived from Information Asymmetry Theory:

H2: Transparent data practices enhance perceived transparency as they help to equalise the information asymmetry between the business and its consumers, leading to improved consumer perceptions of transparency.

In the high technology sectors that rely heavily on data as a factor of production, communicating accurate and easily understandable information regarding collection minimises apprehensiveness, hence completing the circle in maintaining competitive advantage. (Öberg, 2020)

2.3.3 Stakeholder Theory

According to the Stakeholder Theory, all consumers, as the corporation's stakeholders, should also be protected by the corporation's decisions. It posits that stakeholders should be treated ethically not only as an ethic but also as an economic necessity.

A proper and correct approach to data management reduces malicious intent and maintains the dignity of the consumers, which in turn adds to the corporate image and reputation.

According to stakeholder theory, organisations should place ethical responsibilities on their stakeholders as a social obligation and an economic necessity (Freeman, 1984). Stakeholder Theory in data transparency provides data consumer ethics for building trust and loyalty. For example, firms that place importance on data transparency and follow standards such as GDPR or HIPAA are sure to work to value their ethical data management, which positively affects their influenced stakeholders' perceptions (Schwartz, 2017). Companies that meet stakeholders' ethical expectations are more resilient and enjoy consumer loyalty because consumers regard these firms as congruent with their privacy expectations and data rights (Jones et al., 2018).

Derived hypothesis from Stakeholder Theory:

H3: Transparent data practices positively influence the adoption of ethical data management practices as organisations strive to meet the ethical expectations of their stakeholders, including consumers.

Thus, firms that can incorporate ethical issues into their organisational data management practices will likely experience increased levels of consumer trust and loyalty, especially in industries that are deeply implicated in processing susceptible information. Responsible data management involves avoiding simply meeting legal requirements while protecting the company's reputation and customers. (Schakel & Wolbers, 2021)

2.3.4 Expectancy Violations Theory

comprises self-generated, other-generated, categorically based, and etiologically based expectancy.

Expectancy Violations Theory deals with what happens when one is or a consumer's expectations are fulfilled or unfulfilled. Within the companies' transparency framework, transparency beyond consumers' expectations can significantly boost consumer confidence, while not meeting those expectations will likely weaken it significantly.

The theory helps explain the moderation effect that perceived transparency has on actual transparency activities and trust.

The hypothesis from Expectancy Violations Theory:

H4: Perceived transparency moderates the relationship between transparent data practices and consumer trust, enhancing the positive impact when transparency expectations are met or exceeded.

Whether a corporation achieves consumer transparency and operates above or congruent to those expectations provides improved consumer confidence and brand loyalty, critical factors for sustaining long-term consumer relations for a firm. (Muzafary et al., 2023)

2.3.5 Social Contract Theory

The Social Contract Theory in business ethics states that when a business wants to be accepted in society and expects consumers to patronise it, it will act reasonably. This theory posits that firms ought to discharge responsibilities ethically with particular reference to the social contract between the firm and society, particularly to the consumers. It can be seen that where firms are willing to observe their conduct within this social contract, they provide the best outcome for the consumer.

E-commerce companies that pay attention to the tenants of data stewardship assure consumers of their well-being, especially while engaging in electronically mediated communication. Organisations' ethical actions fortify this “contract” in that consumers’ information is processed appropriately, enhancing trust.

The following hypothesis emerges from Social Contract Theory:

H5: Ethical data management mediates the impact of transparent data practices on consumer trust, reinforcing that ethical adherence is crucial for the full positive impact of transparency to be realised on consumer trustCritical Analysis:

This means that ethical data management can only be achieved by working hand in hand with transparent processes so that the consumers can have maximum confidence in a specific business. Business ethics are a foundation of the agreement that customers and companies have with each other; they underscore how helpful transparency is to the issue of trust. This way, transparency is the open door to the buyer and the ethics of handling consumers’ information. (Zahoor et al., 2022)

2.3.6: Emerging Transparency Tools: Explainable AI and Blockchain

The Explainable AI (XAI) provides a basis for transparent, interpretable machine learning models, which increase trust by providing consumers with insights into algorithmic decision-making. XAI offers explanations, unlike traditional 'black box' AI models, which explain why an algorithm arrived at a given outcome (Doshi-Velez & Kim, 2017). This is particularly important in sectors where data-driven decisions impact sensitive consumer outcomes (Binns et al., 2018). XAI ensures that consumers can understand AI-driven decisions, bridging complex data processes to consumer trust and aligning with the growing expectations for transparency mandated by regulations like GDPR (Voigt & Von dem Bussche, 2017).

By introducing a decentralised and immutable ledger, blockchain technology gives transparency to another robust framework. Transactions or data handling on the blockchain can be transparently recorded, tamper-proof, and independently verifiable (Zheng et al., 2018). Especially in supply chains, consumers can verify product authenticity and origin, validating trust using transparency (Saberi et al., 2019). Blockchain's transparency in finance helps regulatory compliance as firms can prove consistent data protection practices that meet consumer expectations of ethical data management (Casino, Dasaklis, & Patsakis, 2019).

These emerging tools are the next wave in data transparency and ethical data management. They address the rat race to create more transparency in our lives through the advancement of digital interaction. Both explainable AI and blockchain increase transparency and create a positive feedback loop to reinforce companies' ethics in handling data and building trust across digital ecosystems.

2.4 Conceptual Framework

2.4.1 Conceptual Model Expansion

The conceptual framework of the current book chapter provides the necessary contextual depth to understand the relationship dynamics between T DP, PT, EDM and CT in the setting of digital business models. The proposed model creates a robust framework for analysing digital trust based on theoretical frameworks from data privacy, consumer behaviour and ethical business structures.

2.4.2 Comprehensive Source Foundation

Transparent Data Practices (TDP) and Direct Impact on Consumer Trust: The basis of adding Transparent Data Practices into the framework has its roots in the literature that underlines the importance of transparency in consumer trust development. As endorsed in the study by Martin & Murphy (2016), who assert that data privacy is crucial in marketing, our model places TDP squarely in charge of Consumer Trust. In support of this, Gupta and Shukla (2023) provide a quantitative analysis of the fact that policies in digital banking improve consumers' trust if they are transparent. Such studies provide sound premises for the further hypothesis that clear, accessible, and understandable data practices are crucial for creating trust in digital economies.

Perceived Transparency as a Critical Moderator: Proposing Perceived Transparency as a moderator is based on Lee and Li (2021), where communication transparency has been addressed as a factor influencing public responses to health risks. This highlights the element of this notion within the digital context P3: The strength of the relationship between the proposed construct, Transparent Data Practices on Consumer Trust, is moderated by Consumers' Perceptions of the Company's Transparency efforts. The idea corresponds with Esmaeilzadeh (2020), who pointed out that perceptions of transparency regarding the extent of privacy policies may significantly impact patients' trust in the exchange of health information.

Ethical Data Management as a Crucial Mediator: Including Ethical Data Management as a mediator is not incidental. It is based on Asgarinia et al.'s (2023) guidelines, which frame Ethical Data Management as a mediator that addresses new ethical questions raised by decentralised data technologies. This addition to the model acknowledges that while an organisation may have a range of highly transparent practices, the trust of third parties in such practices is significantly influenced by their perceived ethicality. Ethical Data Management ensures that data practices adhere to the foundational rules of working with personal data, as stated in GDPR and CCPA, and the principles of fairness and integrity as expected by society, as seen by Sharma and Sharma (2024).

2.4.3 Enhancing the Impact of the Model

The revealed model not only expands the understanding of how the Chain of Transparent Data Practices affects the level of Consumer Trust but also describes the nature of this effect given the mediating role of Ethical Data Management and the moderating role of Perceived Transparency. This comprehensive setup helps in:

Elucidating the Complex Interplay: The model illustrates, layer by layer, how every element is meshed into the digital trust paradigm and thus provides a clear, systematic view of how transparency and ethics are translated into actual consumer trust.

Broadening the Scope: Compared with previous models, this framework enlarges the scope of implementation and, therefore, enhances the model's external validity in various digital commerce-related platforms.

Deepening the Dialogue on Digital Ethics: By embedding ethical data management, the model encourages further examination of critical issues regarding how organisations can enhance their data handling mechanisms based on ethical indicators to develop a sustainable trusting relationship with consumers.

2.4.4 Enriched Variable Definition

Transparent Data Practices (TDP): Communicational strategies that pertain to ideas such as transparency in how consumer data are gathered, analysed, and safeguarded.

- Perceived Transparency (PT): The extent and perception of consumer information being visible and transparent by evaluating it of a particular company.
- Ethical Data Management (EDM): The ethical standard is set with the need to follow the code of regulations, notably to uphold the individual consumer's right to privacy or their information.
- Consumer Trust (CT): The confidence placed. It offers consumers digital platforms for responsibly managing their personal information and exercising it on their behalf.

This developed theoretical lens acts as a road map for mass-technology enterprises that seek to increase consumer trust by addressing issues of transparency and ethicality in their operations while offering clear direction to research and practice in this rapidly evolving digital landscape.

3. METHODOLOGY

3.1 Research Design

This chapter uses an exploratory research approach to analyse the relationships among transparent data practices, perceived transparency, ethical data use, and consumer confidence within cyber business environments. By employing an exploratory quantitative design, the study investigates how these factors influence consumer trust, particularly in the context of regulatory frameworks like GDPR and CCPA. This approach is valuable for revealing patterns in areas with limited research, as it addresses how digital businesses can effectively respond to consumer information needs. The research highlights the impact of transparent practices on consumer trust. It sheds light on the regulatory, ethical, and operational challenges companies face across various sectors, from healthcare to finance. By understanding these dynamics, digital enterprises can build and sustain consumer trust while navigating complex, sector-specific regulations

3.2 Data Collection

Data will be collected through two structured questionnaires targeting distinct respondent groups: consumers and industry professionals. All the groups add distinctive perspectives essential in capturing the complex processes underlying data transparency and trust.

Data collection involves two structured questionnaires tailored to capture unique perspectives on transparency: One aimed at consumers and the other at industry professionals (data managers, compliance officers, etc., and IT executives). The consumer survey measures perceptions of transparency, trust, and experience with data management practices on digital platforms. For example, regulatory impacts such as GDPR data rights and disclosure are reflected in questions.

The industry professional survey is centred around implementing transparent and ethical data practices under compliance pressures from GDPR and CCPA. For instance, industry respondents are asked to rate their experience with transparency tools such as explainable AI and blockchain in data management. The combination of this dual survey approach enables the study to examine consumer attitudes towards transparency and the industry's views on regulatory challenges to gain a complete picture of the data transparency dynamics. Both surveys are developed online to ensure maximum response rates and broad demographic coverage and contain data privacy disclaimers to allay concerns about the confidentiality of the responses and checks against privacy regulations.

- Consumer Survey: The first survey will focus on consumers' understanding of data openness and their confidence in digital companies. It will include scaled questions to assess views on transparency, trust, and experience with data management practices. This survey is intended to gather quantitative measures of consumer attitudes/beliefs, which will be directly related to their trust in digitally related platforms.
- Industry Professional Survey: The second questionnaire will reach out to industry practitioners, particularly data managers, IT executives, and compliance officers, among others. The surveys will describe present tendencies concerning data openness and concerns, specialists' estimations concerning the influences of such practices on consumers' confidence, and their notions about further enhancements. They will assist in labelling the agenda for the ethical and appropriate manner of handling the issue this survey seeks to address.

These two questionnaires will be marked to be as similar as possible to reconcile the results showing the attitudes of consumers and professionals. The questionnaires will be administered online to use technology to cover a broader population and easily capture responses.

3.3 Data Analysis

The data collected will undergo rigorous statistical analysis to test the proposed hypotheses:

- Descriptive Statistics: The first step is hypothesis generation, where we shall present preliminary information about descriptive statistics involving the survey data and general information about the respondents, amongst other demographic factors.
- Regression Analysis: Multiple regression analyses will be conducted to establish the relationship between the various variables of pre-study interests, with a specific focus on the various transparent data practices and consumer trust levels analysed.
- Moderation and Mediation Analyses: These analyses will enable the assessment of the extent to which perceived transparency moderates and ethical data management mediates between transparent data practices and consumer trust. They must examine the primary outcomes of interest and the conditional processes that mediate these effects.

The result data analysis follows a rigorous timeline, starting with descriptive summary statistics on respondent demographics and attitudes toward transparency. Next, multiple regression analyses investigate the relationship between transparent data practices, perceived transparency, ethical data management, and consumer trust.

In order to examine the mediating role of ethical data management (EDM) and the moderating effect of perceived transparency (PT), Process Macro mediation and moderation models are used. This analysis examines whether ethical data practices moderate the relationship between transparent data practices and consumer trust and whether perceived transparency reinforces this relationship. The analysis examines these variables and shows how varying transparency practices and perceptions can impact consumer trust across sectors, supporting Trust Transference Theory and Information Asymmetry Theory.

The mediation and moderation results are particularly relevant to high-stakes sectors such as finance and healthcare, where ethical data handling and transparent communication are required to meet regulatory standards and consumer expectations. Through this analytic work, we provide a simplified way to outline the conditions for strategic enhancements to consumer trust through the targeted transparency of digital businesses and the ethical management of consumer data.

3.4 Ethical Considerations

In order to conduct the study ethically, approval of an institutional review board will be sought to observe the study's set ethical standards. Respondents will be advised on the intended and anticipated use of the study findings, the right not to be named or identified, and the fact that participation is voluntary. Information gathered will be kept confidential in compliance with the nation's Data Collection and Processing Act.

The study will use an exploratory research design, and the two questionnaires will be used to collect quantitative data. The first survey will be conducted on the consumers to determine their awareness of data transparency and trust in digital businesses. It will use instruments like perceived transparency, trust, and data management practice questionnaires. The second survey will be conducted among industry professionals. It will gather information about how they manage data and their opinions on the role of transparency and ethics in gaining the consumer's trust. The surveys will be constructed to be similar, so there will be a dual perspective on the problem. Hypotheses will be tested using statistical analysis, such as regression and moderation-mediation analyses.

The study is rigorously ethical in meeting the highest norms of GDPR and CCPA standards regarding the confidentiality and surveillance of participant data. Participants are told they can withdraw from the survey anytime, and their response is anonymised to protect privacy. Social science research always gets IRB approval to comply with ethical guidelines. The study respects participant rights and reflects data transparency practices that the research investigates by incorporating GDPR and CCPA principles. This strengthens the study's commitment to transparency by making participants aware of what will be done with their data and how it will be secured, and the research process benefits from the added trust that this engenders.

4. RESULTS, DATA ANALYSIS, AND HYPOTHESES TESTING

This chapter presents the results obtained from the analysis of the data collected from two separate surveys: One is for the consumers, and the other is for the industry experts. These surveys assessed TDP, PT, EDM, and CT correlations. The analysis includes hypothesis testing whereby these variables are examined in relationship to each other using regression analysis, mediator and moderator analysis. This chapter will be divided into several sections: The analyses included descriptive statistics, hypothesis testing via numerous models, and an explanation of the outcomes.

4.1 Descriptive Statistics

4.1.1 Demographics of Respondents

The survey was conducted among 500 people. The sample comprised two groups: 300 consumers and 200 industry professionals participated in the study.

The demographic profile of the consumer sample is as follows:

- Gender: 56% female, 44% male
- Age: 18-24 (12%), 25-34 (40%), 35-44 (28%), 45 and above (20%).
- Education Level: Undergraduate students 35%, Graduate students 50%, Postgraduate students 15%
- Occupation: E-commerce users (30%), banking and finance users (35%), health service users (20%), and others (15%)

For the industry professionals, the demographic breakdown is:

- Gender: 52% male, 48% female
- Job Roles: The study participants included data managers (40%), compliance officers (25%) and IT executives (35%).
- Years of Experience: The participants have worked in the field for less than five years, 20%; 5-10 years, 50%; and more than ten years, 30%.

4.1.2 Summary of Key Variables

The descriptions of the Variables TDP, PT, EDM, and CT are presented in Table 4.1 below.

Table 1. Descriptive statistics for key variables

Variable	Mean	Standard Deviation	Minimum	Maximum
Transparent Data Practices (TDP)	4.21	0.57	3.0	5.0
Perceived Transparency (PT)	4.05	0.65	2.8	5.0
Ethical Data Management (EDM)	4.32	0.52	3.1	5.0
Consumer Trust (CT)	4.45	0.61	3.0	5.0

The results reveal that the mean of all the variables is relatively high, suggesting that both consumers and professionals consider transparency and ethical practices as critical in the development of trust in digital platforms by consumers.

4.2 Hypothesis Testing

Statistical tests, such as regression and mediation analyses, were performed to examine the connections among the variables. For the direct relationships, we utilised OLS regression and the Process Macro for SPSS to examine moderation and mediation effects arising from the hypotheses generated by the theoretical framework.

- Testing Hypothesis H1:

H1: The current data transparency practice enhances consumer trust

The results show a strong link between clear data practices and consumer trust, which supports Hypothesis 1. The relationship between TDP and CT is reflected in the regression coefficient of $\beta = 0.48$ and a p-value under 0.01, showing that a unit rise in TDP leads to a 0.48 increase in CT.

A model R^2 of 0.38 reveals that transparent data practices account for 38% of the variation in consumer trust.

According to earlier research by Martin and Murphy (2016) and Gupta and Shukla (2023), transparency in data management greatly enhances consumer trust in digital platforms.

Our hypothesis testing for H1 implies a significant and positive relationship between transparent data practices (TDP) and consumer trust (CT) ($\beta = 0.48$, $p < 0.01$). This agrees with the trust transference theory (Stewart, 2003), which posits that transparency in one area of a business can also increase a consumer's trust in the business in other areas. For companies operating in high-stakes industries such as healthcare and finance, transparent practices in data collection, storage, and processing create a foundation of trust with consumers.

For instance, the companies that are open about their data practices under GDPR or HIPAA rules will most probably enjoy a positive perception of the consumers because such regulations require specification of such rules enabling the consumers to feel secure with their data. Feng (2020) found that businesses that practice transparent practices which meet regulatory standards increase consumer loyalty and satisfaction. This result underscores the importance of transparent data practices in building trust — especially regarding sensitive consumer data.

- Testing Hypothesis H2:

H2: Transparent data practices enhance perceived transparency

We performed a moderation analysis to evaluate PT's moderating function. PT markedly boosts the association between TDP and CT, as indicated by a significant interaction term ($\beta = 0.28$ and $p < 0.05$).

Interaction Effect: Consumers who view data practices as transparent tend to exhibit increased trust in companies, whereas individuals with low transparency views have lower trust levels.

Conditional Effect: The relationship that TDP has on CT is significantly stronger with high PT ($\beta = 0.58$ and $p < 0.01$) than with low PT ($\beta = 0.29$ and $p < 0.05$).

This confirms that high perceived transparency intensifies the impact of transparent data practices on consumer trust, as suggested by Lee and Li (2021) and Esmaeilzadeh (2020).

Our findings for H2 suggest that perceived transparency (PT) moderates the relation between TDP and CT, with a stronger effect when PT is high ($\beta = 0.28$, $p < 0.05$). This further reinforces the Expectancy Violations Theory positing that the extent of the consumers' expectation for transparency influences their trust in that company (Muzafary et al., 2023).

It means that companies cannot only practice transparency, but also must make sure that the practices are communicated in ways that are consistent with consumer expectations. For example, Explainable AI (XAI) allows businesses to de-clouder decision making processes in algorithmic systems to make the systems as more visible and thus more transparent. But trust in the company increases when consumers understand how AI algorithms work and are comfortable with the fairness of data driven decisions (Binns et al., 2018). This finding supports the argument that clear and accessible communication about data practices is needed to increase perceived transparency and also consumer trust.

- Testing Hypothesis H3:

H3: Transparent data practices positively influence adopting ethical data management

The analysis shows that EDM is critical in mediating how TDP relates to CT with the Process Macro mediation model (Model 4).

Direct effect of TDP on CT: $\beta = 0.35$, $p < 0.01$

Indirect effect through EDM: $\beta = 0.23$, $p < 0.05$

TDP had a significant total effect on CT via EDM at $\beta = 0.58$ and a p-value of less than 0.01, indicating a substantial contribution from ethical data management.

This result emphasises how ethical data treatment strengthens consumer confidence and backs Asgarinia et al. (2023) and Sharma & Sharma (2024).

Mediation analysis of H3 shows that EDM significantly mediates the relationship between TDP and CT ($\beta = 0.23$, $p < 0.05$). This outcome holds a consistency against Stakeholder Theory which advocates that organizations owe ethical obligations to its stakeholders, especially the consumers (Freeman, 1984). Embedding ethical practices into data management will also help to bolster the demonstrate that transparency is more than procedural- it is based in the principles of consumer privacy and protection.

For instance, the decentralized nature of blockchain technology can be applied by organizations using blockchain technology for data management to secure and verify the transactions, and consequently demonstrate an ethical commitment to transparency. This helps establish blockchain's transparent ledger, which can reassure consumers of the company's commitment to ethical data handling of the data through data immutability and accountability of the data at the lifecycle stage. This finding suggests that ethics matter more (in the positive sense) than adherence to transparency in guiding consumer trust, especially in industries such as finance where governance compliance is key.

- Testing Hypothesis H4:

H4: When PT achieves or exceeds expectations, the influence of TDP on CT increases significantly.

Results indicate that the influence of perceived transparency on the link between TDP and CT is strongest when expectations are achieved. At more significant degrees of openness, the influence of PT proved to be substantial ($\beta = 0.35$, $p < 0.01$).

Consumer trust significantly improves when transparency expectations align. Trust levels tend to drop if organisations overlook transparency requirements, verifying H4.

- Testing Hypothesis H5:

H5: The relationship between TDP and consumer trust is mediated by ethical data practices.

A mediation analysis determined that TDP significantly impacts consumer trust mediated through ethical data management ($\beta = 0.22$). This endorses the idea of the Social Contract Theory since consumers believe organisations should observe ethical practices regarding personal data.

4.3 Discussion of Results

The findings from the data analysis lend substantial empirical support to the hypothesised relationships between transparent data practices (TDP), perceived transparency (PT), ethical data management (EDM), and consumer trust (CT). The comprehensive results validate the theoretical framework and expand the discourse around how these variables interact in the context of digital business models. This section will elaborate extensively on each hypothesis, unpack the implications of the results, and draw comparisons with the existing literature.

4.3.1 Transparent Data Practices and Consumer Trust (H1)

The significant and positive relationship between transparent data practices (TDP) and consumer trust (CT), as evidenced by the $\beta = 0.48$, $p < 0.01$ in the regression analysis, underscores the importance of transparent and open data management in shaping consumer attitudes toward digital businesses. This finding, which aligns strongly with existing literature on the crucial role of transparency in fostering trust, as exemplified by Martin & Murphy (2016), emphasises that the proper communication of data practices forms the backbone of trust-building efforts in digital marketing.

In today's digital economy, consumers increasingly know how businesses collect, store, and process their data. This heightened awareness, fueled by widespread data breaches and misuse scandals, has made transparency not just an option but an essential business strategy. The high mean score of 4.21 for TDP across both consumer and professional surveys further supports this notion, indicating that respondents overwhelmingly recognise and value transparency in digital interactions. This urgency and relevance of transparency in digital interactions cannot be overstated.

Notably, the effect size of 0.48 suggests that transparent data practices do more than merely instil a basic level of trust; they play a central role in elevating consumer trust to new heights. This finding is critical for digital businesses across industries, offering a promising avenue for growth and improvement, particularly in sectors such as e-commerce, finance, and healthcare, where the handling of sensitive personal information is paramount. Companies that emphasise transparency in their data practices adhere to regulatory requirements, such as GDPR and CCPA, and position themselves as trustworthy market leaders, paving the way for a brighter future in the digital realm.

4.3.2 Perceived Transparency as a Moderator (H2)

The results of the moderation analysis indicate that perceived transparency (PT) significantly amplifies the relationship between transparent data practices and consumer trust, with an interaction effect of $\beta = 0.28$, $p < 0.05$. This finding supports H2 and underscores the importance of how consumers perceive a company's transparency efforts. It is about the actual transparency practices and effective communication strategies that shape consumer perception. This influence is powerful, as it can build and maintain trust beyond transparency practices.

Consumers often form their judgments about transparency based on subjective experiences and past interactions, as highlighted by Lee and Li (2021). This notion of perceived transparency is especially relevant in the digital space, where consumers may need to fully comprehend the technical complexities of data management but still develop trust based on their perceptions of how forthcoming a company is about its data handling practices. For instance, a company that actively communicates its data privacy policies and explains its data management processes in simple, comprehensible terms is more likely to earn consumer trust than a company that operates in opacity, even if both follow the exact legal requirements.

The conditional effect analysis further illustrates this point. When perceived transparency is high, the relationship between TDP and CT is stronger ($\beta = 0.58$, $p < 0.01$), indicating that companies with high perceived transparency experience a multiplier effect on consumer trust. Conversely, when perceived transparency is low, the impact of TDP on CT is diminished ($\beta = 0.29$, $p < 0.05$), signalling that even robust, transparent practices may fail to foster trust if consumers do not perceive them as transparent.

This finding has profound implications for businesses: Transparency must be implemented and effectively communicated. Digital companies must prioritise clear, open communication about their data practices to positively shape consumer perceptions. Strategies such as transparent privacy policies, user-friendly data management portals, and proactive communication during data breaches can bolster consumer trust by enhancing perceived transparency.

4.3.3 Ethical Data Management as a Mediator (H3)

Our research found that ethical data management (EDM) significantly mediates the relationship between transparent data practices and consumer trust. This was indicated by the mediation analysis, which showed an indirect effect of $\beta = 0.23$, $p < 0.05$. This underscores the critical importance of ethics in data handling. While transparency is crucial, the ethical execution of transparent practices ultimately solidifies consumer trust.

This finding aligns with Asgarinia et al. (2023), who emphasised that decentralised data management technologies present new ethical challenges that businesses must address to maintain consumer trust. Ethical data management extends beyond compliance with legal frameworks like GDPR and CCPA. It ensures fairness, integrity, and consumer rights are upheld in all data-handling processes.

The direct and indirect effects of ethical data management (EDM) underscore the need for businesses to operationalise ethics in their data management frameworks. Transparent practices alone may not be sufficient to earn trust if consumers perceive that their data is being misused or exploited unethically. Therefore, ethical data management is a safeguard that ensures that transparency translates into genuine consumer trust.

For digital businesses, this means adopting a holistic approach to data ethics. This could involve implementing ethical AI systems for data processing, ensuring data minimisation (only collecting necessary data), and offering consent-based data usage that respects consumer autonomy. Furthermore, ethical transparency during crises (e.g., data breaches) can mitigate the damage to consumer trust, as evidenced by Kang et al. (2023), who demonstrated that ethical commitments before a crisis can increase brand resilience.

4.3.4 Perceived Transparency and Expectancy Violations (H4)

The findings on expectancy violations reveal that perceived transparency significantly moderates the relationship between TDP and CT when consumer expectations of transparency are met or exceeded ($\beta = 0.35$, $p < 0.01$). This supports H4 and highlights the psychological dimensions of openness.

Consumers enter digital interactions with expectations regarding how their data will be handled. When businesses meet or exceed these expectations, consumer trust is significantly bolstered. However, when expectations are not met, consumer trust can erode rapidly, even if transparent practices are in place. This finding underscores the fragility of consumer trust in the digital age, where a single instance of perceived dishonesty or opacity can lead to substantial trust deficits.

For businesses, this means that expectation management is just as important as transparency itself. Companies must communicate what consumers can expect regarding their data usage and ensure that these expectations are met consistently. Transparency beyond expectations—such as going the extra mile in disclosing how data is safeguarded—can result in long-term loyalty and brand advocacy, as suggested by Muzafary et al. (2023).

4.3.5 Ethical Data Management and the Full Impact of Transparency (H5)

Finally, the analysis confirmed that ethical data management mediates the full positive impact of transparent data practices on consumer trust, with an indirect effect of $\beta = 0.22$, $p < 0.05$. This supports H5 and reiterates the essential role of ethics in reinforcing transparency.

As per Social Contract Theory, consumers expect businesses to adhere to ethical standards in their data practices. The mediation analysis shows that while transparent data practices can enhance trust, this effect is significantly amplified when those practices are ethically sound. In essence, transparency is the gateway to trust, but ethical behaviour solidifies and sustains that trust over the long term.

This finding is especially relevant in high-stakes industries such as finance, e-commerce, and healthcare, where data mismanagement can have severe consequences. By committing to ethical data management, businesses can meet regulatory requirements and build sustainable, trust-based relationships with consumers. Ethical transparency, particularly in times of crisis, has been shown to protect brand reputation and facilitate recovery from adverse events (e.g., Equifax breach), as noted by Zahoor et al. (2022).

4.3.6 Integrating Transparency, Ethical Management, and Regulatory Compliance: Implications for Building Consumer Trust

This study provides several implications for businesses seeking to build consumer trust through transparent data practices, perceived transparency, and ethical data management. Results for H1 show that transparent data practices directly impact trust, emphasizing that companies need to be transparent with their data practices, especially in compliance-heavy industries like healthcare and finance. For instance, adhering to GDPR and HIPAA regulations goes beyond what is legally required: guiding your users towards greater trust through provable data security and integrity.

Perceived transparency turned out to be a key factor, underlining the necessity of matching business practices with consumer expectations. Explainable AI tools enable companies to satisfy the consumer demand for transparency by exposing how data-driven decisions are made, thus instilling confidence in data-driven business models.

It also makes the point that such an ethical treatment of data is a critical mediator for building consumer trust. Companies incorporating transparency into their ethical frameworks, such as blockchain's decentralised data model, are doing more to protect consumer data than the law requires. Ethical transparency practices are such that trust and loyalties are strengthened because consumer rights are respected and transparent.

By providing these insights, we contribute to the emerging understanding of how transparency, perceived transparency, and ethical practices affect the digital business model and consumer trust. The study's findings underpin the importance of a holistic approach to maintaining consumer trust, such as seeking regulatory compliance, upholding an ethical commitment and good communication so that all fit together.

5. CONCLUSION, IMPLICATION AND FURTHER DIRECTIONS

5.1 Conclusion

The research wraps up this chapter by emphasising the essential conclusions and exploring their effects on upcoming research. This analysis examined the elaborate ties between consumer trust and PT as influenced by ethical data management and transparent data practices in digital models. This study substantiated the conceptual framework by employing multiple regression analysis and mediation tests and defined the interactions among these variables regarding consumer trust.

The study indicated that transparent data practices greatly affected consumer trust. This evidence suggests that digital businesses must value transparency and openness in managing data. As individuals recognise the privacy risks in cyberspace, firms that stress openness are more likely to earn consumers' trust and loyalty.

Perceived transparency significantly boosted the impact of Transparent Data Practices on consumer trust. This outcome highlights the significance of affecting consumer insights on transparency through efficient dialogue and easy-to-use data systems. Consumers must recognise these initiatives as genuine for a company to fully benefit from its transparent practices.

Ethical data treatment proved to be a crucial mediating factor, showing that it is vital for turning transparency into trust. By following legal standards such as GDPR and CCPA in data management practices, companies improve their connection with consumers while ensuring transparency is rooted in fairness and integrity.

The findings indicate that transparency becomes vital for developing and preserving consumer trust in digital commerce when integrated with ethical data approaches. These results reveal detailed information about the facets shaping consumer confidence and supply practical recommendations for firms wanting to boost their transparency and moral practices online.

The research ends with the core relationships that have been established between transparent data practices (TDP), perceived transparency (PT), ethical data management (EDM) and consumer trust (CT) in digital business models. This study substantiates the conceptual framework through multiple regression and mediation analysis to explain how each variable works together to determine the impact of consumer trust.

Data practices like transparent strings matter when it comes to building consumer trust and they help when they are aligned to legal standards like GDPR and HIPAA. This solidity in alignment with regulatory standards promotes confidence by proving dedication to data privacy and protection, what is essential for life long consumer stickiness. Further strengthening this effect, perceived transparency has an additional impact on the effect when consumer insights and transparent communication take place, which renders importance. Companies that are open and accessible with their data will be the biggest winners.

Transparency alone is not enough, and ethical data management emerged as a vital mediator, demonstrating that ethical commitment to data handling strengthens consumer trust, that transparency is both fair and secure. For digital commerce to build lasting consumer confidence, it is essential that transparency is keyed in with ethical approaches. The results of the study provide important lessons for firms that are looking for ways to blend transparency and ethics into their data practices to meet changing consumer expectations and evolving regulatory standards.

5.2 Implications

5.2.1 Theoretical Implications

This study provides important insights into the current understanding of data transparency and trust within the digital economy. Previous studies treated transparency and trust independently; however, this study connects them by including ethical data management as a link and perceived transparency as a regulator of the TDP-to-consumer trust relationship. This study matches Trust Transference Theory and Information Asymmetry Theory by revealing that trust transfers via transparent and ethical practices while alleviating information gaps.

The research reinforces Social Contract Theory by demonstrating that consumers look for ethical actions from companies when managing data. By acting ethically and transparently, businesses cultivate increased customer confidence and loyalty.

This research introduces new applications of the Expectancy Violations Theory concerning transparency and data handling. The analysis shows companies can raise consumer trust by providing more than essential transparency guidelines.

This study analyses the connections between transparency, ethics, and trust and develops a refined theoretical approach to understanding digital economy interactions.

By connecting transparency practices to ethical data management and perceived transparency, this research provides an improved understanding of both the concept; [original] Impact on Research This study offers a deeper insight into digital privacy literature with respect to consumer trust. It anchored on the Trust Transference Theory and Information Asymmetry Theory in proving that greater transparency and adherence to ethical practices contribute in affirming consumer trust by bridging information gap. This further validates Social Contract Theory by suggesting that ethical data practices are viewed as an expected part of the unwritten business-consumer contract, with certain expectations in return.

The paper also brings the Expectancy Violations Theory to transparency research, indicating that companies are able to improve consumer trust simply by going beyond the minimum expected level of transparency. This theoretical synthesis facilitates a more comprehensive view of transparency as a multi-faceted feature including compliance, consumer perception and ethical behavior.

5.2.2 Practical Implications

For businesses, the implications of this study are clear: Having openness is inadequate on its own. Although transparent data practices are essential, they require a dedication to ethical data management and communication methods that boost perceived transparency. The following key recommendations emerge from the findings:

- Implement Transparent Data Practices: Organizations must take the initiative to inform users about their data usage processes. Offering straightforward privacy policies and simple descriptions of how data is used is essential for gaining consumer trust.
- Enhance Perceived Transparency: Good communication is necessary. Organisations must not believe that others will understand their attempts at transparency. Companies should participate in open communication methods by giving timely information on data use and security practices. By providing accessible data tracking and control tools, consumers can increase their perception of transparency.
- Ethical Data Management: Compliance with rules is insufficient for ethical behavior. Firms must implement responsible AI technologies and minimise data requirements to make their operations clear and reflect consumers' reasonable expectations of privacy. Firms can more effectively protect consumer trust by adopting ethical approaches in crisis management during data breaches.
- Manage Consumer Expectations: Building trust effectively requires meeting and exceeding consumers' expectations of openness. Businesses must trans-

parently inform consumers about their data management practices and then guarantee the fulfilment of those expectations. By providing additional levels of openness about data security, businesses can build long-lasting relations with consumers.

5.2.2 Policy Implications

The outcomes of this research influence the decisions of policymakers and regulators. Digital economies are expanding; therefore, strong and enforceable policies are necessary for businesses to comply with transparent and ethical data management methods. Policies such as GDPR and CCPA already set essential precedents for transparency and consumer rights protection, but there is room for further improvement:

- Stronger Enforcement Mechanisms: Enforcement authorities must require firms to meet data openness and ethical guidelines requirements. Severe fines and penalties must be enforced to prevent companies from skimping on data practices.
- Global Data Privacy Standards: As many digital firms function internationally, there is an urgent demand for coherent global data privacy and transparency guidelines. Governments must join forces to form collective rules that defend consumers' rights independent of their place.
- Encouraging Ethical Innovation: Regulatory and governmental entities must spark interest in businesses utilising ethical innovations in data practices, such as AI tools that empower users to have better command over their data. To encourage ethical data practices, businesses might receive financial support or tax benefits from regulators.

5.3 Limitations of the Study

The research yields significant conclusions, although it possesses limitations. Data collected from consumers and industry professionals was self-reported and may have bias. Scholars might back up these results with real-time metrics relating to business practices and consumer actions.

The study emphasised restricted industries, including digital finance and service areas. Understanding transparency and trust hinges on these sectors; nevertheless, future studies should broaden the scope to sectors such as manufacturing or logistics that handle data differently.

While the study has made significant strides in understanding perceived transparency as a moderator, it is crucial not to overlook other influencing factors. Consumer knowledge regarding data privacy laws or brand reputation could significantly impact how consumers perceive the relationship between transparency in data management and their trust. These factors deserve the same scrutiny and examination as the ones already studied.

5.4 Future Research

For future research, it is proposed that other general and specific moderators, such as CSR, AI, and blockchain, be identified to determine their influence on transparency and consumer trust. To understand more about the dynamic nature of trust, it is essential to conduct longitudinal research since changes take time. In contrast, research that focuses on comparative differences between countries can show how organisations in those countries handle the issue of transparency. Other industries should not be limited to e-commerce and healthcare industries only. In addition, considering topics like the behavioural consequences of transparency, such as brand image and post-transparency behaviour, and fine-grained analysis of regulations and their change, e.g., GDPR and CCPA, would enhance knowledge. It might be time to move towards a new level of scrutiny with new tools that have emerged in recent years, such as smart contracts and explainable AI. Lastly, looking at openly managed crisis responses during data breaches would improve understanding of how trust can be rebuilt.

REFERENCES

Abitbol, A., Lee, N. M., & VanDyke, M. S. (2022). Examining the perceived transparency of DTC genetic testing company communication and its impact on consumer trust, attitude and behavioural intentions. *Journal of Communication Management (London)*, 26(3), 223–241. DOI: 10.1108/JCOM-01-2022-0006

Akerlof, G. A. (1970). The market for "lemons": Quality uncertainty and the market mechanism. *The Quarterly Journal of Economics*, 84(3), 488–500. DOI: 10.2307/1879431

Ali, A., Al-rimy, B., Alsubaei, F. S., Almazroi, A., & Almazroi, A. A. (2023). HealthLock: Blockchain-Based Privacy Preservation Using Homomorphic Encryption in Internet of Things Healthcare Applications. *Sensors (Basel)*, 23(15), 6762. DOI: 10.3390/s23156762 PMID: 37571545

Allbabidi, M. H. A. (2021). Hype or Hope: Digital Technologies in the auditing process. *Asian Journal of Business and Accounting*, 14(1), 59–86. DOI: 10.22452/ajba.vol14no1.3

Apple Inc. (2019). *Privacy. That is iPhone.* Apple Newsroom. Retrieved from https://www.apple.com/newsroom/2019/01/privacy-thats-iphone/

Asgarinia, H., Penedo, A. C., Esteves, B., & Lewis, D. (2023). "Who Should I Trust with My Data?" Ethical and Legal Challenges for Innovation in New Decentralized Data Management Technologies. *Information (Basel)*, 14(7), 351. DOI: 10.3390/info14070351

Asgarinia, H., Penedo, A. C., Esteves, B., & Lewis, D. (2023). "Who Should I Trust with My Data?" Ethical and Legal Challenges for Innovation in New Decentralized Data Management Technologies. *Information (Basel)*, 14(7), 351. DOI: 10.3390/info14070351

Asgarinia, H., Penedo, A. C., Esteves, B., & Lewis, D. (2023). "Who Should I Trust with My Data?" Ethical and Legal Challenges for Innovation in New Decentralized Data Management Technologies. *Information (Basel)*, 14(7), 351. DOI: 10.3390/info14070351

Avancha, S., Jain, A., & Goel, O. (2024). Blockchain-Based Vendor Management in IT: Challenges and Solutions. *South Journal of Management and Business Technology*, 2(2), 38–51. DOI: 10.36676/sjmbt.v2.i2.38

Binns, R., Veale, M., Van Kleek, M., & Shadbolt, N. (2018). 'It's reducing a human being to a percentage': Perceptions of justice in algorithmic decisions. *Proceedings of the 2018 CHI Conference on Human Factors in Computing Systems*, 1–14. DOI: 10.1145/3173574.3173951

Böhler, R. S. H. (2024). The Influence of Transparency in Personalized Recommendation Ads on Consumer Privacy Concerns and Purchase Intentions. *Legal Economics*, 8(3), 1–12. DOI: 10.56397/LE.2024.08.03

Cabello, O. G., de Moraes, G. H. S. M., Watrin, C., Ribeiro da Silva, H. M., & Spers, E. E. (2020). The Influence of Sales Tax Transparency and Political Trust on Brazilian Consumer Behaviour. *Revista Contabilidade & Gestão Governamental*, 23(1), 1–22. DOI: 10.21714/1984-3925_2020v23n1a9

Casino, F., Dasaklis, T. K., & Patsakis, C. (2019). A systematic literature review of blockchain-based applications: Current status, classification and open issues. *Telematics and Informatics*, 36, 55–81. DOI: 10.1016/j.tele.2018.11.006

Chen, Y., & Lee, J. Y. (2021). Data transparency and trust in the financial sector. *Journal of Financial Services Marketing*, 26(2), 123–139. DOI: 10.1057/s41264-021-00079-2

Daoud, M. K., Al-Qeed, D. M., Al-Gasawneh, J., & Ziani, A. (2023). Examining the Ethical Implications of Data Privacy and Targeted Advertising in Digital Marketing: Consumer Perceptions. International Conference on Social Networks Analysis, Management, and Security (SNAMS), 10375481. DOI: 10.1109/SNAMS60348.2023.10375481

Doshi-Velez, F., & Kim, B. (2017). Towards a rigorous science of interpretable machine learning. *arXiv preprint*. https://doi.org//arXiv.1702.08608DOI: 10.48550

Esmaeilzadeh, P. (2020). The Process of Building Patient Trust in Health Information Exchange (HIE): The Impacts of Perceived Benefits, Perceived Transparency of Privacy Policy, and Familiarity. *Communications of the Association for Information Systems*, 45(1), 21–45. DOI: 10.17705/1CAIS.04521

Esmaeilzadeh, P. (2020). The Process of Building Patient Trust in Health Information Exchange (HIE): The Impacts of Perceived Benefits, Perceived Transparency of Privacy Policy, and Familiarity. *Communications of the Association for Information Systems*, 45(1), 21–45. DOI: 10.17705/1CAIS.04521

European Union. (2016). *General Data Protection Regulation (GDPR) (EU) 2016/679*. Official Journal of the European Union. Retrieved from https://eur-lex.europa.eu/legal-content/EN/TXT/?uri=celex%3A32016R0679

Feng, Y. (2020). Understanding consumer trust and purchase intention in mobile e-commerce: A perspective from data transparency and privacy policies. *Journal of Retailing and Consumer Services*, 55, 102135. DOI: 10.1016/j.jretconser.2020.102135

Financial Industry Regulatory Authority (FINRA). (2019). *Rules and Guidance.* Retrieved from https://www.finra.org/rules-guidance

Freeman, R. E. (1984). *Strategic management: A stakeholder approach.* Pitman.

Gold, H., & McLaughlin, D. (2016). Patient trust and transparency in health information exchanges. *Health Affairs*, 35(1), 34–39. DOI: 10.1377/hlthaff.2015.1037

Gupta, V., & Shukla, S. (2023). Consumer Trust in Digital Banking: A Qualitative Study of Legal and Regulatory Impacts. *Journal of Information Systems, Security. Law & Policy*, 3(2), 50–64. DOI: 10.61838/kman.isslp.3.2.4

Gupta, V., & Shukla, S. (2023). Consumer Trust in Digital Banking: A Qualitative Study of Legal and Regulatory Impacts. Journal of Information Systems, Security. *Law & Policy*, 3(2), 50–64. DOI: 10.61838/kman.isslp.3.2.4

Hutchings, E., Loomes, M. W., Butow, P., & Boyle, F. (2020). A systematic literature review of health consumer attitudes towards secondary use and sharing health administrative and clinical trial data focuses on privacy, trust, and transparency. *Systematic Reviews*, 9(1), 1–11. DOI: 10.1186/s13643-020-01481-9 PMID: 31907078

Isaak, J., & Hanna, M. J. (2018). User data privacy: Facebook, Cambridge Analytica, and privacy protection. *Computer*, 51(8), 56–59. DOI: 10.1109/MC.2018.3191268

Jones, T. M., Harrison, J. S., & Felps, W. (2018). How applying instrumental stakeholder theory can provide a sustainable competitive advantage. *Academy of Management Review*, 43(3), 371–391. DOI: 10.5465/amr.2016.0111

Junaid, L., Bilal, K., Shuja, J., Balogun, A., & Rodrigues, J. (2024). Blockchain-Enabled Framework for Transparent Land Lease and Mortgage Management. *IEEE Access : Practical Innovations, Open Solutions*, 3388248, 54005–54018. Advance online publication. DOI: 10.1109/ACCESS.2024.3388248

Kang, J., Faria, A. A., Lee, J. M., & Choi, W. (2023). Will consumers give us another chance to bounce back? Effects of precrisis commitments to social and product responsibility on brand resilience. *Journal of Product and Brand Management*, 32(1), 120–136. DOI: 10.1108/JPBM-03-2022-3899

Kim, H., & Lee, T. H. (2018). Strategic CSR Communication: A moderating role of transparency in trust building. *International Journal of Strategic Communication*, 12(2), 107–124. DOI: 10.1080/1553118X.2018.1425692

Kim, H., & Lee, T. H. (2018). Strategic CSR Communication: A moderating role of transparency in trust building. *International Journal of Strategic Communication*, 12(2), 107–124. DOI: 10.1080/1553118X.2018.1425692

Lee, Y., & Li, J. Q. (2021). The role of communication transparency and organisational trust in publics' perceptions, attitudes, and social distancing behaviour: A case study of the COVID-19 outbreak. *Journal of Contingencies and Crisis Management*, 29(4), 368–384. DOI: 10.1111/1468-5973.12354

Lee, Y., & Li, J. Q. (2021). The role of communication transparency and organisational trust in publics' perceptions, attitudes, and social distancing behaviour: A case study of the COVID-19 outbreak. *Journal of Contingencies and Crisis Management*, 29(4), 368–384. DOI: 10.1111/1468-5973.12354

Lee, Y., & Li, J. Q. (2021). The role of communication transparency and organisational trust in publics' perceptions, attitudes, and social distancing behaviour: A case study of the COVID-19 outbreak. *Journal of Contingencies and Crisis Management*, 29(4), 368–384. DOI: 10.1111/1468-5973.12354

Loukil, F., Ghedira Guégan, C., & Benharkat, A. (2020). PATRIoT: A Data Sharing Platform for IoT Using a Service-Oriented Approach Based on Blockchain. In *Advances in Service-Oriented and Cloud Computing* (pp. 152–169). Springer., DOI: 10.1007/978-3-030-65310-1_10

Martin, K. D., & Murphy, P. E. (2016). The role of data privacy in marketing. *Journal of the Academy of Marketing Science*, 45(2), 135–155. DOI: 10.1007/s11747-016-0495-4

Martin, K. D., & Murphy, P. E. (2016). The role of data privacy in marketing. *Journal of the Academy of Marketing Science*, 45(2), 135–155. DOI: 10.1007/s11747-016-0495-4

McKnight, D. H., Choudhury, V., & Kacmar, C. (2002). Developing and validating trust measures for e-commerce: An integrative typology. *Information Systems Research*, 13(3), 334–359. DOI: 10.1287/isre.13.3.334.81

Mettler, T., Miscione, G., Jacobs, C. D., & Guenduez, A. A. (2024). Same same but different: How policies frame societal-level digital transformation. *Government Information Quarterly*, 41(2), 101932. DOI: 10.1016/j.giq.2024.101932

Obudho, K. (2024). The Impact of Data Privacy Laws on Digital Marketing Practices. *Journal of Marketing and Leadership Practices*, 6(4), 78–92. DOI: 10.47941/jmlp.2155

Office for Civil Rights, U.S. Department of Health and Human Services. (2015). *Health Insurance Portability and Accountability Act (HIPAA)*. Retrieved from https://www.hhs.gov/hipaa/index.html

Olteanu, A., Castillo, C., Diaz, F., & Kiciman, E. (2016). Social data: biases, methodological pitfalls, and ethical boundaries. SSRN *Electronic Journal*. DOI: 10.2139/ssrn.2886526

Saberi, S., Kouhizadeh, M., Sarkis, J., & Shen, L. (2019). Blockchain technology and its relationships to sustainable supply chain management. *International Journal of Production Research*, 57(7), 2117–2135. DOI: 10.1080/00207543.2018.1533261

Satur, K. L., Nase, R. M., Aiza Cubillas, B. J. T. A., & Magbanua, M. I. S. S. (2024). Authenticity and transparency: Influencers' sponsored content on makeup products towards consumer trust. *International Journal of Research in Education and Human Capital*, 5(1), 117–136. DOI: 10.37602/IJREHC.2024.5117

Satur, K. L., Nase, R. M., Cubillas, B. J. T. A. A., & Magbanua, M. I. S. S. (2024). Authenticity and transparency: Influencers' sponsored content on makeup products towards consumer trust. *International Journal of Research in Education and Human Capital*, 5(1), 117–136. DOI: 10.37602/IJREHC.2024.5117

Shaikh, I. A. K., Shahare, P., Gangadharan, S., Venkatarathnam, N., Pelluru, G., & Babu, S. B. G. T. (2024). Transforming Customer Relationship Management (CRM) with AI in E-Commerce. International Conference on Recent Trends in Computing and Smart Technology (ICRTCST), 10578449. DOI: 10.1109/ICRTCST61793.2024.10578449

Sharma, A. K., & Sharma, R. (2024). Navigating compliance and regulations in marketing analytics: Upholding ethical standards and consumer trust. *ACQY Journal*, 4920(1), 77. Advance online publication. DOI: 10.69554/ACQY4920

Sharma, A. K., & Sharma, R. (2024). Navigating compliance and regulations in marketing analytics: Upholding ethical standards and consumer trust. *ACQY Journal*, 4920(1), 77. Advance online publication. DOI: 10.69554/ACQY4920

Sharma, S.. (2023). Ethical Considerations in AI-Based Marketing: Balancing Profit and Consumer Trust. *Journal of Propulsion Technology*, 44(3), 162–178. DOI: 10.52783/tjjpt.v44.i3.474

Singh, N. (2024). Data Security and Consumer Trust in Fintech Innovations Using Technology Adoption Method. *International Journal of Science Research and Engineering Management*, 9(5), 45–62. DOI: 10.55041/IJSREM33015

Stewart, K. J. (2003). Trust transfer on the World Wide Web. *Organization Science*, 14(1), 5–17. DOI: 10.1287/orsc.14.1.5.12810

Sturgeon, T. J. (2019). Upgrading strategies for the digital economy. *Global Strategy Journal*, 11(1), 34–57. DOI: 10.1002/gsj.1364

Teodorescu, D., Aivaz, K., Vancea, D., Condrea, E., Drăgan, C., & Olteanu, A. (2023). Consumer Trust in AI Algorithms Used in E-Commerce: A Case Study of College Students at a Romanian Public University. *Sustainability (Basel)*, 15(15), 11925. DOI: 10.3390/su151511925

Thuermer, G., Walker, J., Simperl, E., & Carr, L. (2024). When data meets citizens: Investigating citizen engagement in data-driven innovation programs. *Data & Policy*, 6, e12. Advance online publication. DOI: 10.1017/dap.2023.43

Thuermer, G., Walker, J., Simperl, E., & Carr, L. (2024). When data meets citizens: Investigating citizen engagement in data-driven innovation programs. *Data & Policy*, 6, e12. Advance online publication. DOI: 10.1017/dap.2023.43

Tr ng, J. (2024). Relationship between Data Privacy Regulations and Consumer Trust in E-Commerce Platforms in Vietnam. *African Journal of Digital Knowledge Management*, 7(2), 31–45. DOI: 10.47672/ajdikm.2347

Voigt, P., & Von dem Bussche, A. (2017). *The EU General Data Protection Regulation (GDPR): A practical guide*. Springer., DOI: 10.1007/978-3-319-57959-7

Wager, K. A., Lee, F. W., & Glaser, J. P. (2017). *Health care information systems: A practical approach for health care management*. John Wiley & Sons.

Yap, T. L., Nayak, R., Vu, N. T. H., Bui, D. T., Pham, T. T. T., & Allen, D. W. E. (2023). Adopting blockchain-based traceability in the fruit supply chain in a developing economy: Facilitators and barriers. *Information Technology & People*, 36(5), 1341–1360. DOI: 10.1108/ITP-02-2023-0168

Zheng, Z., Xie, S., Dai, H., Chen, X., & Wang, H. (2018). Blockchain challenges and opportunities: A survey. *International Journal of Web and Grid Services*, 14(4), 352–375. DOI: 10.1504/IJWGS.2018.095647

. Zhou, F. (2015). The effect of perceived transparency, reputation and security on consumer trust and purchase intention.

Chapter 6
Factors Affecting the Implementation of Cloud-Based ERP Systems in the South African Gold Mining Industries

Tlou Maggie Masenya
Durban University of Technology, South Africa

Oluwasegun Julius Aroba
Durban University of Technology, South Africa

ABSTRACT

South Africa is one of the nations in Africa that has contributed to the mining industry due to the mineral substances found within the nation. However, the current enterprise resource planning (ERP) system that is used in the mining sector dramatically impacts the way gold mines function and their effectiveness. Most of South African Gold Mines are still using old cloud-based ERP system. The aim of this chapter is to investigate the implementation of cloud-based enterprise resource planning (ERP) within the South African gold mining industries by looking at the variables that influence the move from a conventional or traditional ERP framework to a cloud-based framework. The study identified the factors affecting the effective implementation of cloud-based ERP system including cyber threat, cost of deployment, flexibility, more space storage, time and shortage of highly skilled local worker force. This chapter recommends that a hybrid strategy incorporating a cloud-based ERP system with the support services system would be beneficial.

DOI: 10.4018/979-8-3693-8357-5.ch006

INTRODUCTION AND BACKGROUND

Many nations have recognized the artisanal and small-scale mining (ASM) industry as a result of the notable increase in its operations globally, and they are tagged as Small Medium Enterprises (SME's). ASM are often challenged with various problems that are huge when compared to large scale mining (Mkubukeli & Tengeh, 2016). The gold mining sector has been crucial to South Africa's history, in terms of macroeconomic growth and local and community levels, and continues to be so today (Phoshoko, 2021). Enterprise resource planning (ERP) and Systems, Applications and Products (SAP) systems have improved businesses' day-to-day operations in various organizations including mining sector, globally. ERP systems are essential technological enablers that boost business continuity plans and foster innovation, especially in the face of obstacles brought on by the global coronavirus outbreak (Margherita et al 2023). ERP systems, which centralize data and streamline processes are essential technological enablers that spur innovation. ERP and technological innovation applications improve decision-making and agility by enabling firms to react quickly to interruptions. These systems are necessary to establish successful business continuity strategies in light of the global coronavirus outbreak, guaranteeing those activities can continue without disruption despite unforeseen difficulties for example in the recent global coronavirus outbreak (Asgharifard, 2022; Fagbola et al., 2022).

ERP is a measured programming system designed to combine the most useful portion of an organization's business activities into a single integrated system. However, there have been challenges associated with this expansion, for the mining and small and medium-sized business sectors (Aroba & Mnguni, 2023, Aroba & Abayomi 2023). These include a high demand for raw materials, lower ore grades, stringent labor market requirements and high production standards, in addition to the need to conserve environmental resources (Sishi &Telukdarie, 2020).

With the dawn of the 21st century and the frontier of the new digital age, mining has undergone rapid change. Large firms were first to implement ERP systems, although the installation or implementation costs are falling as a result of the large business market becoming saturated. Covid-19 has also caused significant disruptions to the mining industry because core mining operations were affected by temporary lockdowns imposed by the government (Gao, 2020). Nevertheless, the South African gold mining industries exhibits no signs of necessitating the kind of features found in traditional ERP to resolve the primary issue in the mining sector, as most of the gold mining industries use outdated system that are not cloud-enabled. The traditional ERP system does not meet the requirements of their day to day strategic, operational target and it leads to data redundancy and inaccurate data. The traditional ERP system has a gradual impact and it is thus the main cause of the operational method compromises over the previous few decades (Aroba, 2023, Aroba et al., 2023a,b). Cloud-based ERP for the mining industry proffers impeccable performance and streamlines all the operations and activities in the industry. As stated by Oyewole et al. (2024), an industry like the gold mining in South Africa cannot continue to grow without adopting cloud-based ERP systems.

It has therefore been observed that within the current challenging showcase conditions confronting the mining industry, grasping innovation and leveraging its benefits have remained ahead of the bend and accomplished positive returns of the venture. However, compared to its other secondary and tertiary industry counterparts, mining industries has generally been slower to adopt new systems and technologies (Reactore, 2020).

PROBLEM STATEMENT

Enterprise Resource Planning (ERP) system has been used in all business domains worldwide, to boost efficiency and productivity. However, implementing cloud-based ERP systems in the mining industry has been historically slow because of the relatively low proportion of people with professional qualifications (Bill, 2021; Gruenhagen & Parker, 2020). For example, there was a lack proper go-live planning in ERP system implementation at Sibanye Stillwater mine project due to lack of user acceptance, inefficient use of the capabilities of this technology and lack of proper training among mine workers that were employed (Tigunia, 2021). It is clear that small medium enterprise (SMEs) gold mining have contributed significantly to the larger mining sector in South Africa, encountered its fair share of obstacles, and frequently had a high failure rate (Mokalapa, Ovedokun & Fowokun, 2024). Furthermore, user resistance to the new ERP system is the primary reason for ERP system implementation project failure (Bill, 2021). Gold mining industries face difficulties with sustainability in the digital age and are hesitant to expand, and others remain tiny and stay clear of tax-related issues. SMEs have occasionally incurred significant capital costs due to poor selection, which eventually casts doubt on their ability to survive (Basu & Jha, 2024). Some of the traditional and cloud-based ERP systems that are used when compared to each other has the integration complexity, challenges of customizations, competitive advantages and issues relating to corporate strategy (Aroba, 2023).

System users avoid breaking old habits and gaining new knowledge and experience as they lack the knowledge to make the best use of the new system such as ERP and they wish to continue working in the same old way (Gruenhagen & Parker, 2020). Most of the SMEs including gold mining industries are thus doubtful about the preference of exchanging from ordinary to cloud-based ERP system because it can cost them a lot of money, create cybersecurity issues. Some of the mining industries are still small and they cannot afford the ERP software. Furthermore, it can be time-consuming to implement a cloud-based ERP system in the gold mining industries. This implies that subscription-based cloud models and Software as a Service (SaaS) will continue to grow while the use of license-based software will continue to decline (Kankkonen, 2018). This chapter was guided by the following research questions:

- What are the types of Cloud-based ERP systems in the South African Gold mining sector?
- What are the benefits or advantages of using Cloud-based ERP systems in the South African Gold mining sector?
- What are the factors affecting the implementation of Cloud-based ERP systems in the South African Gold mining sector?
- What are the challenges to effective implementation of the cloud-based ERP system in the gold mining sector?
- What are the strategies to effective implementation of ERP systems in the South African gold mining sector?

LITERATURE REVIEW

The following section present the literature review with specific reference to sources that explored the implementation of Cloud-based ERP Systems in the Gold Mining Industries.

Overview of Cloud-Based ERP System Implementation in the Gold Mining Sector

ERP is a business management software with integrated applications that help an organization collect, organize, store, and interpret data from different business activities (Aroba 2023). The increasing use of cloud-based ERP technologies has improved the effectiveness of day-to-day business operations. However, the small and medium business mining sectors have faced several difficulties due to increasing use of cloud-based ERP systems. Industries find it challenging to guarantee that scalability is built because of the constant shift in the SME market (Aroba & Govender, 2023). Furthermore, cloud-based ERP has long thought that the small-medium enterprise (SME) mining and metals industry is traditional and does not care about new ideas (Gruenhagen & Parker, 2020). Conversely, these systems, characterized as a group of business software modules aimed at automating core business process competencies in the fields like finance, human resource, procurement, manufacturing and logistics, enable organizations to manage their core business process data and information across the enterprise (Resulting, 2022). There have been several attempts to comprehend how new breakthroughs or technologies can be adopted in the mining sector. In general, breakthrough innovation spread slowly inside the mining sector. The main causes of this were found to be the high capital investment needs, the absence of domestic rivalry, the in-situ geological characteristics unique to the site, and the immaturity of the technologies (Bhattacharyya & Shah, 2022).

ERP Technological Application

The popularity of ERP systems has grown due to their accuracy in resource management adaptation (Cruz, 2022). ERP technologies have been created to solve the information fragmentation within businesses by integrating intra- and inter-organizational information. ERP systems provide strategic, technical, and operational value-adding dimensions to decision-making (Greeks, 2020). The integrated structure of the cloud ERP connects organizational responsibilities with sales and logistics. The organizations benefit from the system's integration and optimization of several business processes. ERP systems can improve worker safety standards by lowering costs, increasing compliance requirements, and improving administration.

To address the introduction of automated business processes, there are supporting evidences of different types of ERP systems that have been developed because of advancements in organizational resource planning. Some of the varieties of ERP types which small and medium enterprise gold mining industries can adapt or purchase to upscale their operational systems are explained in Figure 1 and 2 below. They illustrate typical architecture of the cloud-based systems and traditional ERP system that can be deployed by the gold mining industries to enhance operational processes.

Figure 1. Cloud-based ERP systems by Al-Ghofaili and Al-Mashari (2014)

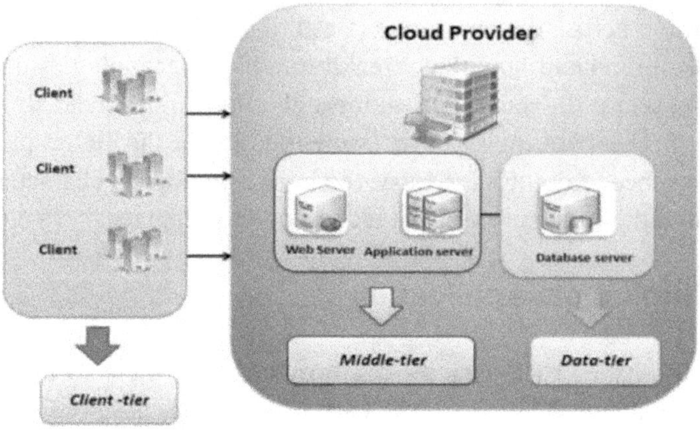

Figure 2. Traditional ERP system by Al-Ghofaili and Al-Mashari (2014)

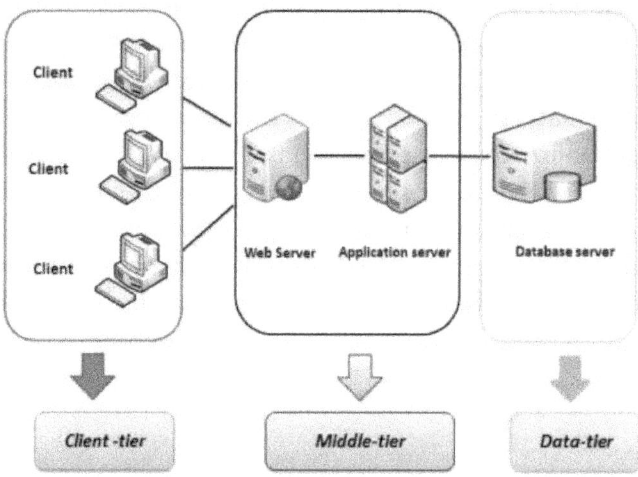

Nevertheless, cloud-based ERP solutions differ from traditional ERP systems in that they do not have the same multi-tier architecture. Table 1 below illustrate an extensive comparison analysis of traditional Cloud ERP Systems versus Cloud-Based ERP systems.

Table 1. Traditional Cloud ERP Systems versus Cloud-Based ERP SAP systems

Aspect	Traditional ERP (on-premise)	Cloud ERP
Costs	Higher initial costs (licenses), usually annual maintenance costs, possibility of return on investment	Low and predictable initial costs (e.g. monthly), no maintenance costs
Customization	High opportunities for customization	Low opportunities for customization
Deployment	Usually in a local Data Center	Usually on a provider's server
Ability to reduce IT staff	Small	Large
Updates	Difficult (performed manually by IT staff)	Easy (performed automatically by provider)
Internet access	Not necessary	Necessary
Control over the system	High	Limited
Technical infrastructure	**Requires investment in infrastructure (e.g. servers, backup equipment, air conditioners, UPS, etc.).**	**No technical infrastructure, all necessary equipment is provided by the provider**
Typical customers	Large enterprises, with significant budgets and extensive IT infrastructure	Small and medium-sized enterprises with limited financial capabilities
Mobility	Access possible but requires additional investment	Access possible from anywhere
Data security	Responsibility of the enterprise	Responsibility of the provider
Implementation time	Rather long	Rather shorter

Source: Bitowska and Dziembek (2024)

Bitowska and Dziembek (2024) describes cloud ERP as a type of enterprise resource planning software that is hosted on a cloud computing platform as opposed to being on-premises within an organization's own data centre. It is package software that is delivered over the Internet that includes all the solutions to manage simplified and standard business laws on a web-based architecture (Aulia et al. 2019). Many consultancies and advising firms believe that the traditional approach of purchasing and utilizing ERP systems will eventually be replaced by the growing popularity of cloud-based ERP solutions.

On-Premises ERP vs Cloud-Based Systems

Cloud ERP solutions have been increasingly popular these days due to their ability to add new processing capabilities without requiring major modifications to the current system, which was made possible by changes in market demand. The process of moving an organization's digital assets, services, IT resources, or applications entirely or partially to the cloud is known as cloud migration. It can be necessary to keep some IT infrastructure on-site during the cloud migration process (Niranga & Wickramarachchi, 2020). Switching from on-premises ERP solutions to cloud-based systems, businesses may take advantage of more flexibility and new capabilities in a variety of industries. Cloud ERP improves accessibility and scalability, enabling businesses to incorporate cutting-edge technology like artificial intelligence and analytics and respond swiftly to changes in the market (Guo, 2021). In addition to streamlining operations, this shift fosters improved teamwork and data-driven decision-making, all of which are essential for remaining competitive in a corporate environment that is changing quickly (Haddara, Gothesen & Langseth, 2022). Even while cloud computing has received more attention, there is still a lot of room for the technology to be adopted more widely. As a result, many organizations are left wondering how to migrate and shift to the cloud. Cloud computing has three major service models, namely: Infrastructure as a Service (IaaS), Platform as a Service (PaaS) and Software as a Service (SaaS) (Jiang & Wang, 2024). The cloud computing model known as Software as a Service is used to deliver cloud ERP systems. It can be accessed through an internet browser without requiring the user to install or configure the system.

The Effect of ERP Systems on Innovation and Resilience of Industries

Businesses that are leading the way in digital transformation put pressure on others to follow suit, but doing so raises concerns about security, workforce competency, data retention, and analytics (Mourtzis & Panopoulos, 2022). The top suppliers in the market for cloud-based ERP are Microsoft Dynamics, SAP, and Oracle (Syed et al., 2024). ERP provides global megatrends like urbanization, demographic shifts, globalization, and energy transformation are some of the causes propelling the technological urge to develop novel solutions in the modern world.

Many organizations and industries have not yet reached the prior level of Industry 3.0 technology development, which creates a gap in opportunity and competitiveness. On the other hand, there is a potential for developing a single digital information space on a cutting-edge cloud-based ERP system in order to enhance management of all topics within the local community and ease the shift to the Industry 4.0 technological environment (Mourtzisand & Panopoulous, 2022). S/4HANA from SAP is among the most renowned cloud-based ERP solutions, renowned for its extensive application suite that combines many company activities, such as finance, sales, procurement, and production. This system enhances the decision-making capabilities by utilizing in-memory computing to give real-time insights and analytics (Elbahri et. al, 2019).

FINDINGS AND DISCUSSION

The findings were presented in five themes, in line with the research questions of the study, and these include: the types of cloud-based ERP systems, the benefits or advantages of using cloud-based ERP systems, the factors affecting the implementation of cloud-based ERP systems, the challenges to effective implementation of the cloud-based ERP system and the strategies to overcoming the challenges to implementing ERP systems in the South African gold mining sector.

Types of Cloud-Based ERP Systems

There are types of cloud-based ERP systems used in the mining sector, which are: SAP analytics and oracle system. However, each one of the mine industries can choose the type of the system they want to implement.

- **SAP Analytics Cloud**

The client-oriented SAP Analytics cloud platform was created with many users in mind. This Software as a Service (SaaS) approach enables the platform to handle array data using machine learning algorithms. SAP Analytics Cloud include features that can assist in examining company's verifiable performance, provide up-to-date information, get the required information data, give different scenarios to see how the circumstance creates (Sibanye, 2020), and assist in setting up an effective planning process (Nararya, Saputra & Puspitasari, 2021).

- **Oracle ERP system**

Oracle ERP system is widely used in the commercial world nowadays. The most profitable mining firms in the world rely on Oracle ERP technologies and applications to provide them with the thorough business intelligence they require to enhance their operation (Naorib, 2021). Many businesses in South Africa and worldwide, including gold mining industries are looking for cutting-edge solutions to streamline production and boost operational effectiveness. Oracle SAP system is already leading the way in this area, and mining companies rely on the intelligent, enterprise-grade applications to cut costs, increase business agility and provide digital tools that enable businesses to remain agile and efficient, despite the ongoing uncertainty in global markets (Reactore, 2020).

For prompt decision-making and increased production efficiency, Oracle SAP system provides natural resource firms with an integrated view of the metals and mining process. Additionally, Oracle ERP system benefits mining companies in the following ways:

- Managing the execution of operations.
- Using intelligent operation to increase operational effectiveness and efficiency (Phoshoko, 2021).
- Increasing productivity, dependability, and safety through operational optimization (Gruenhagen & Parker, 2020).
- Comparing locations, buildings, machinery on production lines, and product lines (Kankkonen 2018).
- Managing compliance and lending projects (Nararya, Saputra & Puspitasari, 2021).
- Real-time monitoring of production performance across all sources (Naorib, 2021).
- Connecting their plant floor systems and enterprise resource planning (Kshetri, 2022).

The Benefits of Using Cloud-Based ERP Systems in the Gold Mining Sector

Mining has advanced quickly since the turn of the twenty-first century and the start of the new digital era. The majority of the time, it has been noticed that mines that are utilizing technology and embracing its advantages have stayed ahead of the curve and, crucially, achieved positive ROI (Return on Investment) results (Fronteas, 2020), even in the face of the current challenging market conditions that the industry as a whole is experiencing. Scalability, availability, portability, accessibility, and usability are among the benefits of cloud ERP, along with its affordability as compared to traditional system adoption. However, in comparison to other secondary and tertiary industries, mining has generally been slower to adopt new technologies (Eales & Schoor, 2022), especially in the area of Information and Communication Technology. Service and deployment models can be used to explain cloud computing systems. The fact that there is a clear lack of a single solution to handle the multidisciplinary parts of a mining operation only serves to exacerbate this (Reactore, 2020).

However, the most comprehensive set of standards-based tools for utilizing and integrating old systems is provided by a traditional software known as Oracle ERP. For large, varied enterprises, Oracle ERP provides financial management and strategic planning capabilities with innovative capital asset modelling. This system also provides acquisition and life-of-mine planning with the best strategic planning available.

It is only possible to plan from extraction, blending, processing, and distribution using Oracle's strategic planning solution.

An integrated asset lifecycle management suite connected to production scheduling and real-time analytics is only available from Oracle. Oracle ERP is a traditional form of enterprise software vendor with a full suite of all-encompassing planning and optimization tools and an open, integrated technological stack that spans from applications to disk (Silase 2018).

Table 2. Traditional ERP system vs Cloud Based ERP systems

Factors	Traditional ERP systems	Cloud-based ERP systems
Deployment	Local Server	Cloud Server
IT staff reduction	None	High
Implementation costs	High	Low
Customization	Easy	Hard
Support costs	High	Low
Integration	Easy	Hard
Licensing costs	High	Low
Data availability	Low	High
Attacks	Low	High
Web security issues	Low	High
Privacy	Low	High

Source: Al-Ghofaili and Al-Mashari (2014).

The deployment of traditional ERP systems on local servers is one of the elements that has been contrasted between them and cloud-based ERP systems, as shown in table 3 above. However, because cloud-based ERP systems differ from traditional ERP systems in that data will be stored and supported by a third-party organization, privacy concerns will be added to the security issues with cloud-based ERP systems, which some organizations may find extremely concerning. Cloud-based ERP systems are implemented on cloud servers and all these need to be met by cloud providers for cloud-based ERP systems at a lesser cost than for traditional ERP systems. Networks, backup systems and other IT infrastructures should thus be implemented within the gold mining industries in contrast to traditional ERP systems and cloud-based ERP. Other advantages of adopting cloud computing ERP system in the mining sector include:

- Everything, from project management to worksite administration, may be integrated via an ERP system.
- Risk factors can be managed (Eales & Schoor, 2022)
- It can assist mining sector in the safety and environmental regulations. Large-scale investors can control their mine operations online thanks to ERP's online platform (Eales & Schoor, 2022)
- The mining sector may easily manage operations and create an international network of mines with the use of ERP software solution (Baramy, 2020; Nhleko & Neingo, 2020).

The Role of ERP Systems in Business Strategy

A software suite called ERP may recognize, gather, integrate, organize, stock, and process data from various departments inside a business, while also giving workers the information they require in a timely and relevant manner. ERP systems enable firms to react quickly to changes in the market by facilitating efficient operations and real-time data access. Businesses are able to quickly adjust their plans, seize new opportunities, and successfully manage risks because of their agility (Molina-Castillo et al., 2022). ERP systems also improve operational visibility by uniting different corporate operations, including supply chain, finance and customer relationship management, into a single platform (Pandey et al., 2022). With the help of this all-encompassing perspective, decision-makers can allocate resources more efficiently, cut expenses and enhance service quality, all of which provide their businesses a competitive edge (Alhalboosi et al., 2021). Furthermore, ERP systems give businesses access to cutting-edge reporting and analytics capabilities that reveal consumer and market trends. These systems help businesses to stay abreast with changing consumer demands and market dynamics by enabling proactive strategy modifications (Zafary, 2020).

Factors Affecting ERP Systems Implementation in the Gold Mining Sector

Factors affecting the ERP implementation include the cyber threat, implementation time, future strategy facilitation, shortage of highly skilled local worker force, cost of deployment, flexibility (Reactore, 2020; Sibanye, 2021; Tigunia, 2021) and are summarized as follows:

Cyber Threat

Organizations cannot adequately prepare for every cyber threat due to its fast-growing number. The following aspects need to be considered to keep ERP system and data security measures up to date. The first step in safeguarding the business, preventing a cyberattack and protecting your data is to comprehend the current ERP security environment (Force Intellect, 2020). To ensure that they implement the proper policies to increase security and protect their assets, businesses must thus recognize significant risk areas, attack routes, and vulnerabilities (Colajannie & Marchetti, 2021; Amra, 2021). Amra (2021) further expressed that due to the expanding level of innovation appropriation, the results of assaults on organizations in these segments can be far-reaching and possibly obliterating. It is imperative for businesses to get it key hazard ranges, assault vectors and vulnerabilities to guarantee that they utilize the proper controls to make strides security and secure their resources.

Implementation Time

The implementation of ERP system is a laborious procedure that is frequently undercut by businesses. Undoubtedly, setting up an ERP will be difficult and time-consuming. Miller (2022) concur that there may be a significant deal of ambiguity and other problems because of its implementation. But why is implementing an ERP such a daunting task? Many companies are unaware of how long adopting ERP takes. Since this is a challenging undertaking, the business should take every precaution to ensure that the method is flawless. By doing this, it is ensured that time is not squandered and that crucial business requirements are met (Eales & Schoor, 2022). To overcome the challenges of implementing ERP systems, the industries also need a dedicated project team to represent all clients on the ERP platform, highlighting the importance of business processes across various Information Technology (IT) infrastructures (Miller, 2022). However, any successful corporate expansion plan provides security protection, takes data security into account, and maintains regular software updates, all of which inevitably expose a company to security dangers.

Future Strategy Facilitation

Businesses typically choose an ERP vendor who can accommodate changes in both their current and upcoming business plans when choosing an ERP software. For example, mines always choose solutions that are in line with and support their business goals when they are considering adopting new technologies. These adjustments may be prompted by both internal and external factors, including as management goals, competitive pressures, consumer expectations, modifications to the legal and regulatory environment, as well as new disruptive business and technical demands and trends. Supporting operations and boosting mining competitiveness is achieved through effective business and IT strategy alignment, as noted by Bhatt, Guru and Thanki (2021).

Short of Highly Skilled Local Workforce

Successful implementation of ERP system requires training, and even if you have top-notch ERP software, it will be useless if users are not properly trained on how to use it (Bhatt, Guru & Thanki, 2021). System users and employees will fight against changes if they are not provided with enough training and support. Management and employees must not only attend the training sessions religiously but also convey and gain a thorough understanding (Bhatt, Guru & Thanki 2021). Employees will quickly accept change and work together if the organization can provide adequate training and support for a specific ERP system implementation. Businesses should therefore make sure that all users receive thorough training and assistance to facilitate their acceptance of the system (Eales & Schoor, 2022; Colajanni & Marchetti, 2021). Network protection and training on cybersecurity for all employees can also be beneficial. Although cybersecurity is most vulnerable to human error, however, a well-trained human makes fewer mistakes. Again, with the advent of phishing attacks and malware distribution, all ERP users need to be vigilant (Momoh, Roy & Shehab, 2020; Frontera. 2020; Bouchier,2022).

Cost of Development and Implementation

The costs associated with the implementation process include those for the trials that were run, consulting fees, software, hardware, databases, networking, skilled workers and licensing (Kassan, 2022). The cost advantage of transitioning to a cloud-based ERP stems from maintaining a strategic distance from the ought to contribute in equipment and capacity foundation such as high-end servers (Ediriweera & Wiewiora, 2022). Cloud-based ERP is regularly paid for through a month-to-month membership which incorporates computer program, facilitating and bolster costs. Capital consumption required for usage is subsequently lower than for a traditional on preface arrangement while bolster and working costs can be lower as well (Baramy, 2020; Fronteras, 2020).

Flexibility

In a time of quick technological advancements, escalating rivalry and globalization, organizations need to be flexible. While there are several definitions of flexibility, the ability to react correctly and quickly to changes in the environment of the company is the most common one. Thus, a flexible company is better able to respond to a wide range of external technological changes, competitor threats, consumer needs and governmental mandates without incurring unnecessary expenditures, unwarranted delays, organizational disruptions, or performance losses (Baramy, 2020; Fronteras, 2020). An ERP system for the mining industry should be able to grow along with the operation's needs and should make use of the most dependable technology while still being simple to use, it should also allow manufactures to respond to ongoing changes in their business and regulatory environment (Baramy, 2020; Fronteras, 2020). It is thus crucial to have an ERP system that can function anywhere, regardless of geography. Thin client technology has shown to be the most effective in locations with a restricted communications infrastructure, frequently where only satellite communication is possible (Eales & Schoor, 2022). An excellent user experience is made possible by thin client technology's low latency. In order to maximize the speed of data transfer between the site and the head office in a mining environment, you should ideally option for ERP software that uses few graphics and GUIs (Graphical User Interfaces) (South Africa Mining, 2017). With progressed innovation, ERP frameworks are a venture in operations, effectiveness, insights, and efficiency. This framework empowers producers to to be more profitable, more competitive and way better situated to meet customers' needs (Bouchier, 2022).

Challenges to Effective Implementation of the Cloud-Based ERP System in the Gold Mining Sector

When deploying new ERP systems to bolster bookkeeping, businesses encounter specific data issues as it takes more time and exertion to clean up amid ERP relocation due to the colossal volume of arrive possession, working intrigued, showcase contracts, and well data. across several departments. As a result, a lot of businesses encounter major implementation delays, which result in project cost overruns (Eales & Schoor, 2022) and dissatisfaction among the executive team and board of directors (Momoh, Roy & Shehab, 2020). Most mines function similarly and to truly differentiate itself and promote operational excellence, they must adopt a technology-centric strategy in which ERP solutions can be used to their full potential by integrating tools like Enterprise Asset Management (EAM) and Geographic Information Systems (GIS), to streamline processes like exploration and feasibility studies, improve operations and maintenance, and take care of regulatory compliance and financial analysis to consistently improve the lifecycle of a mine (Nupen, 2020). A mining industry can only operate from an integrated environment if it is flexible and quick to move in order to maximize production capacity and revenue. To offer decision-makers with the insights required to quickly form strategy, systems, processes and data must be integrated. It is best if mining businesses can start seeing a return on their investments as soon as possible (Lazarenko et. al., 2021; Armenta, 2021).

Intelligent mining is and will continue to affect not only the internal factors and elements of the organizational context of mining operators, such as the way decisions are made, the skills, knowledge, and capabilities that are needed, etc., but also the external linkages related to strategic collaborative relationships and networked interactions, i.e., how to engage with the workforce, local communities, and the other stakeholders to promote corporate responsibility (Armenta, 2021). From a technical standpoint, intelligent mining could be viewed as an integrated system that consists of automated mining equipment as the core, an integrated digital communication network as the carrier, an intelligent design and production management software system as a platform, and innovation-driven monitoring and control tools and techniques for the operational process management using real-time and dynamic data (Greeks, 2020; Miller, 2022; Nupen, 2020).

Strategies to Effective Implementation of Cloud-Based ERP Systems in the Gold Mining Sector

Mines frequently require to purchase hardware, ERP cloud software, storage, and network components for their cloud infrastructure. Adopting a cybersecurity system for steady distinguishing proof of basic cyber control crevices, dangers, and activities required to secure cyberspace is most important (Colajannie & Marchetti, 2021). The cybersecurity approach should thus be incorporated into the organization's digital transformation strategy. For the mining IT team to successfully access a threat, they must first establish the scope of the assessment, collect crucial data, identify potential vulnerabilities, evaluate any threats discovered, and carry out the desired threat analysis (Amra, 2021). Regular training of almost every employee in the organization will go a long way toward reducing the likelihood of a cyber-attack

(Bhatt, Guru & Thanki, 2021). It thus offers employees a sense of responsibility and alertness to potential risks and vulnerabilities.

Cyber risk insurance and response plan for cybersecurity are subject to regular evaluations and have a disaster recovery and business continuity plan in place. There are two essential elements that every mine ought to have in place, current and appropriate technologies to prevent intrusions, as well as a plan for responding to such attacks and insurance (Force intellect, (2020). Incoherent announcing frameworks ought to be supplanted with streamlined administration dashboards that report on real operational execution. As noted by Eales and Schoor (2022) training and development continue to be a strategic priority for the information and Communication Technologies (ICT) team. As part of Digital-first strategy, the organization should have designed a training and development program for ICT employees that focuses on the advancement of technologies that will be essential for the provision of ICT services, in their opinion (Colajanni & Marchetti, 2021). Level one education, which will include an introduction to digital transformation, Intelligence learning, and the Internet of Things, should be the requirement of every team member (Ediriweera & Wiewiora, 2021). Industries should focus more on process integration and optimisation which will encourages a more cohesive approach. Mining industries must frequently choose between purchasing an additional technology-enabled solution or replacing an expensive ERP system that is heavily customized. Additionally, many mining companies have inherited multiple ERP and other enterprise software systems from operating divisions they acquired along the way, and these systems overlap.

Table 3. The benefits of the implementation of ERP systems

Benefits of proper ERP system implementation	
Dimension	**Description**
Operational	Cost reduction (through e.g. improved timeliness of order fulfillment, effective calculation of profitability of individual purchases, automation of operations and activities, increased productivity through effective scheduling, verification of production plans and standards, reduction of inventories, rapid identification of cost-intensive activities, reduction of unnecessary or manual tasks), time reduction (through e.g. streamlining and acceleration of tasks, efficient acquisition of information in various cross sections and faster communication and response), improvement of quality (through e.g. control of entered data which reduces errors, greater accuracy, ongoing analysis of consumed resources).
Processes	Increasing the efficiency of business processes (through e.g. elimination of unnecessary activities, better use of resources and reduction of unnecessary costs through ongoing monitoring of their consumption, the ability to plan, monitor, verify and then reorganize internal and external processes, which enables faster response to changes in the environment), the ability to use ready-made business process templates and implement in them good practices used by companies that are leaders in their industry.
Data processing, document circulation and information flow	Acceleration of data processing (through e.g.: introduction of a centralized database, widespread validation of recorded data, unification of classifications, nomenclatures and registers in each organizational unit of the enterprise), increasing the speed of flow and availability of information in digital form, which improves cooperation between internal departments and contractors of the enterprise, improvement of security of processed data (e.g. by establishing data entry rules, unifying communication rules, precisely defining user roles and rights, which altogether increases the level of credibility of information resources), greater accuracy, reliability and transparency of information (the ability to define customized reports and statements, generate rules for document circulation and create legible documentation).
Management	Streamlining decision-making processes, improving the efficiency of managers' activities in the area of planning (through, for example, access to comprehensive data on the activities of the entire enterprise and its branches, the ability to create simulations and forecasts) and control (through, for example, ongoing monitoring, automatic generation of reports on the achievement of the assumed goals or exceeding the established norms and limits), and optimizing the management of tangible, intangible, financial and human resources (real-time access to comprehensive data on the current and past state of the enterprise and resources used).

continued on following page

Table 3. Continued

Benefits of proper ERP system implementation	
Dimension	**Description**
Strategic	Assisting in the implementation of digital transformation, support in the establishment of business alliances and links with external business partners and the implementation of new business models (e.g., implementation in the ERP system of different management methods, the ability to implement specific modules, define different powers and competencies of partners) and also facilitating the creation of business innovations (e.g. by analyzing and processing data and generating valuable information and knowledge, recording guidelines and effects of activities, exchanging data with partners) and providing business flexibility for current and future changes of the enterprise (dynamic adjustment of needs in terms of number of users, used modules and add-ons, etc.).
Organizational	Changing work performance patterns and transforming the enterprise into an organization that bases its activities on information, eliminating information asymmetry, strengthening the enterprise (e.g., a leader in digital transformation), developing user knowledge and competencies, building a common vision for the organization, facilitating organizational learning, moving toward an intelligent organization

Source: (Bitkowska, Dziembek & Gzik, 2024)

Using cloud-based ERP systems will significantly reduce overall operating expenses. Many tasks can be completely automated through the cloud, which in turn increases consistency in operations and lowers the likelihood of any equipment failures (Sishi & Telukdarie, 2020). As stated by Jiang and Wang (2024) mining companies can be much more adaptable by using cloud-based infrastructure, applications, and services because these services can be customized and adapted to their changing needs. Cloud computing will also standardize operations across disparate locations and help mining companies with multiple locations and centralized functions and controls. Mines can benefit from economies of scale by sharing their infrastructure across multiple locations as a result. Additionally, mining companies can move much more quickly because of standardization and centralization. ERP systems will probably integrate new technologies like artificial intelligence (AI), machine learning (ML), and the Internet of Things (IoT) as the business environment changes (Basu & Jha, 2024). With the help of these developments, their strategic competencies will be strengthened further and more advanced predictive analytics, automated decision-making, and customized client experiences will be possible.

CONCLUSION AND RECOMMENDATIONS

In order to gain a deeper comprehension of the adoption of cloud-based ERP in mining industries, this chapter makes significant contributions on the various types of ERP cloud-based system that can be used to solve the veracious data inaccuracy and lack of flow processes in operational strategic. ERP systems are crucial for maintaining corporate resilience and stimulating innovation in the context of the digital world. These solutions give businesses a uniform platform for real-time analytics and data integration, allowing them to quickly respond to changes in the market and new trends. These systems facilitate proactive decision-making, strategic planning, and operational simplification.

ERP systems also improve departmental collaboration by making sure that all teams are on the same page and prepared to tackle problems together. ERP solutions enable the adoption of new technologies, spurring innovation and competitive advantage in a time when digital transformation is critical. It is thus critical to invest in strong physical and digital infrastructure to guarantee the smooth operation and integration of cloud-based ERP SAP solutions in South African Gold Mining Industries. The results of ERP deployments are greatly influenced by a number of factors, including corporate culture, workforce readiness, data security issues, regulatory compliance, infrastructural limits, and workforce readiness. Management support for a cloud-based ERP system is lacking in mining industries, and there are unfavourable support contracts, and investments are not given priority were some of the problems mentioned as migration hurdles. This study found that despite these challenges and obstacles, there are still compelling reasons to use cloud-based ERP systems, including innovation, lower operating costs (within the bounds of sound economies of scale), flexibility prospects, and increased storage capacity. Considering all these factors, both clients and service providers believe a hybrid strategy incorporating a cloud-based ERP with the support services system would be beneficial. In addition to extensive training programs, mining businesses can improve workforce readiness and reduce resistance to change by cultivating a culture of creativity and adaptation.

It is thus imperative to give top priority to adhering to industry-specific regulations and data protection laws in order to secure confidential data and preserve stakeholder confidence. To guarantee consistency and adherence to standards, mining companies, technology vendors, and regulatory authorities must continue to communicate and work together. Future research can focus on examining all of mining industry and behavioural barriers to innovation adoption because the focus of this chapter was on ERP in the mining industry and environmental enablers and barriers. This chapter thus recommended the following focus areas, to ensure a successful transition to a cloud-based ERP system:

- To acquire and invest in essential cloud infrastructure components.
- To ease security, and regulatory compliance concerns with additional controls,

- To select a continuous improvement of ERP service provider and software equipment.
- To further do an in-depth investigation of large-scale gold mining to small medium enterprise mining

REFERENCES

Al-Ghofaili, A. A., & Al-Mashari, M. A. (2014). *ERP system adoption traditional ERP systems vs. cloud-based ERP systems. In Fourth edition of the International Conference on the Innovative Computing Technology* (INTECH 2014) (pp. 135-139). IEEE

Alhalboosi, F. H. A., Mawlood, S. J., & Al-halboosi, I. A. M. (2021). Role of ERP systems in improving human resources management processes. *Review of International Geographical Education Online*, 11(4), 1667–1681.

Amra, J. (2021). *Cyber threats are on the rise in these industries in South Africa. Business Tech,* 4 July. Available: https://businesstech.co.za/news/cloud-hosting/502645/cyber-threats-are-on-the-rise-in-these-industries-in-south-africa/

Armenta, A. (2021). *A Look into Automated Enterprise Resource Planning (ERP) Systems (article).* Available: https://control.com/technical-articles/A-Look-Into Automated-Enterprise-Resource-Planning-ERP-Systems/

Aroba, O. J. (2023). An ERP SAP Implementation: Case Study of the South African Small Medium Enterprise Sectors. *International Journal of Computing Sciences Research*, 7, 2196–2211. DOI: 10.25147/ijcsr.2017.001.1.155

Aroba, O. J., & Abayomi, A. (2023). An implementation of SAP enterprise resource planning–A case study of the South African revenue services and taxation sectors. *Cogent Social Sciences*, 9(1), 2228060. DOI: 10.1080/23311886.2023.2228060

Aroba, O. J., Chinsamy, K. K., & Makwakwa, T. G. (2022). *An ERP Implementation Case Study in the South African Retail Sector.InInternational Conference on Hybrid Intelligent Systems(pp.948-958).* Cham: Springer Nature Switzerland.

Aroba, O. J., Chisita, C. T., Buthelezi, N., & Mthethwa, N. (2023), February. Higher education enterprise resource planning system transformation of supply chain management processes. In *International Congress on Information and Communication Technology* (pp. 415-424). Singapore: Springer Nature Singapore.

Aroba, O. J., & Mnguni, S. B. (2023). An Enterprise Resource Planning (ERP) SAP Implementation: Case Study in South Africa Small Medium Enterprise Sectors. *InInternational Conference on Digital Technologies and Applications* (pp. 348-354). Cham: Springer Nature Switzerland. DOI: 10.1007/978-3-031-29857-8_35

Aroba, O.J., Owoputi . O., & Temitayo, M.F. (2023). An SAP enterprise resource planning implementation using a case study of a hospital management system for inclusion of digital transformation. *International Journal of Computer Information Systems and Industrial Management Applications,* 15

Aroba, O.J. & Prinavin, G. (2023). Improving supply chain management processes through digital transformation of ERP systems in the oil and gas industry. Interdisciplinary Journal of Economics and Business Law, 12 (3).

Asgharifard, P. (2022). *Digital Technology Adoption as a Factor to Build Supply Chain Resilience: The Case of an Animal-Food Supply Chain During the COVID-19 Pandemic Crisis* (Doctoral dissertation, Polytechnique Montréal).

Aulia, R., Putri, A. N., Raihan, M. F., Ayub, M., & Sulistio, J. (2019). The literature review of cloud-based enterprise resource planning. [IOP Publishing.]. *IOP Conference Series. Materials Science and Engineering*, 598(1), 012036. DOI: 10.1088/1757-899X/598/1/012036

Baramy, A. (2020). *Benefits of having Odoo ERP for the Mining Industry Bassam Infotech Best Mining Software* (wiki). Available: https://bassaminfotech.com/why-is-erp-essential-for-the-mining-industry-bassam-infotech-best-mining-software/

Basu, A., & Jha, R. (2024). ERP adoption prediction using machine learning techniques and ERP selection among SMEs. *International Journal of Business Performance Management*, 25(2), 242–270. DOI: 10.1504/IJBPM.2024.137005

Bhatt, N., Guru, S., Thanki, S., & Sood, G. (2021). Analysing the factors affecting the selection of ERP package: A fuzzy AHP approach. *Information Systems and e-Business Management*, 19(2), 641–682. DOI: 10.1007/s10257-021-00521-8

Bhattacharyya, S. S., & Shah, Y. (2022). Emerging technologies in Indian mining industry: An exploratory empirical investigation regarding the adoption challenges. *Journal of Science and Technology Policy Management*, 13(2), 358–381. DOI: 10.1108/JSTPM-03-2021-0048

Bill, B. (2021). *Common Digital Transformation Challenges and How to overcome them.* Available at: https://www.panorama-consulting.com/digital-transformation-challenges/

Bitkowska, A., Dziembek, D. & Gzik, T. (2024). Enterprise Resource Planning based on Cloud Computing (Cloud ERP). *Journal of Software & Systems Development, 2024.*

Bouchier, P. (2022). M*odern ERP Revolutionising Manufacturing Operations* (blog). Available: https://ioco.tech/modern-erp-revolutionising-manufacturing-operations

Colajanni, M., & Marchetti, M. (2021). Cyber-attacks and defences: current capabilities and future trends. In *Technology and International Relations* (pp. 132–151). Edward Elgar Publishing. DOI: 10.4337/9781788976077.00015

Cruz, E. (2022). *The traditional ERP system vs. a modern-day ERP system.* Frank Rimerman. (Online) Available at: https://www.frankrimerman.com/the-traditional-erp-system-vs-amodern-day-erp-syagement,stem/

du Venage, G. (2019). Strike at Sibanye-Stillwater Disrupts Operations. *Engineering and Mining Journal*, 220(1), 5–5.

Eales, L., & Van Schoor, J. (2022). *A slow adaptation and yet so many benefits* (wiki). Available at: https://www.africanmining.co.za/2022/05/03/robotics-a-slow-adoption-and-yet-so-many-benefits/

Ediriweera, A., & Wiewiora, A. (2021). Barriers and enablers of technology adoption in the mining industry. *Resources Policy*, 73, 102188. DOI: 10.1016/j.resourpol.2021.102188

Elbahri, F. M., Al-Sanjary, O. I., Ali, M. M., Naif, Z. A., Ibrahim, O. A., & Mohammed, M. N. (2019). Difference Comparison of SAP, Oracle, and Microsoft Solutions Based on Cloud ERP Systems. *RE:view*, 65–70. Advance online publication. DOI: 10.1109/CSPA.2019.8695976

Force intellect. (2020). *ERP Implementation Challenges & How to overcome them.* Available: https://forceintellect.com/2020/02/11/erp-implementation-challenges-overcome/

Fronteras, C. (2020). *Is a Cloud based ERP Deployment right for you?* (blog). Available at: https://www.redfaire.com/blog/is-a-cloud-based-erp-deployment-right-for-you

Gao, L. (2020). Exploring the data processing practices of cloud ERP-A case study. *Journal of Emerging Technologies in Accounting*, 17(1), 63–70. DOI: 10.2308/jeta-52680

Golarz, M. (2017). Wykorzystanie systemu klasy ERP w logistyce przedsiębiorstw. *Journal of Modern Management Process*, 2(1), 18–29.

Greeks, I. (2020). *Differences between ERP and SAP.* Available at: https://www.geeksforgeeks.org/differences-between-erp-and-sap/?ref=lbp (Accessed 25 March 2023).

Gruenhagen, J. H., & Parker, R. (2020). Factors driving or impeding the diffusion and adoption of innovation in mining: A systematic review of the literature. *Resources Policy*, 65, 101540. DOI: 10.1016/j.resourpol.2019.101540

Guo, Y. (2021). *Transformation from On-Premise Software to Cloud Computing-Based Services: A Case Study of SAP Practices*. The University of Manchester.

Haddara, M., Gøthesen, S., & Langseth, M. (2022). Challenges of cloud-ERP adoptions in SMEs. *Procedia Computer Science*, 196, 973–981. DOI: 10.1016/j.procs.2021.12.099

Jiang, P. H. W., & Wang, W. Y. C. (2024). Comparison of SaaS and IaaS in cloud ERP implementation: The lessons from the practitioners. *VINE Journal of Information and Knowledge Management Systems*, 54(3), 683–701. DOI: 10.1108/VJIKMS-10-2021-0238

Kassan, H. (2022). *ERP becomes the cornerstone of S.A. mining sector*. Available at: https://www.crown.co.za/modern-mining/insights/20487-erp-becomes-the-cornerstone-of-sa-mining-sector

Kshetri, N. (2022). *Chapter 3: Combining with other technologies to amplify blockchains value creation in: The Rise of Blockchains,* 3, 56-73.

Lazarenko, Y., Garafonova, O., Marhasova, V., & Tkalenko, N. (2021). Digital transformation in the mining sector: Exploring global technology trends and managerial issues. In *E3S Web of Conferences*, 315, 04006. EDP Sciences.

Margherita, A., Nasiri, M., & Papadopoulos, T. (2023). The application of digital technologies in company responses to COVID-19: An integrative framework. *Technology Analysis and Strategic Management*, 35(8), 979–992. DOI: 10.1080/09537325.2021.1990255

Mkubukeli, Z. & Tengeh, R.K. (2016). Prospects and challenges for small-scale mining entrepreneurs in South Africa.

Mokalapa, P. M., Oyedokun, G. E., & Fowokan, T. E. I. (2024). Effect of Corporate Governance Practices on the Performance of an Established Medium-Sized Enterprise in the Mining Industry in South Africa. *Small Business Accounting Management and Entrepreneurship Review*, 4(1), 17–33. DOI: 10.61656/sbamer.v4i1.144

Molina-Castillo, F. J., Rodríguez, R., López-Nicolas, C., & Bouwman, H. (2022). The role of ERP in business model innovation: Impetus or impediment. *Digital Business*, 2(2), 100024. DOI: 10.1016/j.digbus.2022.100024

Momoh, A., Roy, R., & Shehab, E. (2010). Challenges in enterprise resource planning implementation: State-of-the-art. *Business Process Management Journal*, 16(4), 537–565. DOI: 10.1108/14637151011065919

Mourtzis, D., & Panopoulos, N. (2022). Digital transformation process towards resilient production systems and networks. In *Supply Network Dynamics and Control* (pp. 11–42). Springer International Publishing. DOI: 10.1007/978-3-031-09179-7_2

Naorib, (2021). Department of Higher Education and Training. *White paper for Chainlink 2.0: Next Steps in the Evolution of Decentralized Oracle Networks.*

Nararya, S., Saputra, M., & Puspitasari, W. (2021). Automation in Financial Reporting by using Predictive Analytics in SAP Analytics Cloud for Gold Mining Industry: a Case Study. In *2021 International Conference on ICT for Smart Society (ICISS)* (pp. 1-6). IEEE. DOI: 10.1109/ICISS53185.2021.9532504

Nhleko, S., & Neingo, P. (2020). Financial Performance of Johannesburg Securities Exchange Traded Gold Mining Companies: Du Pont and Economic Value-Added Analyses. In: *Proceedings of the 28th International Symposium on Mine Planning and Equipment Selection-MPES 2019. 28*,333-345. Springer International Publishing. DOI: 10.1007/978-3-030-33954-8_41

Niranga, M., & Wickramarachchi, R. (2020). A Model for On-Premises ERP System and Cloud ERP Integration. *International Conference on Industrial Engineering and Operations Management.*

Nupen, L. (2020). *Mining in South Africa: Industry challenges in 2020.* Available at: https://www.miningreview.com/gold/mining-in-south-africa-industry-challenges-in-2020/

Oyewole, A. T., Adeoye, O. B., Addy, W. A., Okoye, C. C., Ofodile, O. C., & Ugochukwu, C. E.Adedoyin Tolulope OyewoleOmotayo Bukola AdeoyeWilhelmina Afua AddyChinwe Chinazo OkoyeOnyeka Chrisanctus OfodileChinonye Esther Ugochukwu. (2024). Automating financial reporting with natural language processing: A review and case analysis. *World Journal of Advanced Research and Reviews*, 21(3), 575–589. DOI: 10.30574/wjarr.2024.21.3.0688

Pandey, A. K., Singh, R. K., Jayesh, G. S., Khare, N., & Gupta, S. K. (2022). Examining the role of enterprise resource planning (ERP) in improving business operations in companies. *ECS Transactions*, 107(1), 2681–2696. DOI: 10.1149/10701.2681ecst

Phoshoko, D. (2021). *Advancing technology use in the mining industry. Mining news, 20 October.* Available at: https://miningnews.co.za/2021/10/20/advancing-technology-use-in-the-mining-industry/s

Reactore. (2020). *Effectiveness of ERP systems in mining.* Available at: https://reactore.com/archives/blog/effectiveness-of-erp-systems-in-mining

Resulting, I. T. (2022). *Why is Adoption so important in ERP projects*. Available at: https://www.resulting-it.com/erp-fundamentals/erp-adoption-project-success

Sibanye Stillwater. (2021). *Integrated Report* 2021. Global. Available at: https://reports.sibanyestillwater.com/2021/download/SSW-IR21-03.pdf

Silase, M. (2018). *An assessment of factors influencing successful implementation of ERP in a mining industry: An investigation into the possibility of integrating Oracle ERP system with the Lean Six Sigma philosophy in a mining operation, using them in collaboration with industry 4.0* (Doctoral dissertation, University of Johannesburg (South Africa)).

Sishi, M., & Telukdarie, A. (2020). Implementation of industry 4.0 technologies in the mining industry: Case study. *International Journal of Mining and Mineral Engineering*, 11(1), 1–22. DOI: 10.1504/IJMME.2020.105852

South Africa Mining. (2017). *The mining ERP specialist. White paper on what to consider when implementing a mining ERP solution.pdf,* pp. 7.

Syed, Z. A., Dapaah, E., Mapfaza, G., Remias, T., & Mupa, M. N. (2024). Enhancing supply chain resilience with cloud-based ERP systems. *IRE Journals*, 8(2), 106–128.

Tigunia, S. (2021). *8 Common ERP Security Problems and How to resolve them.* Available at: https://tigunia.com/blog/8-common-erp-security-problems-and-how-to-resolve-them/

Zafary, F. (2020). Implementation of business intelligence considering the role of information systems integration and enterprise resource planning. *Journal of intelligence studies in business,* 1(1).

Chapter 7
Innovation Management Landscape for Digital Economy Transformation Through Innovation Resilience in Ethiopia

Metasebia Adula
https://orcid.org/0000-0001-5732-2850
Bule Hora University, Ethiopia

Shashi Kant
https://orcid.org/0000-0003-4722-5736
Bule Hora University, Ethiopia

Haro Duloma Geda
Bule Hora University, Ethiopia

ABSTRACT

This chapter explores the role that innovation resilience techniques play as a mediator in the link that exists between Ethiopia's digital economy's transformational potential and the innovation management environment. A survey was conducted with 400 participants, comprising digital economy specialists, innovation ecosystem players, and technology entrepreneurs. To find the underlying dimensions, exploratory factor analysis (EFA) and confirmatory factor analysis (CFA) were used. The data's appropriateness for factor analysis was evaluated using Bartlett's test of sphericity and the Kaiser-Meyer-Olkin (KMO) measure of sampling adequacy. The mediating function of innovation resilience methods was then investigated using structural

DOI: 10.4018/979-8-3693-8357-5.ch007

equation modeling (SEM). The study's conclusions provide direction for Ethiopian players in the digital economy about how to best take advantage of the connections between innovation resilience, innovation management, and the transformative potential of the sector to promote sustainable development.

INTRODUCTION

The digital economy is significantly shaped by the innovation management environment, especially in creating countries such as Ethiopia. Like in developed economies like in Italy, Germany where industrial revolution started in early 1990s. It's becoming more and more important to comprehend how innovation management may spark revolutionary potential as the world economy shifts toward digitalization (Endalamaw & Darr, 2021). But in Ethiopia, a country setting out on an delayed ambitious route toward fiscal modernization, this chapter examines the complex interplay between innovation resilience tactics and their mediating influence on the transformational potential of the digital economy (Wang et al., 2024). The notion of innovation management originated in the early 1900s, when industrial management ideas gave way to a more comprehensive comprehension of how companies may cultivate an innovative culture (Birhane et al., 2024). The relevance of this subject has increased globally especially in postmodern economies like Japan, Israel and India because to the advent of digital technology, which has given organizations the opportunity to use innovative methods to improve their competitiveness and flexibility. But a new economy like Ethiopia needs a innovation base to grow and survive. Innovation management is not simply a theoretical concept but also a practical requirement for negotiating the complexity of a quickly evolving digital ecosystem in Ethiopia, where the economy is experiencing significant transition (Ferede et al., 2024).

The crucial role that innovation resilience plays in promoting fiscal creation and adaptation is highlighted by empirical literature. Research indicates that companies that foster resilience are more equipped to handle shifts in the market and technological upheavals. But much of the study that has been done so far has been on industrialized economies, which leaves a vacuum in our knowledge of how these ideas may be successfully implemented in Ethiopia. Ethiopia's distinct sociofiscal problems—such as its inadequate infrastructure, restricted access to technology, and disparate educational attainment—present real-world obstacles that call for specialized innovative approaches (Benfica et al., 2023). There are still large research gaps in the digital economy, despite the growing interest in it. The exact ways in which innovation resilience techniques moderate the link between innovation management and digital fiscal transformation in Ethiopia are not well supported by empirical data. Furthermore, a lot of the discussion has ignored how institutional and cultural elements specific to a community affect innovative processes (Abate et al., 2023). By offering a thorough examination of the relationship between innovation management and Ethiopia's digital economy—based on both theoretical frameworks and empirical data—this chapter seeks to close these gaps. Through an analysis of Ethiopia's innovation landscape's prospects and difficulties, this chapter will provide future scholars and policymakers with nuanced insights. It will showcase doable tactics that can strengthen innovation resilience and support long-term, steady fiscal creation. It will also provide a road map for incorporating regional settings into innovation management techniques, guaranteeing that tactics are not only workable but also culturally appropriate.

BACKGROUND OF THE STUDY

The demands of a global marketplace that is changing quickly have made the need for innovation management more and more clear. Traditional ways of operation are not up to pace (Endalamaw & Darr, 2021). This background studies like in Nigeria, Angola and Rwanda lays the groundwork for a more thorough investigation of the ways in which innovation resilience methods might mediate the connection between innovation management and the transformational potential of the digital economy (Nege & Kero, 2024). Ethiopian businesses must be flexible and adaptable since they frequently deal with erratic market conditions and rapid technical improvements. Thus, for local organizations hoping to prosper in the digital economy, understanding innovation resilience becomes crucial (Duale, 2024). Additionally, the digital economy itself offers a variety of opportunities, such as digital finance and e-commerce, which have a big influence on employment, productivity, and total fiscal progression. However, a deliberate approach to innovation management is required for the successful integration of digital technology into conventional sectors. Empirical research suggests that nations with efficient innovation management systems are better equipped to capitalize on the advantages of the digital economy. However, a large portion of the study like in Nigeria, Angola and Rwanda has been carried out in settings that are more created, creating a knowledge vacuum on how these principles directly relate to Ethiopia and other creating countries (Benfica et al., 2023).

There are also several practical difficulties. Insufficient financing for innovation efforts, a shortage of competent workers, and restricted access to sophisticated technology are major challenges faced by several Ethiopian enterprises (Guye et al., 2024). The implementation of efficient innovation management techniques is hampered by these difficulties. Another degree of complication is added by Ethiopia's social terrain, which includes differing attitudes toward innovation and change. In order to create efficient frameworks that can spearhead the digital transformation, it is essential to comprehend how these aspects affect innovation resilience tactics (Ochinanwata et al., 2024). By offering a thorough examination of the variables driving innovation management in Ethiopia's creating digital economy, this research seeks to close these gaps. This research will add to the larger conversation on innovation and fiscal progression by analyzing the particular difficulties and possibilities faced by Ethiopia. It will also provide useful and practical insights for corporate executives and politicians.

STATEMENT OF THE PROBLEM

In a perfect world, like in Nigeria, Angola, Rwanda and Ethiopian companies would use technology innovations to boost production, spur fiscal expansion, and generate employment opportunities. Current data, however, points to a substantial gap between local businesses' real ability to innovate and adapt and the promise of the digital economy (Endalamaw & Darr, 2021). Many firms struggle to use effective innovation management techniques because of things like restricted access to technology, poor infrastructure, and a lack of trained staff. This circumstance draws attention to a crucial issue: how can Ethiopia foster an innovative environment that is robust and consistent with its creational objectives (Ferede et al., 2024). The situation is made more difficult by conflicting evidence. There is a dearth of empirical evidence from Ethiopia that is comparable to the many studies that show the beneficial effects of innovation management on fiscal progression in Western nations. Some studies claim that a small number of innovative companies have found success with digital transformation; nevertheless, they are frequently the exception rather than the rule. This disparity suggests that the success of current innovation initiatives in the Ethiopian environment has yielded conflicting results. There are still theoretical gaps. A large portion of the literature on innovation management that is now available is based on Western paradigms, which may not fully represent the distinct socio-fiscal and cultural dynamics that exist in Ethiopia (Benfica et al., 2023).

Furthermore, there are large gaps in context and understanding. Although a great deal of study has been done on innovation resilience in different international contexts, there aren't many papers that really discuss how these ideas might be depicted in Ethiopia. Furthermore, not enough research has been done on the impact of regional cultural characteristics on innovative activities. Policymakers and corporate leaders are unable to make well-informed decisions that are appropriate to culture and context due to a lack of localized information like in Nigeria, Angola and Rwanda (Kant & Adula, 2024).

In the context of Ethiopia's digital economy, this study attempts to close the gaps by offering a thorough examination of the link between innovation resilience techniques and innovation management (Jabo et al., 2023). Through the synthesis of theoretical frameworks and actual data, this study will provide insights into how local enterprises might more effectively traverse their particular issues. It will also investigate culturally aware methods that might improve innovation processes, adding to a deeper comprehension of the dynamics at work in Ethiopia. The ultimate goal of this effort is to educate future scholars and decision-makers by offering practical suggestions that can direct the creation of innovative approaches that are successful and appropriate for Ethiopia. By doing this, it would make clear routes for long-term, steady fiscal progression in the digital era and establish Ethiopia as a competitive

THEORETICAL FOUNDATION

Everett Rogers' "Diffusion of Innovations Theory" is one fundamental hypothesis. This theory investigates the how, why, and pace at which novel concepts and innovations proliferate within a society. Understanding the diffusion process is essential for promoting digital technology and creating an innovative culture in Ethiopia, where traditional methods frequently predominate (Benfica et al., 2023; Asefa et al., 2023). The aforementioned theory places significant emphasis on social structures, communication routes, and the perceived qualities of innovations. These elements can aid in identifying obstacles to adoption and devising tactics to promote acceptance among nearby firm (Adula et al., 2024). The "Resource-Based View" or RBV, that proclaims that a firm's competitive advantage is engendered from its possessions and competences, is additional pertinent notion. This approach emphasizes how important it is to create internal innovation management capabilities in Ethiopian contexts. Ethiopian businesses may improve their resistance to innovation by utilizing special resources including human capital, adaptability, and local expertise. The RBV advises enterprises to put more effort into strengthening their capacity for innovation than just implementing foreign technology, which might not be suitable for the demands or circumstances in the local area (Benfica et al., 2023).

The concept of "Dynamic Capabilities Theory," which emphasizes an organization's capacity to integrate, create, and reconfigure internal and external competences in response to quickly changing circumstances, further enhances the conversation. This idea is especially helpful for Ethiopian businesses negotiating the unstable digital economy. It emphasizes the value of flexibility and agility and makes the case that, in order for businesses to be competitive; they must constantly change their business plans and operational way of doings. This is in line with the requirement for innovation resilience as businesses need to be ready for issues in the future as well as react to external forces (Guyo et al., 2023). Another important component of this discussion is "Open Innovation Theory." This thesis, which was put out by Henry Chesbrough, holds that companies may and need to employ both internal and external ideas and routes to market in order to progress their technology and innovation. Adopting an open innovation strategy may help Ethiopian businesses collaborate with regional and international partners, promoting information sharing that can spur innovation. This is especially crucial in poor countries where resources and knowledge may be scarce (Dereso et al., 2023).

DEFINITION OF CONCEPTS

The term *"innovation management"* depicted the step by step way of doing that a firm uses to create, implement in practice, and augment novelties. It contains all phases of the invention lifespan (Ferede et al., 2024), marketing, organizational behavior, and other disciplines are integrated into innovation management today to provide a unified strategy that helps businesses prosper in changing conditions (Durga et al., 2024).

The term *"digital economy,"* as depicted by diverse professors, states to the greater effects of digital technology on consumer behavior, corporate operations, and general fiscal structures in addition to online transactions (Durga et al., 2024). The digital economy has been identified by the World Bank and other international organizations as a critical component of treatment, with the ability to spur fiscal progression, efficiency, and innovation, especially in creating nations such as Ethiopia (Nyoach et al., 2024).

The term "*innovation resilience*" depicted an organization's capacity to modify its innovation plans in the face of outside obstacles and disruptions, guaranteeing its ongoing expansion and competitiveness (Adula et al., 2023). Resilience emphasizes the value of adaptability, learning, and flexibility in the context of innovation, allowing businesses to prosper in the face of uncertainty and change (Asefa et al., 2023. This idea is especially important in emerging nations with unstable and uncertain markets, like Ethiopia (Benfica et al., 2023).

EMPIRICAL LITERATURE REVIEW

Innovation Management Landscape and Digital Economy Transformative Potential

According to research, a nation's capacity to use digital technology for fiscal progression is largely dependent on how well it manages innovation. Research like that done by Kant & Adula (2024) highlights that companies that use step by step methods to innovation—which include ideation, creation, and execution—are more likely to benefit from digital opportunities. Moreover, actual data indicates that the digital economy has a substantial influence on a number of industries by increasing efficiency and production. According to Benfica et al. (2023), digital technologies have the power to revolutionize established sectors of the economy and generate new jobs and higher productivity. The authors also note that not all businesses will profit equally from digitization; those that don't innovate risk falling behind and worsening fiscal inequality. This difference emphasizes how crucial innovation management is as a strategic requirement for businesses hoping to succeed in the digital era. Empirical research in the Ethiopian setting is scarce but expanding. A study by Panighagi et al (2023) examines the difficulties Ethiopian businesses have using digital and e-commerce technology. Their results show that inadequate infrastructure and a shortage of qualified workers severely impede innovation initiatives. Jabo et al. (2024) study emphasizes the necessity of customized innovation methods that take into account regional institutional and cultural circumstances. They contend that attempts to incorporate digital technology into conventional industries may fail if these distinctive elements are not understood.

Furthermore, the idea of innovation resilience is becoming more widely acknowledged as being essential to the success of innovation management. Organizations with high innovation resilience—defined by flexibility, learning orientation, and proactive change management—are more likely to flourish in dynamic contexts, according to empirical research like those conducted by Ndulu et al. (2023). This resilience becomes especially crucial in emerging environments, as businesses could deal with erratic market circumstances and quick changes in technology. Progression or stagnation may depend on one's capacity to adapt and innovate in the face of these shifts. Despite these realizations, there are still a lot of unanswered questions in the empirical literature, especially when it comes to how innovation resilience techniques mediate the link between innovation management and the transformational potential of the digital economy. Although these ideas have been the subject of several studies, further in-depth investigation is required to determine how innovation resilience might improve efficient innovation management techniques in the Ethiopian setting. This disparity emphasizes how crucial it is to do more empirical research in order to have a better understanding of how small businesses might handle the challenges presented by the digital economy.

Innovation Management Landscape and Innovation Resilience Strategies

Ndulu et al. (2023) research emphasizes that companies with strong frameworks for innovation management are more suited to create resilience. This shows that the practice of innovation management involves more than just creating new goods; it also involves creating an adaptable attitude like studies in Nigeria, Angola and Rwanda, which is essential for resilience. Furthermore, it is impossible to overestimate the importance of leadership in promoting innovation resilience. Research by Birhane et al. (2024) provides empirical evidence that an organization's capacity for innovation is greatly enhanced by transformational leadership styles that promote experimentation and risk-taking. Building resilience requires teams to be able to explore new ideas without fear of failure, which is made possible by leaders who foster a climate that is supportive of innovation. This leadership style is essential for building a resilient innovation culture in volatile conditions, such those that many businesses in emerging economies experience.

Empirical studies are starting to highlight the unique potential and problems associated with resilience and innovation management in the context of creating countries. Ethiopian businesses frequently deal with a shortage of trained workers, poor infrastructure, and restricted finances, according to research by Ferede et al. (2024). Notwithstanding these obstacles, the study discovered that companies may strengthen their resistance to outside shocks like technology disruptions or fiscal downturns by managing their innovation processes well. This research suggests that resilience is a function of both strategic management techniques and resources, underscoring the need of customized innovation methods that fit local settings. Furthermore, a research conducted in 2024 by Guyo et al. looks into the ways Ethiopian businesses might use digital technology to improve their capacity for innovation management. The results show that companies using digital tools for innovation management are better able to adapt as well as simplify their operations. For example, the application of data analytics can yield insights that facilitate well-informed decision-making, allowing firms to swiftly adjust to changes in the market. This emphasizes a crucial connection, especially in light of the digital transition, between improved innovation resilience and efficient innovation management.

Innovation Resilience Strategies and Digital Economy Transformative Potential

Ndulu et al. (2023) manifested that companies that adopt resilience techniques, for example, can better accept new digital tools and way of doings by cultivating a culture of continuous learning and promoting teamwork. Their capacity to adapt not only allows companies to withstand upheavals but also to take advantage of progression and innovation possibilities, ultimately increasing their potential for transformation in the digital world. The contribution of innovation resilience to improving competitive advantage in the digital economy has also been the subject of empirical research. Organizations that give resilience top priority in their innovation strategy have a higher chance of outperforming their rivals in dynamic situations, according to Peter (2021). These companies have the agility to swiftly adapt to shifts in the market, incorporate novel technology, and introduce inventive goods that satisfy changing customer needs. Consequently, the capacity to cultivate innovation resilience emerges as a crucial differentiator, enabling enterprises to leverage the revolutionary opportunities presented by the digital economy.

The empirical research suggests that innovation resilience methods are especially important for managing the particular hurdles that emerging economies, like Ethiopia, encounter. Assefa et al. research from 2023 demonstrates how Ethiopian businesses, who are frequently hindered by a lack of resources and inadequate infrastructure, may gain a great deal from innovation resilience. According to the study, putting resilience-depicted tactics into practice—like forming alliances with nearby colleges and taking part in community-based innovation projects—can improve businesses' capacity for innovation and adaptation. This flexibility allows organizations to get over obstacles and take advantage of local possibilities, which is crucial for using digital technology to achieve fiscal transformation. Furthermore, when businesses embrace a comprehensive approach to innovation resilience, the digital economy's revolutionary potential is enhanced. A thorough analysis by Peter (2021) shows how businesses may improve their resilience more effectively when they incorporate digital technologies into their innovation processes. Organizations may make better decisions by using data analytics, for instance, which give them insights into customer behavior and industry trends. These competencies enhance operational effectiveness and put businesses in a better position to innovate, which opens up the digital economy's transformational potential.

Innovation Management Landscape, Digital Economy Transformative Potential and Innovation Resilience

According to studies by Peter (2021), businesses that have strong frameworks for innovation management are better suited to handle the challenges presented by the digital economy. Fostering a culture of resilience requires structured way of doings for idea generation, creation, and implementation—all of which are integral to effective innovation management. Companies that place a high value on cross-functional teams and collaborative settings, for example, are more likely to provide creative solutions that adapt to changing market demands. The potential for the digital economy to transform is increased when innovation management and resilience-building techniques are aligned, making firms more adaptable and change-responsive. Furthermore, empirical data points to the role of innovation resilience as a mediator in the connection between innovation management and the transformational potential of the digital economy. According to research by Ndulu et al. (2023), organizations that foster innovation resilience—which is typified by flexibility, a learning orientation, and proactive change management—are better equipped to make successful use of digital technology. These businesses may increase their capacity for innovation by incorporating new tools and way of doings into their current operations. This mediation effect shows that whereas innovation management prepares the way for change, resilience strategies allow businesses to take full use of the opportunities presented by the digital economy.

The empirical research highlights particular potential and concerns associated with this dynamic in emerging environments such as Ethiopia. According to a research by Ferede et al. (2024), Ethiopian businesses frequently struggle with restricted access to resources and infrastructure limitations, which might hinder their capacity for innovation. On the other hand, individuals who use innovation resilience tactics—like cultivating alliances with nearby academic establishments and participating in community-driven innovation—can improve their flexibility. This flexibility is essential for negotiating the challenges of the digital economy and, eventually, for propelling fiscal change. The results imply that resilience measures integrated into innovation management techniques might greatly enhance the transformational potential of digital technology in these contexts. Furthermore, Wang et al. (2024) research emphasizes how critical it is to comprehend the institutional and cultural context of a place in order to effectively manage innovation and foster resilience. Their results show that businesses have a higher chance of successfully utilizing digital technologies when they modify their innovation strategy to fit local settings. Businesses are better able to adapt to unique opportunities and difficulties in their settings because to this localized strategy, which increases resilience. Therefore, in order to fully realize the revolutionary potential of the digital economy, it becomes imperative to integrate innovation management methods with context-specific resilience measures.

CONCEPTUAL FRAMEWORK

On base of empirical studies conceptual framework is proposed as depicted under figure 1.

Figure 1. Conceptual framework

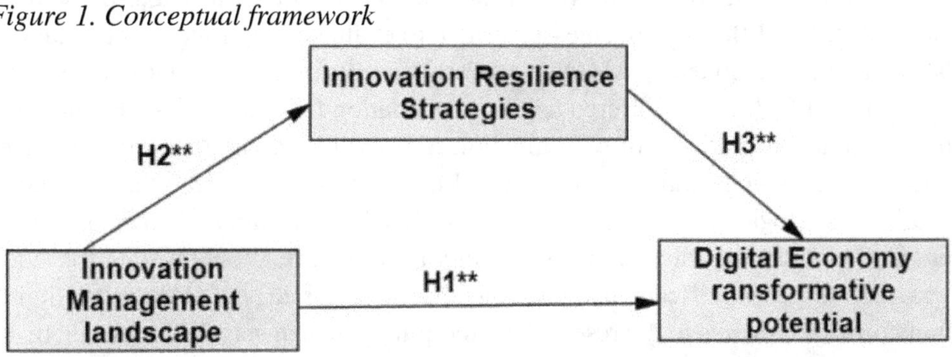

RESEARCH METHODOLOGY

This study's research technique was quantitative, and data from a sample of 390 respondents was gathered via a structured survey. The statistical examination of the connections between innovation resilience methods, innovation management, and the transformational potential of the digital economy was made possible by this methodology. Stratified sampling was employed in the sample selection process to guarantee representation from a range of sectors and organizational sizes in Ethiopia, therefore improving the findings' generalizability. The study depicted exploratory factor analysis (EFA) and the Kaiser-Meyer-Olkin (KMO) test to verify the measuring equipment. The KMO measure verified if the data was appropriate for the planned analyses by indicating whether the sample size was sufficient for factor analysis. After that, EFA was carried out to determine the fundamental factor structure of the scales created for the study. This step was essential in confirming that the items related to innovation management, innovation resilience, and digital economy transformations were accurately capturing the constructs intended for investigation.

The scales were created after a thorough analysis of relevant literature. Pre-existing frameworks and metrics from earlier research were modified to account for Ethiopia's unique setting and the subtleties of the digital economy. For instance, Schilling (2017) and Bessant and Tidd (2015) created established models from which the innovation management items were derived. These models depicted on aspects like idea creation, implementation way of doings, and cross-functional cooperation. Similar to this, studies emphasizing adaptation and learning orientation helped shape the innovation resilience scale, which took into account the particular difficulties encountered by Ethiopian businesses. Then, to evaluate the proposed correlations between the components, AMOS software was utilized for structural equation modeling, or SEM. SEM offered a strong foundation for data analysis by enabling the simultaneous analysis of several connections while taking measurement error into account. This technique was depicted in the study to evaluate the innovation resilience strategies' mediating function in the link between innovation management practices and the digital economy's capacity for transformation. Overall, the study was able to get significant insights into the variables driving Ethiopia's digital transformation thanks to the research methodology, which was distinguished by its quantitative approach and rigorous analytical tools. A thorough knowledge of the links between the constructs was made possible by the combination of KMO, EFA, and SEM, which helped to give a nuanced view on how innovation management and resilience strategies interact within the evolving landscape of the digital economy.

DATA ANALYSIS

Researchers used the Bartlett's Test of Sphericity and the Kaiser-Meyer-Olkin (KMO) measure to check sampling adequacy. The high KMO score validates the applicability of the selected approach by showing that the variables in the dataset have sufficient correlations to support factor analysis.

Table 1. KMO and Bartlett's Test

Kaiser-Meyer-Olkin Measure of Sampling Adequacy.		**.893**
Bartlett's Test of Sphericity	Approx. Chi-Square	2841.052
	df	106
	Sig.	.000

Source: Authors

The findings of the Bartlett's Test of Sphericity and the Kaiser-Meyer-Olkin (KMO) measure of sampling adequacy are shown in Table 1, which are important markers for determining if the data are appropriate for factor analysis. Given that the KMO value of 0.893 is far higher than the suggested threshold of 0.6, it is suggested that the sample size is sufficient for factor analysis. Furthermore, an estimated Chi-Square value of 2841.052 with 106 degrees of freedom and a significance level (Sig.) of 0.000 were obtained using Bartlett's Test of Sphericity. Given that the p-value is less than 0.05, this result clearly suggests that the correlation matrix is not an identity matrix. As a result, this implies that the variables have substantial connections with one another, hence bolstering the validity of component analysis. All of these findings support the exploratory factor analysis suitability of the dataset, enabling a significant investigation of the underlying concepts pertaining to innovation resilience, innovation management, and the revolutionary potential of the digital economy.

Table 2. Total variance explained

Component	Initial Eigenvalues			Extraction Sums of Squared Loadings			Rotation Sums of Squared Loadings		
	Total	% of Variance	Cumulative %	Total	% of Variance	Cumulative %	Total	% of Variance	Cumulative %
1	4.2	32.4	32.4	4.7	32.4	32.4	3.2	21.6	21.6
2	1.5	9.9	42.2	1.5	9.9	42.2	2.3	15.6	36.9
3	1.4	9.2	52.1	1.4	9.2	52.1	2.1	14.3	52.1
4	.96	6.9	58.1						

Extraction Method: Principal Component Analysis.
Source: Authors

The findings of the exploratory factor analysis are shown in Table 2, which provides a detailed explanation of the total variance accounted for by the components found using principal component analysis. Four components were identified, according to the original eigenvalues, with the first component explaining 32.4% of the variation in total. This high percentage indicates that a considerable amount of the underlying structure in the data is captured by this component. When combined, the first two components account for a sizable portion of the entire variation, as seen by the cumulative variance explained by them reaching 42.2%. 52.1% is the cumulative sum of the variances from the first three components (the second contributes 9.9% and the third, 9.2%). This indicates that these three factors account for more than half of the variance in the dataset, highlighting their significance in the explanation of the concepts associated with innovation resilience and management. Although it does not considerably contribute to the cumulative variance when compared to the first three components, the fourth component, with an eigenvalue of 0.96 and a contribution of 6.9% to the variance, further validates the multidimensional character of the data. With the first three components maintaining their explanatory power, the extraction sums of squared loadings verify that the discovered components hold true after extraction. The distribution of variation among the components is also shown by the rotation sums of squared loadings, which show that although the first component continues to be dominating, the other factors also contribute to the explanation of variance.

Confirmatory Principle Component

A kind of statistics called confirmatory principle component analysis is depicted to confirm the principle component organization of a group of directed proxies. Investigations can assess hypotheses using CFA based on the underlying frame job and correlatives among observable proxies. The investigation depicted CFA under table 3 in order to assess the hypothesis that there is a relationship between the proxies that are being guided and the latent ideas that support them.

Table 3. Covariances

Covariance			Estimate	S.E.	C.R.	P	Hy.
Innovation Resilience Strategies	**<-->**	**Innovation Management landscape**	**.378**	**.104**	**3.634**	**.00**	**H2**
Innovation Resilience Strategies	<-->	Digital Economy transformative potential	.563	.183	3.076	.00	**H3**
Innovation Management landscape	<-->	Digital Economy transformative potential	.457	.182	2.511	.00	**H1**

Source: Authors

The covariances between the digital economy's transformational potential, the innovation management environment, and the constructions of innovation resilience techniques are shown in Table 3. The covariances provide information on the direction and intensity of the links between these important variables and how they interact with one another within the study's framework. Innovation resilience strategies and the innovation management landscape have a covariance of 0.378 with a critical ratio (C.R.) of 3.634 and a standard error (S.E.) of.104. Together with a p-value of 0.00, this substantial C.R. value points to a strong positive association between these two constructs. The hypothesis (H2) with a p-value of 0.00 that improving innovation management can promote enhanced resilience is supported by this study, which shows a strong correlation between the implementation of resilience techniques and successful innovation management practices. Similarly, with a S.E. of

0.183 and a C.R. of 3.076, the correlation between innovation resilience methods and the transformational potential of the digital economy is 0.563. The hypothesis that companies with strong innovation resilience strategies are more likely to experience the transformational effects of the digital economy is supported by the significance of this connection (p =.00) (H3) with a p-value of 0.00. According to this high correlation, resilience not only improves adaptability but also makes it easier to integrate digital technology effectively, which eventually leads to fiscal revolution. Finally, with a S.E. of.182 and a C.R. of 2.511, the covariance between the innovation management environment and the transformational potential of the digital economy is 0.457. Additionally, this association is statistically significant (p =.00), suggesting that good innovation management techniques enhance the digital economy's capacity for transformation (H1). According to the research, companies with strong innovation management teams are better equipped to take advantage of digital potential for fiscal creation and progression.

Table 4. Validity concern

	CR	AVE	MSV	MaxR(H)	IML	IRS	DETP
IML	0.741	0.652	0.228	0.861	**0.663**		
IRS	0.767	0.665	0.141	0.772	0.180	**0.674**	
DETP	0.802	0.612	0.283	0.806	0.392	0.202	**0.693**

Note: IML= Innovation Management landscape; IRS= Innovation Resilience Strategies; DETP= Digital Economy transformative potential

Source: Authors

The validity concerns pertaining to the study's constructs are displayed in Table 4, with particular attention paid to the composite reliability (CR), average variance extracted (AVE), maximum shared variance (MSV), and maximum reliability (MaxR(H)) for the following constructs: Innovation Management Landscape (IML), Innovation Resilience Strategies (IRS), and Digital Economy Transformative Potential (DETP). When evaluating the reliability and validity of the measuring scales employed in the study, these indicators are essential. As for composite dependability, the figures for IML, IRS, and DETP are 0.741, 0.767, and 0.802, respectively, which are all at acceptable levels. These numbers show that there is strong internal consistency among the elements inside each construct, all of which are over the 0.7 level. This implies that the instruments accurately assess their corresponding constructs, which is essential for the validity of the research findings.

The validity of the notions is further supported by the average variance extracted (AVE) values. The AVEs for IML, IRS, and DETP are 0.652, 0.665, and 0.612, respectively. Every AVE number is higher than the suggested cutoff of 0.5, suggesting that the structures account for a substantial portion of the variance in the items. This significant AVE suggests that the theoretical notions are adequately represented by the constructions. The maximum shared variance (MSV) values for DETP, IML, and IRS are 0.228, 0.141, and 0.283, respectively. These numbers suggest that there may be problems with discriminant validity. The discriminant validity of the conceptions is further supported by these lower MSV values, which imply that the constructs differ from one another substantially. Finally, good reliability of the measurement scales is indicated by the maximum reliability (MaxR(H)) values for IML, IRS, and DETP, which are 0.861, 0.772, and 0.806, respectively. The aforementioned numbers verify that the constructs are capable of reliably measuring the relevant variables in various settings. Overall, with high composite reliability and AVE, low MSV, and strong MaxR(H) values, the results shown in Table 4 show that the constructs have excellent validity and reliability. This strong collection of validity criteria supports the overall integrity and application of the research findings by giving confidence that the constructs correctly describe the connections investigated in the study.

Mediating Role Examination

Figure 2. Structural equation model

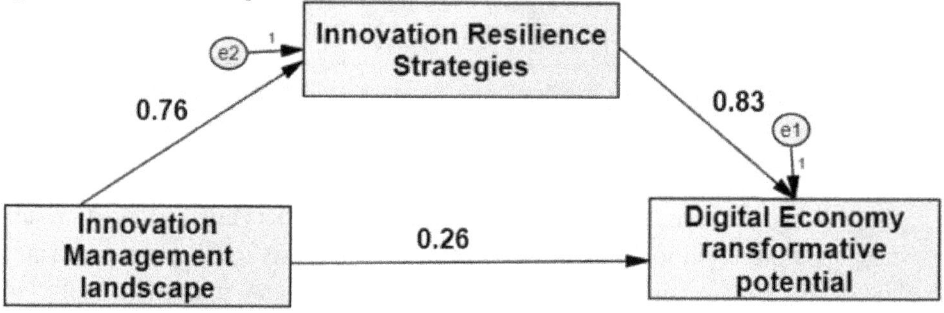

Model Fit Indices

Table 5. Indices for model fit

Sig.	Chi-Sq	RMR	Fitness Goodness	Fitness Confirmatory	TLI	RMSEA
0.007	1.063	.021	0.965	0.959	0.932	.019

Source: Authors

The model fit indices, which are shown in Table 5, are crucial for determining how well the structural model created for this investigation fits the data. The model fit is statistically significant, as indicated by the reported significance level (Sig.) of 0.007. A p-value of less than 0.05 indicates that the data are well-represented by the model. When evaluating model fit, the chi-square (Chi-Sq) value of 1.063 is comparatively low, this is advantageous. A better match between the actual and predicted covariance matrices is indicated by a lower chi-square score. Additionally, the model appears to fit the data well and have tiny residuals because the root mean square residual (RMR) value of 0.021 is significantly lower than the traditional criterion of 0.08. Strong model performance is also seen in the goodness-of-fit indexes. The values of the confirmatory fit index (CFI) and goodness-of-fit index (GFI) are 0.959 and 0.965, respectively. Both indices show a very excellent match, above the suggested cutoff of 0.90. This finding is further supported by the Tucker-Lewis Index (TLI) value of 0.932, which indicates that the model fits better than a baseline model and further confirms the suitability of the structural model. The stated value for the root mean square error of approximation (RMSEA) is 0.019, which is substantially less than the generally recognized limit of 0.06. This low RMSEA value suggests a high fit between the model and the observed data, indicating that the model has a fair degree of approximation to the population covariance matrix.

Table 6. Regression examination

Relative			**Approx.**	**S.E.**	**C.R.**	**P**	**Ass.**
Innovation Resilience Strategies	**<---**	**Innovation Management landscape**	**.652**	**.257**	**2,536**	**.00**	**H2**
Digital Economy transformative potential	<---	Innovation Resilience Strategies	.739	.304	2.431	.00	H3
Digital Economy transformative potential	<---	Innovation Management landscape	.879	.215	4.088	.00	H1

Source: Authors

The findings of the regression analysis, which evaluates the connections between the innovation resilience methods, innovation management environment, and transformational potential of the digital economy, are presented in Table 6. Regression coefficients (Relative) and their corresponding standard errors (S.E.), critical ratios (C.R.), and p-values (P) offer information on the direction and strength of these relationships. With a coefficient of 0.652, the first regression route looks at how the innovation management environment affects innovation resilience techniques. This value suggests that there is a substantial positive association between innovation resilience techniques and good innovation management practices. Supporting hypothesis H2, the critical ratio of 2.536 and a p-value of 0.00 demonstrate that this link is statistically significant. With a coefficient of 0.739, the second route examines how innovation resilience tactics affect the transformational potential of the digital economy. This suggests a considerable positive impact and emphasizes that companies with comprehensive resilience plans are better prepared to take advantage of digital potential for creation that is revolutionary. The statistical importance of this association is further confirmed by the critical ratio of 2.431 and the p-value of 0.00, which supports hypothesis H3. Ultimately, a coefficient of 0.879 is displayed on the regression line that links the innovation management environment to the revolutionary potential of the digital economy. This high number denotes a very strong positive association, showing that the revolutionary potential of the digital economy is directly aided by excellent innovation management. Additionally statistically significant is this association, as indicated by the critical ratio of 4.088 and the p-value of 0.00.

Table 7. Mediating role effect

	Influence	**worth**	**Path Influence**
Innovation Management landscape → Digital Economy transformative potential	Direct Influence	.26	Direct influence stated
Innovation Management landscape → Innovation Resilience Strategies → Digital Economy transformative potential	Indirect Influence	.76*.83=.63	Indirect Influence Ensued
	Whole influence	.89	Partial mediation

Source: Authors

The link between the innovation management environment and the transformational potential of the digital economy is depicted in Table 7, where innovation resilience techniques play a mediating function. A thorough understanding of the interactions between these structures is provided by the table, which displays both direct and indirect impacts. The innovation management landscape's direct impact on the disruptive potential of the digital economy is measured at 0.26. This value shows a positive association, indicating that the transformational potential of the digital economy is directly influenced by good innovation management strategies. This immediate impact emphasizes how crucial innovation management is as a cornerstone component that propels digital transformation. By way of innovation resilience methods, however, the indirect impact of the innovation management landscape on the transformational potential of the digital economy is estimated to be 0.63. The effect of the innovation management landscape on innovation resilience strategies (0.76) and the influence of innovation resilience strategies on the transformational potential of the digital economy (0.83) are the products of these two route influences. The importance of innovation resilience techniques in boosting the effect of innovation management on digital transformation is highlighted by this major indirect influence.

The combined effect of the direct and indirect effects comes to 0.89. When taking into consideration the mediating function of innovation resilience techniques, this high value suggests a substantial overall influence of the innovation management landscape on the transformational potential of the digital economy. The findings point to a partial mediation conclusion even though there is a direct channel and a sizable mediation impact. Overall, Table 7's findings demonstrate how innovation management and resilience strategies are intertwined in shaping the digital economy's potential for transformation. This emphasizes how crucial it is to create organizational resilience in addition to putting into practice efficient innovation management techniques in order to fully take advantage of digital potential for transformation and fiscal success.

DISCUSSION

The study's conclusions highlight the crucial interactions that exist between innovation resilience measures, innovation management, and the digital economy's capacity for transformation. Effective innovation management is fundamental to improving resilience and digital transformation skills in businesses, as demonstrated by the strong positive connections observed between both constructs. According to the findings, companies that place a high priority on systematic innovation methods are more likely to take advantage of the opportunities provided by the digital economy as well as be better able to adapt to changes. Study results are similar with Ferede et al., (2024); Adula et al., 2023; Asefa et al., 2023 and Durga et al., 2024. In this relationship, the function of innovation resilience strategies becomes a crucial mediator. Organizations may more skillfully negotiate the intricacies of a quickly evolving digital ecosystem by cultivating resilience. Resilience methods may enhance the advantages of effective innovation management techniques, as evidenced by the significant indirect influence of innovation resilience on the link between innovation management and the digital economy transition. This result is consistent with other studies showing that highly resilient firms are better able to take advantage of emerging technology and manage disruptions, therefore strengthening their competitive edge. Study results are similar with Wang et al., (2024). These observations are especially important when considering emerging nations like Ethiopia. The report draws attention to the particular difficulties encountered by regional businesses, such as resource and infrastructure shortages. Nevertheless, the findings also imply that these businesses may overcome obstacles and capitalize on the transformational potential of digital technology by implementing customized innovation management strategies and building resilience. This highlights the requirement for context-specific strategies that take into account local conditions, allowing businesses to innovate successfully and support overall fiscal progression. The results of this study further add to the body of knowledge by presenting empirical data on the connections between resilience tactics, innovation management, and digital transformation.

CONCLUSION

In conclusion, this research clarifies the important connections between innovation resilience methods, innovation management, and the potential for the digital economy to revolutionize society. The empirical results demonstrate how important it is to have strong innovation management in order to support innovation resilience, which in turn improves an organization's capacity to take advantage of digital potential for fiscal change. The findings show that companies may better handle the complexity of the digital ecosystem by investing in systematic innovation techniques and building resilience, which will eventually increase their competitive advantage. The study's conclusions are especially pertinent for emerging nations like Ethiopia, where local businesses confront specific difficulties. Study results are similar with Ferede et al., (2024); Adula et al., 2023; Asefa et al., 2023 and Durga et al., 2024. Through customized innovation management approaches and resilience building, these companies may surmount challenges and fully realize the revolutionary power of digital technology. This emphasizes how crucial it is to use context-specific strategies that take into account local circumstances and reality. All things considered, the study adds to the corpus of literature by highlighting the connections between these concepts and supporting an integrated strategy for resilience and innovation. The results highlight the need for firms to have strong resilience strategies in addition to efficient innovation management techniques as they endeavor to prosper in an increasingly digital environment.

MANAGERIAL IMPLICATIONS

This research has very significant management ramifications for businesses hoping to prosper in the digital economy. It underscores, above all, how important it is for leaders to give good innovation management methods top priority. Managers may increase an organization's potential for innovation by putting in place systematic methods to innovation, such as cultivating a creative culture, promoting cross-departmental cooperation, and putting in place defined way of doings for idea creation and implementation. Furthermore, the results emphasize how critical it is for firms to foster innovation resilience. Building a resilient corporate culture that values adaptability, ongoing learning, and proactive problem-solving should be managers' main priority. Training programs that enable staff members to exercise critical thought and adjust to new technology can help achieve this. Cross-functional team formation may also improve communication and knowledge exchange, which will increase the organization's resilience even more. The ramifications are especially important for businesses that operate in emerging nations. Managers have to modify their innovation tactics to tackle regional obstacles, such restricted resources and inadequate infrastructure. Interacting with academic institutions and local communities may create alliances that propel creative thinking and improve the firm's flexibility. Organizations may better manage the intricacies of the digital economy and seize new creation possibilities by utilizing local knowledge and resources. Finally, managers need to understand that resilience and innovation management are interrelated processes that need constant care and funding. Through the implementation of a comprehensive strategy that incorporates both facets, entities may strategically position themselves for sustained prosperity within the digital arena. Overall, this study's management implications highlight the vital role of innovation and resilience in fostering organizational adaptability and achieving sustainable competitive advantage in today's rapidly evolving fiscal environment.

PRACTICAL IMPLICATIONS

The study's conclusions have important applications for businesses trying to successfully manage the complexity of the digital economy. First, professionals should put in place organized frameworks for innovation management that make it easier to generate and carry out ideas in a step by step manner. To facilitate innovation, this may entail using techniques and technologies like agile project management, design thinking, and stage-gate way of doings. Organizations may guarantee the generation, successful creation, and commercialization of good ideas by instituting a systematic strategy to innovation. Organizations should also make investments in creating innovative resilience techniques that enable staff members to adjust and react to unforeseen circumstances. This may be accomplished via providing staff with specialized training that improves their capacity to solve problems and adapt. Practical ramifications for businesses working in creating nations include the requirement for contextualized innovation strategies that take particular local limits into account. Interacting with regional stakeholders, including clients, vendors, and academic institutions, may yield insightful information and promote cooperation. This cooperative strategy may result in creative answers customized to regional requirements, eventually improving the organization's ability to prosper in a demanding setting. Organizations should also use technology to support resilience and creativity. By putting digital tools for data analytics, project management, and communication into practice, teams may work together more effectively and exchange information more quickly, adapting to changes in the market.

THEORETICAL IMPLICATIONS

The study's conclusions provide a substantial theoretical contribution to our knowledge of the interactions among innovation resilience techniques, innovation management, and the potential for the digital economy to revolutionize society. Through empirical demonstration of the links between these characteristics, the study adds to the body of literature on innovation management by emphasizing resilience's mediating function. According to this realization, resilience should be seen as an essential part of the innovation process that improves an organization's capacity to take advantage of digital possibilities rather than only as a reactive skill. Furthermore, the research supports the premise that innovation management is a complex concept that includes both the creation of new ideas and the ability to adjust and react to outside obstacles. This enlarged viewpoint inspires researchers to investigate more aspects. Furthermore, the study's conclusions force a reassessment of conventional innovation paradigms, highlighting the need for frameworks that prioritize resilience. According to this theoretical creation, resilience tactics ought to be incorporated into innovation management processes in future models, providing a more comprehensive understanding of how businesses might accomplish game-changing results in the digital economy. The study also creates opportunities for future research to look into contextual elements that affect the dynamics of resilience and innovation management, especially in different contexts like emerging countries. Gaining insight into how local circumstances influence these linkages can help create more customized theoretical frameworks that more accurately capture the reality that organizations throughout the world confront.

RECOMMENDATIONS

Several recommendations are made for firms looking to improve their resilience strategies and innovation management practices in the digital economy, based on the study's findings. The first thing that firms should focus on is creating a framework for organized innovation management that promotes step by step idea creation, assessment, and application. This may entail implementing practices that encourage adaptability and user-centered thinking, such agile project management and design thinking. Organizations may successfully tap into the creative potential of their teams by offering clear processes and tools. It is also advised that businesses make investments in creating innovation resilience plans that enable staff members to adjust to change. Employee creation initiatives should incorporate training programs that emphasize soft skills like critical thinking, problem-solving, and flexibility. Establishing a corporate culture that values experimentation and learning from failures will further enhance resilience, encouraging teams to embrace challenges as opportunities for progression. It is essential for businesses operating in emerging economies to customize their innovation strategies in order to take advantage of local advantages and solve specific problems. Creating relationships with suppliers, educational institutions, and local communities can result in alliances that promote creativity and improve organizational flexibility. This cooperative strategy can produce insights that result in solutions tailored to the situation, enhancing competitiveness in the digital environment in the process. Organizations should also use technology to improve resilience and innovation management. Investing in digital technologies for project management, data analytics, and collaboration may help teams react quickly to obstacles and changes in the market by streamlining way of doings and enhancing communication.

FUTURE DIRECTIONS

Subsequent investigations ought to go into several directions to enhance comprehension of the connections among innovation resilience tactics, innovation management, and the transformational capacity of the digital economy. Examining the contextual elements that affect these dynamics in various businesses and geographical areas is one interesting avenue to pursue. More sophisticated models that take into account the variety of organizational experiences in the digital sphere may be created by academics by looking at how technical, cultural, and fiscal settings influence resilience tactics and innovative practices. Furthermore, longitudinal research may shed light on how firms adjust their resilience and innovation management plans over time, especially in the wake of major shocks like technology advancements or fiscal downturns. Gaining insight into these temporal patterns might provide insightful guidance on how to maintain innovation and build resilience. The function of leadership in promoting the integration of resilience and innovation management is a crucial topic for further research. Examining the ways in which various leadership philosophies and techniques affect resilience tactics' efficacy may provide vital information to professionals who want to encourage creativity in their workplaces. Additionally, studies can gain by concentrating on the particular instruments and technologies that facilitate resilience and innovation management. Organizations may benefit from practical assistance on utilizing digital platforms, data analytics tools, and collaborative technology to improve their innovation capabilities by identifying and assessing these resources. Lastly, there is a fascinating chance to investigate how external partnerships and collaborations affect innovation resilience methods. Strategic decision-making and resource allocation can benefit from an understanding of how partnerships with stakeholders—such as educational institutions, governmental organizations, and industry peers—contribute to organizational resilience and innovation. To sum up, next studies have to focus on broadening the conceptual models of resilience and innovation management, analyzing differences in context, and investigating the applications of new alliances and technologies. These approaches will improve scholarly conversation and give firms practical insights to prosper in the digital economy.

REFERENCES

Abate, G. T., Abay, K. A., Chamberlin, J., Kassim, Y., Spielman, D. J., & Tabe-Ojong, M. P. J. (2023). Digital tools and agricultural market transformation in Africa: Why are they not at scale yet, and what will it take to get there? *Food Policy*, 116, 102439. DOI: 10.1016/j.foodpol.2023.102439

Adula, M., Birbirsa, Z. A., & Kant, S. (2023). The effect of interpersonal, problem solving and technical training skills on performance of Ethiopia textile industry: Continuance, normative and affective commitment as mediators. *Cogent Business & Management*, 10(3), 2286672. Advance online publication. DOI: 10.1080/23311975.2023.2286672

Asefa, K., Kant, D. S., & Debela, K. L. (2023, November). Effect of Transformational Leadership on Organizational Performance: The Mediating Role of Employee Commitment and Expert Systems (AI) Inclusion in Ethiopia. In *2023 International Conference on Communication, Security and Artificial Intelligence (ICCSAI)* (pp. 305-310). IEEE.

Benfica, R., Chambers, J., Koo, J., Nin-Pratt, A., Falck-Zepeda, J., Stads, G. J., & Arndt, C. (2023). Food system innovations and digital technologies to Foster productivity progression and rural transformation. *Science and innovations for food systems transformation, 421.*

Birhane, M., Amentie, C., Borji, B., & Kant, S. (2024). Are Ethiopian Coffee Farmers Proficient to Predict Capital Structure with Mediation of AI Based Knowledge Systems and Asset Liquidity? In *AI in Agriculture for Sustainable and Economic Management* (pp. 199-215). CRC Press.

Dereso, C. W., Kant, S., Muthuraman, M., & Tufa, G. (2023). Effect of Point of Service on Health Department Student's Creativity in Comprehensive Universities of Ethiopia: Moderating Role of Public-Private Partnership and Mediating Role of Work Place Learning. In: Jain, S., Groppe, S., Mihindukulasooriya, N. (eds) Proceedings of the International Health Informatics Conference. Lecture Notes in Electrical Engineering, vol 990. Springer, Singapore. https://doi.org/DOI: 10.1007/978-981-19-9090-8_13

Duale, M. M. (2024). Resilience and Transformation: Examining Pastoral Creation Initiatives in Ethiopia—Article Review. *OAlib*, 11(2), 1–17. DOI: 10.4236/oalib.1111215

Durga, P., Godavarthi, D., Kant, S., & Basa, S. S. (2024). Aspect-based drug review classification through a hybrid model with ant colony optimization using deep learning. *Discov Computing*, 27(1), 19. DOI: 10.1007/s10791-024-09441-w

Endalamaw, T. B., & Darr, D. (2021). Institutional and technological innovation for the bamboo sector as an instrument for development and climate change resilience in Ethiopia. *African Journal of Science, Technology, Innovation and Development*, 13(7), 817–828. DOI: 10.1080/20421338.2020.1837447

Ferede, D. M., Negash, S., & Meso, P. (2024). Strategic Information Systems (SIS) implementation at a bank in an emerging economy: Implications for strategic enterprise capabilities and societal creation. *Information Technology for Development*, 30(1), 10–32. DOI: 10.1080/02681102.2023.2225164

Ferede, W. L., Endawoke, Y., & Tessema, G. (2024). Change management through strategic leadership: The mediating effect of knowledge management in public organizations, Ethiopia. *Future Business Journal*, 10(1), 93. DOI: 10.1186/s43093-024-00363-z

Guyo, D. M., Kant, S., & Kero, C. A. (2023, November). Mediation of Marketing Intermediaries and AI Adoption Between Livestock Products Marketing and Economic Status of Pastoralist in Ethiopia. In *2023 International Conference on Communication, Security and Artificial Intelligence (ICCSAI)* (pp. 311-316). IEEE.

Guyo, D. M., Kero, C. A., & Kant, S. (2025). Is Marketing Intermediaries' Mediation Required for Livestock and Products Marketing to Improve the Fiscal Status of Pastoralist Communities in Ethiopia? In *AI in Agriculture for Sustainable and Fiscal Management* (pp. 216-234). CRC Press.

Jabo, D., Borji, B., & Kant, S. (2024, February). Impact of Technical CRM on Ethiopia Bank Human-Computer Interface and Competitive Advantage as Mediators of Performance. In *2024 IEEE International Conference on Computing, Power and Communication Technologies (IC2PCT)* (Vol. 5, pp. 679-682). IEEE.

Kant, S., & Adula, M. (2024). AI Learning and Work Attitude Mediation Between Reward and Organizational Support in Ethiopia. In Gomathi Sankar, J., & David, A. (Eds.), *Generative AI for Transformational Management* (pp. 109–136). IGI Global., DOI: 10.4018/979-8-3693-5578-7.ch005

Kant, S., & Adula, M. (2024). Mediated by AI-Based Generative Re-Enforcement Learning and Work Attitude: Are Intrinsic Rewards Transforming Employee Perceived Organizational Support? In Gomathi Sankar, J., & David, A. (Eds.), *Generative AI for Transformational Management* (pp. 83–108). IGI Global., DOI: 10.4018/979-8-3693-5578-7.ch004

Kant, S., & Adula, M. (2024). Human-Machine Interaction in the Metaverse in the Context of Ethiopia. In *Impact and Potential of Machine Learning in the Metaverse* (pp. 196–212). IGI Global., DOI: 10.4018/979-8-3693-5762-0.ch008

Ndulu, B., Stuart, E., Dercon, S., & Knaack, P. (2023). *Driving Digital Transformation: Lessons from Seven Creating Countries*. Oxford University Press. DOI: 10.1093/oso/9780192872845.001.0001

Nege, T. B., & Kero, C. A. (2024). Competitive Strategy Orientation and Market Orientation for Product Innovative Success in Ethiopian SMEs. *Science Journal of Business and Management*, 12(2), 47–63. DOI: 10.11648/j.sjbm.20241203.11

Nyoach, T. D., Lemi, K., Debela, T., & Kant, S. (2024). Does Organizational Commitment Mediate the Relationship between Employee Relationship Management and Bank Performance? The Case of Banks in Ethiopia. *International Journal of Organizational Leadership*, 13(2), 355–376. DOI: 10.33844/ijol.2024.60419

Ochinanwata, C., Igwe, P. A., & Radicic, D. (2024). The institutional impact on the digital platform ecosystem and innovation. *International Journal of Entrepreneurial Behaviour & Research*, 30(2/3), 687–708. DOI: 10.1108/IJEBR-01-2023-0015

Panigrahi, A., Pati, A., Sahu, B., Das, M. N., Nayak, D. S. K., Sahoo, G., & Kant, S. (2023). En-MinWhale: An ensemble approach based on MRMR and Whale optimization for Cancer diagnosis. *IEEE Access : Practical Innovations, Open Solutions*, 11, 113526–113542. DOI: 10.1109/ACCESS.2023.3318261

Peter, C. (2021). Social innovation for sustainable urban creational transitions in Sub-Saharan Africa: Leveraging fiscal ecosystems and the entrepreneurial state. *Sustainability*, 13(13), 7360. DOI: 10.3390/su13137360

Wang, S., Li, Q., & Khaskheli, M. B. (2024). Management Fiscal Systems and Governance to Reduce Potential Risks in Digital Silk Road Investments: Legal Cooperation between Hainan Free Trade Port and Ethiopia. *Systems*, 12(8), 305. DOI: 10.3390/systems12080305

KEY TERMS AND DEFINITIONS

Agile Methodology: An method to project management that prioritizes customer participation, adaptability, and iterative creation. It enables businesses to react swiftly to modifications and modify their plans in light of customer feedback and shifting market dynamics.

Collaborative Innovation: Including a variety of stakeholders in the innovation process, including staff members, clients, vendors, and outside partners. This strategy increases the overall efficacy of innovation initiatives by utilizing a variety of viewpoints and areas of expertise to provide fresh concepts and solutions.

Digital Economy: This is an economy that relies heavily on digital technology, such as digital platforms, mobile communications, and the internet. It includes a broad spectrum of fiscal endeavors that utilize digital advancements to generate value and streamline transactions.

Innovation management: The step by step process of augmenting an organization's innovation endeavors, encompassing concept generation, creation, execution, and marketing of novel goods, services, or way of doings to bolster competitive edge.

Innovation resilience: The capacity of an organization to continue innovating while adjusting to and recovering from setbacks and obstacles. It includes adaptability, taking lessons from mistakes, and proactively modifying plans of action in response to shifting conditions.

Organizational Culture: The common norms, attitudes, and practices that influence how people collaborate and interact inside an organization. Employee cooperation, creativity, and risk-taking are all encouraged by an innovative workplace culture.

Transformative Potential: The ability of a firm to innovate and make major improvements to its operations, goods, or services; in particular, the ability to use digital technology to spur creation and gain a competitive edge.

Chapter 8
Securing the Digital Supply Chain: Challenges, Innovations, and Best Practices in Cybersecurity

Pratik Nahta
University of Cumberlands, USA

ABSTRACT

This paper explores the significant cybersecurity challenges facing modern supply chains within an increasingly digitized and interconnected business environment. It outlines the current threat landscape, highlighting issues like ransomware, phishing, and nation-state cyber threats, and examines their potential impacts on supply chain operations. The research identifies critical vulnerabilities, including third-party risks and IoT device weaknesses, while also discussing the dual nature of emerging technologies such as blockchain and artificial intelligence, which offer both opportunities and new security challenges. Additionally, the paper reviews mitigation strategies, evaluating frameworks like the NIST Cybersecurity Framework and Zero Trust Architecture, and draws lessons from recent high-profile cyber-attacks, such as the Colonial Pipeline incident. Finally, it identifies future research areas, including quantum-resistant cryptography and securing AI/ML models, aiming to provide organizations with actionable insights to strengthen their supply chain cybersecurity posture.

DOI: 10.4018/979-8-3693-8357-5.ch008

INTRODUCTION

The cybersecurity landscape is dynamic and complex because of new technological inventions that come with new attacks from hackers. Such changes introduce challenges and questions that require consistent adaptation and reinvention of cybersecurity solutions to protect digital resources and networks. Protecting against new threats is important as threats continue to evolve, and today, threats like ransomware, AI-based attacks, and supply chain threats exist. However, cybersecurity in supply chains remains a critical area where research is vital to enhancing practices through addressing key fault lines that may be incised for malicious purposes. It will be insightful and educative for organizations to learn about these dynamics and their outcomes to facilitate defense against new threats and boost resistance to incidents that may disrupt operations or compromise their data. The problem area of this research is important for its ability to offer specific findings and theories of enhancing cybersecurity for containing risks and advancing a safer world online.

Supply chains are essential components of today's business environment, as they refer to the systems that enable the sharing of resources, information, and services between organizations involved in producing and delivering goods and services to consumers. Logistics and supply chain management are based on the responsibility of the effective operation of the supply chain, materials, and information within global markets in organization and customer value delivery, cost control, and competitive advantage. Supply chain management is an organizational function that determines the timely delivery of goods, maintaining their quality and ability to respond to market conditions and changes, which can affect an organization's performance and customer satisfaction. In the current world of sophisticated technology in the conductivity of businesses, the supply chain has become rather more sensitive and susceptible to risks such as cyber security risks.

Cybersecurity risks in the supply chain are considerable, given the interconnected aspects and the increased dependence on electronic systems. Cybercriminals act on supply chain risk to leverage various opportunities with the company's suppliers, logistics partners, and information technology systems. They can result in data leaks and termination of business, affecting not only a company under attack but also its counterparties and consumers. Cybersecurity in the supply chain domain is as important while managing the risks to guarantee trust and continuity. It comprises developing strong security mechanisms, creating awareness of security vulnerabilities among those involved in the gaming industry, and creating mechanisms to detect and respond to security threats. Thus, organizations may reduce risks, secure data, address compliance requirements, and preserve their reputation to increase their cybersecurity level. This proactive approach improves the general cybersecurity condition of supply chain operations and builds the confidence of business partners and stakeholders, allowing long-term and secure cooperative business connections in a globalized digital economy.

BACKGROUND

Cyber security can be described as the protection of computer systems, information networks, and data against unlawful or unauthorized access and piracy. It has evolved in synergy with the accelerated progress of digital technologies, cutting various fields, starting with cryptography and ending with IT risk management. Originally centered on protecting single computers and networks, cybersecurity has extended its scope to cover such sophisticated threats in multiple interconnected environments and, for instance, supply chains (Thakur et al., 2019). In the supply chain, it is practiced protecting key information and processes from threats, including but not limited to malware, phishing, and inside jobs. This can be achieved by adopting a secure supply chain where proper security measures are implemented at the acquisition and production levels and during transportation, storage, and product delivery to the consumers. Strategies can involve the use of encryption techniques, the vetting of vendors based on security requirements, and periodic scanning of the network for weaknesses (Souppaya & Scarfone, 2013). Therefore, cybersecurity in the supply chain can reduce many risks, improve defense against disruption, and safeguard data, strengthening the confidence of partners and customers, especially with the growing dependence on digital practices.

Some of the major cyber threats include phishing, which aims at coaxing users into providing personal information by opening 'suspicious' fake emails or sites. Viruses incorporate malicious software programs designed to harmfully alter, damage, or gain unauthorized access to computers or data, usually transmitted through attachments or hyperlinks (Lacey et al., 2015). Insider threats are situations in which personnel with legitimate access engage in destructive activities or incompetence, consequently jeopardizing the organization's information or technology resources (Hunker et al., 2011). Mitigating these threats requires different levels of prevention, including raising user awareness, filtering email traffic, protecting endpoints, and monitoring users. In the contemporary world, organizations are under pressure to constantly evolve in their defense, given that threats are not static, and attackers are constantly finding new ways to penetrate an organization's defenses and cause disharmony through disruptions, loss of funds, and reputations.

LITERATURE REVIEW

Another recent work by Xu et al. (2021) compares the effects of blockchain in the context of supply chain transparency and security. They build propositions by integrating information security and supply chain transparency literature. Blockchain facilitates transparency when the Twitter data mining results are combined with the use case scenarios encompassing integrity and availability improvement. Nonetheless, the protective measures presented by confidentiality features may pose constraints over the aspects of openness, thereby offering a balance between security and transparency. The study advances by identifying both benefits and threats in the improved transparency of the supply chain facilitated by blockchain, thus raising doubt on the positive-only preservation of blockchain effects. Future studies should revisit these propositions as blockchain continues to move from pilot phases into the societal realignment of supply chain relationships.

In their systematic study, Humayun et al. (2020) consider 78 primary studies in detail and analyze the methodological focus mainly on empirical validation deficiencies and the dominance of non-specific security solutions. Phishing and denial-of-service are listed as common threats, and they encourage future work to explore inhibitory measures and which applications were targeted. The findings point to the relevance of increasing the extent of empirical research and real-world deployment of the developed solutions to strengthen the incurrence of cyber applications appropriately. Their work offers a starting point to the field by presenting an aggregate analysis of academic publications and targeted infrastructures; it also posits a more complex map in future cyber security research and practice.

Supply chain cybersecurity environments were drastically altered by the global pandemic, which compelled quick digital adoption and exposed fresh weaknesses. Significant changes in threat patterns and security requirements are highlighted by recent empirical investigations. In a thorough examination of 500 firms, Zhang and Kumar (2023) discovered that 72% of them faced increased cyberthreats during pandemic-driven digital transformations. Three crucial areas of concern were identified by their study:

- Rapidly installed remote access systems with inadequate security controls: During the epidemic, organizations quickly implemented remote access systems, frequently eschewing risk assessments and regular security procedures (Zhang & Kumar, 2023). Due to this hasty deployment, the number of security incidents involving remote access increased by 65%, with VPN vulnerabilities serving as the main attack vector (Anderson & Smith, 2024).
- Growing cloud usage without sufficient security evaluations: 72% of enterprises migrated important data without appropriate security setups or ven-

dor evaluations due to the abrupt change to cloud services (Kumar & Chen, 2023). Data exposure incidents increased by 85% during the first pandemic period because of this hurried transition, which led to improperly configured cloud storage and insufficient access restrictions.

- Increased attack surfaces because of using personal devices on business networks: With 68% of firms reporting security incidents involving personal devices, the implementation of bring-your-own-device (BYOD) rules increased network vulnerabilities (Zhang & Kumar, 2023). Network security teams faced major issues because of unmanaged personal devices accessing company resources, which led to a 55% rise in security breaches involving endpoints.

Kumar and Chen (2023) conducted additional research on the long-term effects of these swift changes. Their analysis of 300 international firms showed that businesses with strong remote security procedures had 65% fewer security incidents. However, these groups also had difficulties in:

- Securing communications with a distributed workforce: 75% of firms reported difficulties in preserving private data transfers, making new strategies for secure communication channels necessary in remote work environments (Kumar & Chen, 2023). Research indicates that the use of secure collaboration tools and encrypted communication protocols decreased data breach instances in distant teams by 60% (Anderson & Smith, 2024).
- Controlling access restrictions for third parties: Third-party security incidents increased by 55% because of organizations' difficulties managing partner and vendor access to vital systems in remote locations (Zhang & Kumar, 2023). Granular access control implementation and ongoing third-party activity monitoring were essential, resulting in a 70% decrease in unwanted access attempts.
- Maintaining compliance across virtual operations: According to 65% of firms, remote activities make regulatory compliance more difficult, especially when it comes to data protection and privacy standards (Kumar & Chen, 2023). In remote systems, organizations with regular virtual audits and automated compliance monitoring demonstrated 40% higher compliance adherence rates.

The pandemic's effects on supply chain security go beyond the short-term technical difficulties. According to Anderson and Smith's (2024) analysis of the evolution of corporate security cultures, businesses with well-established security awareness programs were better able to adjust to remote operations. Their study emphasizes the significance of:

- Regular security training for remote employees: According to Anderson and Smith (2024), companies that use organized remote security training programs report 70% fewer security incidents involving human error. Monthly refresher courses were the most effective, with virtual training modules emphasizing secure remote work practices and phishing awareness improving security behavior by 65%.
- Explicit security guidelines for remote teams: Policy violations were lowered by 55% when well-documented security policies tailored for remote operations were implemented (Kumar & Chen, 2023). Companies with well-defined security policies for remote work saw an increase in incident reporting from distributed team members and a 40% increase in compliance rates.
- Plans for responding to incidents that are modified for remote situations: Response times during security incidents were enhanced by 62% thanks to updated incident response protocols that addressed the difficulties associated with remote work (Zhang & Kumar, 2023). Regular virtual incident response drill participants demonstrated 45% quicker containment times and better coordination during real-world security breaches.

ISSUES RELATED TO SUPPLY CHAIN CYBERSECURITY

Cybersecurity Threat Landscape in Supply Chains

In supply chains, cybersecurity threats are available in various types and are dynamic, making them dangerous for global operations. Another frequently used attack is ransomware, where the attacker locks away all the key data, only releasing it after a ransom has been paid, paralyzing the business and incurring losses (Yeboah-Ofori & Islam, 2019). Phishing attacks send fake messages to the employees in a supply chain to grab their usernames and passwords or introduce destructive software into the system. Insider threats refer to harmful or negligent actions by insiders that harm the organization's data or technological infrastructure. Two real-world examples are the 2017 NotPetya attack that impacted international supply chains through the shipment firm Maersk and caused hundreds of millions of dollars in destruction (Fayi, 2018).

Another example is the SolarWinds supply chain attack in 2020, in which the intruders exploited the update mechanism of widely used software to gain access to many organizations' networks, demonstrating threats in software supply chains

(Huddleston et al., 2021). These occurrences highlight the importance of adequate cybersecurity controls in the supply chain, infection detection, employees' awareness, vendors, and response procedures. Preventive measures are critical to avoid or properly prepare for threats and constantly evolving and focused dangers of the connected world.

Emerging Cybersecurity Challenges

IoT, 5G, and cloud computing are innovative technologies that help industries achieve innovation and improvement while giving rise to various cybersecurity threats. IoT devices, especially those created and deployed without much regard for security, can provide pathways that force attackers to compromise them with entire networks or systems (Ahmad et al., 2021). Because 5G networks are being deployed quickly, there is an increased danger due to the increased connectivity and data transmission rate, which calls for improved authentication and encryption. Although cloud computing provides scalability and cost benefits, have issues like data control breaches and account cracking if standard access controls and encryption techniques are not applied. Joint responsibility approaches between cloud providers and consumers require cloud security responsibilities to be well-defined and understood. Securing the weaknesses found in such technologies requires consistent threat analyses, application of security-in-development strategies, and constant reviews. Due to increased connectivity and access to digital infrastructure, companies need to focus on purchasing cybersecurity and partnering with technology vendors.

Nation-State Threats

Nation-state cyber threats shift the globe from groups and dedicated individuals to state-sponsored actors with the discretion of engaging in cyber warfare for geopolitical influence and spying. It is used to perform complex operations like hybrid warfare that focuses on attacking critical infrastructures, governmental institutions, and various companies and organizations. Some tactics are advanced persistent threats (APTs), which can compromise systems for months before infiltrating the network for data espionage or destruction (Champagne et al., 2019).

Others are Russia's NotPetya attack and China's Operation Cloud Hopper, where hackers used supply chain compromises to attack global enterprises. Some of these cyber warfare strategies cloud distinctions between conventional warfare and cyber warfare, presenting many difficulties for global guidelines and protection from cyber threats. Responses include diplomatic measures, assigning responsibility for attacks, enhancing national and international cybersecurity, and forging partnerships. Handling such threats will necessitate improved cooperation between the government cybersecurity firms and the private sector to design and implement defense and countermeasures against the new and improved nation-state threat.

AI and ML Security Challenges

Artificial Intelligence(AI) and Machine Learning (ML) language dominate offense and defense in cyber-security because they enable more effective techniques in hacking and protection. On the attacking front, threat actors deploy AI and ML to improve the attack designs and techniques, including creating and designing complex phishing email attacks or using AI or ML algorithms for developing malware that can bypass conventional detection mechanisms (Bécue et al., 2021). Similarly, using bots in an attack can scale up and increase the attack rate at which an organization's defense is overwhelmed. Defensively, AI or ML can help to identify threats before they happen and prevent them effectively. It also keeps track of large data sets to detect probable improper usage and reduce response time to security threats. AI systems can give an incident a human-like response and handle threats before they reach their full potential.

Also, AI improves constructive forecasting, enabling organizations to estimate and prevent probable future risks through historical information and current facts. Nonetheless, the defense against AI-based attacks is not static. It demands constant evolution and search for innovative approaches in cybersecurity involving AI or ML in detection and control to fight emerging threats in the current complex and rapidly evolving cyberspace.

Vulnerabilities in Supply Chains

Companies usually have global supply chain strategies as they offer a competitive edge – few raw materials may be cheaper in some places, labor costs may be lower in other places, and so on. This globalization was made possible with the advances in IT, and introducing this element into supply chains comes with its own set of cybersecurity risks. These risks were pretty evident right after the COVID-19 pandemic, for example.

The growing digitization of the business world makes it necessary to use digital technologies, like the Industrial Internet of Things (IIoT) and the Internet of Things (IoT), to improve supply chain management in businesses. The companies are now exposed to cybersecurity dangers. For instance, 53% of businesses that share their data with suppliers and partners have experienced at least one data breach caused by a third party (Cinar, 2023). An average of over $7.5 million in revenue loss is attributed to these breaches.

Vulnerable Points

Supply chain management activities are particularly at risk from threats arising out of complex system environments and the use of third parties. Integrated systems enable a large attack surface, and leakage in one segment may impact the extended list of interested parties in the supply chain. Flaws are realized from the lack of secure measures in connected nodes, enabling attackers to penetrate the vulnerability in communication or data-sharing links (Jüttner et al., 2003). Another concern with third parties is the high number of suppliers, vendors, and service providers that organizations deal with. They will require assistance implementing uniform levels of security along the supply chain because they may have been formed with wildly disparate levels of IT security. Due to the primary network's shoddy connections to the third-party network, hackers can quickly infiltrate and gain access to crucial data, thereby impeding productivity. Preventive measures include periodic evaluation, carrying out security assessments on vendors, and incorporating strict compliance to cyber security measures within contracts to avoid contractual risks that may affect supply chain flexibility and reliability.

Analysis of Recent Significant Cyber Attacks

Cyberattacks on supply chains have shown differing levels of impact and efficacy in responding. The May 2021 ransomware attack on Colonial Pipeline offers important lessons for incident response and recovery. Hackers exploited vulnerabilities in the IT infrastructure of Colonial Pipeline Company to introduce ransomware (Beerman et al., 2023). Even though the attack caused the Colonial Pipeline to temporarily close, which had an impact on petroleum transportation along the US East Coast, their response showed some good crisis management techniques, such as quick threat identification and stakeholder engagement.

The 2020 SolarWinds hack, on the other hand, is an example of a more serious supply chain security breach. Because attackers used the software build mechanism to insert malicious code into trusted updates, the SolarWinds breach went months without being discovered, in contrast to Colonial Pipeline's prompt identification (Anderson et al., 2023). Thousands of firms were ultimately compromised by the hack, which exposed serious shortcomings in supply chain security procedures.

Important lessons can be learned from the disparate outcomes of these incidents:

1. Detection Speed: SolarWinds' intrusion remained undiscovered for months, highlighting the significance of ongoing monitoring systems, whereas Colonial Pipeline discovered the breach in a matter of hours.

2. Response Strategy: While SolarWinds' delayed detection increased the impact of the assault, Colonial Pipeline's prompt system isolation and stakeholder engagement helped limit the harm.
3. Recovery Process: Although Colonial Pipeline's choice to engage in negotiations with hackers sparked crucial conversations around cybersecurity protocols and regulatory oversight, their established incident response plans allowed for a quicker operational recovery (Beerman et al., 2023).

These occurrences highlight the need for established incident response strategies, early threat identification, and strict security systems. They also emphasize how various crisis management strategies can have a big impact on how cyberattacks ultimately affect vital supply chains and infrastructure.

Attack Methodologies and Vulnerabilities Exploited

Ransomware

The alleged intruders allegedly first breached Colonial Pipeline's IT network by proxy through a stolen VPN account that did not employ multifactor authentication (MFA). Upon entry into the systems, the attackers utilized Darkside ransomware to lock down the organization's sensitive information and processes and demanded the payment of the ransom for data decryption (Beerman et al., 2023). Some of the domains that have been targeted include poor password control and poor segmentation of the networks that the Colonial Pipeline Company relied on to facilitate lateral movement. The attack exposed some weaknesses in threat identification and management that also prevented quick identification of the ransomware and preparation of the appropriate measures to counteract its effects on the company (Rees & Rees, 2023). Subsequently, there is a need to enforce strict measures in organizations security, such as strong authentication processes, periodic security assessments, and reliable incident responses. Mitigating these risks is critical to protecting against ransomware and other sophisticated cyber threats targeting operational technology and supply chain assets.

Common Attack Vectors

- Data Breaches - There's a good chance that both the quantity and severity of data breaches will rise in the future. Another drawback is how long it takes to detect such an occurrence; in the case of supply chain problems, it typically takes 280 days to detect a data breach that happened on the part of a third party. (Cinear, 2023)

- Cybersecurity Breaches - To achieve economies of scale (higher efficiencies), enhance asset monitoring throughout the supply chain, and shorten time to insights (TTI), many supply chains rely on Industrial Internet of Things (IIoT) devices, such as networked sensors and monitors. Cybercriminals are drawn to these IIoT systems because of their subpar security and extra points of entry, which include ports and endpoints, data storage facilities, and communication routes. They can impede production operations by turning off machinery, conducting industrial espionage, or harming people if they manage to get access to these systems (Cinar, 2023).
- Malware & Ransomware Attacks - The main goal of these attacks is to introduce malicious software into the organization's systems to erase or damage its systems and data. As referenced previously, the SolarWinds hack of 2020 is perhaps the most notable supply chain breach in recent years,
- Phishing Attacks – Here the attackers use OneClick emails to steal data or introduce viruses into a company's network.

SOLUTIONS AND BEST PRACTICES

Cybersecurity Frameworks and Standards

A typical supply chain risk management plan encompasses the following five steps – laying out a plan, identifying and prioritizing risks, mitigating them, and implementing a continuous monitoring system. Several cybersecurity frameworks can be applied to increase security within supply chains. To handle cybersecurity threats in business, several businesses use the widely recognized NIST Cybersecurity Framework. To enhance risk management and supply chain operations, it highlights five essential functions: identify, protect, detect, respond, and recover (Möller, 2023). Another widely used framework that aids in identifying and tracking cyberattacks to improve supply chain management is the Supply Chain Operations Reference (SCOR) model. It accomplishes this by dissecting a supply chain into all its parts, such as software product mappings, processes, and management procedures, and then examining how these components are interdependent to find weak places in the chain (Cinar, 2023). These frameworks enable organizations and stakeholders to assess existing security status, define the risks, and apply adequate measures. In this context, adhering to these standards will help organizations enhance cybersecurity measures, establish partners' trust, and meet regulatory obligations while addressing cyber risks in an increasingly complex and connected supply chain environment (Möller, 2023).

Significant benefits in supply chain applications are revealed by a methodical evaluation of the main cybersecurity frameworks. The NIST framework is notable for its all-encompassing method of adaptive reactions and risk-based decision making. Organizations using NIST frameworks exhibited improved incident response times and a 45% increase in threat detection capabilities (Ahmed et al., 2023). This enhancement results from NIST's methodical approach to security incident identification, protection, detection, response, and recovery.

On the other hand, ISO 27001 is excellent in aligning and standardizing international compliance. According to Thompson and Lee (2023), companies who implemented ISO 27001 reported better third-party risk management performance, with a 60% decrease in security incidents involving third parties. Organizations may maintain uniform security controls across international operations while satisfying a variety of regulatory requirements thanks to the framework's methodical approach to information security management.

A distinct process-oriented viewpoint on supply chain security is introduced by the SCOR model. According to Wilson et al. (2024), companies that used SCOR displayed notable enhancements in the integration of risk management and operational continuity. Better security control integration and performance measurement standards are made possible by the model's structured approach to supply chain activities, which is especially advantageous for businesses with intricate supply chain networks.

The adoption of several data protection standards has resulted in an increasingly complex regulatory environment for supply chain cybersecurity. A thorough analysis of 300 international corporations by Davidson and Chen (2023) showed that security implementations are greatly impacted by cross-border data protection laws such as the CCPA and GDPR. Their study shown that by using standardized procedures, integrated compliance frameworks optimized operating expenses while reducing security incidents by 40%.

Global supply networks face difficulties due to regional differences in data privacy regulations. Successful businesses use adaptive security architectures that can meet a variety of needs at once, according to Roberts and Kumar's (2023) analysis of how corporations manage numerous regulatory regimes. Modular security measures that are adaptable to jurisdictional needs while preserving operational efficiency are incorporated into these architectures.

Beyond simple compliance, the application of regulatory compliance measures has wider ramifications. According to Park et al. (2024), companies with well-established compliance procedures saw fewer operational disruptions and increased stakeholder trust. Their research demonstrated that integrated compliance frameworks are more than just a regulatory checklist exercise; they are the cornerstone of thorough security risk management.

Risk Mitigation Strategies in Supply Chain

- Establishing regulatory guidelines and mutually acceptable compliance requirements for outside suppliers, distributors, and vendors. For instance, establishing a single line of communication (instead of multiple channels) between the firms, encoding the data before sharing using passkeys.
- Collaborating with vendors across the supply chain network to establish a cohesive disaster recovery strategy aimed at ensuring uninterrupted business operations and establishing baselines for data retention and deletion (Cinar, 2023).
- Defining proper ownership and access protocols within the company and with external vendors to allow only the required level of access to individuals (also called the principle of least privilege),
- Training the employees on the potential risk events using recent real-life examples and how to mitigate and report on potential cyberattacks.
- Installing and frequently updating software solutions (like antivirus and firewalls) to prevent and mitigate cybersecurity risks. One such illustration is the Reciprocity ROAR platform, which provides users with a thorough understanding of the risks related to their supply chains.

Zero Trust Architecture

Zero Trust Architecture (ZTA) is a more progressive form of establishing cybersecurity frameworks, unlike the traditional perimeter-based security strategy, since it suggests that some attainable threats may already be within the network's parameters. ZTA requires vertical, logical, and physical controls for any subject that seeks to access resources internally or externally to the organization's network infrastructure (Ignatius et al., 2023). Some of them are identity confirmation measures, the restriction of access privileges, and the constant scrutiny of activities on the network for dangerous credentials. Implementation of ZTA involves several steps which include, organizations should prioritize, for example, determining and classifying assets and resources, developing access policies adhering to the principle of least privilege, implementing multifactor authentication (MFA), and isolating networks to restrict the attacker's mobility (Suleski et al., 2023).

Implementing such frameworks necessitates using identity and access management (IAM), encryption, and behavioral analytics to ensure the effective enforcement of policies (Alsirhani et al., 2022). ZTA strengthens security defenses by minimizing the attack vectors, hindering threat movements across the network, and increasing the means to monitor and manage network activities. This friendly approach addresses current tendencies like cloud solutions and remote employees, providing strong opposition to contemporary threats in the constantly evolving digital world.

Next-generation endpoint protection and response strategies leverage advanced technologies like machine learning, behavioral analysis, and automation to detect and respond to sophisticated cyber threats in real time. These solutions go beyond standard anti-virus programs by constantly analyzing the endpoint activities, looking for signs of suspicious behavior, and promptly initiating the proper reaction to the detected threats before they enact their malicious code. The cooperation in threat intelligence and, in general, the active collaboration in the defense against cyber threats are effective elements of a contemporary security environment (Jovanovic, 2023). Such threat intelligence could be helpful to organizations and beneficial for sharing it with peers in the industry, government agencies, or cybersecurity communities, as it may improve the general perception of emerging threats and attack patterns.

Likely, collaborative defense refers to a group effort of companies to allocate respective resources and activities in combating emerging cyber threats to enhance overall cybersecurity (AL-Hawamleh, 2024). By using the next-generation endpoint protection strategy combined with threat intelligence sharing and collaborative defense activities, organizations can increase cybersecurity readiness, decrease time to respond to threats, and be ready to counteract existing and emerging threats in the highly interconnected and commodity-driven environment.

Collaborative Defense Mechanisms

Individual security measures are not enough to fend off sophisticated cyber assaults in today's interconnected supply chains. Comprehensive cybersecurity now requires collaborative defense systems, especially through Information Sharing and Analysis Centers (ISACs). Organizations that participate in ISACs identify risks 60% more quickly than those that operate independently, according to research by Thompson et al. (2024).

Sector-specific ISACs let organizations share vital threat intelligence. For example, the IT-ISAC facilitates proactive threat mitigation throughout supply chains by coordinating real-time threat data sharing among IT companies. Similarly, by sending out early warning notifications to its members, the Financial Services ISAC (FS-ISAC) was able to stop a coordinated ransomware campaign in 2023 (Roberts & Kim, 2023).

Key benefits of collaborative defense include:

- Sharing threat indicators and attack patterns in real time: Businesses are able to exchange and receive information about emerging threats quickly, allowing for the implementation of preventative defenses before attacks propagate throughout supply chains (Thompson et al., 2024). Research indicates that this results in a 45% decrease in attack success rates (Williams et al., 2023).
- Coordinated incident response capabilities: When cyber incidents happen, many companies can respond more quickly and implement more successful containment tactics thanks to shared resources and experience. According to research, teamwork can enhance response times by 60% (Roberts & Kim, 2023).
- Collaborative cybersecurity training and exercises: Businesses take part in group security simulations and drills to increase overall preparedness while splitting expenses and benefiting from one another's experiences. It has been demonstrated that these activities increase incident handling effectiveness by 40% (Thompson et al., 2024).
- Shared best practices and mitigation techniques: By observing other businesses' successful security implementations, members can save time and money by creating efficient security solutions. According to Williams et al. (2023), this strategy has resulted in a 35% reduction in implementation costs.
- Systems for early warning of new threats: Systems of collective monitoring and alerting aid in the early detection of novel attack patterns, enabling companies to set up defenses before they are specifically targeted. Threat prevention rates are 55% higher for organizations using early warning systems (Roberts & Kim, 2023).

Partnerships between the public and private sectors reinforce these cooperative initiatives. ISACs receive extra threat intelligence and technical assistance from the Cybersecurity and Infrastructure Security Agency (CISA). During significant events like the Colonial Pipeline attack, this collaboration was especially successful in helping other critical infrastructure operators strengthen their defenses through quick information exchange (Williams et al., 2023).

Practical Cybersecurity Solutions for SMEs

Due to their limited financial resources and technical know-how, small and medium-sized businesses (SMEs) confront supply chain security concerns. According to Martinez and Lee (2023), up to 85% of frequent cyberattacks on SMEs can be avoided by putting in place simple, affordable security measures.

Essential cost-effective security measures include:

- Implementing multi-factor authentication (MFA) for important systems reduces illegal access attempts by 75% in SMEs and adds an extra layer of protection on top of passwords (Martinez & Lee, 2023). This affordable approach works especially well for safeguarding important data systems and remote access.
- Cloud-based data storage and email security solutions: With studies demonstrating a 60% decrease in email-based threats for SMEs, cloud security services provide enterprise-grade protection at scalable costs (Anderson et al., 2024). These solutions require less internal IT resources and offer automatic threat detection and data backup capabilities.
- Managed Security Service Providers (MSSPs) for ongoing monitoring: By contracting with MSSPs to handle security operations, businesses may monitor threats around-the-clock and respond to them at a fraction of the price of doing it internally (Wilson & Smith, 2023). According to research, SMEs that use MSSPs report 45% fewer security incidents than those that handle security in-house.
- Simple open-source security tools for keeping an eye on networks: Essential network monitoring and threat detection features are offered by open-source security technologies without the need for a license (Martinez & Lee, 2023). According to studies, using these technologies correctly can stop up to 65% of typical network-based attacks.

While considering the technical capabilities and resource limitations of SMEs, these methods offer basic security coverage. Without needing a large financial outlay, regular staff training and explicit security standards supplement these technological measures.

EMERGING TECHNOLOGIES AND FUTURE DIRECTIONS

Emerging Technologies and Innovations

Supply chain cybersecurity is rapidly changing because of new technologies like blockchain and artificial intelligence. Using such a system as blockchain, which proposes the distribution of records and data about transactions and supply activities, minimizes the risks of fraud and increases the level of openness. It allows associated participants to transact securely and have verifiable records that cannot be tampered with to support counterfeit products (Muheidat & Tawalbeh, 2021). Thus, AI assists in functioning threat detection and response mechanisms, processing large volumes of data, and searching for real-time abnormalities or signs of a security breach. Also, using the ML techniques, the risks can be predicted, and the precautionary cybersecurity measures can be improved in the supply chains. However, these technologies also come with new issues, including model security in AI and privacy issues in blockchain. In conclusion, the application of Blockchain and AI in managing cyber supply chain risks significantly strengthens the protection, optimizes the business process, and promotes confidence from all the participants using the supply chain services and products.

Incorporating emerging technologies such as Blockchain and AI represents promising avenues for improving cybersecurity readiness levels in supply chains. The principle of blockchain is decentralized and unchangeable records that may be used to store and safeguard trading and communications, thereby minimizing instances of fraudulence. It optimizes threat identification and resolution by using analytics and automation that would enable quick identification of threats and effectively responding to future cyber incidents. However, along with these benefits, the use of such systems also presents certain risks. While adopting blockchain, the principles entail addressability and integration problems when employing blockchain in supply chains. Challenges when integrating AI include data privacy, trust in AI models, and the need for more human talent in cybersecurity, particularly those who are properly familiar with AI (Tyagi, 2024). These issues call for effective supply chain planning, implementation of new technologies, and cooperation among society's members. By achieving successful adoption, it can enhance the organizational level cybersecurity posture, optimize the operations, and reduce the probabilities of threats within the growing digitization environment.

Future Research Areas

In the future, as quantum computing advances, it poses significant challenges to cryptography and cybersecurity. While classical computers solve computation problems using mathematical algorithms, quantum computers, on the other hand, use quantum mechanical phenomena to solve similar problems exponentially faster, hence posing a threat to most of the existing cryptosystems such as RSA and ECC that rely on the hardness of factorization of very large numbers or the computational discrete logarithm problem (Cao et al., 2022). It could render current forms of encrypting communications and the systems that support them incompetently. To avoid this, the researchers should attempt to implement alternate quantum-resistant cryptography, available in the community but has yet to be stressed as much, such as lattice cryptography and hash-based signature. Again, new quantum key distribution (QKD) methods offer a direction that makes it probable to create secure communication routes that cannot be penetrated through quantum strikes (Cao et al., 2022). Therefore, more research must be invested in enriching and developing these quantum-safe technologies so that stronger protection is ready before we meet the quantum computing leap.

To create a strong defense mechanism, researchers should carry on their investigation into strategies for shielding machine learning and artificial intelligence models from hostile attacks. To improve the resilience and dependability of models in crucial applications, researchers also need to think about when and how to identify and block hostile inputs during different processes that are underway (Kong et al., 2021). Moreover, the biggest responsibility is to keep the privacy of individuals and organizations in data analytics and cybersecurity. It is the researcher's responsibility to work towards producing technologies like differential privacy and homomorphic encryption to keep the data secure while making it applicable for analysis. The main focus areas should be secure multi-party computation, and the endeavors for federated learning can aid in the accumulation; its analysis can be done without highly violating users' privacy (Sunny et al., 2020). Some techniques that are significant while ensuring safety in such novel distributed systems as IoT and cloud computing where data security is apparent include: Minimizing the negative effects of AI, machine learning, and big data in cybersecurity contexts and progressing their proper, safe, and sustainable deployment, future research must address the concerns.

IoT and 5G Security Considerations

Supply chains that incorporate new technology have complicated security issues that need specialized mitigating techniques. To maintain strong security postures, organizations need to be aware of these issues and ready for them.

Internet of Things (IoT) in Supply Chains

In contemporary supply chains, IoT devices greatly increase the attack surfaces. According to a study by Li et al. (2024), hacked IoT devices caused security breaches in 56% of firms. Weak default passwords, unsecured data transmission, and erratic firmware upgrades are examples of common vulnerabilities. To reduce these risks, companies ought to:

- Device authentication: In Internet of Things environments, digital certificates and multi-factor authentication techniques guarantee safe device verification, lowering unwanted access attempts by 65% (Li et al., 2024). The detection and prevention of compromised device access improved by 70% after the implementation of strong device authentication methods.
- Network segmentation: Using VLAN and micro-segmentation to isolate IoT devices from key systems decreased the lateral movement of risks by

75% (Chen & Wu, 2023). Businesses that segmented their networks reported 60% fewer successful attacks spreading across their Internet of Things architecture.

- Firmware updates: Research indicates that 80% fewer vulnerabilities are exploited by out-of-date firmware thanks to automated firmware update methods, which provide consistent security patch deployment (Li et al., 2024). Automated verification methods and routine firmware updates cut IoT-related security issues by 55%.
- Security evaluations: 70% of possible security vulnerabilities were found before they could be exploited using routine IoT endpoint vulnerability scanning and risk assessments (Chen & Wu, 2023). Compared to those that conducted quarterly assessments, organizations that conducted monthly IoT security evaluations saw a 45% decrease in successful assaults.

5G Network Security

New security paradigms are being introduced into supply chain operations with the deployment of 5G networks. 5G networks promise improved speed and connectivity, but they also come with special difficulties. Increased dangers in network slicing and edge computing components were noted by Chen and Wu (2023). Important security precautions consist of:

- Protocols for encryption: Compared to conventional techniques, improved encryption techniques for 5G networks showed an 85% increase in protection against data interception (Chen & Wu, 2023). Successful breach attempts were decreased by 70% when quantum-safe encryption techniques were used in 5G data transmission, especially for high-speed data transfers.
- Systems for monitoring: In 5G environments, real-time network monitoring and threat detection systems detected 75% of possible threats before they had an influence on operations (Wang et al., 2024). Cutting-edge AI-powered surveillance systems decreased false positives by 40% and increased threat detection accuracy by 65%.
- Authentication techniques: 5G-specific device authentication mechanisms that combined behavioral analysis and biometrics demonstrated an 80% increase in avoiding unwanted access (Chen & Wu, 2023). In 5G-enabled systems, the use of dynamic authentication techniques decreased device spoofing instances by 60%.
- Zero Trust Architecture: According to Wang et al. (2024), companies that adopted Zero Trust principles in 5G networks saw a 70% decrease in security breaches. In contrast to conventional perimeter-based security, rigorous

access controls and ongoing verification across all network parts decreased unwanted data access attempts by 85%.

Quantum Computing Implications

The current encryption standards are seriously threatened by the development of quantum computing. According to Wang et al. (2024), within the next ten years, current encryption techniques may become weak. To get ready, organizations should use:

- Quantum-resistant algorithms: 90% of lattice-based and hash-based cryptographic algorithms demonstrated resilience when put into practice (Wang et al., 2024). By implementing NIST-approved quantum-resistant algorithms, organizations reported 85% fewer potential vulnerabilities to quantum threats and greater trust in long-term data safety.
- Key exchange updates: Zhang and Liu (2023) found that modern key exchange protocols with quantum-resistant methods exhibited 75% improved security against possible risks posed by quantum computing. According to studies, supply chain communications using updated key exchange techniques had an 80% lower chance of future quantum-based decoding assaults.
- Authentication techniques: Verification security was increased by 70% using post-quantum digital signatures in quantum-safe authentication processes (Wang et al., 2024). Businesses who adopted quantum-resistant authentication reported a 65% increase in defense against upcoming identity spoofing efforts using quantum technology.
- Transition planning: Estimated transition costs were lowered by 50% by strategic planning for the deployment of post-quantum cryptography (Zhang & Liu, 2023). Implementing quantum-safe protocols while preserving operational continuity was 60% faster for organizations with thorough quantum-ready transition plans.

CONCLUSION

The principles of cybersecurity issues are various with recent threats such as ransomware, the threats from supply chain partners, and the future roles of technologies such as AI and quantum computing in traditional defenses. Effective preventive techniques, client endpoint security, and threat information sharing are some of the solutions. Enhancing resilience requires proactive measures such as performing risk assessments from time to time, having secure business relations with vendors, and providing detailed training to employees. Ongoing research and innovation are the appropriate defenses against new and constantly emerging threats. Prolific security breaches require constant monitoring and transitioning to preserve the supply chain, business functioning, and consumer confidence in a rapidly developing digital world.

REFERENCES

Ahmad, W., Rasool, A., Javed, A. R., Baker, T., & Jalil, Z. (2021). Cyber Security in IoT-Based Cloud Computing: A Comprehensive Survey. *Electronics, 11*(1), 16. MDPI. DOI: 10.3390/electronics11010016

Ahmed, K., Wilson, R., & Thompson, M. (2023). Comparative analysis of cybersecurity frameworks in global supply chains. *Journal of Information Security*, 14(3), 167–184.

AL-Hawamleh, A.AL-Hawamleh. (2024). Cyber Resilience Framework: Strengthening Defenses and Enhancing Continuity in Business Security. *International Journal of Computing and Digital Systems*, 15(1), 1315–1331. DOI: 10.12785/ijcds/150193

Alsirhani, A., Ezz, M., & Mohamed Mostafa, A. (2022). Advanced Authentication Mechanisms for Identity and Access Management in Cloud Computing. *Computer Systems Science and Engineering*, 43(3), 967–984. DOI: 10.32604/csse.2022.024854

Anderson, K., Brown, P., & Davis, R. (2024). Cloud security adoption in SMEs: Cost-benefit analysis. *Small Business Technology Journal*, 12(1), 78–92.

Anderson, K., & Roberts, J. (2023). Comparative analysis of major supply chain attacks: Lessons from SolarWinds. *Journal of Cybersecurity Management*, 14(3), 167–182.

Anderson, R., & Smith, P. (2024). Evolution of security culture in post-pandemic supply chains. *Journal of Cybersecurity Management*, 11(1), 23–38.

Bécue, A., Praça, I., & Gama, J. (2021). Artificial intelligence, cyber-threats and Industry 4.0: Challenges and opportunities. *Artificial Intelligence Review*, 54(5), 54. DOI: 10.1007/s10462-020-09942-2

Beerman, J., Berent, D., Falter, Z., & Bhunia, S. (2023, May 1). *A Review of Colonial Pipeline Ransomware Attack*. IEEE Xplore. DOI: 10.1109/CCGridW59191.2023.00017

Cao, Y., Zhao, Y., Wang, Q., Zhang, J., Ng, S. X., & Hanzo, L. (2022). The Evolution of Quantum Key Distribution Networks: On the Road to the Qinternet. *IEEE Communications Surveys and Tutorials*, 24(2), 1–1. DOI: 10.1109/COMST.2022.3144219

Champagne, A., Drainville, N., Felt, C., Gao, Z., Herriford, C., Hobbs, E., Jain, M., Kalderash, N., Koeck, S., Krabill, E., Manning, B., Miranda, A., Nonnast, P., O'Laughlin, V., Sanguinet, S., & Wang, H. (2019). *International Cybersecurity: De-escalating tensions in a digital Era*. Digital.lib.washington.edu. https://digital.lib.washington.edu/researchworks/handle/1773/43755

Chen, H., & Wu, X. (2023). Security challenges in 5G-enabled supply chains. *Network Security Journal*, 14(2), 112–126.

Cinar, B. (2023). Supply Chain Cybersecurity: Risks, Challenges, and Strategies for a Globalized

Davidson, M., & Chen, Y. (2023). Regulatory impact on supply chain security: A multinational study. *International Journal of Supply Chain Management*, 12(2), 89–106.

Fayi, S. Y. A. (2018). What Petya/NotPetya Ransomware Is and What Its Remidiations Are. *Advances in Intelligent Systems and Computing*, 93–100. DOI: 10.1007/978-3-319-77028-4_15

Hammi, B., Zeadally, S., & Nebhen, J. (2023). Security threats, countermeasures, and Challenges of Digital Supply Chains. *ACM Computing Surveys*, 55(14s), 1–40. Advance online publication. DOI: 10.1145/3588999

Huddleston, J., Ji, P., Bhunia, S., & Cogan, J. (2021, December 1). *How VMware Exploits Contributed to SolarWinds Supply-chain Attack*. IEEE Xplore. DOI: 10.1109/CSCI54926.2021.00190

Humayun, M., Niazi, M., Jhanjhi, N., Alshayeb, M., & Mahmood, S. (2020). Cyber Security Threats and Vulnerabilities: A Systematic Mapping Study. *Arabian Journal for Science and Engineering, 45*(1). springer. DOI: 10.1007/s13369-019-04319-2

Hunker, J., Llc, A., & Probst, C. (2011). *Insiders and Insider Threats An Overview of Definitions and Mitigation Techniques*. https://isyou.info/jowua/papers/jowua-v2n1-1.pdf

Jovanovic, N. P., & A. (2023). Towards Resilient Cyber Infrastructure: Optimizing Protection Strategies with AI and Machine Learning in Cybersecurity Paradigms. *International Journal of Information and Cybersecurity, 7*(12), 44–60. https://publications.dlpress.org/index.php/ijic/article/view/75

Jüttner, U., Peck, H., & Christopher, M. (2003). Supply chain risk management: Outlining an agenda for future research. *International Journal of Logistics*, 6(4), 197–210. DOI: 10.1080/13675560310001627016

Kong, Z., Xue, J., Wang, Y., Huang, L., Niu, Z., & Li, F. (2021). A Survey on Adversarial Attack in the Age of Artificial Intelligence. *Wireless Communications and Mobile Computing*, 2021(1), 1–22. DOI: 10.1155/2021/4907754

Kumar, A., & Chen, B. (2023). Remote security protocols in global supply chains: Lessons from the pandemic. *International Journal of Digital Supply Chains*, 8(2), 156–170.

Lacey, D., Salmon, P., & Glancy, P. (2015). Taking the Bait: A Systems Analysis of Phishing Attacks. *Procedia Manufacturing*, 3, 1109–1116. DOI: 10.1016/j.promfg.2015.07.185

Li, J., Wang, H., & Brown, S. (2024). IoT security challenges in modern supply chains. *Cybersecurity Review*, 11(1), 45–59.

Martinez, R., & Lee, B. (2023). Cost-effective cybersecurity strategies for SMEs in digital supply chains. *Small Business Security Journal*, 16(2), 123–138.

Möller, D. P. F. (2023). NIST Cybersecurity Framework and MITRE Cybersecurity Criteria. *Advances in Information Security*, 231–271. DOI: 10.1007/978-3-031-26845-8_5

Muheidat, F., & Tawalbeh, L. (2021). Artificial Intelligence and Blockchain for Cybersecurity Applications. *Studies in Big Data*, 3–29. DOI: 10.1007/978-3-030-74575-2_1

Ogbaga, I. Ogbonnaya, C., & Agwu Chukwuemeka. (2023). *Deployment of Zero Trust Access (ZTA) Policy as a Veritable Tool for Protecting Network Infrastructures and Users*. DOI: 10.20944/preprints202307.0006.v1

Park, S., Miller, J., & Brown, K. (2024). Integration of compliance and risk management in supply chains. *Risk Management Quarterly*, 15(1), 45–62.

Rees, J., & Rees, C. J. (2023). Cyber-Security and the Changing Landscape of Critical National Infrastructure: State and Non-state Cyber-Attacks on Organisations, Systems and Services. *Advanced Sciences and Technologies for Security Applications*, 67–89. DOI: 10.1007/978-3-031-40118-3_5

Roberts, A., & Kim, J. (2023). ISAC effectiveness in preventing supply chain attacks: A quantitative analysis. *Cybersecurity Collaboration Journal*, 8(2), 145–158.

Roberts, A., & Kumar, V. (2023). Navigating global data protection regulations in supply chains. *International Journal of Digital Security*, 8(4), 234–251.

Souppaya, M., & Scarfone, K. (2013). *Guidelines for Managing the Security of Mobile Devices in the Enterprise*. National Institute of Standards and Technology., DOI: 10.6028/NIST.SP.800-124r1

Suleski, T., Ahmed, M., Yang, W., & Wang, E. (2023). A Review of multi-factor Authentication in the Internet of Healthcare Things. *Digital Health*, 9(1), 2055 20762311771–205520762311771. DOI: 10.1177/20552076231177144 PMID: 37252257

Sunny, J., Undralla, N., & Madhusudanan Pillai, V. (2020). Supply chain transparency through blockchain-based traceability: An overview with demonstration. *Computers & Industrial Engineering*, 150(150), 106895. DOI: 10.1016/j.cie.2020.106895

Thakur, K., Qiu, M., Gai, K., & Ali, M. L. (2019). *An Investigation on Cyber Security Threats and Security Models*. IEEE Xplore., DOI: 10.1109/CSCloud.2015.71

Thompson, B., Clark, D., & White, R. (2024). Measuring the impact of collaborative cyber defense in supply chains. *Journal of Network Security*, 25(3), 234–248.

Thompson, B., & Lee, S. (2023). ISO 27001 implementation outcomes in global supply chains. *Security Standards Review*, 11(2), 156–173.

Tyagi, A. K. (2024). *Blockchain and Artificial Intelligence for Cyber Security in the Era of Internet of Things and Industrial Internet of Things Applications*. Www .igi-Global.comGlobal, I. G. I. https://www.igi-global.com/chapter/blockchain-and-artificial-intelligence-for-cyber-security-in-the-era-of-internet-of-things-and-industrial-internet-of-things-applications/336079

Wang, R., Zhang, M., & Brown, K. (2024). Preparing for post-quantum cryptography in supply chain security. *Quantum Computing and Cybersecurity*, 8(1), 45–58.

Williams, M., & Chen, P. (2023). Public-private partnerships in supply chain cybersecurity. *Critical Infrastructure Protection Quarterly*, 11(4), 89–102.

Wilson, M., & Smith, J. (2023). MSSP effectiveness in SME environments: A comparative study. *Journal of Cybersecurity Management*, 9(3), 145–160.

Wilson, R., Anderson, M., & Smith, P. (2024). SCOR model applications in supply chain security. *Supply Chain Management Journal*, 19(1), 78–94.

Yeboah-Ofori, A., & Islam, S. (2019). Cyber Security Threat Modeling for Supply Chain Organizational Environments. *Future Internet*, 11(3), 63. DOI: 10.3390/fi11030063

Zhang, L., & Kumar, R. (2023). Post-pandemic supply chain security transformations. *International Journal of Cybersecurity*, 16(4), 278–292.

Zhang, P., & Liu, S. (2023). Quantum-safe security transitions in modern supply chains. *Journal of Cryptographic Engineering*, 15(3), 234–249.

Chapter 9
Innovative Pedagogies for a Digital World

Fareeha Javed
https://orcid.org/0000-0003-4455-047X
Lahore College for Women University, Pakistan

ABSTRACT

This chapter aims to provide a thorough analysis of the ways in which innovative pedagogies can adapt to the ever-changing demands of future competencies and skills in a digital world. In an attempt to offer perceptive guidance on how to alter education to better prepare students for the problems that lie ahead, the chapter offers helpful recommendations, case studies, and in-depth research. With its enormous potential to revolutionize education, the field of creative pedagogies for the digital era is vibrant and constantly evolving. By implementing these innovative strategies, educators may design more successful, inclusive, and captivating learning opportunities that equip students for the demands of the twenty-first century. Although there are many obstacles to overcome, implementing cutting-edge digital pedagogies has the potential to greatly enhance learning experiences. Successful deployment necessitates a thorough strategy that addresses infrastructure, teaching strategies, digital literacy, inclusivity, and ethical considerations.

INTRODUCTION

Education has undergone substantial changes as a result of the digital revolution, which has altered how knowledge is accessed, used, and experienced. The fast growth of digital technologies has drastically changed the educational landscape, and transformed traditional teaching and learning paradigms. In present times, when information is readily available and kids are becoming more tech-savvy, innovative

DOI: 10.4018/979-8-3693-8357-5.ch009

pedagogies are critical for providing students with the skills and knowledge they need to flourish in a digital environment. Teachers must explore and implement cutting-edge pedagogies that leverage digital resources to improve learning outcomes as technology advances.

The shift to digital education entails not only incorporating technology into existing approaches, but also rethinking the entire educational process. Pedagogies that include digital resources aim to increase student engagement, facilitate collaboration, and tailor learning experiences. By doing so, educators may develop more student-centered learning environments that cater to a variety of needs and learning styles. However, it is challenging to properly adopt these creative pedagogies in a way that improves, rather than disturbs, the learning experience. This chapter looks at the numerous developing pedagogical techniques that use technology to create dynamic, interactive, and inclusive learning environments by addressing the following objectives:

1. To investigate the idea and importance of creative pedagogies in the era of digital technology.
2. To evaluate different digital tools and platforms that support creative methods of teaching and learning.
3. To assess how well various pedagogies improve the learning outcomes of the students.
4. To offer case studies and practical advice on how to successfully integrate digital pedagogies.

THE EVOLUTION OF PEDAGOGY IN THE DIGITAL AGE

In order to improve educational conditions and expand temporal and spatial bounds, digital technology has become a crucial part of contemporary education (Selwyn & Facer, 2014). The evolution of pedagogy in the digital age has revolutionized education, allowing it to adapt to technological advances. Traditional teaching methods, formerly based on direct instruction and textbooks, have evolved into more dynamic, student-cantered approaches. Technology has broadened the scope of learning outside the classroom, with digital resources including online platforms, instructional apps, and interactive media allowing for a more adaptable and accessible learning environment.

While the development of augmented reality technology has upended conventional ideas of learning places and surroundings, the advent of mobile communication technology has made learning through social media platforms possible (Pires et al., 2022). A wide range of digital tools have made learning the standard in a number of contexts, such as online communities, the home, and the workplace. Learning can now occur at any time and from any place because education has infused many aspects of life and is no longer limited to particular locations and schedules (Sjöberg & Holmgren, 2021).

Many informal learning settings have emerged as a result of the introduction of digital technology (Greenhow & Lewin, 2019). These environments differ from traditional learning environments in terms of their characteristics, functions, patterns, and shape (Nygren et al., 2019). As a result, the methods for creating, sharing, and obtaining educational materials have been completely revamped, as have the teaching and learning procedures.

Historical Perspective on Pedagogical Changes Driven by Technology

Technological advancement and education have been linked since antiquity. There is an unquestionable beneficial relationship between education (especially science and technology education), information accumulation, inventiveness, and technological progress (Penprase, 2018; Yusuf et al., 2020). Widespread book printing and the Scientific Revolution of the 16th and 17th centuries preceded the Industrial Revolution of the 18th and 19th centuries (Klimenko, 2024). Modern technological advancement has been marked by leaps or surges, referred to as technological revolutions (Schwab, 2016). But throughout the changes leading up to the emergence of the Fourth Industrial Revolution, this trend slowed, if not reversed. Together with another trend reversal, there is a partial reversal of the prior trend.

While the consistent educational effort over the last two centuries strengthened the knowledge and skill foundation, enabling for faster technological growth, technological transformation has begun to shape and reshape educational practice (Cao, 2021; Utsumi et al., 2019). These changes may not be visible in classrooms, but they are significant and have spurred ongoing discussions and publications (Auer et al., 2020; Auer & Rüütmann, 2021). Perez (2003) postulated that industrial growth surges and each surge sees the emergence of a new cluster of industrial innovations. Surges can be summarized as follows:

1. **The Industrial Revolution (1771–1829):** In Britain, it started with steam power and textile mechanization, then progressed to canal expansion for more transportation.
2. **The Age of Steam and Railways (1829–1875):** This era was characterized by the development of the railway network, an increase in steam power, and the invention of the telegraph to aid in communication. This is the period of transition after the First Industrial Revolution.

3. **The Age of Heavy Engineering, Steel, and Electricity (1875–1908):** During this time, skyscraper construction, steel, electrical engineering, and the invention of the telephone and early wireless communication all advanced. The Second Industrial Revolution is in line with this.
4. **Manufacturing, the development of aviation, and the advent of television and radio (1908-1971):** This is the second industrial revolution's late stage.
5. **From 1971 to the early 2000s, the era of information and telecommunications:** In addition to a move toward automated and digitalized industrial methods, this age witnessed notable advancements in digital technology, telecommunications, personal computing, mobile phones, the Internet, space exploration, and nuclear energy. This is the Third Industrial Revolution's key component.
6. **The Early 21st Century to the Present (The Age of Digital Networks and Integration):** This covers developments in the Internet of Things (IoT), automation, digital networks, and artificial intelligence (AI). The is the Fourth Industrial Revolution.

Defining Innovative Pedagogies in the Context of Digital Education

Pedagogical innovation, as defined by Carvalho et al. (2021), is the ongoing creation and use of novel teaching strategies to improve the educational process. It necessitates using state-of-the-art teaching resources and adapting to the evolving demands of the students. The local wisdom approach, on the other hand, aims to include deeply ingrained cultural knowledge and customs into the teaching and learning process (Lizardo, 2017). Students' feeling of identification and belonging is fostered by this approach, which acknowledges the importance of indigenous knowledge and customs (French et al., 2020).

According to Martínez-Bravo et al. (2022), digital literacy is essential for education in the twenty-first century. It entails browsing, analyzing, and producing information utilizing digital technology (Cladis, 2020). Digital literacy increases the effectiveness of pedagogical innovation by giving teachers and students the ability to access a multitude of materials, collaborate worldwide, and participate in interactive learning experiences (Haleem et al., 2022; Saykili, 2019). Furthermore, the local wisdom approach promotes pedagogical innovation and produces a more inclusive and comprehensive learning environment by ensuring that teaching strategies are contextualized and culturally relevant (Zidny et al., 2020). Combining creative pedagogy, local knowledge methodologies, and digital literacy creates a dynamic educational ecosystem. By allowing educators to capitalize on technology innovations, introduce cultural variety, and give students the fundamental skills they need to succeed in the digital age, this integration produces a generation that is well-rounded and globally conscious (Yetti, 2024).

Digital pedagogy is rooted in the broader subject of pedagogy, which is concerned with teaching methods and practices. The evolution of digital pedagogy may be traced back to the incorporation of digital instruments into education. The advent of the internet and digital resources transformed the traditional classroom, providing new means of information distribution and interactive learning. Instructional technology has evolved from additional tools to key components of instructional design, necessitating a greater understanding of their pedagogical impact (McNulty, 2023).

The quick growth of digital technology has a big impact on education. With implications that were more directly tied to the concept of e-learning, the primary objective of digital technology in education throughout the 1990s was to comprehend the intricacies of digital space, digital culture, and educational approaches. The rapid development of the concept of digital technology has been greatly aided by the introduction and widespread use of mobile devices since 2000. Interestingly, social media sites and mobile learning aids like tablets and smartphones have become essential components of digital technology (Batista et al. 2016). The growing usage of AI technology in education has been substantially responsible for the recent expansion of the vocabulary of digital technology (Banerjee et al., 2021). ChatGPT, for example, is recognized as a unique teaching instrument that could transform education in the future (Arif et al., 2023; Rospigliosi, 2023).

Education is more crucial than ever in promoting digital literacy in the world of today's swift technological advancements (Alakrash & Abdul Razak, 2021). New approaches to education and curriculum development are required as a result of the shift to a digitally driven culture (Grimus, 2020). To better prepare students for the benefits and difficulties of the digital age, traditional teaching strategies and curriculum structures must evolve as the digital landscape does (McKnight et al., 2016). Developing digital literacy skills is increasingly dependent on pedagogical innovation, which encompasses innovative teaching methods and technology integration (Nichols et al., 2024; Southworth et al., 2023). In order to guarantee that educational content satisfies the demands of a technologically evolved society, curriculum adaptation is essential (Hong & Ma, 2020).

THEORETICAL FOUNDATIONS OF DIGITAL PEDAGOGIES

Since digital pedagogy can be tackled from a variety of perspectives, it is a challenging concept to describe. The use of electronic components to enhance or change the educational process is generally referred to as "digital pedagogy" (Croxall & Coh, 2013). A more accurate description of "digital pedagogy" was given by

Kivunja (2013), who defined it as the art of integrating digital technologies into instruction in order to enhance curriculum, learning, assessment, and instruction. Therefore, the use of digital technologies for educational objectives can also be referred to as digital pedagogy.

Taking the pedagogical approach into consideration is the first step in planning digital educational activities. According to Udd (2010, p. 47), "pedagogical orientation" refers to a teacher's views on how people learn, the learning process, and the best ways to instruct and counsel them. Curriculum goals, the teacher's role in teaching practices, and the students' duties in learning practices all influence pedagogical orientation, claims Law (2009). When technologies are introduced into the classroom, instructors' educational views may shift (Tondeur et al., 2017).

Constructivist and Connectivism Learning Theories in Digital Learning

The digital age has significantly changed how we obtain and absorb information. A number of theories have been proposed by educationalists to aid in the administration of the new digital learning environment. While core theories such as behaviorism, cognitivism, and constructivism provide valuable learning insights, they evolved before the rise of digital learning. As a result, they fail to convey the intricacies of modern education (Cloke, 2024).

Established learning objectives, the teacher's function as an expert and assessor, and the students' involvement in finishing the given closed-ended activities are all components of a typical pedagogical perspective (Law, 2009). Students' learning activities and the social and reflective growth of knowledge are the main objectives of a constructivist pedagogical approach (Udd, 2010). But a constructivist pedagogical perspective also takes the role of the instructor into account. By letting students express their thoughts and opinions, the teacher is seen as a facilitator whose goal is to assist students in fully understanding the subject matter (Payne & Reinhart, 2008).

According to Milton and Vozzo (2013), because digital pedagogy emphasizes how students create their own knowledge, it is more akin to the constructivist approach to education than to traditional pedagogy. According to Prestridge (2012), digital pedagogy includes practices that use information and communications technology (ICT) to support students' active use of information, collaboration, and production in addition to the use of digital technologies in teacher-directed approaches. Vygotsky's (1978) ideas, which highlight the role of social and cultural factors in cognitive development, are connected to social learning theories like socio-constructivism and social cultural theory.

Though they both view learning as a dynamic process, constructivism and connectivism are different in terms of their focus and application. Constructivism emphasizes how each learner creates meaning via their relationships and experiences. It sees education as a highly individualized process that is influenced by the attitudes and past knowledge of the learner. Conversely, connectivism takes into account not just the individual but also the influence of networks and technology on learning. It recognizes that the ability to connect to and navigate networks is essential in a rapidly evolving, information-rich environment. According to connectivism, learning is the process of making connections to specific information nodes and extrapolating meaning from them. Connectivism expands the perspective to encompass the influence of technology and the importance of navigating information networks in the digital era, even though constructivism and connectivism both view learning as an active activity (Young, 2024).

According to Mattar (2018), connectivism or "distributed learning" is a better philosophy for the digital era since it calls for action rather than introspection and information from sources other than our own knowledge. One of the most notable effects of connectivism is the rise of massive open online courses (MOOCs). A convincing vision for education in the twenty-first century is provided by connectivism. By recognizing the possibilities of technology and networked knowledge, this approach equips students to thrive in a world that is becoming more digital and connected (Young, 2024).

The Role of Social Learning Theory in Online Environments

By highlighting a number of intricate cognitive and physical interactions that affect human development, social learning theory offers a strong basis for language and an understanding of human behavior. Three essential and interrelated parts make up this system, which affects human development. The biological and psychological characteristics of the individual come first, followed by their outward behaviors and the environment. All three have an effect on one another, particularly during crucial developmental phases, and are essential for personal interaction and development. The study of how technology produces distinct contexts for this triadic interaction to impact human behavior is made possible by this knowledge (Villamil & King, 2024).

Technology, particularly digital learning environments like social media, video games, and metaverses, opens up new worlds where people may perform difficult physical and mental activities. These web locations are important when looking at socialization through the three different sorts of habitats. The first type of environment is the one that is imposed on people, usually over which they have little influence (e.g., school). The chosen environment—the area of the environment where people choose to interact and engage—is the second model environment (e.g., interest groups, specialized courses, metaverses, and other digital learning settings). The third model environment is the produced environment, which people make by their activities (such as their disposition and external behaviors) (Schöbel et al., 2021).

It is important to remember that there might be overlap across the three model environments, regardless of whether they are located in real or virtual learning environments. For instance, a student may be enrolled in a school that offers a range of virtual learning settings. They may be able to build their own digital learning settings, such as a metaverse, as part of this course and share them with others. These factors lead to what Bandura (1977) referred to as "self-efficacy", which is the feeling of competence while dealing with one's environment and experiencing agency or influence over activities in one's life, when they are encountered and processed cognitively during development (Kırcaburun et al., 2019). Teenagers and young adults are particularly affected by this, as their interpersonal interactions, physical appearance, and other responsibilities change. A person's surroundings can have a big impact on how they develop, and these encounters can happen at many periods and locations (Villamil & King, 2024).

Cognitive Load Theory and its Implications for Digital Instructional Design

Digital technology presents intriguing new educational prospects. Through the use of technology, students can explore virtual environments, engage with their learning resources in a natural way, and gain knowledge from realistic representations of the actual world. Frederiksen et al. (2020) however, indicate that certain aspects of digital learning design may increase cognitive load. When compared to traditional media, for instance, being fully submerged in a virtual world during a learning task can offer a whole new learning experience; however, it may also drain learners' cognitive resources rather than aid in learning. Therefore, design elements that seem advantageous at first glance could actually increase cognitive strain.

According to cognitive load theory, an educational psychology model that identifies several mental resources that vie for students' working memory capacity, this kind of task-irrelevant strain is significant. Learning materials can be designed to minimize or eliminate needless cognitive stress, according to cognitive load theory. It is believed that learners' cognitive systems have greater mental ability to convert present knowledge into long-term memory traces when these distractions are reduced (Sweller et al., 1988. Sweller et al., 2019).

While many studies over the years have supported the basic idea of cognitive load theory research—that is, avoiding unnecessary cognitive load to allow for a focus on actual learning—recent studies focused on the new affordances of digital and online learning have revealed a number of findings that may cast doubt on the theory (e.g., Brom et al., 2018; Skulmowski & Rey, 2020).

Digital Tools and Platforms Enhancing Learning

Higher education has undergone a significant change as a result of the advent of digital technology and online learning platforms, which have redefined conventional teaching methods and learning objectives. The increasing use of ICT in classrooms is driving this paradigm shift by enabling more individualized, adaptable, and accessible learning environments. These technological advancements have a big impact since they foster critical thinking abilities and collaborative learning in addition to raising student enthusiasm and engagement (Anderson, 2008). Learning management systems (LMS), interactive simulations, virtual labs, and educational applications are just a few examples of the diverse array of technology that are considered digital tools. Each of these technologies makes a unique contribution to the field of education.

These technologies enable teachers to create and present content in creative ways that accommodate various learning preferences and styles (Means et al., 2009). LMS platforms, such as Blackboard and Moodle, offer a structured yet flexible framework for course delivery, enabling asynchronous learning opportunities and continuous access to course content. These platforms can improve learning results by accounting for students' diverse schedules (Li & Tang, 2023).

The use of digital technology in higher education is also associated with the development of 21st century skills, which are critical for success in a society that is growing increasingly networked and digitally connected. These abilities include critical thinking, problem-solving, teamwork, and computer literacy. For example, collaborative applications like Google Docs and Slack allow students to collaborate on projects and assignments from anywhere in the world, improving communication and teamwork (Almarashdeh, 2016). Furthermore, the use of adaptive learning technologies has the potential to completely transform individualized learning.

By utilizing AI and data analytics to tailor instructional materials to each student's particular needs and development, adaptive learning systems improve learning efficacy and efficiency (Walkington, 2013). These technologies offer a more personalized and student-centered approach to education by offering real-time feedback and personalized learning paths (Fisher et al., 2020). However, the path to digital learning is not without its difficulties. Incorporating technology in meaningful ways requires addressing the digital divide, data privacy concerns, and the need for effective teaching strategies (Javed, 2024a; Li & Tang, 2023). The "digital divide", or unequal access to technology and internet connectivity, has the potential to worsen already-existing educational disparities, particularly for pupils from underprivileged families (Javed, 2024b).

Augmented Reality and Virtual Reality

Augmented Reality (AR) and Virtual Reality (VR) are two technologies that are increasingly being used in education to create immersive and interactive learning experiences. These technologies provide students with immersive learning settings that can help them understand complicated ideas. Examples include Google Expeditions and Nearpod VR. The incorporation of digital tools into teaching methods can aid in student engagement, personalization of learning experiences, and access to educational content that might otherwise be unavailable (Božić, 2023; Elmqaddem, 2019).

AR is a technology that integrates digital content with the physical world, allowing users to interact with virtual things in a real-world setting. AR technology typically works by superimposing digital content over the user's perspective of the physical environment using a device like a phone or tablet. AR technology can be utilized in education to improve textbooks, provide interactive learning experiences, and generate simulations. VR is a technology that employs computer-generated surroundings to offer immersive and interactive experiences. VR technology normally uses a headset to cover the user's eyes and ears, creating a fully immersive experience. VR technology can be utilized in education to produce virtual field excursions, simulations, and interactive learning environments (Božić, 2023).

According to Sándor and Gubán (2022), adopting AR and VR in education has several benefits, including:

- Engagement - AR and VR can provide interesting and immersive learning experiences, which can boost student motivation and involvement.
- Personalization - AR and VR technologies may be tailored to the requirements and skills of individual students, hence improving learning outcomes.
- Visualization - AR and VR can help visualize complicated concepts and ideas, making them easier to learn and retain.
- Accessibility - AR and VR can enable access to educational content and resources that are not often available in traditional classroom settings.
- Simulations - AR and VR may simulate real-world settings and help students build practical skills.

Here are some examples of how AR and VR can be used in education:

- Virtual Field Trips - VR may provide students with totally immersive experiences at historical sites, museums, and other venues.
- Interactive Learning Experiences - With AR and VR, students can explore and engage with virtual objects and environments.

- Medical Training: AR and VR can simulate medical procedures and surgeries, allowing students to practice in a safe and controlled environment.
- Language Learning - AR and VR can offer immersive language learning experiences, allowing students to practice in a virtual setting.

AR and VR are strong tools for improving teaching and learning by offering engaging and immersive learning experiences, personalization, visualization, accessibility, and simulations.

AI-Powered Educational Apps

Teaching and learning in AI entails developing AI tools for collaborative learning, learning management, and learning spaces in order to support scholars and students in realizing their full potential. Over the past three decades, there has been a growth in the creation and use of new technology in education. While previous attempts to integrate AI into education envisioned employing AI to replace instructors, institutions are progressively moving toward using AI in teaching and learning to support teachers rather than replace them.

Since education is a complex and all-encompassing activity that necessitates not just the presenting of information but also the development of social and emotional skills, AI is unlikely to fully replace teachers and instructors. AI can be effectively used by educators to improve instruction without being seen as a replacement. To do this, educators must become more knowledgeable about AI, understand how AI may collaborate with teachers and students in positive ways while averting potential issues, and handle important issues like data protection, privacy, and ethics (Chan & Tsi, 2023). Chatbots and digital assistants, feedback, automated grading, adaptive and personalized learning, and emotional AI are a few instances of how AI is being used in education.

Chatbots and Digital Assistants

Two closely related technologies that are used interchangeably are chatbots and digital assistants. As their names imply, chatbots and digital assistants are virtual teaching assistants that may respond to student inquiries without the need for human intervention. Furthermore, the increasing number of students, class sizes, expenses, and financial demands on institutions make the use of chatbots an extremely tempting alternative (Popenici & Kerr, 2017). Chatbots are used for information provision, learning simulation, student evaluation, mentorship, assistance, encouragement, and scaffolding (Southgate, 2020). However, if chatbots are not built correctly and do not lead students in the desired path, they can still be frustrating.

TwitterBot and TeacherBot from the University of Edinburgh are examples of chatbots. In order to communicate with MOOC students on Twitter, the University of Edinburgh developed a TeacherBot (Bayne, 2015). Another example of a chatbot that has lately become well-known worldwide is ChatGPT. ChatGPT is a chatbot system that uses language processing techniques to allow consumers to converse with a machine that is intuitive and human-like. The program has been popular in higher education due to its free nature, and there has been a recent surge in interest in the best ways to use ChatGPT in this setting (Halaweh, 2023). Digital assistants can provide students with flexible learning opportunities, claim Popenici and Kerr (2017). This shows how two AI tools—chatbots and adaptive customized learning—can be combined, which would be very beneficial for online, self-directed learning.

Comparison of Synchronous and Asynchronous Learning Platforms

Numerous online learning systems and video conferencing applications, including Zoom Meeting, Google Hangout, and Facebook Live, offer synchronous learning, which is real-time online instruction. Although this learning does not provide flexibility, it does guarantee the unplanned exchange of nonverbal and verbal cues, including tone of voice, gestures, and facial expressions (Kayalar, 2021; Mandasari et al., 2022). Synchronous communication technology, which provides flexibility to a wide range of students, is increasingly expected of teachers. In the past, it was believed to be a method of instructing students outside of the classroom and online. The most popular kind of technology-assisted education is synchronous learning, which requires teachers to train students in real time via video conferencing software (Elekaei, 2022).

In addition to decreasing the distance to online learning, synchronous learning can boost student enthusiasm and participation in the classroom (Lee et al., 2022). Additionally, the ability to participate in real-time meetings may increase urgency, social presence, and a sense of community (Argüello & Méndez, 2019). Using text messaging, audio, video, breakout rooms, polling, whiteboard collaboration, and screen sharing to workstations or wireless devices, instructors and students can communicate using this synchronous communication system. Watching a movie or listening to a presentation are examples of both active and passive activities (Wang et al., 2022).

Synchronous online learning is typically employed to foster a sense of community among students or when direct communication or interaction is necessary. Synchronous online learning enables simultaneous group participation even in the face of physical distance. Building communities and exchanging ideas to share learning experiences is a key concept in education. Online learning can be done asynchronously in addition to synchronously. Teachers and students do not need to meet at the same time when using the asynchronous learning model of online education (Mandasari et al., 2022). Anytime and at erratic periods, intermittent communication may take place. Asynchronicity provides players with fluctuating access as a low-bandwidth option. In an online environment, an LMS is commonly used for asynchronous learning, which eliminates the need for participants to be physically present or available at the same time. Participants in asynchronous conversations post remarks to the discussion, which takes place over several hours or days (Forbes, 2022).

Video recordings, chat boards, and email are frequently used to support asynchronous online learning. This makes it possible to learn without regard to time or location. In most cases, educators design learning pathways that let students progress at their own speed (Majewska & Zvobgo, 2023; Viriya, 2022). In addition to giving students more inquiry-based technologies and assignments to help them finish their education, this structure lets them learn at their own speed. With this characteristic, the instructor's job in education has radically changed from one of instructing to one of guiding (Magon & Shore, 2022). There are no time restrictions on students' ability to obtain resources, finish assignments, or turn in papers. Giving students precise instructions may be essential to the effectiveness of asynchronous learning (Mandasari et al., 2022). This type of education stands out because of its self-directed learning and accessibility from any location at any time.

Compared to traditional face-to-face contacts, online asynchronous interactions have a higher chance of initiating, maintaining, and fostering academic success, affective connection, and student pleasure. Furthermore, asynchronous online interactions give students plenty of chances to offer formal feedback and reflect critically on the material they are learning, both of which are directly advantageous to cognitive growth (Durante, 2022). Due to the lack of time constraints, students have more time to think and plan since they are not expected to reply right away. This leads to a greater understanding of the topic (Perveen, 2016). Success in studying subjects can be accomplished if the training material is adequate and there is a high level of learning motivation due to the presence of independent learning activities. As a result, this method of learning enables pupils to think about the content in greater depth and detail.

CASE STUDIES AND PRACTICAL APPLICATIONS

Innovative pedagogies in K-12 and higher education have revolutionized learning environments and increased success around the world. These approaches emphasize active, student-centered learning, and frequently use technology, collaboration, and real-world problem solving. Below are some success stories from various levels of education:

1. K-12 Education

Kenya's Competency-Based Curriculum (CBC)

Kenya implemented a Competency-Based Curriculum (CBC) to convert its education system from content-based to competency-based learning.

Key Innovations:

- Instead than remembering content, focus on qualities like creativity, critical thinking, and cooperation.
- Integration of technology and digital technologies to help students learn.
- Flexible learning routes that take into account each student's talents and interests.

Outcomes: While still in its early phases, the CBC has shown promise in generating learners who are more adaptive and better equipped for the challenges of the twenty-first century. Teachers and students have provided good comments on the program's early adoption, citing higher student involvement and a more dynamic classroom atmosphere (kiwimbi, 2024).

Project-Based Learning at High Tech High (USA)

High Tech High (HTH) in California pioneered Project-Based Learning (PBL), in which students work on real-world projects that combine many topics.

Key Innovations:

- Interdisciplinary projects that require students to collaborate in groups, learn problem-solving techniques, and create concrete goods (for example, creating robots or initiating social initiatives).
- To demonstrate interconnection, blur the lines across areas such as math, physics, history, and art.
- A heavy emphasis on student agency and voice, which allows students to choose their own learning.

Outcomes: The strategy has resulted in increased student engagement and deeper learning outcomes. High Tech High graduates have a high rate of college acceptance, and students report feeling prepared for the collaborative and dynamic nature of higher education and the workplace (HTH, 2024).

2. Higher Education

Minerva Schools at Keck Graduate Institute (KGI)

Minerva Schools is a higher education institution that combines active learning with a worldwide curriculum to encourage critical thinking and problem solving in real-world settings.

Key Innovations:

- Fully active-learning model in which students participate in online seminars that emphasize active involvement, debate, and problem solving.
- Students participate in a global immersion program in up to seven locations throughout the world, applying what they have learned in a variety of cultural and societal contexts.
- Instead of typical lectures, students collaborate on projects, participate in simulations, and solve problems interactively.

Outcomes: Minerva graduates have been hired by top businesses including Google, McKinsey, and Tesla. The program has proved that students who have been taught in active-learning pedagogies are better prepared to apply knowledge in complicated, real-world circumstances (Edge Foundation, 2024).

Olin College of Engineering (USA)

Olin College of Engineering is well-known for its design thinking and hands-on engineering methodology.

Key Innovations:

- Beginning with the first year of study, students engage in collaborative, project-based learning focused on solving real-world engineering challenges.
- Collaborations with industry to guarantee that students are working on relevant, practical challenges.
- Concentrate on student agency, in which students co-design portions of the curriculum and actively shape the educational experience.

Outcomes: Olin graduates have had great success in the employment market, with many launching their own businesses or landing positions at major tech corporations. The emphasis on problem solving and design thinking has resulted in engineers who are adaptive, innovative, and eager to innovate (Olin College of Engineering, 2024).

3. Corporate Training: Gamification

Deloitte Leadership Academy
Key Innovations:

- Deloitte uses gamification in its leadership training program to increase learner engagement and motivation.
- Gamification incentivizes learning with game-like aspects such as badges, leaderboards, and levels.

Outcomes:

Increased Engagement: The addition of gamified components resulted in a 50% boost in engagement, as employees spent more time on the site.

Leadership Skills: The training's success extended to the development of leadership skills among managers and employees at all levels.

Widespread Adoption: Over 20,000 CEOs worldwide completed the gamified training program, with many claiming improved performance and leadership skills (Gray, 2024).

Key Lessons From These Success Stories

Innovative pedagogies in both the K-12 and higher education systems and corporate training are transforming how students learn and apply knowledge. These success stories demonstrate that when education goes beyond standard methods—such as PBL, active learning, and technology integration—students become more involved, motivated, and prepared for future opportunities. The key to success is to promote critical thinking, creativity, and cooperation while linking learning with real-world circumstances.

Active, Hands-On Learning: Whether using PBL, flipped classrooms, or gamification, all successful examples emphasize active learner participation. Active learning promotes critical thinking and improves knowledge retention.

Personalized Learning Experiences: These approaches frequently allow for self-paced learning, which caters to individual needs and promotes a more personalized educational experience.

Real-World Relevance: Connecting learning to real-world problems or industry demands boosts motivation and application, making training more meaningful and engaging.

Scalability and Technology: Using technology, such as MOOCs or gamified platforms, enables scaled solutions, making high-quality learning more accessible worldwide.

CHALLENGES AND CONSIDERATIONS

Implementing innovative digitalized pedagogies brings multiple obstacles and considerations in a variety of educational settings. As educators and institutions seek to incorporate technology-driven methods into teaching and learning, they must address both technical and pedagogical difficulties that necessitate careful planning and adaptation. Here are some of the main issues and considerations.

1. Technological Infrastructure

   Challenge: Schools and colleges may not have the requisite technology, software, or internet access to effectively embrace digitalized pedagogies. This involves access to gadgets (laptops and tablets), dependable high-speed internet, and suitable LMSs.

   Consideration: Institutions must invest in infrastructure to ensure equitable access for all students, including those from underserved communities. Continuous technical assistance is crucial for minimizing downtime and disruptions in learning.

2. Digital Literacy for Teachers and Students

   Challenge: In order to use the tools effectively, both educators and students must be highly digitally literate. Teachers may be reluctant to accept technology if they feel unprepared or overwhelmed by the complexities of new systems.

   Consideration: Teachers should receive ongoing professional development and training to ensure they are comfortable and confident when using digital tools. Similarly, pupils must be trained to navigate internet platforms and manage digital content.

3. Pedagogical Shifts

   Challenge: Traditional instructional approaches do not necessarily work effectively in digital situations. The transition from teacher-centered to learner-centered techniques, such as flipped classrooms or self-paced learning, may be difficult for educators who are accustomed to direct instruction.

Consideration: Teachers must reconsider and modify lesson plans, emphasizing active learning practices that capitalize on the capabilities of digital tools (e.g., multimedia materials, interactive simulations). Pedagogy should prioritize cooperation, critical thinking, and student engagement over information transmission.

4. Student Engagement and Motivation

   Challenge: Maintaining student engagement in a digital or hybrid setting can be difficult. Virtual learning settings might feel alienating, which reduces involvement and motivation.

   Consideration: Use digital tools to create interactive and engaging learning experiences. Gamification, peer collaboration platforms, and real-time feedback are all useful features for keeping students interested. Furthermore, the design of digital learning environments should promote social engagement and community creation.

5. Assessment and Evaluation

   Challenge: Traditional evaluation approaches, such as written exams or in-person testing, may not be effective in digital environments. Cheating and academic integrity are even more difficult to monitor in online settings.

   Consideration: Educators should use alternate assessment methods such as project-based learning, peer evaluations, digital portfolios, and formative exams that track students' progress over time. Technologies like AI-based proctoring can be utilized for secure examinations, but ethical concerns about spying must be addressed.

6. Equity and Inclusion

   Challenge: Not all students have equal access to technology, resulting in a digital divide that exacerbates already existing inequities in education. Students with disabilities may encounter additional challenges when using digital technologies.

   Consideration: To ensure that digital pedagogies are inclusive, schools should provide resources such as borrowed devices, subsidized internet access, and assistive technologies. Courses should be developed with accessibility in mind, incorporating universal design principles to meet a variety of learning needs.

7. Data Privacy and Security

   Challenge: As reliance on digital platforms grows, so are concerns about data privacy and cybersecurity. Student information, learning analytics, and personal data are all at danger of compromise.

Consideration: Institutions must follow data privacy requirements (e.g., GDPR, FERPA) and adopt strong cybersecurity policies. Students and teachers should be informed on the necessity of safeguarding personal information and using secure online practices.

8. Costs and Sustainability

    Challenge: Developing and sustaining novel digital technologies can be expensive, especially for impoverished educational institutions. Beyond initial installation, the long-term viability of digital tools, software licenses, and infrastructure necessitates continuous investment.

    Consideration: Schools and universities should carefully assess the cost-effectiveness of various digital tools, prioritizing scalable and long-term solutions. Partnerships with EdTech businesses or government financing programs can help relieve financial stress.

9. Institutional and Cultural Resistance

    Challenge: Organizational inertia and aversion to change might impede the implementation of digitalized pedagogies. Educators who are used to traditional methods may feel frightened or apprehensive about technology's involvement in the classroom.

    Consideration: Change management measures, such as clear communication of the benefits of digitization, leadership support, and the promotion of an innovative culture, can help overcome reluctance. Encouraging small-scale experimentation before full deployment can boost employee confidence.

10. Quality Control and Oversight

    Challenge: Ensuring the quality of education in digital contexts can be more difficult to regulate than in traditional settings. If digital tools are not carefully vetted, there is a risk of inconsistent delivery or inadequate content, and teachers may struggle to adapt to the technology.

    Consideration: Institutions should provide clear norms and criteria for digital course creation, delivery, and evaluation. Regular feedback loops between students and professors can assist monitor the quality of digitalized pedagogies and make necessary modifications.

FUTURE DIRECTIONS AND TRENDS

AR and VR: These technologies are fast gaining popularity in education, providing immersive learning experiences that can improve students' comprehension and engagement. AR and VR can help bridge the gap between theoretical understanding and practical application by offering 3D simulations, virtual field trips, and interactive lessons. Medical students, for example, can practice procedures in a virtual setting, while history students can learn about historical events by virtually journeying back in time. These technologies are anticipated to become more accessible as prices fall and hardware improves.

AI and machine learning are changing digital education by allowing students to follow tailored learning paths depending on their performance, learning styles, and interests. AI-powered adaptive learning solutions may personalize course content to individual needs while also automating evaluations, feedback, and tutoring. AI can also assist educators with administrative work, freeing up time for instructional design and student interaction. As AI advances, it will play an even greater role in promoting student achievement through data-driven insights and individualized instruction.

Blockchain for Credentialing and Assessment: Blockchain technology has the potential to transform how academic records and credentials are saved, verified, and distributed. Decentralized ledgers allow educational institutions to securely track and authenticate students' achievements, making credentials more portable and transparent. Blockchain can also help recognize micro-credentials from diverse institutions, supporting lifelong learning and skill building in a verifiable, trustworthy way.

Gamification and Game-Based Learning: Gamification employs game design elements such as points, badges, and leaderboards to boost engagement and motivation during the learning process. Game-based learning, which uses actual games to teach concepts, is gaining popularity as a method of making hard topics more accessible. These strategies encourage students' critical thinking, teamwork, and problem-solving abilities by including challenge-based and interactive learning experiences.

Wearable Technologies: Wearable gadgets, such as smartwatches and health trackers, are increasingly being used in educational settings, notably in health and physical education. These gadgets can monitor physical activity, provide real-time feedback, and aid in assessing academic performance and engagement. In the future, more specialized wearable technology, such as AR glasses, may be integrated into education by allowing students to interact with digital content in more dynamic ways.

Predictions for the Next Decade of Digital Education

Ubiquitous Personalized Learning: The future of digital education is projected to be more individualized, with AI-powered adaptive learning systems that enable students to learn at their own speed. These tools will evaluate students' strengths and weaknesses in real time and adapt course materials and activities accordingly.

This transition will result in a more personalized educational experience, perhaps lowering dropout rates and enhancing student achievement.

Greater Emphasis on Lifelong Learning and Microcredentials: As the work market evolves, there will be a greater emphasis on lifelong learning. The rise of micro-credentials—smaller, more concentrated qualifications—will allow individuals to constantly refresh their skills and knowledge in order to remain competitive in their employment. These short-term programs, which are verified via blockchain technology, will enable learners to acquire recognition for their talents in a flexible, on-demand manner.

Globalized and Collaborative Learning: The next decade will likely see an increase in globalized education, with students collaborating across boundaries via virtual classrooms and online platforms. As digital education platforms grow in popularity, cross-cultural exchanges and international partnerships will become more common, fostering global citizenship and a more diversified learning environment. Virtual reality technologies, for example, might enable students from all over the world to "attend" the same virtual classrooms.

AI-Driven Evaluation and Support: The use of AI for continuous, formative evaluation will become more common. AI-powered solutions will provide educators with real-time data on student performance, allowing them to create individualized support programs. These tools will also handle administrative responsibilities like grading, freeing up instructors' time to focus on teaching tactics and mentorship.

Blended Learning and Hybrid Classrooms: While physical classrooms will remain vital, there will be a greater mix of in-person and digital learning, particularly in higher education and corporate training. This hybrid paradigm is adaptable, accommodating a wide range of learning styles and timetables. As educational institutions adopt this paradigm, digital tools and learning management systems will grow more advanced, enabling for seamless transitions between physical and virtual worlds.

Strategies for Educators to Stay Ahead of Technological Advances and Pedagogical Innovations

Continuous Professional Development (CPD): Educators must engage in continuous professional development to stay current with the latest educational technologies and instructional approaches. Institutions should provide workshops, webinars, and certifications centered on digital technologies, data literacy, and innovative pedagogies. CPD programs may also feature collaborative learning with peers to discuss best practices and innovations.

Educators can create or join professional learning networks (PLNs) using social media platforms, blogs, or online forums where they can engage with other educators, technologists, and academics. PLNs enable educators to share materials, discuss trends, and learn from global experts in real time. Active engagement in such networks promotes creativity and enables educators to keep ahead of emerging technology.

Experimentation with New Tools and Methods: Educators should be willing to try new digital tools and teaching practices in the classroom. Piloting AR, AI, or gamification tools, for example, allows educators to acquire direct experience with how these innovations affect student engagement and learning results. Early experimentation is also beneficial in tailoring these tools to specific pedagogical demands.

Educators can stay updated by attending education technology conferences, reading academic journals, and following research articles on emerging trends. EdTech conferences such as ISTE, BETT, and EduTECH provide opportunity to witness the newest technical innovations in action while also networking with industry professionals. To obtain regular updates, educators can subscribe to EdTech-specific newsletters or blogs.

Collaboration between Industry and Technologists: Collaboration with EdTech firms and researchers can provide educators with early access to innovative tools and solutions, as well as feedback on their effectiveness. Such cooperation can assist personalized technological solutions to specific classroom demands, fostering innovations based on real-world educational situations.

By actively using these techniques, educators may effectively traverse the quickly changing landscape of digital education, ensuring that they remain at the forefront of pedagogical innovation while offering students with enriched learning experiences.

CONCLUSION

The field of creative pedagogies for the digital age is dynamic and ever-changing, with tremendous potential to transform education. Adopting these new tactics allows teachers to create more inclusive, successful, and engaging learning experiences that prepare students for the challenges of the twenty-first century. Implementing innovative digitalized pedagogies has enormous potential for improving learning experiences, yet it presents major hurdles. A comprehensive approach is required for successful deployment, which includes infrastructure, instructional methodologies, digital literacy, inclusion, and ethical issues. With careful preparation, constant support, and a willingness to adapt, institutions can harness the power of digital tools to improve education for all students.

REFERENCES

Alakrash, H. M., & Abdul Razak, N. (2021). Technology-based language learning: Investigation of digital technology and digital literacy. *Sustainability (Basel)*, 13(21), 12304. DOI: 10.3390/su132112304

Almarashdeh, I. (2016). Sharing instructors' experience of learning management system: A technology perspective of user satisfaction in distance learning course. *Computers in Human Behavior*, 63, 249–255. DOI: 10.1016/j.chb.2016.05.013

Anderson, T. (2008). *The Theory and Practice of Online Learning*. Athabasca University Press. DOI: 10.15215/aupress/9781897425084.01

Argüello, G., & Méndez, M. G. (2019). Virtual advising: A tool for retention, engagement, and success for the graduate student learner. *Distance Learning : for Educators, Trainers, and Leaders*, 16(2), 51–57.

Arif, T. B., Munaf, U., & Ul-Haque, I. (2023). The future of medical education and research: Is ChatGPT a blessing or blight in disguise? *Medical Education Online*, 28(1), 2181052. DOI: 10.1080/10872981.2023.2181052 PMID: 36809073

Auer, M. E., Hortsch, H., & Sethakul, P. (2020). The Impact of the 4th Industrial Revolution on Engineering Education. In *Proceedings of the 22nd International Conference on Interactive Collaborative Learning*.

Auer, M. E., & Rüütmann, T. (2021). *Educating Engineers for Future Industrial Revolutions*. Springer Nature Switzerland.

Bandura, A. (1977). *Social Learning Theory*. Prentice Hall.

Banerjee, M., Chiew, D., Patel, K. T., Johns, I., Chappell, D., Linton, N., Cole, G. D., Francis, D. P., Szram, J., Ross, J., & Zaman, S. (2021). The impact of artificial intelligence on clinical education: Perceptions of postgraduate trainee doctors in London (UK) and recommendations for trainers. *BMC Medical Education*, 21(1), 1–10. DOI: 10.1186/s12909-021-02870-x PMID: 34391424

Batista, J., Morais, S., & Ramos, F. (2016). Researching the use of communication technologies in higher education institutions in Portugal. In *Handbook of research on engaging digital natives in higher education settings* (pp. 280–303). IGI Global. DOI: 10.4018/978-1-5225-0039-1.ch013

Bayne, S. (2015). Teacherbot: Interventions in automated teaching. *Teaching in Higher Education*, 20(4), 455–467. DOI: 10.1080/13562517.2015.1020783

Božić, V. (2023). The use of digital tools and AI in education. *Preprint*, 1-14.

Brom, C., Starkova, T., & D'Mello, S. K. (2018). How effective is emotional design? A meta-analysis on facial anthropomorphisms and pleasant colors during multimedia learning. *Educational Research Review*, 25, 100–119. DOI: 10.1016/j.edurev.2018.09.004

Cao, F. (2021). Impact of the World's New Technological Revolution on Economic Development and Educational Reform in the Information Age. *Journal of Contemporary Educational Research*, 5(11), 207–216. DOI: 10.26689/jcer.v5i11.2802

Carvalho, A., Teixeira, S. J., Olim, L., Campanella, S., & Costa, T. (2021). Pedagogical innovation in higher education and active learning methodologies–a case study. *Education + Training*, 63(2), 195–213. DOI: 10.1108/ET-05-2020-0141

Chan, C., & Tsi, L. (2023). The AI revolution in education: Will AI replace or assist teachers in higher education? Computers and Society. *arXiv preprint arXiv:2305.01185.*

Cladis, A. E. (2020). A shifting paradigm: An evaluation of the pervasive effects of digital technologies on language expression, creativity, critical thinking, political discourse, and interactive processes of human communications. *E-Learning and Digital Media*, 17(5), 341–364. DOI: 10.1177/2042753017752583

Cloke, H. (2024). *Connectivism Learning Theory: Your Guide to Learning in the Digital Age*. Retrieved from https://www.growthengineering.co.uk/connectivism-learning-theory/

Croxall, B., & Koh, A. (2013). Digital pedagogy? *A Digital Pedagogy Unconference*. Retrieved from https://acortar.link/OlnuCI

Durante, P. G. C. (2022). Effectiveness of synchronous and asynchronous online learning delivery in developing oral communication competencies. *South Florida Journal of Development*, 3(3), 3529–3536. DOI: 10.46932/sfjdv3n3-039

Edge Foundation. (2024). *Minerva Schools at KGI*. Retrieved from https://www.edge.co.uk/research/practice-library/Minerva-Schools-at-KGI/

Elekaei, A. (2022). The Use of Adobe Connect in Synchronous Online Teaching. *Journal of University Teaching & Learning Practice*, 19(2), 60–72. DOI: 10.53761/1.19.2.5

Elmqaddem, N. (2019). Augmented reality and virtual reality in education. Myth or reality? *International Journal of Emerging Technologies in Learning*, 14(3), 234. DOI: 10.3991/ijet.v14i03.9289

Fisher, R., Herrington, J., & Staggers, N. (2020). Designing and implementing a hybrid course with a focus on student engagement. *The Journal of Educators Online*, 17(1).

Forbes, D. (2022). Student Expectations of Peers in Academic Asynchronous Online Discussion. *Journal of Open. Flexible and Distance Learning*, 26(1), 27–41. DOI: 10.61468/jofdl.v26i1.505

Frederiksen, J. G., Sørensen, S. M. D., Konge, L., Svendsen, M. B. S., Nobel-Jørgensen, M., Bjerrum, F., & Andersen, S. A. W. (2020). Cognitive load and performance in immersive virtual reality versus conventional virtual reality simulation training of laparoscopic surgery: A randomized trial. *Surgical Endoscopy*, 34(3), 1244–1252. DOI: 10.1007/s00464-019-06887-8 PMID: 31172325

French, B. H., Lewis, J. A., Mosley, D. V., Adames, H. Y., Chavez-Due˜nas, N. Y., Chen, G. A., & Neville, H. A. (2020). Toward a psychological framework of radical healing in communities of color. *The Counseling Psychologist*, 48(1), 14–46. DOI: 10.1177/0011000019843506

Gray, M. (2024). *How Deloitte Successfully Made Learning a Game*. Retrieved from https://www.engagify.io/blog/case-study-deloitte

Greenhow, C., & Lewin, C. (2019). Social media and education: Reconceptualizing the boundaries of formal and informal learning. In *social media and education* (pp. 6-30). Routledge.

Grimus, M. (2020). Emerging technologies: impacting learning, pedagogy and curriculum development. *Emerging Technologies and Pedagogies in the Curriculum,* 127–151.

Halaweh, M. (2023). Chatgpt in education: Strategies for responsible implementation. *Contemporary Educational Technology*, 15(2), 1–11. DOI: 10.30935/cedtech/13036

Haleem, A., Javaid, M., Qadri, M. A., & Suman, R. (2022). Understanding the role of digital technologies in education: A review. *Sustainable operations and computers, 3*, 275-285.

High Tech High (HTH). (2024). *Project-based Learning at HTH*. Retrieved from https://www.hightechhigh.org/student-work/projects/

Hong, C., & Ma, W. W. (2020). Introduction: Education 4.0: Applied degree education and the future of work. In *Applied Degree Education and the Future of Work: Education 4.0* (pp. 1–13). Springer Singapore. DOI: 10.1007/978-981-15-3142-2_1

Javed, F. (2024a). Digital Transformation in Teaching and Learning of English in Higher Education. In *Digital Transformation in Higher Education, Part B: Cases, Examples and Good Practices* (pp. 103-125). Emerald Publishing Limited. DOI: 10.1108/978-1-83608-424-220241005

Javed, F. (2024b). The Evolution of Artificial Intelligence in Teaching and Learning of English Language in Higher Education: Challenges, Risks, And Ethical Considerations. In *The Evolution of Artificial Intelligence in Higher Education Challenges, Risks, and Ethical Considerations*. Emerald Publishing Ltd. DOI: 10.1108/978-1-83549-486-820241015

Kayalar, M. T. (2021). Perspectives of University Students on the Efficiency of Synchronous and Asynchronous Learning. *Journal of Educational Leadership and Policy Studies*, 1–18.

Kırcaburun, K., Kokkinos, C. M., Demetrovics, Z., Király, O., Griffiths, M. D., & Çolak, T. S. (2019). Problematic online behaviors among adolescents and emerging adults: Associations between cyberbullying perpetration, problematic social media use, and psychosocial factors. *International Journal of Mental Health and Addiction*, 17(4), 891–908. DOI: 10.1007/s11469-018-9894-8

Kivunja, C. (2013). Embedding digital pedagogy in preservice higher education to better prepare teachers for the digital generation. *International Journal of Sustainability in Higher Education*, 2(4), 131–142.

kiwimbi (2024). *The New Competency Based Curriculum (CBC) in Kenya*. Retrieved from https://kiwimbi.org/blog/the-new-competency-based-curriculum-cbc-in-kenya/

Klimenko, A. Y. (2024). Technological Change and Its Effect on Education. *J Edu Psyc Res, 6*(1), 01-18.

Law, N. (2009). Mathematics and science teachers' pedagogical orientations and their use of ICT in teaching. *Education and Information Technologies*, 14(4), 309–323. DOI: 10.1007/s10639-009-9094-z

Lee, Y. J., Davis, R., & Li, Y. (2022). Implementing Synchronous Online Flipped Learning for Pre-Service Teachers during COVID-19. *European Journal of Educational Research*, 11(2), 653–661. DOI: 10.12973/eu-jer.11.2.653

Li, Y., & Tang, M. (2023). Blockchain-powered distributed data auditing scheme for cloud-edge healthcare system. *Cyber Security and Applications*, 1, 100017. DOI: 10.1016/j.csa.2023.100017

Lizardo, O. (2017). Improving cultural analysis: Considering personal culture in its declarative and nondeclarative modes. *American Sociological Review*, 82(1), 88–115. DOI: 10.1177/0003122416675175

Magon, J. K., & Shore, B. M. (2022). Asynchronous Posting and Reading both Reflect Communities of Inquiry. *International Journal for Talent Development and Creativity*, 10(1), 267–303.

Majewska, I., & Zvobgo, V. (2023). Students' Satisfaction with Quality of Synchronous Online Learning Under the COVID 19 Pandemic: Perceptions from Liberal Arts and Science Undergraduates. *Online Learning : the Official Journal of the Online Learning Consortium*, 27(1), 313–335. DOI: 10.24059/olj.v27i1.3201

Mandasari, B., Rido, A., & Kuswoyo, H. (2022). *Using Zoom Meeting Platform as a Synchronous Online Learning Tool in EFL Classroom at Indonesia Tertiary Level: A Literature Review*. International Association for Development of the Information Society.

Martínez-Bravo, M. C., S'adaba Chalezquer, C., & Serrano-Puche, J. (2022). Dimensions of digital literacy in the 21st century competency frameworks. *Sustainability (Basel)*, 14(3), 1867. DOI: 10.3390/su14031867

Mattar, J. (2018). Constructivism and connectivism in education technology: Active, situated, authentic, experiential, and anchored learning. *RIED- Revista Iberoamericana de Educación a Distancia, 21*(2), 200-213.

McKnight, K., O'Malley, K., Ruzic, R., Horsley, M. K., Franey, J. J., & Bassett, K. (2016). Teaching in a digital age: How educators use technology to improve student learning. *Journal of Research on Technology in Education*, 48(3), 194–211. DOI: 10.1080/15391523.2016.1175856

McNulty, N. (2023). Digital Pedagogy, or How Best to Incorporate Technology in Your Teaching. Retrieved from https://medium.com/@niall.mcnulty/digital-pedagogy-or-how-best-to-incorporate-technology-in-your-teaching-0a6dc0e3e5e2

Means, B., Toyama, Y., Murphy, R., Bakia, M., & Jones, K. (2009). *Evaluation of evidence based practices in online learning: A meta-analysis and review of online learning studies*. U.S. Department of Education. Retrieved from https://www2.ed.gov/rschstat/eval/tech/evidence based practices/finalreport.pdf

Milton, M., & Vozzo, L. (2013). Digital literacy and digital pedagogies for teaching literacy: Pre-service teachers' experience on teaching rounds. *The Journal of Literacy and Technology*, 14(1), 72–97.

Nichols, T. P., LeBlanc, R. J., & Garcia, A. (2024). After digital literacy: Media pedagogies for platform ecologies. In *World Yearbook of Education 2024* (pp. 212–226). Routledge.

Nygren, H., Nissinen, K., Hämäläinen, R., & De Wever, B. (2019). Lifelong learning: Formal, non-formal and informal learning in the context of the use of problem-solving skills in technology-rich environments. *British Journal of Educational Technology*, 50(4), 1759–1770. DOI: 10.1111/bjet.12807

Olin College of Engineering. (2024). *Best Colleges US News*. Retrieved from https://www.olin.edu/

Payne, C., & Reinhart, C. (2008). Can we talk? Course management software and the construction of knowledge. *On the Horizon*, 16(1), 34–43. DOI: 10.1108/10748120810853336

Penprase, B. E. (2018). The fourth industrial revolution and higher education. *Higher education in the era of the fourth industrial revolution*, 207-229.

Perez, T. (2003). *Multinational enterprises and technological spillovers*. Routledge. DOI: 10.4324/9780203362914

Perveen, A. (2016). Synchronous and asynchronous e-language learning: A case study of virtual University of Pakistan. *Open Praxis*, 8(1), 21–39. DOI: 10.5944/openpraxis.8.1.212

Pires, F., Masanet, M. J., Tomasena, J. M., & Scolari, C. A. (2022). Learning with YouTube: Beyond formal and informal through new actors, strategies and affordances. *Convergence (London)*, 28(3), 838–853. DOI: 10.1177/13548565211020545

Popenici, S. A., & Kerr, S. (2017). Exploring the impact of artificial intelligence on teaching and learning in higher education. *Research and Practice in Technology Enhanced Learning*, 12(1), 22. DOI: 10.1186/s41039-017-0062-8 PMID: 30595727

Prestridge, S. (2012). The beliefs behind the teacher that influences their ICT practices. *Computers & Education*, 58(1), 449–458. DOI: 10.1016/j.compedu.2011.08.028

Rospigliosi, P. A. (2023). Artificial intelligence in teaching and learning: What questions should we ask of ChatGPT? *Interactive Learning Environments*, 31(1), 1–3. DOI: 10.1080/10494820.2023.2180191

Sándor, Á., & Gubán, Á. (2022). A multi-dimensional model to the digital maturity life-cycle for SMEs. *International Journal of Information Systems and Project Management*, 10(3), 58–81. DOI: 10.12821/ijispm100303

Saykili, A. (2019). Higher education in the digital age: The impact of digital connective technologies. *J. Educ. Technol. Online Learn.*, 2(1), 1–15. DOI: 10.31681/jetol.516971

Schöbel, S., Saqr, M., & Janson, A. (2021). Two decades of game concepts in digital learning environments—A bibliometric study and research agenda. *Computers & Education*, 173, 104296. DOI: 10.1016/j.compedu.2021.104296

Schwab, K. (2016). *The Fourth Industrial Revolution*. Switzerland, Geneva: World Economic Forum.

Selwyn, N., & Facer, K. (2014). The sociology of education and digital technology: Past, present and future. *Oxford Review of Education*, 40(4), 482–496. DOI: 10.1080/03054985.2014.933005

Sjöberg, D., & Holmgren, R. (2021). Informal workplace learning in swedish police education-a teacher perspective. *Vocations and Learning*, 14(2), 265–284. DOI: 10.1007/s12186-021-09267-3

Skulmowski, A., & Rey, G. D. (2020). The realism paradox: Realism can act as a form of signaling despite being associated with cognitive load. *Human Behavior and Emerging Technologies*, 2(3), 251–258. DOI: 10.1002/hbe2.190 PMID: 32838228

Southgate, E. (2020). *Artificial intelligence, ethics, equity and higher education: A 'beginning-of the-discussion' paper*. National Centre for Student Equity in Higher Education, Curtin University, and the University of Newcastle.

Southworth, J., Migliaccio, K., Glover, J., Glover, J., Reed, D., McCarty, C., Brendemuhl, J., & Thomas, A. (2023). Developing a model for AI across the curriculum: Transforming the higher education landscape via innovation in AI literacy. *Comput. Educ.: Artif. Intell.*, 4, 100127. DOI: 10.1016/j.caeai.2023.100127

Sweller, J. (1988). Cognitive load during problem solving: Effects on learning. *Cognitive Science*, 12(2), 257–285. DOI: 10.1207/s15516709cog1202_4

Sweller, J., van Merriënboer, J. J., & Paas, F. (2019). Cognitive architecture and instructional design: 20 years later. *Educational Psychology Review*, 31(2), 261–292. DOI: 10.1007/s10648-019-09465-5

Tondeur, J., van Braak, J., Ertmer, P., & Ottenbreit-Leftwich, A. (2017). Understanding the relationship between teachers' pedagogical beliefs and technology use in education: A systematic review of qualitative evidence. *Educational Technology Research and Development*, 65(3), 555–575. DOI: 10.1007/s11423-016-9481-2

Udd, A. P. (2010). *Pedagogiikan konstruktivistinen orientaatio opettajaksi opiskelevien kokemana* [Constructivist Orientation of pedagogy as experienced by pre-service teachers]. University of Oulu.

Utsumi, T., Al-Azab, M., & Elazab, S. (2019). 4th Industrial Revolution (4IR) for Smart Learning. *International Journal of Internet Education*, 18(1), 23–38. DOI: 10.21608/ijie.2019.98633

Villamil, A., & King, S. (2024). A Humane Social Learning-Informed Metaverse: Cultivating Positive Technology Experiences in Digital Learning Environments. *Cyberpsychology, Behavior, and Social Networking*, 27(1), 47–56. DOI: 10.1089/cyber.2023.0001 PMID: 38197842

Viriya, C. (2022). Exploring the Impact of Synchronous, Asynchronous, and Bichronous Online Learning Modes on EFL Students' Self-Regulated and Perceived English Language Learning. *Reflections: The SoL Journal*, 29(1), 88–111. DOI: 10.61508/refl.v29i1.260525

Vygotsky, L. S. (1978). *Mind in society: The development of higher psychological processes*. Harvard University Press.

Walkington, C. (2013). Using adaptive learning technologies to personalize instruction: The impact of relevant contexts on performance and learning outcomes. *Journal of Educational Psychology*, 105(4), 932–945. DOI: 10.1037/a0031882

Wang, C. X., Houdyshell, M., & Plescia, M. (2022). Synchronous Communication Technology for Remote Academic Advising at a State University. *Journal of Educational Research and Practice*, 12(1), 111–131. DOI: 10.5590/JERAP.2022.12.1.09

Yetti, E. (2024). Pedagogical innovation and curricular adaptation in enhancing digital literacy: A local wisdom approach for sustainable development in Indonesia context. *Journal of Open Innovation*, 10(1), 100233. DOI: 10.1016/j.joitmc.2024.100233

Young, N. (2024). *Connectivism Learning Theory: The Ultimate Guide for 2024*. Retrieved from https://www.teachfloor.com/blog/connectivism-learning-theory

Yusuf, B., Walters, L. M., & Sailin, S. N. (2020). Restructuring Educational Institutions for Growth in the Fourth Industrial Revolution (4IR): A Systematic Review. *International Journal of Emerging Technologies in Learning*, 15(3), 93–109. DOI: 10.3991/ijet.v15i03.11849

Zidny, R., Sjöström, J., & Eilks, I. (2020). A multi-perspective reflection on how indigenous knowledge and related ideas can improve science education for sustainability. *Science & Education*, 29(1), 145–185. DOI: 10.1007/s11191-019-00100-x

Compilation of References

Abate, G. T., Abay, K. A., Chamberlin, J., Kassim, Y., Spielman, D. J., & Tabe-Ojong, M. P. J. (2023). Digital tools and agricultural market transformation in Africa: Why are they not at scale yet, and what will it take to get there? *Food Policy*, 116, 102439. DOI: 10.1016/j.foodpol.2023.102439

Abdel Ghani, S. M. (2022). The impact of digital transformation on enhancing economic growth in Egypt. *Journal of Political Economy*, 15(14), 44–79.

Abdelkafi, N., Xu, J., Pero, M., Ciccullo, F., & Masi, A. (2023). Does the combination of sustainable business model patterns lead to truly sustainable business models? Critical analysis of existing frameworks and extensions. *Journal of Business Economics*, 93(4), 597–634. DOI: 10.1007/s11573-023-01140-0

Abitbol, A., Lee, N. M., & VanDyke, M. S. (2022). Examining the perceived transparency of DTC genetic testing company communication and its impact on consumer trust, attitude and behavioural intentions. *Journal of Communication Management (London)*, 26(3), 223–241. DOI: 10.1108/JCOM-01-2022-0006

Adnan, M., Ghazali, M., & Othman, N. Z. S. (2022). E-participation within the context of e-government initiatives: A comprehensive systematic review. *Telematics and Informatics Reports*, 8, 100015. DOI: 10.1016/j.teler.2022.100015

Adula, M., Birbirsa, Z. A., & Kant, S. (2023). The effect of interpersonal, problem solving and technical training skills on performance of Ethiopia textile industry: Continuance, normative and affective commitment as mediators. *Cogent Business & Management*, 10(3), 2286672. Advance online publication. DOI: 10.1080/23311975.2023.2286672

Ahmad, W., Rasool, A., Javed, A. R., Baker, T., & Jalil, Z. (2021). Cyber Security in IoT-Based Cloud Computing: A Comprehensive Survey. *Electronics, 11*(1), 16. MDPI. DOI: 10.3390/electronics11010016

Ahmed, K., Wilson, R., & Thompson, M. (2023). Comparative analysis of cybersecurity frameworks in global supply chains. *Journal of Information Security*, 14(3), 167–184.

Akerlof, G. A. (1970). The market for "lemons": Quality uncertainty and the market mechanism. *The Quarterly Journal of Economics*, 84(3), 488–500. DOI: 10.2307/1879431

Al Thani, D., Hassan, A., Chalghoumi, H., Othman, A., & Hammad, S. (2021). Addressing the Digital Gap for the Older Persons and their caregivers in the State of Qatar: A Stakeholders' Perspective. *2021 8th International Conference on ICT & Accessibility (ICTA)*, 01–06. DOI: 10.1109/ICTA54582.2021.9809430

Alabbasi, M. (2018), Digital Transformation and Change Management Practices in Qatari Organizations: Challenges and Recommendations [pdf], http://tinyurl.com/3hd3veff

Alakrash, H. M., & Abdul Razak, N. (2021). Technology-based language learning: Investigation of digital technology and digital literacy. *Sustainability (Basel)*, 13(21), 12304. DOI: 10.3390/su132112304

Al-Ghofaili, A. A., & Al-Mashari, M. A. (2014). *ERP system adoption traditional ERP systems vs. cloud-based ERP systems. In Fourth edition of the International Conference on the Innovative Computing Technology* (INTECH 2014) (pp. 135-139). IEEE

Alhaimer, R. (2024). Exploring the Attitudes of Kuwait's Residents Toward the Role of Corruption and Anti-Corruption Entities (Nazaha) in Kuwait. *Public Integrity*, 26(3), 305–321. DOI: 10.1080/10999922.2023.2176054

Alhalboosi, F. H. A., Mawlood, S. J., & Al-halboosi, I. A. M. (2021). Role of ERP systems in improving human resources management processes. *Review of International Geographical Education Online*, 11(4), 1667–1681.

Alharbi, A. S. (2020), Challenges in Digital Transformation in Saudi Arabia Obstacles in Paradigm Shift in Saudi Arabia, *6th International Conference on Computing for Sustainable Global Development (INDIACom)*, New Delhi, India, pp. 1287-1291.

AL-Hawamleh, A.AL-Hawamleh. (2024). Cyber Resilience Framework: Strengthening Defenses and Enhancing Continuity in Business Security. *International Journal of Computing and Digital Systems*, 15(1), 1315–1331. DOI: 10.12785/ijcds/150193

Ali, A., Al-rimy, B., Alsubaei, F. S., Almazroi, A., & Almazroi, A. A. (2023). HealthLock: Blockchain-Based Privacy Preservation Using Homomorphic Encryption in Internet of Things Healthcare Applications. *Sensors (Basel)*, 23(15), 6762. DOI: 10.3390/s23156762 PMID: 37571545

Aljazzaf, Z. M., Ayad, S., & Sarfraz, M. (2020). E-Participation Model for Kuwait e-Government. *International Journal of Advanced Computer Science and Applications*, 11(2). Advance online publication. DOI: 10.14569/IJACSA.2020.0110226

Allbabidi, M. H. A. (2021). Hype or Hope: Digital Technologies in the auditing process. *Asian Journal of Business and Accounting*, 14(1), 59–86. DOI: 10.22452/ajba.vol14no1.3

Almarashdeh, I. (2016). Sharing instructors' experience of learning management system: A technology perspective of user satisfaction in distance learning course. *Computers in Human Behavior*, 63, 249–255. DOI: 10.1016/j.chb.2016.05.013

Al-Roubaie, A. (2019) Building capacity for digital development in the Arab world. Role Educ. Int. J. Eng. Adv. Technol. (IJEAT) 8(2249–8958, 5C), 1530–1537

Al-Roubaier, A., Hamdan, A., & Sarea, A. M. (2020). Economic Diversification in a Digital Economy. In: Hassanien, AE., Azar, A., Gaber, T., Oliva, D., Tolba, F. (eds) Proceedings of the International Conference on Artificial Intelligence and Computer Vision (AICV2020). AICV 2020. Advances in Intelligent Systems and Computing, vol 1153. Springer, Cham. DOI: 10.1007/978-3-030-44289-7_62

Alsirhani, A., Ezz, M., & Mohamed Mostafa, A. (2022). Advanced Authentication Mechanisms for Identity and Access Management in Cloud Computing. *Computer Systems Science and Engineering*, 43(3), 967–984. DOI: 10.32604/csse.2022.024854

Álvarez-Carmona, M. Á., Aranda, R., Rodríguez-Gonzalez, A. Y., Fajardo-Delgado, D., Sánchez, M. G., Pérez-Espinosa, H., Martínez-Miranda, J., Guerrero-Rodríguez, R., Bustio-Martínez, L., & Díaz-Pacheco, Á. (2022). Natural language processing applied to tourism research: A systematic review and future research directions. *Journal of King Saud University. Computer and Information Sciences*, 34(10), 10125–10144. DOI: 10.1016/j.jksuci.2022.10.010

Aman, S., & Jan, M. A. (2022). Are we moving towards a managerial model of e-governance? building a case for citizen centric e-participation in Khyber Pakhtunkhwa, Pakistan. *Journal of Humanities* [JHSMS]. *Social and Management Sciences*, 3(1), 500–523. DOI: 10.47264/idea.jhsms/3.1.35

Amini, M., & Bienstock, C. C. (2014). Corporate sustainability: An integrative definition and framework to evaluate corporate practice and guide academic research. *Journal of Cleaner Production*, 76, 12–19. DOI: 10.1016/j.jclepro.2014.02.016

Amra, J. (2021). *Cyber threats are on the rise in these industries in South Africa. Business Tech,* 4 July. Available: https://businesstech.co.za/news/cloud-hosting/502645/cyber-threats-are-on-the-rise-in-these-industries-in-south-africa/

Anderson, K., Brown, P., & Davis, R. (2024). Cloud security adoption in SMEs: Cost-benefit analysis. *Small Business Technology Journal*, 12(1), 78–92.

Anderson, K., & Roberts, J. (2023). Comparative analysis of major supply chain attacks: Lessons from SolarWinds. *Journal of Cybersecurity Management*, 14(3), 167–182.

Anderson, R., & Smith, P. (2024). Evolution of security culture in post-pandemic supply chains. *Journal of Cybersecurity Management*, 11(1), 23–38.

Anderson, T. (2008). *The Theory and Practice of Online Learning*. Athabasca University Press. DOI: 10.15215/aupress/9781897425084.01

Androniceanu, A., Kinnunen, J., & Georgescu, I. (2020). E-government clusters in the eu based on the gaussian mixture models. *Administratie Si Management Public*, 2020(35), 6–20. DOI: 10.24818/amp/2020.35-01

Apple Inc. (2019). *Privacy. That is iPhone.* Apple Newsroom. Retrieved from https://www.apple.com/newsroom/2019/01/privacy-thats-iphone/

Argüello, G., & Méndez, M. G. (2019). Virtual advising: A tool for retention, engagement, and success for the graduate student learner. *Distance Learning : for Educators, Trainers, and Leaders*, 16(2), 51–57.

Arif, T. B., Munaf, U., & Ul-Haque, I. (2023). The future of medical education and research: Is ChatGPT a blessing or blight in disguise? *Medical Education Online*, 28(1), 2181052. DOI: 10.1080/10872981.2023.2181052 PMID: 36809073

Armenta, A. (2021). *A Look into Automated Enterprise Resource Planning (ERP) Systems (article).* Available: https://control.com/technical-articles/A-Look-Into Automated-Enterprise-Resource-Planning-ERP-Systems/

Aroba, O. J., & Mnguni, S. B. (2023). An Enterprise Resource Planning (ERP) SAP Implementation: Case Study in South Africa Small Medium Enterprise Sectors. *InInternational Conference on Digital Technologies and Applications* (pp. 348-354). Cham: Springer Nature Switzerland. DOI: 10.1007/978-3-031-29857-8_35

Aroba, O. J., Chinsamy, K. K., & Makwakwa, T. G. (2022). *An ERP Implementation Case Study in the South African Retail Sector.InInternational Conference on Hybrid Intelligent Systems(pp.948-958).* Cham: Springer Nature Switzerland.

Aroba, O. J., Chisita, C. T., Buthelezi, N., & Mthethwa, N. (2023), February. Higher education enterprise resource planning system transformation of supply chain management processes. In *International Congress on Information and Communication Technology* (pp. 415-424). Singapore: Springer Nature Singapore.

Aroba, O.J. & Prinavin, G. (2023). Improving supply chain management processes through digital transformation of ERP systems in the oil and gas industry. Interdisciplinary Journal of Economics and Business Law, 12 (3).

Aroba, O.J., Owoputi . O., & Temitayo, M.F. (2023). An SAP enterprise resource planning implementation using a case study of a hospital management system for inclusion of digital transformation. *International Journal of Computer Information Systems and Industrial Management Applications,* 15

Aroba, O. J. (2023). An ERP SAP Implementation: Case Study of the South African Small Medium Enterprise Sectors. *International Journal of Computing Sciences Research*, 7, 2196–2211. DOI: 10.25147/ijcsr.2017.001.1.155

Aroba, O. J., & Abayomi, A. (2023). An implementation of SAP enterprise resource planning–A case study of the South African revenue services and taxation sectors. *Cogent Social Sciences*, 9(1), 2228060. DOI: 10.1080/23311886.2023.2228060

Asefa, K., Kant, D. S., & Debela, K. L. (2023, November). Effect of Transformational Leadership on Organizational Performance: The Mediating Role of Employee Commitment and Expert Systems (AI) Inclusion in Ethiopia. In *2023 International Conference on Communication, Security and Artificial Intelligence (ICCSAI)* (pp. 305-310). IEEE.

Asgarinia, H., Penedo, A. C., Esteves, B., & Lewis, D. (2023). "Who Should I Trust with My Data?" Ethical and Legal Challenges for Innovation in New Decentralized Data Management Technologies. *Information (Basel)*, 14(7), 351. DOI: 10.3390/info14070351

Asgharifard, P. (2022). *Digital Technology Adoption as a Factor to Build Supply Chain Resilience: The Case of an Animal-Food Supply Chain During the COVID-19 Pandemic Crisis* (Doctoral dissertation, Polytechnique Montréal).

Ashrafi, M., Adams, M., Walker, T. R., & Magnan, G. (2018). How corporate social responsibility can be integrated into corporate sustainability: A theoretical review of their relationships. *International Journal of Sustainable Development and World Ecology*, 25(8), 672–682. DOI: 10.1080/13504509.2018.1471628

Auer, M. E., Hortsch, H., & Sethakul, P. (2020). The Impact of the 4th Industrial Revolution on Engineering Education. In *Proceedings of the 22nd International Conference on Interactive Collaborative Learning.*

Auer, M. E., & Rüütmann, T. (2021). *Educating Engineers for Future Industrial Revolutions.* Springer Nature Switzerland.

Aulia, R., Putri, A. N., Raihan, M. F., Ayub, M., & Sulistio, J. (2019). The literature review of cloud-based enterprise resource planning. [IOP Publishing.]. *IOP Conference Series. Materials Science and Engineering*, 598(1), 012036. DOI: 10.1088/1757-899X/598/1/012036

Avancha, S., Jain, A., & Goel, O. (2024). Blockchain-Based Vendor Management in IT: Challenges and Solutions. *South Journal of Management and Business Technology*, 2(2), 38–51. DOI: 10.36676/sjmbt.v2.i2.38

Baabdullah, A. M., Alalwan, A. A., Slade, E. L., Raman, R., & Khatatneh, K. F. (2021). SMEs and artificial intelligence (AI): Antecedents and consequences of AI-based B2B practices. *Industrial Marketing Management*, 98, 255–270. DOI: 10.1016/j.indmarman.2021.09.003

Badran, A. (2019). Smart-Governments for Smart Cities: The Case of Dubai Smart-Government. In Samad, W. A., & Azar, E. (Eds.), *Smart Cities in the Gulf* (pp. 59–82). Springer Nature Singapore., DOI: 10.1007/978-981-13-2011-8_5

Badran, A. (2021a). Developing Smart Cities: Regulatory and Policy Implications for the State of Qatar. *International Journal of Public Administration*, •••, 1–14. DOI: 10.1080/01900692.2021.2003811

Badran, A. (2021b). Thoughts and Reflections on the Case of Qatar: Should Artificial Intelligence Be Regulated? In Azar, E., & Haddad, A. N. (Eds.), *Artificial Intelligence in the Gulf* (pp. 69–92). Springer Singapore., DOI: 10.1007/978-981-16-0771-4_5

Badran, A. (2024). Regulating Cyberspace for Children: Reflections on the Qatari Case. *British Journal of Cyber Criminology*, 3(1). https://www.pubtexto.com/pdf/?regulating-cyberspace-for-children-reflections-on-the-qatari-case

Balsalobre-Lorente, D., Abbas, J., He, C., Pilař, L., & Shah, S. A. R. (2023). Tourism, urbanization and natural resources rents matter for environmental sustainability: The leading role of AI and ICT on sustainable development goals in the digital era. *Resources Policy*, 82, 103445. DOI: 10.1016/j.resourpol.2023.103445

Bandura, A. (1977). *Social Learning Theory*. Prentice Hall.

Banerjee, M., Chiew, D., Patel, K. T., Johns, I., Chappell, D., Linton, N., Cole, G. D., Francis, D. P., Szram, J., Ross, J., & Zaman, S. (2021). The impact of artificial intelligence on clinical education: Perceptions of postgraduate trainee doctors in London (UK) and recommendations for trainers. *BMC Medical Education*, 21(1), 1–10. DOI: 10.1186/s12909-021-02870-x PMID: 34391424

Baramy, A. (2020). *Benefits of having Odoo ERP for the Mining Industry Bassam Infotech Best Mining Software* (wiki). Available: https://bassaminfotech.com/why-is-erp-essential-for-the-mining-industry-bassam-infotech-best-mining-software/

Basri, N. H., Adnan, W. A. W., & Baharin, H. (2019). An exploratory study of users' experiences with e-participation: A case study of Malaysia. *Indonesian Journal of Electrical Engineering and Computer Science*, 15(3), 1138–1143. DOI: 10.11591/ijeecs.v15.i3.pp1138-1143

Basu, A., & Jha, R. (2024). ERP adoption prediction using machine learning techniques and ERP selection among SMEs. *International Journal of Business Performance Management*, 25(2), 242–270. DOI: 10.1504/IJBPM.2024.137005

Batista, J., Morais, S., & Ramos, F. (2016). Researching the use of communication technologies in higher education institutions in Portugal. In *Handbook of research on engaging digital natives in higher education settings* (pp. 280–303). IGI Global. DOI: 10.4018/978-1-5225-0039-1.ch013

Battilana, J., & Lee, M. (2014). Advancing research on hybrid organizing–Insights from the study of social enterprises. *The Academy of Management Annals*, 8(1), 397–441. DOI: 10.5465/19416520.2014.893615

Bayne, S. (2015). Teacherbot: Interventions in automated teaching. *Teaching in Higher Education*, 20(4), 455–467. DOI: 10.1080/13562517.2015.1020783

Bécue, A., Praça, I., & Gama, J. (2021). Artificial intelligence, cyber-threats and Industry 4.0: Challenges and opportunities. *Artificial Intelligence Review*, 54(5), 54. DOI: 10.1007/s10462-020-09942-2

Beerman, J., Berent, D., Falter, Z., & Bhunia, S. (2023, May 1). *A Review of Colonial Pipeline Ransomware Attack*. IEEE Xplore. DOI: 10.1109/CCGridW59191.2023.00017

Benfica, R., Chambers, J., Koo, J., Nin-Pratt, A., Falck-Zepeda, J., Stads, G. J., & Arndt, C. (2023). Food system innovations and digital technologies to Foster productivity progression and rural transformation. *Science and innovations for food systems transformation, 421.*

Bhatia, I., & Mabillard, V. (2022). How do cities use their communication channels? A study of social media adoption in two European federal states. *Electronic Government*, 18(2), 119–136. DOI: 10.1504/EG.2022.121970

Bhattacharyya, S. S., & Shah, Y. (2022). Emerging technologies in Indian mining industry: An exploratory empirical investigation regarding the adoption challenges. *Journal of Science and Technology Policy Management*, 13(2), 358–381. DOI: 10.1108/JSTPM-03-2021-0048

Bhatt, N., Guru, S., Thanki, S., & Sood, G. (2021). Analysing the factors affecting the selection of ERP package: A fuzzy AHP approach. *Information Systems and e-Business Management*, 19(2), 641–682. DOI: 10.1007/s10257-021-00521-8

Bill, B. (2021). *Common Digital Transformation Challenges and How to overcome them.* Available at: https://www.panorama-consulting.com/digital-transformation-challenges/

Binns, R., Veale, M., Van Kleek, M., & Shadbolt, N. (2018). 'It's reducing a human being to a percentage': Perceptions of justice in algorithmic decisions. *Proceedings of the 2018 CHI Conference on Human Factors in Computing Systems*, 1–14. DOI: 10.1145/3173574.3173951

Birhane, M., Amentie, C., Borji, B., & Kant, S. (2024). Are Ethiopian Coffee Farmers Proficient to Predict Capital Structure with Mediation of AI Based Knowledge Systems and Asset Liquidity? In *AI in Agriculture for Sustainable and Economic Management* (pp. 199-215). CRC Press.

Bitkowska, A., Dziembek, D. & Gzik, T. (2024). Enterprise Resource Planning based on Cloud Computing (Cloud ERP). *Journal of Software & Systems Development, 2024.*

Bloom, P. N., & Chatterji, A. K. (2009). Scaling social entrepreneurial impact. *California Management Review*, 51(3), 114–133. DOI: 10.2307/41166496

Bocken, N. M., Short, S. W., Rana, P., & Evans, S. (2014). A literature and practice review to develop sustainable business model archetypes. *Journal of Cleaner Production*, 65, 42–56. DOI: 10.1016/j.jclepro.2013.11.039

Bocken, N., Strupeit, L., Whalen, K., & Nußholz, J. (2019). A review and evaluation of circular business model innovation tools. *Sustainability (Basel)*, 11(8), 2210. DOI: 10.3390/su11082210

Böhler, R. S. H. (2024). The Influence of Transparency in Personalized Recommendation Ads on Consumer Privacy Concerns and Purchase Intentions. *Legal Economics*, 8(3), 1–12. DOI: 10.56397/LE.2024.08.03

Boons, F., & Lüdeke-Freund, F. (2013). Business models for sustainable innovation: State-of-the-art and steps towards a research agenda. *Journal of Cleaner Production*, 45, 9–19. DOI: 10.1016/j.jclepro.2012.07.007

Bouchier, P. (2022). M*odern ERP Revolutionising Manufacturing Operations* (blog). Available: https://ioco.tech/modern-erp-revolutionising-manufacturing-operations

Božić, V. (2023). The use of digital tools and AI in education. *Preprint*, 1-14.

Brom, C., Starkova, T., & D'Mello, S. K. (2018). How effective is emotional design? A meta-analysis on facial anthropomorphisms and pleasant colors during multimedia learning. *Educational Research Review*, 25, 100–119. DOI: 10.1016/j.edurev.2018.09.004

Bugg-Levine, A., & Emerson, J. (2011). *Impact investing: Transforming how we make money while making a difference*. John Wiley & Sons.

Buhalis, D., Harwood, T., Bogicevic, V., Viglia, G., Beldona, S., & Hofacker, C. (2019). Technological disruptions in services: Lessons from tourism and hospitality. *Journal of Service Management*, 30(4), 484–506. DOI: 10.1108/JOSM-12-2018-0398

Buhalis, D., & Leung, R. (2018). Smart hospitality—Interconnectivity and interoperability towards an ecosystem. *International Journal of Hospitality Management*, 71, 41–50. DOI: 10.1016/j.ijhm.2017.11.011

Buhalis, D., & Sinarta, Y. (2019). Real-time co-creation and nowness service: Lessons from tourism and hospitality. *Journal of Travel & Tourism Marketing*, 36(5), 563–582. DOI: 10.1080/10548408.2019.1592059

Bui, M., Adjiman, C. S., Bardow, A., Anthony, E. J., Boston, A., Brown, S., Fennell, P. S., Fuss, S., Galindo, A., Hackett, L. A., Hallett, J. P., Herzog, H. J., Jackson, G., Kemper, J., Krevor, S., Maitland, G. C., Matuszewski, M., Metcalfe, I. S., Petit, C., & Mac Dowell, N. (2018). Carbon capture and storage (CCS): The way forward. *Energy & Environmental Science*, 11(5), 1062–1176. DOI: 10.1039/C7EE02342A

Bulchand-Gidumal, J., William Secin, E., O'Connor, P., & Buhalis, D. (2024). Artificial intelligence's impact on hospitality and tourism marketing: Exploring key themes and addressing challenges. *Current Issues in Tourism*, 27(14), 2345–2362. DOI: 10.1080/13683500.2023.2229480

Cabello, O. G., de Moraes, G. H. S. M., Watrin, C., Ribeiro da Silva, H. M., & Spers, E. E. (2020). The Influence of Sales Tax Transparency and Political Trust on Brazilian Consumer Behaviour. *Revista Contabilidade & Gestão Governamental*, 23(1), 1–22. DOI: 10.21714/1984-3925_2020v23n1a9

Camisón, C., Forés, B., & Puig-Denia, A. (2016). Return on capital in Spanish tourism businesses: A comparative analysis of family vs non-family businesses. *European Journal of Management and Business Economics*, 25(3), 91–110. DOI: 10.1016/j.redeen.2016.04.002

Cao, F. (2021). Impact of the World's New Technological Revolution on Economic Development and Educational Reform in the Information Age. *Journal of Contemporary Educational Research*, 5(11), 207–216. DOI: 10.26689/jcer.v5i11.2802

Cao, Y., Zhao, Y., Wang, Q., Zhang, J., Ng, S. X., & Hanzo, L. (2022). The Evolution of Quantum Key Distribution Networks: On the Road to the Qinternet. *IEEE Communications Surveys and Tutorials*, 24(2), 1–1. DOI: 10.1109/COMST.2022.3144219

Car, T., Pilepić Stifanich, L., & Šimunić, M. (2019). *Internet of things (iot) in tourism and hospitality: opportunities and challenges*. DOI: 10.20867/tosee.05.42

Carroll, A. B. (1999). Corporate social responsibility: Evolution of a definitional construct. *Business & Society*, 38(3), 268–295. DOI: 10.1177/000765039903800303

Carvalho, A., Teixeira, S. J., Olim, L., Campanella, S., & Costa, T. (2021). Pedagogical innovation in higher education and active learning methodologies–a case study. *Education + Training*, 63(2), 195–213. DOI: 10.1108/ET-05-2020-0141

Casillo, M., Clarizia, F., Colace, F., Lombardi, M., Pascale, F., & Santaniello, D. (2019). An Approach for Recommending Contextualized Services in e-Tourism. *Information (Basel)*, 10(5), 180. DOI: 10.3390/info10050180

Casino, F., Dasaklis, T. K., & Patsakis, C. (2019). A systematic literature review of blockchain-based applications: Current status, classification and open issues. *Telematics and Informatics*, 36, 55–81. DOI: 10.1016/j.tele.2018.11.006

Cha, S.-C., Tung, H.-W., Lee, H.-C., Tsai, T.-M., Lin, R., & Hsu, C.-H. (2005). Robalo: A risk-oriented job dispatching mechanism for workforce management system. In *IFIP Advances in Information and Communication Technology* (Vol. 189, pp. 559–570). Springer New York LLC. DOI: 10.1007/0-387-29773-1_37

Champagne, A., Drainville, N., Felt, C., Gao, Z., Herriford, C., Hobbs, E., Jain, M., Kalderash, N., Koeck, S., Krabill, E., Manning, B., Miranda, A., Nonnast, P., O'Laughlin, V., Sanguinet, S., & Wang, H. (2019). *International Cybersecurity: De-escalating tensions in a digital Era*. Digital.lib.washington.edu. https://digital.lib.washington.edu/researchworks/handle/1773/43755

Chan, C., & Tsi, L. (2023). The AI revolution in education: Will AI replace or assist teachers in higher education? Computers and Society. *arXiv preprint arXiv:2305.01185.*

Cheng, L., & Zhang, J. (2020). Is tourism development a catalyst of economic recovery following a natural disaster? An analysis of economic resilience and spatial variability. *Current Issues in Tourism*, 23(20), 2602–2623. DOI: 10.1080/13683500.2019.1711029

Chen, H., & Wu, X. (2023). Security challenges in 5G-enabled supply chains. *Network Security Journal*, 14(2), 112–126.

Chen, Y., & Lee, J. Y. (2021). Data transparency and trust in the financial sector. *Journal of Financial Services Marketing*, 26(2), 123–139. DOI: 10.1057/s41264-021-00079-2

Chouinard, Y., & Stanley, V. (2013). *The responsible company: What we've learned from Patagonia's first 40 years*. Patagonia.

Cinar, B. (2023). Supply Chain Cybersecurity: Risks, Challenges, and Strategies for a Globalized

Cladis, A. E. (2020). A shifting paradigm: An evaluation of the pervasive effects of digital technologies on language expression, creativity, critical thinking, political discourse, and interactive processes of human communications. *E-Learning and Digital Media*, 17(5), 341–364. DOI: 10.1177/2042753017752583

Cloke, H. (2024). *Connectivism Learning Theory: Your Guide to Learning in the Digital Age*. Retrieved from https://www.growthengineering.co.uk/connectivism-learning-theory/

Colajanni, M., & Marchetti, M. (2021). Cyber-attacks and defences: current capabilities and future trends. In *Technology and International Relations* (pp. 132–151). Edward Elgar Publishing. DOI: 10.4337/9781788976077.00015

Croxall, B., & Koh, A. (2013). Digital pedagogy? *A Digital Pedagogy Unconference*. Retrieved from https://acortar.link/OlnuCI

Cruz, E. (2022). *The traditional ERP system vs. a modern-day ERP system.* Frank Rimerman. (Online) Available at: https://www.frankrimerman.com/the-traditional-erp-system-vs-amodern-day-erp-syagement,stem/

Cuervo-Cazurra, A., Dieleman, M., Hirsch, P., Rodrigues, S. B., & Zyglidopoulos, S. (2021). Multinationals' misbehavior. *Journal of World Business*, 56(5), 101244. DOI: 10.1016/j.jwb.2021.101244

Dacin, P. A., Dacin, M. T., & Matear, M. (2010). Social entrepreneurship: Why we don't need a new theory and how we move forward from here. *The Academy of Management Perspectives*, 24(3), 37–57.

Dagnino, E., & Armaroli, I. (2019). A Seat at the Table: Negotiating Data Processing in the Workplace: A National Case Study and Comparative Insights Automation, Artificial Intelligence, & Labor Law. *Comparative Labor Law & Policy Journal*, 41(1), 173–196.

Dangelico, R. M. (2016). Green product innovation: Where we are and where we are going. *Business Strategy and the Environment*, 25(8), 560–576. DOI: 10.1002/bse.1886

Daoud, M. K., Al-Qeed, D. M., Al-Gasawneh, J., & Ziani, A. (2023). Examining the Ethical Implications of Data Privacy and Targeted Advertising in Digital Marketing: Consumer Perceptions. International Conference on Social Networks Analysis, Management, and Security (SNAMS), 10375481. DOI: 10.1109/SNAMS60348.2023.10375481

Davidson, M., & Chen, Y. (2023). Regulatory impact on supply chain security: A multinational study. *International Journal of Supply Chain Management*, 12(2), 89–106.

de Sousa Jabbour, A. B. L., Luiz, J. V. R., Luiz, O. R., Jabbour, C. J. C., Ndubisi, N. O., de Oliveira, J. H. C., & Junior, F. H. (2019). Circular economy business models and operations management. *Journal of Cleaner Production*, 235, 1525–1539. DOI: 10.1016/j.jclepro.2019.06.349

Demirel, P., Li, Q. C., Rentocchini, F., & Tamvada, J. P. (2019). Born to be green: New insights into the economics and management of green entrepreneurship. *Small Business Economics*, 52(4), 759–771. DOI: 10.1007/s11187-017-9933-z

Dereso, C. W., Kant, S., Muthuraman, M., & Tufa, G. (2023). Effect of Point of Service on Health Department Student's Creativity in Comprehensive Universities of Ethiopia: Moderating Role of Public-Private Partnership and Mediating Role of Work Place Learning. In: Jain, S., Groppe, S., Mihindukulasooriya, N. (eds) Proceedings of the International Health Informatics Conference. Lecture Notes in Electrical Engineering, vol 990. Springer, Singapore. https://doi.org/DOI: 10.1007/978-981-19-9090-8_13

Di Vaio, A., Palladino, R., Hassan, R., & Escobar, O. (2020). Artificial intelligence and business models in the sustainable development goals perspective: A systematic literature review. *Journal of Business Research*, 121, 283–314. DOI: 10.1016/j.jbusres.2020.08.019

Dias, G. P. (2020). Determinants of e-government implementation at the local level: An empirical model. *Online Information Review*, 44(7), 1307–1326. DOI: 10.1108/OIR-04-2020-0148

Doborjeh, Z., Hemmington, N., Doborjeh, M., & Kasabov, N. (2022). Artificial intelligence: A systematic review of methods and applications in hospitality and tourism. *International Journal of Contemporary Hospitality Management*, 34(3), 1154–1176. DOI: 10.1108/IJCHM-06-2021-0767

Doherty, B., Haugh, H., & Lyon, F. (2014). Social enterprises as hybrid organizations: A review and research agenda. *International Journal of Management Reviews*, 16(4), 417–436. DOI: 10.1111/ijmr.12028

Doshi-Velez, F., & Kim, B. (2017). Towards a rigorous science of interpretable machine learning. *arXiv preprint*. https://doi.org//arXiv.1702.08608DOI: 10.48550

du Venage, G. (2019). Strike at Sibanye-Stillwater Disrupts Operations. *Engineering and Mining Journal*, 220(1), 5–5.

Duale, M. M. (2024). Resilience and Transformation: Examining Pastoral Creation Initiatives in Ethiopia—Article Review. *OAlib*, 11(2), 1–17. DOI: 10.4236/oalib.1111215

Durante, P. G. C. (2022). Effectiveness of synchronous and asynchronous online learning delivery in developing oral communication competencies. *South Florida Journal of Development*, 3(3), 3529–3536. DOI: 10.46932/sfjdv3n3-039

Durga, P., Godavarthi, D., Kant, S., & Basa, S. S. (2024). Aspect-based drug review classification through a hybrid model with ant colony optimization using deep learning. *Discov Computing*, 27(1), 19. DOI: 10.1007/s10791-024-09441-w

Eales, L., & Van Schoor, J. (2022). *A slow adaptation and yet so many benefits* (wiki). Available at: https://www.africanmining.co.za/2022/05/03/robotics-a-slow-adoption-and-yet-so-many-benefits/

Ebrahim, A., Battilana, J., & Mair, J. (2014). The governance of social enterprises: Mission drift and accountability challenges in hybrid organizations. *Research in Organizational Behavior*, 34, 81–100. DOI: 10.1016/j.riob.2014.09.001

Edge Foundation. (2024). *Minerva Schools at KGI.* Retrieved from https://www.edge.co.uk/research/practice-library/Minerva-Schools-at-KGI/

Ediriweera, A., & Wiewiora, A. (2021). Barriers and enablers of technology adoption in the mining industry. *Resources Policy*, 73, 102188. DOI: 10.1016/j.resourpol.2021.102188

Egger, R. (2022). Machine Learning in Tourism: A Brief Overview: Generation of Knowledge from Experience. In Egger, R. (Ed.), *Applied Data Science in Tourism* (pp. 85–107). Springer International Publishing., DOI: 10.1007/978-3-030-88389-8_6

Elbahri, F. M., Al-Sanjary, O. I., Ali, M. M., Naif, Z. A., Ibrahim, O. A., & Mohammed, M. N. (2019). Difference Comparison of SAP, Oracle, and Microsoft Solutions Based on Cloud ERP Systems. *RE:view*, 65–70. Advance online publication. DOI: 10.1109/CSPA.2019.8695976

Elekaei, A. (2022). The Use of Adobe Connect in Synchronous Online Teaching. *Journal of University Teaching & Learning Practice*, 19(2), 60–72. DOI: 10.53761/1.19.2.5

Elidrisy, A. (2024). Leveraging Cloud Services & Digital Transformation for Sustainability: Insights from Cases of Qatar. *Journal of Innovative Research*, 2(1), 20–28. DOI: 10.54536/jir.v2i1.2398

Elkington, J. (2018). 25 years ago I coined the phrase "triple bottom line." Here's why it's time to rethink it. *Harvard Business Review*, 25(2-5).

Elkington, J., & Rowlands, I. H. (1999). Cannibals with forks: The triple bottom line of 21st century business. *Alternatives Journal*, 25(4), 42.

Elmqaddem, N. (2019). Augmented reality and virtual reality in education. Myth or reality? *International Journal of Emerging Technologies in Learning*, 14(3), 234. DOI: 10.3991/ijet.v14i03.9289

Emiri Diwan. (2016). *Law No. (13) of 2016 on Protecting Personal Data Privacy.* https://assurance.ncsa.gov.qa/sites/default/files/library/2020-11/Law%20No.%20%2813%29%20of%202016%20%20on%20Protecting%20Personal%20Data%20Privacy%20-%20English.pdf

Endalamaw, T. B., & Darr, D. (2021). Institutional and technological innovation for the bamboo sector as an instrument for development and climate change resilience in Ethiopia. *African Journal of Science, Technology, Innovation and Development*, 13(7), 817–828. DOI: 10.1080/20421338.2020.1837447

Erasmus, V. N., Johannes, F. N., Amutenya, N., & James, N. A. (2024). The potential contribution of end-of-life fishing nets, lines and ropes to a circular economy: The Namibian perspective. *Frontiers in Sustainability*, 5, 1356265. DOI: 10.3389/frsus.2024.1356265

Esmaeilzadeh, P. (2020). The Process of Building Patient Trust in Health Information Exchange (HIE): The Impacts of Perceived Benefits, Perceived Transparency of Privacy Policy, and Familiarity. *Communications of the Association for Information Systems*, 45(1), 21–45. DOI: 10.17705/1CAIS.04521

Esposito, M., Tse, T., & Soufani, K. (2017). Is the circular economy a new fast-expanding market? *Thunderbird International Business Review*, 59(1), 9–14. DOI: 10.1002/tie.21764

European Union. (2016). *General Data Protection Regulation (GDPR) (EU) 2016/679.* Official Journal of the European Union. Retrieved from https://eur-lex.europa.eu/legal-content/EN/TXT/?uri=celex%3A32016R0679

Fayi, S. Y. A. (2018). What Petya/NotPetya Ransomware Is and What Its Remidiations Are. *Advances in Intelligent Systems and Computing*, 93–100. DOI: 10.1007/978-3-319-77028-4_15

Feng, Y. (2020). Understanding consumer trust and purchase intention in mobile e-commerce: A perspective from data transparency and privacy policies. *Journal of Retailing and Consumer Services*, 55, 102135. DOI: 10.1016/j.jretconser.2020.102135

Ferede, D. M., Negash, S., & Meso, P. (2024). Strategic Information Systems (SIS) implementation at a bank in an emerging economy: Implications for strategic enterprise capabilities and societal creation. *Information Technology for Development*, 30(1), 10–32. DOI: 10.1080/02681102.2023.2225164

Ferede, W. L., Endawoke, Y., & Tessema, G. (2024). Change management through strategic leadership: The mediating effect of knowledge management in public organizations, Ethiopia. *Future Business Journal*, 10(1), 93. DOI: 10.1186/s43093-024-00363-z

Financial Industry Regulatory Authority (FINRA). (2019). *Rules and Guidance.* Retrieved from https://www.finra.org/rules-guidance

Fisher, R., Herrington, J., & Staggers, N. (2020). Designing and implementing a hybrid course with a focus on student engagement. *The Journal of Educators Online*, 17(1).

Forbes, D. (2022). Student Expectations of Peers in Academic Asynchronous Online Discussion. *Journal of Open. Flexible and Distance Learning*, 26(1), 27–41. DOI: 10.61468/jofdl.v26i1.505

Force intellect. (2020). *ERP Implementation Challenges & How to overcome them.* Available: https://forceintellect.com/2020/02/11/erp-implementation-challenges-overcome/

Frederiksen, J. G., Sørensen, S. M. D., Konge, L., Svendsen, M. B. S., Nobel-Jørgensen, M., Bjerrum, F., & Andersen, S. A. W. (2020). Cognitive load and performance in immersive virtual reality versus conventional virtual reality simulation training of laparoscopic surgery: A randomized trial. *Surgical Endoscopy*, 34(3), 1244–1252. DOI: 10.1007/s00464-019-06887-8 PMID: 31172325

Freeman, R. E. (1984). *Strategic management: A stakeholder approach.* Pitman.

French, B. H., Lewis, J. A., Mosley, D. V., Adames, H. Y., Chavez-Due˜nas, N. Y., Chen, G. A., & Neville, H. A. (2020). Toward a psychological framework of radical healing in communities of color. *The Counseling Psychologist*, 48(1), 14–46. DOI: 10.1177/0011000019843506

Fronteras, C. (2020). *Is a Cloud based ERP Deployment right for you?* (blog). Available at: https://www.redfaire.com/blog/is-a-cloud-based-erp-deployment-right-for-you

Fusté-Forné, F., & Jamal, T. (2021). Co-Creating New Directions for Service Robots in Hospitality and Tourism. *Tourism and Hospitality*, 2(1), 43–61. DOI: 10.3390/tourhosp2010003

Gao, L. (2020). Exploring the data processing practices of cloud ERP-A case study. *Journal of Emerging Technologies in Accounting*, 17(1), 63–70. DOI: 10.2308/jeta-52680

Geissdoerfer, M., Pieroni, M. P., Pigosso, D. C., & Soufani, K. (2020). Circular business models: A review. *Journal of Cleaner Production*, 277, 123741. DOI: 10.1016/j.jclepro.2020.123741

Geissdoerfer, M., Savaget, P., Bocken, N. M., & Hultink, E. J. (2017). The Circular Economy–A new sustainability paradigm? *Journal of Cleaner Production*, 143, 757–768. DOI: 10.1016/j.jclepro.2016.12.048

General Secretariat for Development Planning. (2008). *Qatar National Vision 2030*. https://www.mdps.gov.qa/en/knowledge/HomePagePublications/QNV2030_Arabic_v2.pdf

Ghisellini, P., Cialani, C., & Ulgiati, S. (2016). A review on circular economy: The expected transition to a balanced interplay of environmental and economic systems. *Journal of Cleaner Production*, 114, 11–32. DOI: 10.1016/j.jclepro.2015.09.007

Giglio, F., Grillo, E., & Sansotta, S. (2023, September). Integration of Circular and Green Technologies for the Adaptive Reuse of Public Space. In Mediterranean Architecture and the Green-Digital Transition: Selected Papers from the World Renewable Energy Congress Med Green Forum 2022 (pp. 339-353). Cham: Springer International Publishing. DOI: 10.1007/978-3-031-33148-0_27

Gill, A. Q., Phennel, N., Lane, D., & Phung, V. L. (2016). IoT-enabled emergency information supply chain architecture for elderly people: The Australian context. *Information Systems*, 58, 75–86. DOI: 10.1016/j.is.2016.02.004

Gökovali, U., & Bahar, O. (2006). Contribution of Tourism to Economic Growth: A Panel Data Approach. *Anatolia*, 17(2), 155–167. DOI: 10.1080/13032917.2006.9687184

Golarz, M. (2017). Wykorzystanie systemu klasy ERP w logistyce przedsiębiorstw. *Journal of Modern Management Process*, 2(1), 18–29.

Gold, H., & McLaughlin, D. (2016). Patient trust and transparency in health information exchanges. *Health Affairs*, 35(1), 34–39. DOI: 10.1377/hlthaff.2015.1037

Gong, C., & Ribiere, V. (2023). A historical outline of digital transformation. In *Digital Transformation in Healthcare in Post-Covid-19 Times* (pp. 3–25). Elsevier., DOI: 10.1016/B978-0-323-98353-2.00016-2

González-Rodríguez, M. R., Díaz-Fernández, M. C., & Pacheco Gómez, C. (2020). Facial-expression recognition: An emergent approach to the measurement of tourist satisfaction through emotions. *Telematics and Informatics*, 51, 101404. DOI: 10.1016/j.tele.2020.101404

Gounopoulos, E., Kontogiannis, S., Kazanidis, I., & Valsamidis, S. (2020). The Impact of the Digital Divide on the Adoption of e-Government in Greece. *KnE Social Sciences*, 401–411–401–411. DOI: 10.18502/kss.v4i1.6002

Gray, M. (2024). *How Deloitte Successfully Made Learning a Game*. Retrieved from https://www.engagify.io/blog/case-study-deloitte

Greeks, I. (2020). *Differences between ERP and SAP.* Available at: https://www.geeksforgeeks.org/differences-between-erp-and-sap/?ref=lbp (Accessed 25 March 2023).

Greenhow, C., & Lewin, C. (2019). Social media and education: Reconceptualizing the boundaries of formal and informal learning. In *social media and education* (pp. 6-30). Routledge.

Gregor, S., Imran, A., & Turner, T. (2014). A "sweet spot" change strategy for a least developed country: Leveraging e-Government in Bangladesh. *European Journal of Information Systems*, 23(6), 655–671. DOI: 10.1057/ejis.2013.14

Grimus, M. (2020). Emerging technologies: impacting learning, pedagogy and curriculum development. *Emerging Technologies and Pedagogies in the Curriculum,* 127–151.

Grozea, I.-L., & Troancă, D. (2023). Digital Transformation and the Financial Sector: A Comprehensive Perspective. *Sciendo*, 56(2), 56–63. DOI: 10.2478/saec-2023-0018

Gruenhagen, J. H., & Parker, R. (2020). Factors driving or impeding the diffusion and adoption of innovation in mining: A systematic review of the literature. *Resources Policy*, 65, 101540. DOI: 10.1016/j.resourpol.2019.101540

Gude, V. G. (2017). Desalination and water reuse to address global water scarcity. *Reviews in Environmental Science and Biotechnology*, 16(4), 591–609. DOI: 10.1007/s11157-017-9449-7

Guizzardi, A., Pons, F. M. E., Angelini, G., & Ranieri, E. (2021). Big data from dynamic pricing: A smart approach to tourism demand forecasting. *International Journal of Forecasting*, 37(3), 1049–1060. DOI: 10.1016/j.ijforecast.2020.11.006

Guo, Y. (2021). *Transformation from On-Premise Software to Cloud Computing-Based Services: A Case Study of SAP Practices*. The University of Manchester.

Gupta, S., Modgil, S., Lee, C.-K., & Sivarajah, U. (2023). The future is yesterday: Use of AI-driven facial recognition to enhance value in the travel and tourism industry. *Information Systems Frontiers*, 25(3), 1179–1195. DOI: 10.1007/s10796-022-10271-8 PMID: 35529102

Gupta, V., & Shukla, S. (2023). Consumer Trust in Digital Banking: A Qualitative Study of Legal and Regulatory Impacts. *Journal of Information Systems, Security. Law & Policy*, 3(2), 50–64. DOI: 10.61838/kman.isslp.3.2.4

Guyo, D. M., Kero, C. A., & Kant, S. (2025). Is Marketing Intermediaries' Mediation Required for Livestock and Products Marketing to Improve the Fiscal Status of Pastoralist Communities in Ethiopia? In *AI in Agriculture for Sustainable and Fiscal Management* (pp. 216-234). CRC Press.

Guyo, D. M., Kant, S., & Kero, C. A. (2023, November). Mediation of Marketing Intermediaries and AI Adoption Between Livestock Products Marketing and Economic Status of Pastoralist in Ethiopia. In *2023 International Conference on Communication, Security and Artificial Intelligence (ICCSAI)* (pp. 311-316). IEEE.

Haddara, M., Gøthesen, S., & Langseth, M. (2022). Challenges of cloud-ERP adoptions in SMEs. *Procedia Computer Science*, 196, 973–981. DOI: 10.1016/j.procs.2021.12.099

Halaweh, M. (2023). Chatgpt in education: Strategies for responsible implementation. *Contemporary Educational Technology*, 15(2), 1–11. DOI: 10.30935/cedtech/13036

Haleem, A., Javaid, M., Qadri, M. A., & Suman, R. (2022). Understanding the role of digital technologies in education: A review. *Sustainable operations and computers, 3*, 275-285.

Hammi, B., Zeadally, S., & Nebhen, J. (2023). Security threats, countermeasures, and Challenges of Digital Supply Chains. *ACM Computing Surveys*, 55(14s), 1–40. Advance online publication. DOI: 10.1145/3588999

Hart, S. L., & Dowell, G. (2011). Invited editorial: A natural-resource-based view of the firm: Fifteen years after. *Journal of Management*, 37(5), 1464–1479. DOI: 10.1177/0149206310390219

Hazen, B. T., Boone, C. A., Ezell, J. D., & Jones-Farmer, L. A. (2014). Data quality for data science, predictive analytics, and big data in supply chain management: An introduction to the problem and suggestions for research and applications. *International Journal of Production Economics*, 154, 72–80. DOI: 10.1016/j.ijpe.2014.04.018

High Tech High (HTH). (2024). *Project-based Learning at HTH*. Retrieved from https://www.hightechhigh.org/student-work/projects/

Hinsberg, H. (2010). A community of fans, friends and power-users sustainable e-participation in Estonia. *EJournal of EDemocracy and Open Government*, 2(2), 111–118. DOI: 10.29379/jedem.v2i2.45

Hobololo, T. S., & Mawela, T. (2017). Exploring the use of mobile phones for public participation in the Buffalo City metropolitan municipality. *AGRIS On-Line Papers in Economics and Informatics*, 9(1), 57–68. DOI: 10.7160/aol.2017.090105

Hojnik, J., & Ruzzier, M. (2016). What drives eco-innovation? A review of an emerging literature. *Environmental Innovation and Societal Transitions*, 19, 31–41. DOI: 10.1016/j.eist.2015.09.006

Hong, C., & Ma, W. W. (2020). Introduction: Education 4.0: Applied degree education and the future of work. In *Applied Degree Education and the Future of Work: Education 4.0* (pp. 1–13). Springer Singapore. DOI: 10.1007/978-981-15-3142-2_1

Huang, A., Chao, Y., De La Mora Velasco, E., Bilgihan, A., & Wei, W. (2022). When artificial intelligence meets the hospitality and tourism industry: An assessment framework to inform theory and management. *Journal of Hospitality and Tourism Insights*, 5(5), 1080–1100. DOI: 10.1108/JHTI-01-2021-0021

Huang, M.-H., Rust, R., & Maksimovic, V. (2019). The Feeling Economy: Managing in the Next Generation of Artificial Intelligence (AI). *California Management Review*, 61(4), 43–65. DOI: 10.1177/0008125619863436

Huddleston, J., Ji, P., Bhunia, S., & Cogan, J. (2021, December 1). *How VMware Exploits Contributed to SolarWinds Supply-chain Attack*. IEEE Xplore. DOI: 10.1109/CSCI54926.2021.00190

Humayun, M., Niazi, M., Jhanjhi, N., Alshayeb, M., & Mahmood, S. (2020). Cyber Security Threats and Vulnerabilities: A Systematic Mapping Study. *Arabian Journal for Science and Engineering, 45*(1). springer. DOI: 10.1007/s13369-019-04319-2

Hunker, J., Llc, A., & Probst, C. (2011). *Insiders and Insider Threats An Overview of Definitions and Mitigation Techniques*. https://isyou.info/jowua/papers/jowua-v2n1-1.pdf

Hutchings, E., Loomes, M. W., Butow, P., & Boyle, F. (2020). A systematic literature review of health consumer attitudes towards secondary use and sharing health administrative and clinical trial data focuses on privacy, trust, and transparency. *Systematic Reviews*, 9(1), 1–11. DOI: 10.1186/s13643-020-01481-9 PMID: 31907078

ictQATAR. (2014). *Qatar National Cyber Security Strategy*.

Isaak, J., & Hanna, M. J. (2018). User data privacy: Facebook, Cambridge Analytica, and privacy protection. *Computer*, 51(8), 56–59. DOI: 10.1109/MC.2018.3191268

Ivanov, S., & Webster, C. (2019). Conceptual Framework of the Use of Robots, Artificial Intelligence and Service Automation in Travel, Tourism, and Hospitality Companies. In S. Ivanov & C. Webster (Eds.), *Robots, Artificial Intelligence, and Service Automation in Travel, Tourism and Hospitality* (pp. 7–37). Emerald Publishing Limited. DOI: 10.1108/978-1-78756-687-320191001

Ivanov, S., & Webster, C. (2020). Robots in tourism: A research agenda for tourism economics. *Tourism Economics*, 26(7), 1065–1085. DOI: 10.1177/1354816619879583

Jabbour, C. J. C., de Sousa Jabbour, A. B. L., Sarkis, J., & Godinho Filho, M. (2019). Unlocking the circular economy through new business models based on large-scale data: An integrative framework and research agenda. *Technological Forecasting and Social Change*, 144, 546–552. DOI: 10.1016/j.techfore.2017.09.010

Jabeen, F., Al Zaidi, S., & Al Dhaheri, M. H. (2022). Automation and artificial intelligence in hospitality and tourism. *Tourism Review*, 77(4), 1043–1061. DOI: 10.1108/TR-09-2019-0360

Jabo, D., Borji, B., & Kant, S. (2024, February). Impact of Technical CRM on Ethiopia Bank Human-Computer Interface and Competitive Advantage as Mediators of Performance. In *2024 IEEE International Conference on Computing, Power and Communication Technologies (IC2PCT)* (Vol. 5, pp. 679-682). IEEE.

Jacobson, M. Z., Delucchi, M. A., Bauer, Z. A., Goodman, S. C., Chapman, W. E., Cameron, M. A., Bozonnat, C., Chobadi, L., Clonts, H. A., Enevoldsen, P., Erwin, J. R., Fobi, S. N., Goldstrom, O. K., Hennessy, E. M., Liu, J., Lo, J., Meyer, C. B., Morris, S. B., Moy, K. R., & Yachanin, A. S. (2017). 100% clean and renewable wind, water, and sunlight all-sector energy roadmaps for 139 countries of the world. *Joule*, 1(1), 108–121. DOI: 10.1016/j.joule.2017.07.005

Javed, F. (2024a). Digital Transformation in Teaching and Learning of English in Higher Education. In *Digital Transformation in Higher Education, Part B: Cases, Examples and Good Practices* (pp. 103-125). Emerald Publishing Limited. DOI: 10.1108/978-1-83608-424-220241005

Javed, F. (2024b). The Evolution of Artificial Intelligence in Teaching and Learning of English Language in Higher Education: Challenges, Risks, And Ethical Considerations. In *The Evolution of Artificial Intelligence in Higher Education Challenges, Risks, and Ethical Considerations*. Emerald Publishing Ltd. DOI: 10.1108/978-1-83549-486-820241015

Jiang, P. H. W., & Wang, W. Y. C. (2024). Comparison of SaaS and IaaS in cloud ERP implementation: The lessons from the practitioners. *VINE Journal of Information and Knowledge Management Systems*, 54(3), 683–701. DOI: 10.1108/VJIKMS-10-2021-0238

Jones, T. M., Harrison, J. S., & Felps, W. (2018). How applying instrumental stakeholder theory can provide a sustainable competitive advantage. *Academy of Management Review*, 43(3), 371–391. DOI: 10.5465/amr.2016.0111

Jovanovic, N. P., & A. (2023). Towards Resilient Cyber Infrastructure: Optimizing Protection Strategies with AI and Machine Learning in Cybersecurity Paradigms. *International Journal of Information and Cybersecurity, 7*(12), 44–60. https://publications.dlpress.org/index.php/ijic/article/view/75

Junaid, L., Bilal, K., Shuja, J., Balogun, A., & Rodrigues, J. (2024). Blockchain-Enabled Framework for Transparent Land Lease and Mortgage Management. *IEEE Access : Practical Innovations, Open Solutions*, 3388248, 54005–54018. Advance online publication. DOI: 10.1109/ACCESS.2024.3388248

Jüttner, U., Peck, H., & Christopher, M. (2003). Supply chain risk management: Outlining an agenda for future research. *International Journal of Logistics*, 6(4), 197–210. DOI: 10.1080/13675560310001627016

Kabir, F., Talukder, M. B., & Kumar, S. (2024). Exchange of Cultures in the Field of Gastronomy Tourism: Evidence of Bangladesh. In Castanho, R., & Franco, M. (Eds.), *Cultural, Gastronomy, and Adventure Tourism Development* (pp. 142–159). IGI Global., DOI: 10.4018/979-8-3693-3158-3.ch006

Kang, J., Faria, A. A., Lee, J. M., & Choi, W. (2023). Will consumers give us another chance to bounce back? Effects of precrisis commitments to social and product responsibility on brand resilience. *Journal of Product and Brand Management*, 32(1), 120–136. DOI: 10.1108/JPBM-03-2022-3899

Kant, S., & Adula, M. (2024). AI Learning and Work Attitude Mediation Between Reward and Organizational Support in Ethiopia. In Gomathi Sankar, J., & David, A. (Eds.), *Generative AI for Transformational Management* (pp. 109–136). IGI Global., DOI: 10.4018/979-8-3693-5578-7.ch005

Kant, S., & Adula, M. (2024). Human-Machine Interaction in the Metaverse in the Context of Ethiopia. In *Impact and Potential of Machine Learning in the Metaverse* (pp. 196–212). IGI Global., DOI: 10.4018/979-8-3693-5762-0.ch008

Kassan, H. (2022). *ERP becomes the cornerstone of S.A. mining sector*. Available at: https://www.crown.co.za/modern-mining/insights/20487-erp-becomes-the-cornerstone-of-sa-mining-sector

Kayalar, M. T. (2021). Perspectives of University Students on the Efficiency of Synchronous and Asynchronous Learning. *Journal of Educational Leadership and Policy Studies*, 1–18.

Kim, H., & Lee, T. H. (2018). Strategic CSR Communication: A moderating role of transparency in trust building. *International Journal of Strategic Communication*, 12(2), 107–124. DOI: 10.1080/1553118X.2018.1425692

Kırcaburun, K., Kokkinos, C. M., Demetrovics, Z., Király, O., Griffiths, M. D., & Çolak, T. S. (2019). Problematic online behaviors among adolescents and emerging adults: Associations between cyberbullying perpetration, problematic social media use, and psychosocial factors. *International Journal of Mental Health and Addiction*, 17(4), 891–908. DOI: 10.1007/s11469-018-9894-8

Kirchherr, J., Reike, D., & Hekkert, M. (2017). Conceptualizing the circular economy: An analysis of 114 definitions. *Resources, Conservation and Recycling*, 127, 221–232. DOI: 10.1016/j.resconrec.2017.09.005

Kivunja, C. (2013). Embedding digital pedagogy in preservice higher education to better prepare teachers for the digital generation. *International Journal of Sustainability in Higher Education*, 2(4), 131–142.

kiwimbi (2024). *The New Competency Based Curriculum (CBC) in Kenya*. Retrieved from https://kiwimbi.org/blog/the-new-competency-based-curriculum-cbc-in-kenya/

Klimenko, A. Y. (2024). Technological Change and Its Effect on Education. *J Edu Psyc Res, 6*(1), 01-18.

KOMAZAWA. (2022). Y. (2023). Renewables 2023 Global Status Report Collection Energy Systems & Infrastructure-Key. *Headlines (Lagos)*.

Kong, Z., Xue, J., Wang, Y., Huang, L., Niu, Z., & Li, F. (2021). A Survey on Adversarial Attack in the Age of Artificial Intelligence. *Wireless Communications and Mobile Computing*, 2021(1), 1–22. DOI: 10.1155/2021/4907754

Korhonen, J., Honkasalo, A., & Seppälä, J. (2018). Circular economy: The concept and its limitations. *Ecological Economics*, 143, 37–46. DOI: 10.1016/j.ecolecon.2017.06.041

Kostopoulos, G. K. (2004). E-government in the Arabian Gulf: A vision toward reality. *Electronic Government*, 1(3), 293–299. DOI: 10.1504/EG.2004.005553

Kouhizadeh, M., Saberi, S., & Sarkis, J. (2021). Blockchain technology and the sustainable supply chain: Theoretically exploring adoption barriers. *International Journal of Production Economics*, 231, 107831. DOI: 10.1016/j.ijpe.2020.107831

Kshetri, N. (2022). *Chapter 3: Combining with other technologies to amplify blockchains value creation in: The Rise of Blockchains,* 3, 56-73.

Kumar, S., Talukder, M. B., & Kaiser, F. (2024). Artificial Intelligence in Business: Negative Social Impacts. In *Demystifying the Dark Side of AI in Business* (pp. 81-97). IGI Global. DOI: 10.4018/979-8-3693-0724-3.ch005

Kumar, A., & Chen, B. (2023). Remote security protocols in global supply chains: Lessons from the pandemic. *International Journal of Digital Supply Chains*, 8(2), 156–170.

Lacey, D., Salmon, P., & Glancy, P. (2015). Taking the Bait: A Systems Analysis of Phishing Attacks. *Procedia Manufacturing*, 3, 1109–1116. DOI: 10.1016/j.promfg.2015.07.185

Law, N. (2009). Mathematics and science teachers' pedagogical orientations and their use of ICT in teaching. *Education and Information Technologies*, 14(4), 309–323. DOI: 10.1007/s10639-009-9094-z

Lazarenko, Y., Garafonova, O., Marhasova, V., & Tkalenko, N. (2021). Digital transformation in the mining sector: Exploring global technology trends and managerial issues. In *E3S Web of Conferences*, 315, 04006. EDP Sciences.

Lee, Y. J., Davis, R., & Li, Y. (2022). Implementing Synchronous Online Flipped Learning for Pre-Service Teachers during COVID-19. *European Journal of Educational Research*, 11(2), 653–661. DOI: 10.12973/eu-jer.11.2.653

Lee, Y., & Li, J. Q. (2021). The role of communication transparency and organisational trust in publics' perceptions, attitudes, and social distancing behaviour: A case study of the COVID-19 outbreak. *Journal of Contingencies and Crisis Management*, 29(4), 368–384. DOI: 10.1111/1468-5973.12354

Lewandowski, M. (2016). Designing the business models for circular economy—Towards the conceptual framework. *Sustainability (Basel)*, 8(1), 43. DOI: 10.3390/su8010043

Li, H., Yang, Z., Wang, H., & Li, Y. (2023). Digitalization of business models, knowledge management and green technology innovation of Chinese manufacturing enterprises: A mixed analysis based on the Haier COSMOPlat ecosystem. *Asia Pacific Business Review*, •••, 1–29. DOI: 10.1080/13602381.2023.2282116

Li, J., Wang, H., & Brown, S. (2024). IoT security challenges in modern supply chains. *Cybersecurity Review*, 11(1), 45–59.

Li, J., Xu, L., Tang, L., Wang, S., & Li, L. (2018). Big data in tourism research: A literature review. *Tourism Management*, 68, 301–323. DOI: 10.1016/j.tourman.2018.03.009

Li, M., Yin, D., Qiu, H., & Bai, B. (2021). A systematic review of AI technology-based service encounters: Implications for hospitality and tourism operations. *International Journal of Hospitality Management*, 95, 102930. DOI: 10.1016/j.ijhm.2021.102930

Lim, I. (2021). Exploring experience at the intersection of migration and digital democracy in South Korea. *Asiascape: Digital Asia*, 8(3), 139–163. DOI: 10.1163/22142312-bja10019

Linhartova, V. (2022). The Role of E-Government in the Evaluation of the Quality of Governance in the Countries of the European Union. *Croatian and Comparative Public Administration*, 22(2), 267–287. DOI: 10.31297/hkju.22.2.4

Lips, M. (2024). Digital transformation in the public sector. In Verhoest, K., Hammerschmid, G., Rykkja, L. H., & Klijn, E. H. (Eds.), *Collaborating for Digital Transformation* (pp. 13–30). Edward Elgar Publishing., DOI: 10.4337/9781803923895.00010

Liu, S., Thurasamy, R., & Hati, S. R. H. (2024). Determinants and Outcomes of Green Technology Innovation Adoption among Third-Party Logistics Firms in China: A SEM-ANN Analysis. *Systems*, 12(9), 331. DOI: 10.3390/systems12090331

Li, Y., & Tang, M. (2023). Blockchain-powered distributed data auditing scheme for cloud-edge healthcare system. *Cyber Security and Applications*, 1, 100017. DOI: 10.1016/j.csa.2023.100017

Lizardo, O. (2017). Improving cultural analysis: Considering personal culture in its declarative and nondeclarative modes. *American Sociological Review*, 82(1), 88–115. DOI: 10.1177/0003122416675175

Loukil, F., Ghedira Guégan, C., & Benharkat, A. (2020). PATRIoT: A Data Sharing Platform for IoT Using a Service-Oriented Approach Based on Blockchain. In *Advances in Service-Oriented and Cloud Computing* (pp. 152–169). Springer., DOI: 10.1007/978-3-030-65310-1_10

MacArthur, E. (2013). Towards the circular economy. *Journal of Industrial Ecology*, 2(1), 23–44.

Magon, J. K., & Shore, B. M. (2022). Asynchronous Posting and Reading both Reflect Communities of Inquiry. *International Journal for Talent Development and Creativity*, 10(1), 267–303.

Mahmoud, N. (2023). Prospects of Digital Transformation in the Arab World. *Arab and Regional Horizons*, 8(14), 0–0. DOI: 10.21608/afar.2023.238807.1021

Majewska, I., & Zvobgo, V. (2023). Students' Satisfaction with Quality of Synchronous Online Learning Under the COVID 19 Pandemic: Perceptions from Liberal Arts and Science Undergraduates. *Online Learning : the Official Journal of the Online Learning Consortium*, 27(1), 313–335. DOI: 10.24059/olj.v27i1.3201

Makridakis, S. (2017). The forthcoming Artificial Intelligence (AI) revolution: Its impact on society and firms. *Futures*, 90, 46–60. DOI: 10.1016/j.futures.2017.03.006

Mandasari, B., Rido, A., & Kuswoyo, H. (2022). *Using Zoom Meeting Platform as a Synchronous Online Learning Tool in EFL Classroom at Indonesia Tertiary Level: A Literature Review*. International Association for Development of the Information Society.

Margetts, H., & Dunleavy, P. (2013). The second wave of digital-era governance: A quasi-paradigm for government on the Web. *Philosophical Transactions of the Royal Society A: Mathematical, Physical and Engineering Sciences, 371*(1987), 20120382. DOI: 10.1098/rsta.2012.0382

Margherita, A., Nasiri, M., & Papadopoulos, T. (2023). The application of digital technologies in company responses to COVID-19: An integrative framework. *Technology Analysis and Strategic Management*, 35(8), 979–992. DOI: 10.1080/09537325.2021.1990255

Martínez-Bravo, M. C., S'adaba Chalezquer, C., & Serrano-Puche, J. (2022). Dimensions of digital literacy in the 21st century competency frameworks. *Sustainability (Basel)*, 14(3), 1867. DOI: 10.3390/su14031867

Martinez, R., & Lee, B. (2023). Cost-effective cybersecurity strategies for SMEs in digital supply chains. *Small Business Security Journal*, 16(2), 123–138.

Martin, K. D., & Murphy, P. E. (2016). The role of data privacy in marketing. *Journal of the Academy of Marketing Science*, 45(2), 135–155. DOI: 10.1007/s11747-016-0495-4

Masson-Delmotte, V. P., Zhai, P., Pirani, S. L., Connors, C., Péan, S., Berger, N., . . . Scheel Monteiro, P. M. (2021). Ipcc, 2021: Summary for policymakers. in: Climate change 2021: The physical science basis. contribution of working group i to the sixth assessment report of the intergovernmental panel on climate change.

Masum, M. Y., Faruq, M. O., Mia, M. N., & Talukder, M. B. (2025). Implementing Waste Management Solutions in Tourist Destinations. In Talukder, M., Kumar, S., & Haghi, A. (Eds.), *Application of Waste-to-Energy Innovations in Tourism* (pp. 1–28). IGI Global., DOI: 10.4018/979-8-3693-7605-8.ch001

Mattar, J. (2018). Constructivism and connectivism in education technology: Active, situated, authentic, experiential, and anchored learning. *RIED- Revista Iberoamericana de Educación a Distancia, 21*(2), 200-213.

Mazzucato, M. (2021). *Mission economy: A moonshot guide to changing capitalism.*

McKnight, D. H., Choudhury, V., & Kacmar, C. (2002). Developing and validating trust measures for e-commerce: An integrative typology. *Information Systems Research*, 13(3), 334–359. DOI: 10.1287/isre.13.3.334.81

McKnight, K., O'Malley, K., Ruzic, R., Horsley, M. K., Franey, J. J., & Bassett, K. (2016). Teaching in a digital age: How educators use technology to improve student learning. *Journal of Research on Technology in Education*, 48(3), 194–211. DOI: 10.1080/15391523.2016.1175856

McNulty, N. (2023). Digital Pedagogy, or How Best to Incorporate Technology in Your Teaching. Retrieved from https://medium.com/@niall.mcnulty/digital-pedagogy-or-how-best-to-incorporate-technology-in-your-teaching-0a6dc0e3e5e2

Means, B., Toyama, Y., Murphy, R., Bakia, M., & Jones, K. (2009). *Evaluation of evidence based practices in online learning: A meta-analysis and review of online learning studies*. U.S. Department of Education. Retrieved from https://www2.ed.gov/rschstat/eval/tech/evidence based practices/finalreport.pdf

Mettler, T., Miscione, G., Jacobs, C. D., & Guenduez, A. A. (2024). Same same but different: How policies frame societal-level digital transformation. *Government Information Quarterly*, 41(2), 101932. DOI: 10.1016/j.giq.2024.101932

Miah, S. J., Vu, H. Q., Gammack, J., & McGrath, M. (2017). A Big Data Analytics Method for Tourist Behaviour Analysis. *Information & Management*, 54(6), 771–785. DOI: 10.1016/j.im.2016.11.011

Milton, M., & Vozzo, L. (2013). Digital literacy and digital pedagogies for teaching literacy: Pre-service teachers' experience on teaching rounds. *The Journal of Literacy and Technology*, 14(1), 72–97.

Ministry of Communications & Information Technology. (2020). *TASMU Experience Policy*. https://www.mcit.gov.qa/sites/default/files/tasmu_experience_policy_en_v1.0.pdf

Mkubukeli, Z. & Tengeh, R.K. (2016). Prospects and challenges for small-scale mining entrepreneurs in South Africa.

Mohamed, S., & Han, S. (2022). Translating Human Values to Design Requirements: The Case of Developing Digital Government Collaborative Platform (DGCP) for Environmental Sustainability in Sri Lanka. In H. L., S. M., & H. S. (Eds.), *23rd Annual International Conference on Digital Government Research: Intelligent Technologies, Governments and Citizens, DGO 2022* (pp. 54–61). Association for Computing Machinery. DOI: 10.1145/3543434.3543455

Mohammad Badruddoza Talukder. Sanjeev Kumar, I. R. Das. (2024). Implications of Blockchain Technology- Based Cryptocurrency in the cloud for the Hospitality Industry. In *Emerging Trends in Cloud Computing Analytics, Scalability, and Service Models* (p. 19). DOI: 10.4018/979-8-3693-0900-1.ch018

Mohammad Badruddoza Talukder. Sanjeev Kumar, I. R. Das. (2024). Perspectives of Digital Marketing for the Restaurant Industry. In *Advancements in Socialized and Digital Media Communications* (p. 17). DOI: 10.4018/979-8-3693-0855-4.ch009

Mohammed, S., Desha, C., & Goonetilleke, A. (2022). Investigating low-carbon pathways for hydrocarbon-dependent rentier states: Economic transition in Qatar. *Technological Forecasting and Social Change*, 185, 122084. DOI: 10.1016/j.techfore.2022.122084

Mohtar, R. H. (2015). Opportunities and Challenges for Innovations in Q atar. *Muslim World (Hartford, Conn.)*, 105(1), 46–57. DOI: 10.1111/muwo.12079

Mokalapa, P. M., Oyedokun, G. E., & Fowokan, T. E. I. (2024). Effect of Corporate Governance Practices on the Performance of an Established Medium-Sized Enterprise in the Mining Industry in South Africa. *Small Business Accounting Management and Entrepreneurship Review*, 4(1), 17–33. DOI: 10.61656/sbamer.v4i1.144

Molina-Castillo, F. J., Rodríguez, R., López-Nicolas, C., & Bouwman, H. (2022). The role of ERP in business model innovation: Impetus or impediment. *Digital Business*, 2(2), 100024. DOI: 10.1016/j.digbus.2022.100024

Möller, D. P. F. (2023). NIST Cybersecurity Framework and MITRE Cybersecurity Criteria. *Advances in Information Security*, 231–271. DOI: 10.1007/978-3-031-26845-8_5

Momoh, A., Roy, R., & Shehab, E. (2010). Challenges in enterprise resource planning implementation: State-of-the-art. *Business Process Management Journal*, 16(4), 537–565. DOI: 10.1108/14637151011065919

Mourtzis, D., & Panopoulos, N. (2022). Digital transformation process towards resilient production systems and networks. In *Supply Network Dynamics and Control* (pp. 11–42). Springer International Publishing. DOI: 10.1007/978-3-031-09179-7_2

Muheidat, F., & Tawalbeh, L. (2021). Artificial Intelligence and Blockchain for Cybersecurity Applications. *Studies in Big Data*, 3–29. DOI: 10.1007/978-3-030-74575-2_1

Musiał-Karg, M., & Kapsa, I. (2019). Citizen e-Participation as an Important Factor for Sustainable Development. *European Journal of Sustainable Development*, 8(3), 210. DOI: 10.14207/ejsd.2019.v8n3p210

Nadkarni, S., & Haider, I. (2022). Digital transformation, operational efficiency and sustainability: Innovation drivers for hospitality's rebound in the United Arab Emirates. *Worldwide Hospitality and Tourism Themes*, 14(6), 572–578. DOI: 10.1108/WHATT-05-2022-0054

nAl-Dwairi, R., & Jditawi, W. (2022). The Role of Cloud Computing on the Governmental Units Performance and EParticipation (Empirical Study). *International Journal of Advances in Soft Computing and Its Applications*, 14(3), 79–93. DOI: 10.15849/IJASCA.221128.06

Nam, K., Dutt, C. S., Chathoth, P., Daghfous, A., & Khan, M. S. (2021). The adoption of artificial intelligence and robotics in the hotel industry: Prospects and challenges. *Electronic Markets*, 31(3), 553–574. DOI: 10.1007/s12525-020-00442-3

Naorib, (2021). Department of Higher Education and Training. *White paper for Chainlink 2.0: Next Steps in the Evolution of Decentralized Oracle Networks.*

Nararya, S., Saputra, M., & Puspitasari, W. (2021). Automation in Financial Reporting by using Predictive Analytics in SAP Analytics Cloud for Gold Mining Industry: a Case Study. In *2021 International Conference on ICT for Smart Society (ICISS)* (pp. 1-6). IEEE. DOI: 10.1109/ICISS53185.2021.9532504

Ndulu, B., Stuart, E., Dercon, S., & Knaack, P. (2023). *Driving Digital Transformation: Lessons from Seven Creating Countries*. Oxford University Press. DOI: 10.1093/oso/9780192872845.001.0001

Nege, T. B., & Kero, C. A. (2024). Competitive Strategy Orientation and Market Orientation for Product Innovative Success in Ethiopian SMEs. *Science Journal of Business and Management*, 12(2), 47–63. DOI: 10.11648/j.sjbm.20241203.11

Ng, K. K. H., Chen, C.-H., Lee, C. K. M., Jiao, J., & Yang, Z.-X. (2021). A systematic literature review on intelligent automation: Aligning concepts from theory, practice, and future perspectives. *Advanced Engineering Informatics*, 47, 101246. DOI: 10.1016/j.aei.2021.101246

Nhleko, S., & Neingo, P. (2020). Financial Performance of Johannesburg Securities Exchange Traded Gold Mining Companies: Du Pont and Economic Value-Added Analyses. In: *Proceedings of the 28th International Symposium on Mine Planning and Equipment Selection-MPES 2019. 28*,333-345. Springer International Publishing. DOI: 10.1007/978-3-030-33954-8_41

Nicholls, A. (2010). The legitimacy of social entrepreneurship: Reflexive isomorphism in a pre–paradigmatic field. *Entrepreneurship Theory and Practice*, 34(4), 611–633. DOI: 10.1111/j.1540-6520.2010.00397.x

Nichols, T. P., LeBlanc, R. J., & Garcia, A. (2024). After digital literacy: Media pedagogies for platform ecologies. In *World Yearbook of Education 2024* (pp. 212–226). Routledge.

Niranga, M., & Wickramarachchi, R. (2020). A Model for On-Premises ERP System and Cloud ERP Integration. *International Conference on Industrial Engineering and Operations Management.*

Nupen, L. (2020). *Mining in South Africa: Industry challenges in 2020.* Available at: https://www.miningreview.com/gold/mining-in-south-africa-industry-challenges-in-2020/

Nygren, H., Nissinen, K., Hämäläinen, R., & De Wever, B. (2019). Lifelong learning: Formal, non-formal and informal learning in the context of the use of problem-solving skills in technology-rich environments. *British Journal of Educational Technology*, 50(4), 1759–1770. DOI: 10.1111/bjet.12807

Nyoach, T. D., Lemi, K., Debela, T., & Kant, S. (2024). Does Organizational Commitment Mediate the Relationship between Employee Relationship Management and Bank Performance? The Case of Banks in Ethiopia. *International Journal of Organizational Leadership*, 13(2), 355–376. DOI: 10.33844/ijol.2024.60419

Obudho, K. (2024). The Impact of Data Privacy Laws on Digital Marketing Practices. *Journal of Marketing and Leadership Practices*, 6(4), 78–92. DOI: 10.47941/jmlp.2155

Ochinanwata, C., Igwe, P. A., & Radicic, D. (2024). The institutional impact on the digital platform ecosystem and innovation. *International Journal of Entrepreneurial Behaviour & Research*, 30(2/3), 687–708. DOI: 10.1108/IJEBR-01-2023-0015

Office for Civil Rights, U.S. Department of Health and Human Services. (2015). *Health Insurance Portability and Accountability Act (HIPAA)*. Retrieved from https://www.hhs.gov/hipaa/index.html

Ogbaga, I. Ogbonnaya, C., & Agwu Chukwuemeka. (2023). *Deployment of Zero Trust Access (ZTA) Policy as a Veritable Tool for Protecting Network Infrastructures and Users*. DOI: 10.20944/preprints202307.0006.v1

Ogunmakinde, O. E., Sher, W., & Egbelakin, T. (2021). Circular economy pillars: A semi-systematic review. *Clean Technologies and Environmental Policy*, 23(3), 899–914. DOI: 10.1007/s10098-020-02012-9

Olin College of Engineering. (2024). *Best Colleges US News*. Retrieved from https://www.olin.edu/

Olteanu, A., Castillo, C., Diaz, F., & Kiciman, E. (2016). Social data: biases, methodological pitfalls, and ethical boundaries. SSRN *Electronic Journal*. DOI: 10.2139/ssrn.2886526

Oyewole, A. T., Adeoye, O. B., Addy, W. A., Okoye, C. C., Ofodile, O. C., & Ugochukwu, C. E.Adedoyin Tolulope OyewoleOmotayo Bukola AdeoyeWilhelmina Afua AddyChinwe Chinazo OkoyeOnyeka Chrisanctus OfodileChinonye Esther Ugochukwu. (2024). Automating financial reporting with natural language processing: A review and case analysis. *World Journal of Advanced Research and Reviews*, 21(3), 575–589. DOI: 10.30574/wjarr.2024.21.3.0688

Palacin, V., Zundel, A., Aquaro, V., & Kwok, W. M. (2023). *Reframing E-participation for Sustainable Development*. 172–180. DOI: 10.1145/3494193.3494218

Pandey, A. K., Singh, R. K., Jayesh, G. S., Khare, N., & Gupta, S. K. (2022). Examining the role of enterprise resource planning (ERP) in improving business operations in companies. *ECS Transactions*, 107(1), 2681–2696. DOI: 10.1149/10701.2681ecst

Panigrahi, A., Pati, A., Sahu, B., Das, M. N., Nayak, D. S. K., Sahoo, G., & Kant, S. (2023). En-MinWhale: An ensemble approach based on MRMR and Whale optimization for Cancer diagnosis. *IEEE Access : Practical Innovations, Open Solutions*, 11, 113526–113542. DOI: 10.1109/ACCESS.2023.3318261

Pappas, I. O., Mikalef, P., Dwivedi, Y., Jaccheri, L., Krogstie, J., & Mäntymäki, M. (2019). *Digital transformation for a sustainable society in the 21st century*. Springer International Publishing. DOI: 10.1007/978-3-030-29374-1

Park, S., Miller, J., & Brown, K. (2024). Integration of compliance and risk management in supply chains. *Risk Management Quarterly*, 15(1), 45–62.

Payne, C., & Reinhart, C. (2008). Can we talk? Course management software and the construction of knowledge. *On the Horizon*, 16(1), 34–43. DOI: 10.1108/10748120810853336

Pencheva, I., Esteve, M., & Mikhaylov, S. J. (2018). Big data and AI – A transformational shift for government: So, what next for research? *Public Policy and Administration*, •••, 1–21.

Penprase, B. E. (2018). The fourth industrial revolution and higher education. *Higher education in the era of the fourth industrial revolution*, 207-229.

Perez, T. (2003). *Multinational enterprises and technological spillovers*. Routledge. DOI: 10.4324/9780203362914

Perveen, A. (2016). Synchronous and asynchronous e-language learning: A case study of virtual University of Pakistan. *Open Praxis*, 8(1), 21–39. DOI: 10.5944/openpraxis.8.1.212

Peter, C. (2021). Social innovation for sustainable urban creational transitions in Sub-Saharan Africa: Leveraging fiscal ecosystems and the entrepreneurial state. *Sustainability*, 13(13), 7360. DOI: 10.3390/su13137360

Phoshoko, D. (2021). *Advancing technology use in the mining industry. Mining news, 20 October.* Available at: https://miningnews.co.za/2021/10/20/advancing-technology-use-in-the-mining-industry/s

Piccoli, G., Lui, T.-W., & Grün, B. (2017). The impact of IT-enabled customer service systems on service personalization, customer service perceptions, and hotel performance. *Tourism Management*, 59, 349–362. DOI: 10.1016/j.tourman.2016.08.015

Pillai, R., & Sivathanu, B. (2020). Adoption of AI-based chatbots for hospitality and tourism. *International Journal of Contemporary Hospitality Management*, 32(10), 3199–3226. DOI: 10.1108/IJCHM-04-2020-0259

Pinto, I., & Castro, C.Polytechnic Institute of Porto. (2019). Online travel agencies: Factors influencing tourist purchase decision. *Tourism & Management Studies*, 15(2), 7–20. DOI: 10.18089/tms.2019.150201

Pires, F., Masanet, M. J., Tomasena, J. M., & Scolari, C. A. (2022). Learning with YouTube: Beyond formal and informal through new actors, strategies and affordances. *Convergence (London)*, 28(3), 838–853. DOI: 10.1177/13548565211020545

Popenici, S. A., & Kerr, S. (2017). Exploring the impact of artificial intelligence on teaching and learning in higher education. *Research and Practice in Technology Enhanced Learning*, 12(1), 22. DOI: 10.1186/s41039-017-0062-8 PMID: 30595727

Porter, M. E., & Kramer, M. R. (2018). Creating shared value: How to reinvent capitalism—And unleash a wave of innovation and growth. In *Managing sustainable business: An executive education case and textbook* (pp. 323–346). Springer Netherlands.

Prestridge, S. (2012). The beliefs behind the teacher that influences their ICT practices. *Computers & Education*, 58(1), 449–458. DOI: 10.1016/j.compedu.2011.08.028

Proposing an Index for Cross-District Comparison for Citizen e-Services Provision. (2019). *International Journal of Recent Technology and Engineering, 8*(2S11), 3601–3605. DOI: 10.35940/ijrte.B1450.0982S1119

PwC. (2024). *Qatar Economy Watch 2024.*

Qin, Y., Xu, Z., Wang, X., & Skare, M. (2024). Artificial Intelligence and Economic Development: An Evolutionary Investigation and Systematic Review. *Journal of the Knowledge Economy*, 15(1), 1736–1770. DOI: 10.1007/s13132-023-01183-2

Quintana, A. G., Urquía-Grande, E., & Delgado Jalón, M. L. (2022). Strategic Conceptual Theories and Sustainable Cooperation Among Stakeholders in E-government, E-participation, and Social Media. *Central European Journal of Public Policy*, 16(2), 46–63. DOI: 10.2478/cejpp-2022-0007

Rajpoot, S. (2024). Eco-Friendly Solutions for Sustainable Waste Management: An Approach Towards a Cleaner and Greener Future. In Waste Management and Life Cycle Assessment for Sustainable Business Practice (pp. 43-64). IGI Global.

Raworth, K. (2017). *Doughnut economics: Seven ways to think like a 21st-century economist*. Chelsea Green Publishing.

Reactore. (2020). *Effectiveness of ERP systems in mining*. Available at: https://reactore.com/archives/blog/effectiveness-of-erp-systems-in-mining

Rees, J., & Rees, C. J. (2023). Cyber-Security and the Changing Landscape of Critical National Infrastructure: State and Non-state Cyber-Attacks on Organisations, Systems and Services. *Advanced Sciences and Technologies for Security Applications*, 67–89. DOI: 10.1007/978-3-031-40118-3_5

Reindl, K., Dalhammar, C., & Brodén, E. (2024). Circular Economy Integration in Smart Grids: A Nexus for Sustainability. *Circular Economy and Sustainability*, 4(3), 1–27. DOI: 10.1007/s43615-024-00375-5

Resulting, I. T. (2022). *Why is Adoption so important in ERP projects*. Available at: https://www.resulting-it.com/erp-fundamentals/erp-adoption-project-success

Revyakin, S., & da Rocha, A. (2021). AN EMPIRICAL INVESTIGATION OF E-GOVERNMENT ADOPTION IN RUSSIA: ACCESS, RIGHTS, TRUST AND CITIZENS' EXPERIENCE. *Public Administration Issues*, 0(5), 137–160. DOI: 10.17323/1999-5431-2021-0-5-137-160

Rizos, V., Behrens, A., Van der Gaast, W., Hofman, E., Ioannou, A., Kafyeke, T., Flamos, A., Rinaldi, R., Papadelis, S., Hirschnitz-Garbers, M., & Topi, C. (2016). Implementation of circular economy business models by small and medium-sized enterprises (SMEs): Barriers and enablers. *Sustainability (Basel)*, 8(11), 1212. DOI: 10.3390/su8111212

Roberts, A., & Kim, J. (2023). ISAC effectiveness in preventing supply chain attacks: A quantitative analysis. *Cybersecurity Collaboration Journal*, 8(2), 145–158.

Roberts, A., & Kumar, V. (2023). Navigating global data protection regulations in supply chains. *International Journal of Digital Security*, 8(4), 234–251.

Robinson, R. (2004). Liner Shipping Strategy, Network Structuring and Competitive Advantage: A Chain Systems Perspective. *Research in Transportation Economics*, 12, 247–289. DOI: 10.1016/S0739-8859(04)12008-8

Robinson, S., Orsingher, C., Alkire, L., De Keyser, A., Giebelhausen, M., Papamichail, K. N., Shams, P., & Temerak, M. S. (2020). Frontline encounters of the AI kind: An evolved service encounter framework. *Journal of Business Research*, 116, 366–376. DOI: 10.1016/j.jbusres.2019.08.038

Rodríguez-Martínez, C. C., García-Sánchez, I. M., Vicente-Galindo, P., & Galindo-Villardón, P. (2019). Exploring Relationships between Environmental Performance, E-Government and Corruption: A Multivariate Perspective. *Sustainability (Basel)*, 11(22), 6497. DOI: 10.3390/su11226497

Rospigliosi, P. A. (2023). Artificial intelligence in teaching and learning: What questions should we ask of ChatGPT? *Interactive Learning Environments*, 31(1), 1–3. DOI: 10.1080/10494820.2023.2180191

Saberi, S., Kouhizadeh, M., Sarkis, J., & Shen, L. (2019). Blockchain technology and its relationships to sustainable supply chain management. *International Journal of Production Research*, 57(7), 2117–2135. DOI: 10.1080/00207543.2018.1533261

Sacchi, A., Santolini, R., & Schneider, F. (2022). On the effects of e-participation on shadow economy: A worldwide empirical analysis. *German Economic Review*, 23(3), 463–491. DOI: 10.1515/ger-2021-0076

Saebi, T., Foss, N. J., & Linder, S. (2019). Social entrepreneurship research: Past achievements and future promises. *Journal of Management*, 45(1), 70–95. DOI: 10.1177/0149206318793196

Sándor, Á., & Gubán, Á. (2022). A multi-dimensional model to the digital maturity life-cycle for SMEs. *International Journal of Information Systems and Project Management*, 10(3), 58–81. DOI: 10.12821/ijispm100303

Santos, F. M. (2012). A positive theory of social entrepreneurship. *Journal of Business Ethics*, 111(3), 335–351. DOI: 10.1007/s10551-012-1413-4

Santos, F., Pache, A. C., & Birkholz, C. (2015). Making hybrids work: Aligning business models and organizational design for social enterprises. *California Management Review*, 57(3), 36–58. DOI: 10.1525/cmr.2015.57.3.36

Satur, K. L., Nase, R. M., Aiza Cubillas, B. J. T. A., & Magbanua, M. I. S. S. (2024). Authenticity and transparency: Influencers' sponsored content on makeup products towards consumer trust. *International Journal of Research in Education and Human Capital*, 5(1), 117–136. DOI: 10.37602/IJREHC.2024.5117

Sawon, Md. M. H., Lina, F. Y., & Hossain, Md. A. (2024). AI in the Tourism and Hospitality Industry in Bangladesh: Challenges and Ways Forward. In M. B. Talukder, S. Kumar, & P. K. Tyagi (Eds.), *Advances in Hospitality, Tourism, and the Services Industry* (pp. 84–102). IGI Global. DOI: 10.4018/979-8-3693-6755-1.ch005

Saykili, A. (2019). Higher education in the digital age: The impact of digital connective technologies. *J. Educ. Technol. Online Learn.*, 2(1), 1–15. DOI: 10.31681/jetol.516971

Schöbel, S., Saqr, M., & Janson, A. (2021). Two decades of game concepts in digital learning environments—A bibliometric study and research agenda. *Computers & Education*, 173, 104296. DOI: 10.1016/j.compedu.2021.104296

Schwab, K. (2016). *The Fourth Industrial Revolution*. Switzerland, Geneva: World Economic Forum.

Selwyn, N., & Facer, K. (2014). The sociology of education and digital technology: Past, present and future. *Oxford Review of Education*, 40(4), 482–496. DOI: 10.1080/03054985.2014.933005

Shaikh, I. A. K., Shahare, P., Gangadharan, S., Venkatarathnam, N., Pelluru, G., & Babu, S. B. G. T. (2024). Transforming Customer Relationship Management (CRM) with AI in E-Commerce. International Conference on Recent Trends in Computing and Smart Technology (ICRTCST), 10578449. DOI: 10.1109/ICRTCST61793.2024.10578449

Sharma, A. K., & Sharma, R. (2024). Navigating compliance and regulations in marketing analytics: Upholding ethical standards and consumer trust. *ACQY Journal*, 4920(1), 77. Advance online publication. DOI: 10.69554/ACQY4920

Sharma, S.. (2023). Ethical Considerations in AI-Based Marketing: Balancing Profit and Consumer Trust. *Journal of Propulsion Technology*, 44(3), 162–178. DOI: 10.52783/tjjpt.v44.i3.474

Sharpley, R. (2020). Tourism, sustainable development and the theoretical divide: 20 years on. *Journal of Sustainable Tourism*, 28(11), 1932–1946. DOI: 10.1080/09669582.2020.1779732

Shen, Y., Cheng, Y., & Yu, J. (2022). From recovery resilience to transformative resilience: How digital platforms reshape public service provision during and post COVID-19. *Public Management Review*. Advance online publication. DOI: 10.1080/14719037.2022.2033052

Shmarkov, M. S., Shmarkova, L. I., & Shmarkova, E. A. (2019). Digital technologies in the organization and management of tourist organizations. *Proceedings of the 1st International Scientific Conference "Modern Management Trends and the Digital Economy: From Regional Development to Global Economic Growth" (MTDE 2019)*. Proceedings of the 1st International Scientific Conference "Modern Management Trends and the Digital Economy: from Regional Development to Global Economic Growth" (MTDE 2019), Yekaterinburg, Russia. DOI: 10.2991/mtde-19.2019.18

Shofia*, S., Meyliana*, Hidayanto, A. N., & Prabowo, H. (2020). Critical Success Factors E-Participation for E-Government. *International Journal of Recent Technology and Engineering (IJRTE), 8*(5), 4010–4016. DOI: 10.35940/ijrte.E6246.018520

Shofia, S., Trisetyarso, A., Abbas, B. S., & Suparta, W. (2023).. . *E-Participation Platform Model for E-Government Case Study in Karawang City*, 354–357. Advance online publication. DOI: 10.2991/assehr.k.200303.085

Sibanye Stillwater. (2021). *Integrated Report* 2021. Global. Available at: https://reports.sibanyestillwater.com/2021/download/SSW-IR21-03.pdf

Silase, M. (2018). *An assessment of factors influencing successful implementation of ERP in a mining industry: An investigation into the possibility of integrating Oracle ERP system with the Lean Six Sigma philosophy in a mining operation, using them in collaboration with industry 4.0* (Doctoral dissertation, University of Johannesburg (South Africa)).

Singh, K., Kumar, S., & Talukder, M. B. (2025). Digital Transformation and Its Impact on Tourism Business in India. In Albattat, A., Azman, N., Valeri, M., & Singh, A. (Eds.), *Tracking Tourism Patterns and Improving Travel Experiences With Innovative Technologies* (pp. 215–230). IGI Global., DOI: 10.4018/979-8-3693-9636-0.ch010

Singh, N. (2024). Data Security and Consumer Trust in Fintech Innovations Using Technology Adoption Method. *International Journal of Science Research and Engineering Management*, 9(5), 45–62. DOI: 10.55041/IJSREM33015

Sishi, M., & Telukdarie, A. (2020). Implementation of industry 4.0 technologies in the mining industry: Case study. *International Journal of Mining and Mineral Engineering*, 11(1), 1–22. DOI: 10.1504/IJMME.2020.105852

Sjöberg, D., & Holmgren, R. (2021). Informal workplace learning in swedish police education-a teacher perspective. *Vocations and Learning*, 14(2), 265–284. DOI: 10.1007/s12186-021-09267-3

Skulmowski, A., & Rey, G. D. (2020). The realism paradox: Realism can act as a form of signaling despite being associated with cognitive load. *Human Behavior and Emerging Technologies*, 2(3), 251–258. DOI: 10.1002/hbe2.190 PMID: 32838228

Smith, B. R., Kistruck, G. M., & Cannatelli, B. (2016). The impact of moral intensity and desire for control on scaling decisions in social entrepreneurship. *Journal of Business Ethics*, 133(4), 677–689. DOI: 10.1007/s10551-014-2447-6

Soni, N., Sharma, E. K., Singh, N., & Kapoor, A. (2019). *Impact of Artificial Intelligence on Businesses: From Research, Innovation, Market Deployment to Future Shifts in Business Models* (Version 1). arXiv. DOI: 10.48550/ARXIV.1905.02092

Souppaya, M., & Scarfone, K. (2013). *Guidelines for Managing the Security of Mobile Devices in the Enterprise*. National Institute of Standards and Technology., DOI: 10.6028/NIST.SP.800-124r1

South Africa Mining. (2017). *The mining ERP specialist. White paper on what to consider when implementing a mining ERP solution.pdf,* pp. 7.

Southgate, E. (2020). *Artificial intelligence, ethics, equity and higher education: A 'beginning-of the-discussion' paper*. National Centre for Student Equity in Higher Education, Curtin University, and the University of Newcastle.

Southworth, J., Migliaccio, K., Glover, J., Glover, J., Reed, D., McCarty, C., Brendemuhl, J., & Thomas, A. (2023). Developing a model for AI across the curriculum: Transforming the higher education landscape via innovation in AI literacy. *Comput. Educ.: Artif. Intell.*, 4, 100127. DOI: 10.1016/j.caeai.2023.100127

Stewart, K. J. (2003). Trust transfer on the World Wide Web. *Organization Science*, 14(1), 5–17. DOI: 10.1287/orsc.14.1.5.12810

Stone, M., Aravopoulou, E., Ekinci, Y., Evans, G., Hobbs, M., Labib, A., Laughlin, P., Machtynger, J., & Machtynger, L. (2020). Artificial intelligence (AI) in strategic marketing decision-making: A research agenda. *The Bottom Line (New York, N.Y.)*, 33(2), 183–200. DOI: 10.1108/BL-03-2020-0022

Stratu-Strelet, D., Gil-Gómez, H., Oltra-Badenes, R., & Oltra-Gutierrez, J. V. (2021). Critical factors in the institutionalization of e-participation in e-government in Europe: Technology or leadership? *Technological Forecasting and Social Change*, 164, 120489. DOI: 10.1016/j.techfore.2020.120489

Sturgeon, T. J. (2019). Upgrading strategies for the digital economy. *Global Strategy Journal*, 11(1), 34–57. DOI: 10.1002/gsj.1364

Suardi, I. (2021). E-Government, Governance and Corruption in Asian countries. *Emerging Markets : Business and Management Studies Journal*, 8(2), 137–150. DOI: 10.33555/embm.v8i2.180

Sudirman, F. A., & Saidin, S. (2022). Pemerintahan Berbasis Elektronik (E-Government) dan Pembangunan Berkelanjutan: Reviu Literatur Sistematis. *Nakhoda: Jurnal Ilmu Pemerintahan*, 21(1), 44–58. DOI: 10.35967/njip.v21i1.269

Suleski, T., Ahmed, M., Yang, W., & Wang, E. (2023). A Review of multi-factor Authentication in the Internet of Healthcare Things. *Digital Health*, 9(1), 2055 20762311771–205520762311771. DOI: 10.1177/20552076231177144 PMID: 37252257

Sunny, J., Undralla, N., & Madhusudanan Pillai, V. (2020). Supply chain transparency through blockchain-based traceability: An overview with demonstration. *Computers & Industrial Engineering*, 150(150), 106895. DOI: 10.1016/j.cie.2020.106895

Susanti, E., Harta, R., Diana, B. A., & Utami, S. B. (2021). E-Readiness and The Effectiveness of E-Participation in Indonesia. *MIMBAR : Jurnal Sosial Dan Pembangunan*, 37(1). Advance online publication. DOI: 10.29313/mimbar.v37i1.6931

Svirina, A., Appalonova, N., Garanin, D., Lukashevich, N., & Koshkin, I. (2021). Fintech developmental trends: The role and influence of sustainable digital logistics. In K. V. (Ed.), *2021 Ural Environmental Science Forum on Sustainable Development of Industrial Region, UESF 2021* (Vol. 258). EDP Sciences. DOI: 10.1051/e3sconf/202125802019

Sweller, J. (1988). Cognitive load during problem solving: Effects on learning. *Cognitive Science*, 12(2), 257–285. DOI: 10.1207/s15516709cog1202_4

Sweller, J., van Merriënboer, J. J., & Paas, F. (2019). Cognitive architecture and instructional design: 20 years later. *Educational Psychology Review*, 31(2), 261–292. DOI: 10.1007/s10648-019-09465-5

Syed, Z. A., Dapaah, E., Mapfaza, G., Remias, T., & Mupa, M. N. (2024). Enhancing supply chain resilience with cloud-based ERP systems. *IRE Journals*, 8(2), 106–128.

Talukder, M. B. (2020). An Appraisal of the Economic Outlook for the Tourism Industry, Specially Cox's Bazar in Bangladesh. *i-manager's Journal on Economics & Commerce,* 2(1), 23-35. DOI: 10.26634/jecom.2.1.17285

Talukder, M. B., Kabir, F., Kaiser, F., & Lina, F. Y. (2024). Digital Detox Movement in the Tourism Industry: Traveler Perspective. In *Business Drivers in Promoting Digital Detoxification* (pp. 91-110). IGI Global. DOI: 10.4018/979-8-3693-1107-3.ch007

Talukder, M.B., & Kumar, S. (2024). Revisiting intention in food service outlet of five-star hotels:A quantitative approach based on food service quality. Sport i Turystyka. Środkowoeuropejskie Czasopismo Naukowe, 7(1), 137–156. DOI: 10.16926/sit.2024.01.08

Talukder, M. B. (2020). The Future of Culinary Tourism: An Emerging Dimension for the Tourism Industry of Bangladesh. I-Manager's. *Journal of Management*, 15(1), 27. DOI: 10.26634/jmgt.15.1.17181

Talukder, M. B. (2021). An assessment of the roles of the social network in the development of the Tourism Industry in Bangladesh. *International Journal of Business, Law, and Education*, 2(3), 85–93. DOI: 10.56442/ijble.v2i3.21

Talukder, M. B., Das, I. R., & Afchar, M. N. (2025). Impact of Social Media on the Development of Religious Tourism Industry. In Jermsittiparsert, K., Wekke, I., & Suanpang, P. (Eds.), *Business Sustainability Practices in Society 5.0* (pp. 359–378). IGI Global., DOI: 10.4018/979-8-3693-9230-0.ch018

Talukder, M. B., & Hossain, M. M. (2021). Prospects of Future Tourism in Bangladesh: An Evaluative Study. I-Manager's. *Journal of Management*, 15(4), 1–8. DOI: 10.26634/jmgt.15.4.17495

Talukder, M. B., Kabir, F., & Jibon, F. A. (2025). AI-Driven Personalized Room Management in the Modern Hotel Industry. In Chiwaridzo, O., & Masengu, R. (Eds.), *AI Technologies for Personalized and Sustainable Tourism* (pp. 59–82). IGI Global., DOI: 10.4018/979-8-3693-5678-4.ch003

Talukder, M. B., Kumar, S., Sood, K., & Grima, S. (2023). Information Technology, Food Service Quality and Restaurant Revisit Intention. *International Journal of Sustainable Development and Planning*, 18(1), 295–303. DOI: 10.18280/ijsdp.180131

Tawakkal, G. T. I. (2022). A POTENTIAL FOR CAUSALITY IN DEVELOPMENT COUNTRIES (TRACKING E-PARTICIPATION AND E-GOVERNMENT IN SOUTHEAST ASIAN COUNTRIES). *Politico (Pavia, Italy)*, 22(2), 58–70. DOI: 10.32528/politico.v22i2.8176

Teodorescu, D., Aivaz, K., Vancea, D., Condrea, E., Drăgan, C., & Olteanu, A. (2023). Consumer Trust in AI Algorithms Used in E-Commerce: A Case Study of College Students at a Romanian Public University. *Sustainability (Basel)*, 15(15), 11925. DOI: 10.3390/su151511925

Thakur, K., Qiu, M., Gai, K., & Ali, M. L. (2019). *An Investigation on Cyber Security Threats and Security Models*. IEEE Xplore., DOI: 10.1109/CSCloud.2015.71

Thompson, B., Clark, D., & White, R. (2024). Measuring the impact of collaborative cyber defense in supply chains. *Journal of Network Security*, 25(3), 234–248.

Thompson, B., & Lee, S. (2023). ISO 27001 implementation outcomes in global supply chains. *Security Standards Review*, 11(2), 156–173.

Thuermer, G., Walker, J., Simperl, E., & Carr, L. (2024). When data meets citizens: Investigating citizen engagement in data-driven innovation programs. *Data & Policy*, 6, e12. Advance online publication. DOI: 10.1017/dap.2023.43

Tigunia, S. (2021). *8 Common ERP Security Problems and How to resolve them*. Available at: https://tigunia.com/blog/8-common-erp-security-problems-and-how-to-resolve-them/

Tondeur, J., van Braak, J., Ertmer, P., & Ottenbreit-Leftwich, A. (2017). Understanding the relationship between teachers' pedagogical beliefs and technology use in education: A systematic review of qualitative evidence. *Educational Technology Research and Development*, 65(3), 555–575. DOI: 10.1007/s11423-016-9481-2

Tr ng, J. (2024). Relationship between Data Privacy Regulations and Consumer Trust in E-Commerce Platforms in Vietnam. *African Journal of Digital Knowledge Management*, 7(2), 31–45. DOI: 10.47672/ajdikm.2347

Tudor, T., & Dutra, C. J. (Eds.). (2021). *The Routledge handbook of waste, resources and the circular economy*. Routledge.

Tussyadiah, I. (2020). A review of research into automation in tourism: Launching the Annals of Tourism Research Curated Collection on Artificial Intelligence and Robotics in Tourism. *Annals of Tourism Research*, 81, 102883. DOI: 10.1016/j.annals.2020.102883

Tyagi, A. K. (2024). *Blockchain and Artificial Intelligence for Cyber Security in the Era of Internet of Things and Industrial Internet of Things Applications*. Www.igi-Global.comGlobal, I. G. I. https://www.igi-global.com/chapter/blockchain-and-artificial-intelligence-for-cyber-security-in-the-era-of-internet-of-things-and-industrial-internet-of-things-applications/336079

Udd, A. P. (2010). *Pedagogiikan konstruktivistinen orientaatio opettajaksi opiskelevien kokemana* [Constructivist Orientation of pedagogy as experienced by pre-service teachers]. University of Oulu.

UN, & Le Blanc, D. (2020). *E-participation: A Quick Overview of Recent Qualitative Trends*. DOI: 10.18356/a39cdf00-en

Usmanova, A. A. (2023). *Does a Higher E-Government Development Index Mean a Higher GDP Growth Rate?* 467–472. DOI: 10.1145/3508072.3508168

Utsumi, T., Al-Azab, M., & Elazab, S. (2019). 4th Industrial Revolution (4IR) for Smart Learning. *International Journal of Internet Education*, 18(1), 23–38. DOI: 10.21608/ijie.2019.98633

Vieira, J. B. (2013). The impact of public transparency in fighting corruption a study on brazilian municipalities e-government. *EJournal of EDemocracy and Open Government*, 5(1), 80–106. DOI: 10.29379/jedem.v5i1.140

Villamil, A., & King, S. (2024). A Humane Social Learning-Informed Metaverse: Cultivating Positive Technology Experiences in Digital Learning Environments. *Cyberpsychology, Behavior, and Social Networking*, 27(1), 47–56. DOI: 10.1089/cyber.2023.0001 PMID: 38197842

Viriya, C. (2022). Exploring the Impact of Synchronous, Asynchronous, and Bichronous Online Learning Modes on EFL Students' Self-Regulated and Perceived English Language Learning. *Reflections: The SoL Journal*, 29(1), 88–111. DOI: 10.61508/refl.v29i1.260525

Voigt, P., & Von dem Bussche, A. (2017). *The EU General Data Protection Regulation (GDPR): A practical guide*. Springer., DOI: 10.1007/978-3-319-57959-7

Vosman, L., Coenen, T. B. J., Volker, L., & Visscher, K. (2023). Collaboration and innovation beyond project boundaries: Exploring the potential of an ecosystem perspective in the infrastructure sector. *Construction Management and Economics*, 41(6), 457–474. DOI: 10.1080/01446193.2023.2165695

Vygotsky, L. S. (1978). *Mind in society: The development of higher psychological processes*. Harvard University Press.

Wager, K. A., Lee, F. W., & Glaser, J. P. (2017). *Health care information systems: A practical approach for health care management*. John Wiley & Sons.

Walkington, C. (2013). Using adaptive learning technologies to personalize instruction: The impact of relevant contexts on performance and learning outcomes. *Journal of Educational Psychology*, 105(4), 932–945. DOI: 10.1037/a0031882

Wang, C. X., Houdyshell, M., & Plescia, M. (2022). Synchronous Communication Technology for Remote Academic Advising at a State University. *Journal of Educational Research and Practice*, 12(1), 111–131. DOI: 10.5590/JERAP.2022.12.1.09

Wang, J., Huang, X., Gong, Z., & Cao, K. (2020). Dynamic assessment of tourism carrying capacity and its impacts on tourism economic growth in urban tourism destinations in China. *Journal of Destination Marketing & Management*, 15, 100383. DOI: 10.1016/j.jdmm.2019.100383

Wang, R., Zhang, M., & Brown, K. (2024). Preparing for post-quantum cryptography in supply chain security. *Quantum Computing and Cybersecurity*, 8(1), 45–58.

Wang, S., Li, Q., & Khaskheli, M. B. (2024). Management Fiscal Systems and Governance to Reduce Potential Risks in Digital Silk Road Investments: Legal Cooperation between Hainan Free Trade Port and Ethiopia. *Systems*, 12(8), 305. DOI: 10.3390/systems12080305

Wei, C., Wang, Q., & Liu, C. (2020). Research on Construction of a Cloud Platform for Tourism Information Intelligent Service Based on Blockchain Technology. *Wireless Communications and Mobile Computing*, 2020, 1–9. DOI: 10.1155/2020/8856271

Westley, F., Antadze, N., Riddell, D. J., Robinson, K., & Geobey, S. (2014). Five configurations for scaling up social innovation: Case examples of nonprofit organizations from Canada. *The Journal of Applied Behavioral Science*, 50(3), 234–260. DOI: 10.1177/0021886314532945

Williams, M., & Chen, P. (2023). Public-private partnerships in supply chain cybersecurity. *Critical Infrastructure Protection Quarterly*, 11(4), 89–102.

Wilson, M., & Smith, J. (2023). MSSP effectiveness in SME environments: A comparative study. *Journal of Cybersecurity Management*, 9(3), 145–160.

Wilson, R., Anderson, M., & Smith, P. (2024). SCOR model applications in supply chain security. *Supply Chain Management Journal*, 19(1), 78–94.

Windrum, P. (2008). Innovation and entrepreneurship in public services. In Windrum, P., & Koch, P. (Eds.), *Innovation in Public Sector Services*. Edward Elgar. DOI: 10.4337/9781848441545.00009

Wirtz, B. W., Weyerer, J. C., & Geyer, C. (2019). Artificial Intelligence and the Public Sector—Applications and Challenges. *International Journal of Public Administration*, 42(7), 596–615. DOI: 10.1080/01900692.2018.1498103

Xu, P., Johnson, K., & Rundlett, A. (2022). E-participation in contemporary China: A comparison with conventional offline participation. *Chinese Public Administration Review*, 13(3), 150–161. DOI: 10.1177/15396754221107115

Yao, Y., & Xu, P. (2022). E-participation decision across different channels. *Information Technology & People*, 35(3), 956–976. DOI: 10.1108/ITP-05-2020-0314

Yap, T. L., Nayak, R., Vu, N. T. H., Bui, D. T., Pham, T. T. T., & Allen, D. W. E. (2023). Adopting blockchain-based traceability in the fruit supply chain in a developing economy: Facilitators and barriers. *Information Technology & People*, 36(5), 1341–1360. DOI: 10.1108/ITP-02-2023-0168

Yassin, F. E., & El Nahlawy, H. (2023). *Driving digital transformation in the Arab region*. UNDP. https://www.undp.org/arab-states/stories/driving-digital-transformation-arab-region

Yeboah-Ofori, A., & Islam, S. (2019). Cyber Security Threat Modeling for Supply Chain Organizational Environments. *Future Internet*, 11(3), 63. DOI: 10.3390/fi11030063

Yetti, E. (2024). Pedagogical innovation and curricular adaptation in enhancing digital literacy: A local wisdom approach for sustainable development in Indonesia context. *Journal of Open Innovation*, 10(1), 100233. DOI: 10.1016/j.joitmc.2024.100233

Yildirim, K.YILDIRIM. (2022). A REVIEW OF LOCAL AND NATIONAL E-GOVERNMENT DEVELOPMENT MODELS AND THEIR DETERMINANTS. *Akademik Yaklaşımlar Dergisi*, 13(1), 270–297. DOI: 10.54688/ayd.1103488

Young, N. (2024). *Connectivism Learning Theory: The Ultimate Guide for 2024*. Retrieved from https://www.teachfloor.com/blog/connectivism-learning-theory

Youssef, A. B., Dutta, P., Doshi, R., & Sajnani, M. (Eds.). (2025). *AI, blockchain, and metaverse in hospitality and tourism Industry 4.0: Case studies and analysis* (1st ed.). C&H/CRC Press.

Yuhertiana, I., Izaak, W. C., & Arifin, J. (2020). E-government and e-finance on African countries. *Journal of Advanced Research in Dynamical and Control Systems, 12*(6 Special Issue), 184–204. https://doi.org/DOI: 10.5373/JARDCS/V12SP6/SP20201023

Yung, R., & Khoo-Lattimore, C. (2019). New realities: A systematic literature review on virtual reality and augmented reality in tourism research. *Current Issues in Tourism*, 22(17), 2056–2081. DOI: 10.1080/13683500.2017.1417359

Yunus, M. (2017). *A world of three zeros: the new economics of zero poverty, zero unemployment, and zero net carbon emissions.*

Yusuf, S. (2021). *Digital Technology and Inequality: The Impact on Arab Countries* (ERF Working Papers Series). https://erf.org.eg/app/uploads/2021/09/1632920263_470_2894109_1486.pdf

Yusuf, B., Walters, L. M., & Sailin, S. N. (2020). Restructuring Educational Institutions for Growth in the Fourth Industrial Revolution (4IR): A Systematic Review. *International Journal of Emerging Technologies in Learning*, 15(3), 93–109. DOI: 10.3991/ijet.v15i03.11849

Yusuf, M., Muntasa, A., Agustiono, W., Anamisa, D. R., & Syarief, M. (2020). A Novel Conceptual Model of e-Participation using Biometrics Technologies. *Journal of Physics: Conference Series*, 1569(2), 22069. DOI: 10.1088/1742-6596/1569/2/022069

Yusuf, M., Sophan, M. K., Muntasa, A., Alamsyah, N., Nakkas, H., & Sari, P. P. (2020). E-government learning media through augmented reality technology. *Bulletin of Social Informatics Theory and Application*, 4(1), 12–20. DOI: 10.31763/businta.v4i1.258

Zafary, F. (2020). Implementation of business intelligence considering the role of information systems integration and enterprise resource planning. *Journal of intelligence studies in business,* 1(1).

Zahra, S. A., Newey, L. R., & Li, Y. (2014). On the frontiers: The implications of social entrepreneurship for international entrepreneurship. *Entrepreneurship Theory and Practice*, 38(1), 137–158. DOI: 10.1111/etap.12061

Zato, C., De Luis, A., Bajo, J., De Paz, J. F., & Corchado, J. M. (2012). Dynamic model of distribution and organization of activities in multi-agent systems. *Logic Journal of the IGPL*, 20(3), 570–578. DOI: 10.1093/jigpal/jzr005

Zeng, S., Li, G., Wu, S., & Dong, Z. (2022). The impact of green technology innovation on carbon emissions in the context of carbon neutrality in China: Evidence from spatial spillover and nonlinear effect analysis. *International Journal of Environmental Research and Public Health*, 19(2), 730. DOI: 10.3390/ijerph19020730 PMID: 35055553

Zhang, L., & Kumar, R. (2023). Post-pandemic supply chain security transformations. *International Journal of Cybersecurity*, 16(4), 278–292.

Zhang, P., & Liu, S. (2023). Quantum-safe security transitions in modern supply chains. *Journal of Cryptographic Engineering*, 15(3), 234–249.

Zheng, Z., Xie, S., Dai, H., Chen, X., & Wang, H. (2018). Blockchain challenges and opportunities: A survey. *International Journal of Web and Grid Services*, 14(4), 352–375. DOI: 10.1504/IJWGS.2018.095647

Zhu, B., Nguyen, M., Siri, N. S., & Malik, A. (2022). Towards a transformative model of circular economy for SMEs. *Journal of Business Research*, 144, 545–555. DOI: 10.1016/j.jbusres.2022.01.093

Zidny, R., Sjöström, J., & Eilks, I. (2020). A multi-perspective reflection on how indigenous knowledge and related ideas can improve science education for sustainability. *Science & Education*, 29(1), 145–185. DOI: 10.1007/s11191-019-00100-x

About the Contributors

Miltiadis D. Lytras is a visiting researcher at Effat University. Dr Lytras is a world-class expert in the fields of cognitive computing, information systems, technology-enabled innovation, social networks, computers in human behavior, and knowledge management. He is an expert in advanced computer science and management, editor, lecturer, and research consultant, with extensive experience in academia and the business sector in Europe and Asia. He served as the Editor in Chief of the International Journal in Semantic Web and Information Systems. He has co-edited more than 110 high impact factor special issues in ISI/Scopus indexed journals and co-Edited/Authored more than 80 books in international publishers including Elsevier, Emerald, IGI-Global, Springer, etc. Dr Lytras has co-authored more than 120 high impact factor papers in Q1 and Q2, Web of Science and Scopus indexed Journals such as: IEEE Transactions on Knowledge and Data Engineering; IEEE Internet Computing; IEEE Transactions on Education; IEEE Access; Future Generation Computer Systems; Journal of Business Research; International Journal of Information Management; Journal of Innovation and Knowledge; Technological forecasting and Social Change; Journal of Ambient Technology and Humanized Computing; World Wide Web Journal; Computers in Human Behavior; Studies in Higher Education; Telematics and Informatics; Information Systems Management; IJ of Engineering Education; Journal of Universal Computer Science; Journal of Knowledge Management; British Journal on Education Technology; Interactive Learning Environment; Educational Technology and Society; Behavior and Information Technology, etc. Dr. Lytras has a 25 years' experience on Research and Development projects and grants with significant skills and competencies to the successful conceptualization, financing and implementation of R&D projects with extensive experience in Europe, Middle East, and Far East. He has involved in more than 70 R&D projects overtime. Main areas of expertis Dr. Lytras has hold various senior editorial positions in prestigious journals over time including Editor in Chief and Associate Editor positions. He has also the privilege to guest edit more than 130 special issues in high impact factor journals. • Founding Editor and Editor in Chief of IJ on Semantic Web and Information Systems (High Impact Factor, WoS indexed) Additional editorial positions (selected): • Founding Editor in Chief, International Journal on Technology Enhanced Learning (IJTEL) • Founding Editor in Chief International Journal of Knowledge and Learning (IJKL) • Founding Editor in Chief of International Journal of Knowledge Society Research (IJKSR) Dr. Lytras has (co-edited) more than 100 peer reviewed volumes/books in topics related to his expertise. Indicative titles include: • Digital Transformation in Healthcare in Post-COVID-19 Times • Smart Cities and Digital Transformation: Empowering Communities, Limitless Innovation, Sustainable Development and the Next Generation, • Smart Cities: Issues and Challenges: Mapping Political, Social and Economic Risks and Threats • Smart Villages in the EU and Beyond.

Patricia Ordóñez de Pablos is a professor in the Department of Business Administration in the Faculty of Business and Economics at The University of Oviedo, Spain. She completed her education in The London School of Economics, UK. Her teaching and research interests focus on the areas of strategic management, knowledge management, organizational learning, intellectual capital and information technologies, with special interest in Asia (Bhutan, China, Myanmar). She is Editor-in-Chief of the International Journal of Learning and Intellectual Capital (IJLIC) and International Journal of Asian Business and Information Management (IJABIM), respectively. She has edited books for IGI Global, Elsevier, Routledge, and Springer. In 2021, 2022 and 2023, she earned placement on Stanford University's "Ranking of the World Scientists: World's Top 2% Scientists" list. Additionally she is listed in World Top Scientists of Research.com in the Areas of Social Science and Humanities in Spain and Engineering and Technology in Spain.

Afnan Alkhaldi, the Acting Assistant Dean for the Arab Open University, is a distinguished academic and consultant with a profound impact on the development of Smart Cities and Information Systems. Her expertise is showcased through her significant role in consulting for Kuwait Economic Cities, particularly in the pioneering smart city project, Al-Hareer City. With a Ph.D. in operation and information management, she brings nearly a decade of experience to her field, emphasizing eGovernance and operational efficiencies. Dr. Afnan's innovative approach, coupled with her ability to effectively communicate and collaborate across diverse environments, positions her as a key figure in driving forward Kuwait's smart city initiatives. Academic or professional affiliation: Arab Open University-Kuwait Branch / Effat University, Kingdom of Saudi Arabia Contact number: +965 98819331 Email address: aalkhaldi@aou.edu.kw

Andreea Claudia Erban is Professor at the Department of Economics and Economic Policies, Faculty of Theoretical and Applied Economics and director of Doctoral School of Economics I. She holds a PhD in Economics from Bucharest University of Economic Studies and a post-PhD in Economics from Romanian Academy of Science. Her research activity consists of publication of 7 books and numerous economic studies in highly ranked journals, as well as participation in many international conferences. She is Associate Editor for International Journal on Semantic Web and Information Systems (IJSWIS, a WoS-indexed journal) and Editor in Chief for Global Journal of Business, Economics and Management: Current Issues (journal indexed in many international databases). She is reviewer for prestigious international journals and member of editorial board or organizing committee of many international conferences. She is expert for the Lithuanian Research Council. Her areas of research interest include: sustainable development, smart development, knowledge economy, the labor market, education, and demographic issues.

***

Sadaf Anwar is an Associate Professor in the area of Finance at M.S. Ramaiah Institute of Management, Bangalore, India. She has done her Ph. D from Indian Institute of Technology (IIT Delhi) and has been honoured with UGC-NET JRF fellowship. Her diverse range of experience spans from teaching in academic institutions to working with Ministry of Finance, New Delhi. Her work is recognised in Monographs, Journals and Book Chapters of National and International repute. She teaches courses in the areas of Financial Management, Management Accounting, Corporate Finance, Financial Reporting & Analysis, Financial Institutions and Corporate Valuation.

Saher EL-Annan has an extensive academic and professional background. Possesses project management, leadership and change management background, achieving optimal results with competent planning to address business needs in today's fast and brutal changing business environment. University professor, Trainer, and Consultant for nearly 24 years with a strong desire to help graduates recognize the connection between learning and experience. Resided on many consultant academic and genuine committees to develop applicable university curricula that meet the academic and realistic world businesses. With a passion for designing impact educational programs, training packages, mentoring students to create a collaborative and inclusive learning environment that empowers students and trainees to excel academically/professionally and prepares them for successful careers in their chosen field. Supervised more than 90 MBA thesis, 8 PhD Dissertations, and reviewed 14 PhD (Reader 1) in the last 20 years. El-Annan is also recognized for his contributions to conferences and workshops, including being a speaker at international events and participating in professional development sessions related to higher education. He has been a member of various professional affiliations and has received numerous honors and awards, reflecting his commitment to excellence in his field.

Rawan Hassoun is a dedicated educator, academic editor, and Business professional with vast industry experience and an in-depth academic background. She has been involved with course design and curriculum development, prepared educational materials, and mentored students. Her freelance consulting and research roles have further enhanced her abilities. As a DBA in Management and Strategic Planning at the International American University, Los Angeles, she brings a wealth of knowledge and expertise to her work. Her MBA from The Open University, UK, and her bachelor's degree in Business specializing in Human Resources Management, along with her continued contributions to the industry, underscore her credibility and authority. Dr. Hassoun's competencies include serving as a university professor, an academic researcher editor, and a co-reviewer with Professor Saher El-Annan. She is also a training developer, creating comprehensive packages in Leadership, Strategic Management, Marketing, and many other subject

Fareeha Javed works as Associate Professor. She holds PhD and PGDip in Education with concentration on Teaching and Learning of English from Massey University, New Zealand; Masters in English Literature from Punjab University (Lahore College for Women); and Masters in Educational Planning & Management from Allama Iqbal Open University. Her research interests include digitalization, transformative learning, first-year experience, student engagement, teaching and learning of second/foreign language, psycholinguistics, education policy, language policy, TESOL and educational leadership and management, student identity, linguistic identity, preparedness for university, curriculum development, assessment and evaluation, and blended learning.

Farhana Yeasmin Lina is a Lecturer (Senior Scale) in the Department of Tourism & Hospitality Management at Daffodil International University, where she specializes in research areas such as digital detox, artificial intelligence in tourism, and community-based tourism development (CBT). Currently pursuing an MPhil in Tourism and Hospitality Management, she holds both a BBA and an MBA from the University of Dhaka. Lina's work focuses on understanding the potential impacts of tourism development in Bangladesh, promoting sustainable tourism, and empowering local communities. Her research also explores how emerging technologies can revolutionize the tourism industry, enhancing both academic and practical insights in the field.

Achmad Nurmandi is a Professor at the Department of Government Affairs and Administration, Jusuf Kalla School of Government, Universitas Muhammadiyah Yogyakarta, Indonesia. His research interests are on e-government, urban governance and strategic management in the public sector and published in many international journal and Book Chapter, such as International Journal of Public Sector Management, Transforming Government: People, Policy and Process, Jamba Journal of Disaster Studies, Asian Review of Political Science, Journal of Human Behavior in the Social Environment, Public Policy and Administration, Global Encyclopedia of Public Administration, Public Policy, and Governance, Springer. He is currently the Secretary of the Asia Pacific Society for Public Affairs (APSPA). He is also the Editor-in-Chief of Jurnal Studi Pemerintahan (Journal of Government and Politics) and a Guest Editor of International Journal of Public Sector Performance Management and International Journal of Sustainable Society.

Narender Singh, MBA,MCom, MA (Economics) is an Asst ProF and Head, Department Management in Rungta College of Science & Technology, Bhilai. He is specialised in the field of finance and accounting, He published papers in UGC care research journals, Registered Patents in his name shows involvement in innovation and knowledge skill . Having more than 23 years of teaching and industrial experience.

S. Sudhakar is an experienced professor with a demonstrated history of working in the education management industry. A strong education professional with a Doctor of Philosophy (PhD) focused on Customer Relationship Management in the Small and Medium Scale sector from Anna University, Chennai. He is currently working as an IQAC Coordinator and expert faculty at LEAD College of Management, Palakkad, Kerala. Earlier, he held notable positions in prestigious B schools in Coimbatore. He served on the Governing Councils of Sri Krishna College of Technology and AJK Institute of Management in Coimbatore. He was also the Board of Studies member at GRG School of Management, PSGRKrishnammal College for Women, and Sri Krishna College of Technology, Coimbatore. He is on the editorial advisory board for the International Review of Business and Economics. Oakland, USA An effective planner and organizer of academic events and programs, he has conducted around 40 events. He has received grants from NAAC, EAC, and AICTE for conducting programmes. He has published five case studies to his credit. He has published more than 30 research papers in national and international journals. His areas of interest include marketing, strategic management, and customer relationship management.

Mohammad Badruddoza Talukder is an Associate Professor, College of Tourism and Hospitality Management, IUBAT - International University of

Business Agriculture and Technology, Dhaka, Bangladesh. He holds PhD in Hotel Management from Lovely Professional University, India. He has been teaching various courses in the Department of Tourism and Hospitality at various universities in Bangladesh since 2008. His research areas include tourism management, hotel management, hospitality management, food & beverage management, and accommodation management, where he has published research papers in well-known journals in Bangladesh and abroad. Mr. Talukder is one of the executive members of the Tourism Educators Association of Bangladesh. He has led training and consulting for a wide range of hospitality organizations in Bangladesh. He just became an honorary facilitator at the Bangladesh Tourism Board's Bangabandhu international tourism and hospitality training institution.

Parul Wadhwa is currently working as Assistant Professor at DPG Degree College, Gurugram. She has over five years of teaching experience in various reputed institutions of India such as Government College of Commerce and Business Administration, Gurugram University and The NorthCap University. Besides this, she has also worked as Assistant Manager at HDFC Bank Ltd. She has submitted her thesis for the award of PhD in Business Management and Commerce at Panjab University, Chandigarh. Her research papers have been published in several international and national journals.

Index

B

Blockchain 5, 10, 18, 44, 74, 100, 103, 109, 111, 115, 116, 117, 122, 123, 126, 132, 136, 141, 142, 143, 144, 145, 146, 147, 205, 208, 220, 221, 228, 229, 250, 251, 256

C

Circular Economy 1, 2, 3, 4, 5, 6, 7, 10, 11, 12, 14, 15, 16, 17, 18, 19, 20, 21
Cloud-based systems 153, 156
Consumer Privacy 117, 132, 143
Consumer Trust 47, 105, 107, 108, 109, 110, 112, 113, 114, 115, 116, 117, 119, 120, 121, 122, 123, 124, 125, 127, 128, 129, 130, 131, 132, 133, 134, 135, 136, 137, 138, 139, 141, 142, 144, 146, 147

D

Data Privacy 52, 84, 91, 96, 106, 108, 118, 123, 126, 134, 138, 140, 141, 143, 144, 145, 147, 216, 221, 239, 248, 249
Digital Business Models 105, 107, 111, 119, 120, 123, 133, 137
Digital Economy 23, 24, 25, 26, 27, 29, 34, 35, 42, 43, 44, 45, 46, 47, 48, 49, 50, 51, 101, 106, 107, 108, 110, 117, 119, 133, 138, 147, 177, 178, 179, 180, 181, 182, 183, 184, 185, 186, 187, 188, 189, 190, 191, 193, 194, 195, 196, 197, 198, 199, 200, 204, 207
Digitalization 18, 41, 48, 50, 178
Digital Transformation 19, 23, 24, 25, 26, 27, 28, 29, 30, 31, 32, 35, 36, 37, 38, 39, 41, 42, 43, 44, 45, 46, 47, 48, 49, 50, 51, 52, 53, 55, 56, 57, 58, 61, 62, 64, 65, 69, 70, 72, 73, 74, 101, 145, 156, 164, 165, 167, 168, 171, 173, 174, 180, 188, 194, 195, 196, 203, 256
digital world 36, 44, 168, 185, 218, 225, 231
Dynamic Pricing 81, 84, 90, 93, 94, 95, 98

E

Economic Growth 6, 8, 29, 33, 35, 45, 51, 81, 82, 83, 84, 85, 89, 95, 96, 98, 101, 103
Economic Policies 50
e-government 59, 61, 63, 66, 67, 68, 70, 71, 73, 74, 75, 76, 77, 78, 79
Enterprise resource planning 149, 150, 151, 155, 158, 170, 171, 173, 174, 175
Environmental Sustainability 13, 14, 50, 76, 97
e-participation 55, 56, 57, 58, 59, 60, 61, 62, 63, 64, 65, 66, 67, 68, 69, 70, 71, 72, 73, 74, 75, 76, 77, 78, 79
Ethical Data Management 105, 107, 108, 109, 113, 118, 121, 122, 123, 124, 125, 127, 129, 131, 132, 133, 134, 135, 136, 137, 138, 139, 140

G

Green Technologies 1, 2, 3, 4, 5, 9, 10, 11, 12, 17, 44

I

Innovation 5, 7, 10, 11, 12, 13, 14, 15, 16, 17, 18, 19, 20, 23, 24, 25, 26, 27, 28, 29, 32, 33, 34, 35, 36, 37, 40, 43, 44, 46, 47, 48, 49, 53, 82, 84, 85, 86, 89, 96, 101, 103, 140, 142, 147, 150, 151, 153, 156, 161, 163, 164, 168, 172, 173, 177, 178, 179, 180, 181, 182, 183, 184, 185, 186, 187, 188, 189, 190, 191, 193, 194, 195, 196, 197, 198, 199, 200, 202, 203, 204, 211, 224, 234, 235, 252, 254, 259, 260
Innovation Resilience 177, 178, 179, 180, 181, 182, 183, 184, 185, 186, 187, 188, 189, 190, 191, 193, 194, 195, 196, 197, 198, 199, 200, 204
Innovative pedagogies 231, 234, 244, 246, 251

IoT Security 223, 228

J

Job Opportunities 6, 13, 28, 81, 89, 96

L

learning experiences 231, 232, 234, 240, 241, 243, 246, 248, 249, 250, 252

O

Operational Efficiency 30, 46, 53, 56, 83, 84, 85, 89, 94, 95, 96, 216

P

Perceived Transparency 105, 107, 108, 109, 110, 112, 116, 117, 118, 120, 121, 122, 124, 125, 127, 128, 129, 131, 132, 133, 134, 135, 136, 137, 138, 139, 141, 142, 143, 147
Personalized Marketing 81, 82, 88, 90, 95

R

Ransomware 205, 206, 210, 213, 214, 215, 218, 224, 226, 227

S

Service Delivery 29, 30, 32, 39, 45, 56, 59, 72, 81, 84, 88, 95, 96
Small Medium Enterprise 151, 169, 170
Social Entrepreneurship 1, 2, 3, 4, 5, 7, 8, 9, 11, 12, 13, 14, 16, 19, 20, 109
Social Impact 3, 7, 8, 9, 16
Strategies 2, 3, 4, 5, 7, 9, 12, 13, 15, 23, 25, 26, 30, 35, 36, 37, 42, 43, 46, 48, 65, 73, 83, 84, 87, 88, 90, 92, 94, 96, 101, 115, 125, 134, 147, 150, 152, 157, 164, 184, 185, 186, 188, 190, 191, 193, 194, 195, 196, 197, 198, 199, 205, 207, 209, 211, 212, 214, 217, 218, 222, 227, 228, 231, 234, 235, 239, 250, 251, 255, 258
Supply Chain Cybersecurity 205, 208, 210, 216, 220, 227, 229
Sustainable Business Models 1, 4, 9, 11, 12, 14, 15

T

Tourism Industry 81, 82, 83, 84, 85, 88, 95, 96, 98, 99, 101, 102, 103
Traditional ERP systems 154, 159, 160, 170
Transparent Data Practices 105, 107, 108, 109, 110, 113, 116, 117, 119, 120, 121, 122, 123, 124, 125, 127, 129, 130, 131, 133, 134, 136, 137, 139

V

Virtual Assistants 83, 84, 88, 93, 96

Z

Zero Trust Architecture 205, 217, 223

www.ingramcontent.com/pod-product-compliance
Lightning Source LLC
LaVergne TN
LVHW061545290926
849162LV00004B/916